General editor: TERENCE HAWKES

Marxist Shakespeares

Marxist Shakespeares uses the rich analytic resources of the Marxist tradition to redefine what the study of Shakespeare can mean. The essays collected here reveal that Marxism remains an inescapable challenge to prevailing modes of literary scholarship, essential to addressing such issues as:

- the relationship of texts to social class
- the historical construction of the aesthetic
- the utopian dimensions of literary production
- the role of literature in nationalist and anti-nationalist projects

This book offers new insights into the historical conditions within which Shakespeare's representations of class and gender emerged, and into Shakespeare's role in the world-wide culture industry stretching from Hollywood to the Globe Theatre.

Marxist Shakespeares will be a vital resource for students of Shakespeare as it examines Marx's own readings of Shakespeare, Derrida's engagement with Marx, and the importance of Pierre Bourdieu, Georges Bataille, and Alice Clark within a continuing tradition of Marxist thought.

Jean E. Howard teaches Early Modern literature at Columbia University. She is the author of *The Stage and Social Struggle in Early Modern England* (1994) and co-author, with Phyllis Rackin, of *Engendering a Nation: A Feminist Account of Shakespeare's English Histories* (1997).

Scott Cutler Shershow teaches English literature and literary theory at Miami University, Ohio. He is the author of *Puppets and Popular Culture* (1996), and of articles on Renaissance drama, popular culture and cultural studies.

ACCENTS ON SHAKESPEARE
General Editor: TERENCE HAWKES

It is more than twenty years since the New Accents series helped to establish 'theory' as a fundamental and continuing feature of the study of literature at undergraduate level. Since then, the need for short, powerful 'cutting edge' accounts of and comments on new developments has increased sharply. In the case of Shakespeare, books with this sort of focus have not been readily available. **Accents on Shakespeare** aims to supply them.

Accents on Shakespeare volumes will either 'apply' theory, or broaden and adapt it in order to connect with concrete teaching concerns. In the process, they will also reflect and engage with the major developments in Shakespeare studies of the last ten years.

The series will lead as well as follow. In pursuit of this goal it will be a two-tiered series. In addition to affordable, 'adoptable' titles aimed at modular undergraduate courses, it will include a number of research-based books. Spirited and committed, these second-tier volumes advocate radical change rather than stolidly reinforcing the status quo.

IN THE SAME SERIES

Shakespeare and Appropriation
Edited by Christy Desmet and Robert Sawyer

Shakespeare Without Women
Dympna Callaghan

Philosophical Shakespeares
Edited by John J. Joughin

Shakespeare and Modernity: Early Modern to Millennium
Edited by Hugh Grady

Marxist Shakespeares
Edited by Jean E. Howard and Scott Cutler Shershow

Marxist Shakespeares

Edited by
JEAN E. HOWARD and
SCOTT CUTLER SHERSHOW

London and New York

First published 2001
by Routledge
2 Park Square, Milton Park,
Abingdon, Oxon, OX14 4RN

Simultaneously published
in the USA and Canada
by Routledge
270 Madison Ave,
New York NY 10016

Routledge is an imprint of the
Taylor & Francis Group

Transferred to Digital Printing 2006

Typeset in Baskerville by
RefineCatch Limited, Bungay, Suffolk

British Library Cataloguing in Publication Data

A catalogue record for this book is available from the British Library

Library of Congress Cataloging in Publication Data

Marxist Shakespeares / Jean E. Howard and Scott Cutler Shershow.
p. cm — (Accents on Shakespeare)
Includes bibliographical references and index.
1. Shakespeare, William, 1564–1616—Political and social views. 2. Literature and society—England—History—16th century. 3. Women and literature—England—History—16th century. 4. Marxist criticism. I. Howard, Jean E. (Jean Elizabeth), 1948– II. Shershow, Scott Cutler, 1953– III. Series.

PR3024.M39 2000
822.3′3—dc21 00–030823

ISBN 0–415–20234–5 (pbk)
ISBN 0–415–20233–7 (hbk)

Contents

Contributors

Denise Albanese is Associate Professor of English and Cultural Studies at George Mason University in Fairfax, Virginia. She is the author of *New Science, New World* (Duke University Press, 1996), and she works on critical science and technology studies as well as on early modern culture and Shakespeare performance. She is currently at work on a study of Kenneth Branagh, "popular" Shakespeare, and the place of American Anglophilia in global culture.

Crystal Bartolovich is an Assistant Professor of English and Textual Studies at Syracuse University. She has published essays on a range of topics in Marxism and early modern cultural studies; currently, she is completing a book manuscript, *Boundary Disputes: Notes on the Socialization of Culture.*

Barbara E. Bowen is Associate Professor of English at Queens College and the Graduate Center of the City University of New York. She has published a book on *Troilus and Cressida* and articles on African American literature and the politics of academic labor. She has been active for twenty years in the labor movement and is a union leader at CUNY. Her current research project is a book on Aemelia Lanyer.

Dympna Callaghan is William P. Tolley Professor in the Humanities at Syracuse University. She is author of *Woman and Gender in Renaissance Tragedy* (Harvester, 1989) and *Shakespeare Without Women* (Routledge,

1999); co-author of *The Weyward Sisters: Shakespeare and Feminist Politics* (Blackwell, 1994), and co-editor of *Feminist Readings in Early Modern Culture: Emerging Subjects* (Cambridge University Press, 1996). In addition, she has edited two collections, *A Feminist Companion to Shakespeare* (Blackwell, 2000) and *The Duchess of Malfi Casebook* (Macmillan, 2000).

Walter Cohen is Professor of Comparative Literature at Cornell University, where he is also Vice Provost and Dean of the Graduate School. He has published *Drama of a Nation: Public Theater in Renaissance England and Spain* (Cornell University Press, 1985) and co-edited *The Norton Shakespeare* (Norton, 1997).

Richard Halpern is Professor of English at the University of California at Berkeley. He is author of *The Poetics of Primitive Accumulation: English Renaissance Culture and the Genealogy of Capital* (Cornell University Press, 1991) and *Shakespeare Among the Moderns* (Cornell University Press, 1997).

Jean E. Howard teaches English at Columbia University. Her recent books include *The Stage and Social Struggle in Early Modern England* (Routledge, 1994) and, with Phyllis Rackin, *Engendering a Nation: A Feminist Account of Shakespeare's English Histories* (Routledge, 1997). She is one of the editors of *The Norton Shakespeare* (Norton, 1997) and General Editor of the Bedford Text and Context Shakespeare Series. She is at work on a new book, *Theater of a City: Social Change and Generic Innovation on the Early Modern Stage.*

Natasha Korda is an Assistant Professor of English at Wesleyan University. She is currently working on a book manuscript entitled *Household Stuff: Shakespeare's Domestic Economics*, and is co-editing an anthology with Jonathan Gil Harris entitled *Staged Properties: Props and Property in Early Modern English Drama.*

Kiernan Ryan is Professor of English at Royal Holloway, University of London, and a Fellow of New Hall, University of Cambridge. He is the author of *Shakespeare* (Harvester Wheatsheaf, 1989; 3rd edn., Macmillan, 2001) and the editor of *King Lear: Contemporary Critical Essays* (Macmillan, 1993), *New Historicism and Cultural Materialism: A Reader* (Arnold, 1996), *Shakespeare: The Last Plays* (Longman, 1999), and *Shakespeare: Texts and Contexts* (2000).

Scott Cutler Shershow is Associate Professor of English at Miami University in Oxford, Ohio. He is the author of *Laughing Matters: The Paradox of Comedy* (University of Massachusetts Press, 1986), *Puppets and*

"Popular" Culture (Cornell University Press, 1996), and, more recently, of articles on early modern drama, cultural studies, and literary theory.

Peter Stallybrass is Professor of English at the University of Pennsylvania where he also directs the seminar on the History of Material Texts. With Allon White he wrote *The Politics and Poetics of Transgression* (Cornell University Press, 1986), and with David Scott Kastan he edited *Staging The Renaissance* (Routledge, 1991). He recently completed a book with Ann Rosalind Jones entitled *Renaissance Clothing and the Materials of Memory* (Cambridge University Press, forthcoming). His essays on Marx and materiality have just been published in Portuguese under the title of *Marx's Coat* (Belo Horizonte, Brazil: Autentica, 1999).

Richard Wilson is Professor of Renaissance Studies and Director of the Shakespeare Programme at the University of Lancaster. He is the author of *Will Power: Essays on Shakespearean Authority* (Harvester Wheatsheaf, 1993) and the editor, with Richard Dalton, of *New Historicism and Renaissance Drama* (Longman 1992). He has also edited *Christopher Marlowe* (Longman 1999) and *Julius Caesar* (MacMillan 2000). His study of Shakespeare and Catholicism, *Secret Shakespeare*, is forthcoming from Manchester University Press.

Acknowledgements

The editors of this volume would especially like to thank Terry Hawkes for his expert advice and witty encouragement in bringing this volume to fruition. We are also deeply grateful to all our contributors for their excellent essays and their good cheer through the long process of putting such a complicated volume together. As always, Jean E. Howard would like to thank her students, all of them, for the intellectual stimulation they so constantly provide; and, as always, to give the most special thanks to Jim, Katie, and Caleb. Scott Cutler Shershow wants to thank Barry Chabot, Peter Rose, Tim Melley, Jean Howard and, especially, Scott Michaelsen for discussion of Marxist theory, and Frances Dolan for intellectual companionship and for the boundless generosity that almost, but not quite, goes without saying.

General editor's preface

In our century, the field of literary studies has rarely been a settled, tranquil place. Indeed, for over two decades, the clash of opposed theories, prejudices and points of view has made it more of a battlefield. Echoing across its most beleaguered terrain, the student's weary complaint "Why can't I just pick up Shakespeare's plays and read them?" seems to demand a sympathetic response.

Nevertheless, we know that modern spectacles will always impose their own particular characteristics on the vision of those who unthinkingly don them. This must mean, at the very least, that an apparently simple confrontation with, or pious contemplation of, the text of a four-hundred-year-old play can scarcely supply the grounding for an adequate response to its complex demands. For this reason, a transfer of emphasis from "text" towards "context" has increasingly been the concern of critics and scholars since the Second World War: a tendency that has perhaps reached its climax in more recent movements such as "New Historicism" or "Cultural Materialism".

A consideration of the conditions, social, political or economic within which the play came to exist, from which it derives, and to which it speaks will certainly make legitimate demands on the attention of any well-prepared student nowadays. Of course, the serious pursuit of those interests will also inevitably start to undermine ancient and inherited prejudices, such as the supposed distinction between "foreground" and "background" in literary studies. And even the slightest awareness of the pressures of gender or of race, or the most cursory glance at the role played by that strange creature "Shakespeare" in our cultural politics, will reinforce a similar turn towards questions that sometimes appear scandalously "non-literary." It seems clear that very different and unsettling notions of the ways in which literature might be addressed can hardly be avoided. The worrying truth is that nobody can just pick up Shakespeare's plays and read them. Perhaps – even more worrying – they never could.

The aim of *Accents on Shakespeare* is to encourage students and teachers to explore the implications of this situation by means of an engagement with the major developments in Shakespeare studies of the last ten years. It will offer a continuing and challenging reflection on those ideas through a series of multi- and single-author books which will also supply the basis for adapting or augmenting them in the light of changing concerns.

Accents on Shakespeare also intends to lead as well as follow. In pursuit of this goal, the series will operate on more than one level. In addition to titles aimed at modular undergraduate courses, it will include a number of books embodying polemical, strongly argued cases aimed at expanding the horizons of a specific aspect of the subject and at challenging the preconceptions on which it is based. These volumes will not be learned "monographs" in any traditional sense. They will, it is hoped, offer a platform for the work of the liveliest younger scholars and teachers at their most outspoken and provocative. Committed and contentious, they will be reporting from the forefront of current critical activity and will have something new to say. The fact that each book in the series promises a Shakespeare inflected in terms of a specific urgency should ensure that, in the present as in the recent past, the accent will be on change.

Terence Hawkes

1

Introduction:
Marxism now, Shakespeare now

JEAN E. HOWARD AND
SCOTT CUTLER SHERSHOW

In one account of his intellectual trajectory as a member of the Birmingham Centre for Cultural Studies, Stuart Hall talks of his own personal and the group's collective struggle, over a number of years, with Marxism (Hall 1992). He came to Marxism, he insists, unwillingly. Like many of his generation, he early on experienced the profound revulsion from Soviet state communism occasioned among other things by the movement of Soviet tanks into Budapest in 1956. If Marxism meant Soviet totalitarianism, he wanted nothing to do with it. Nor did Marxism easily satisfy Hall's requirements for a subtle and comprehensive mode of *cultural* analysis. Its rigidities and vulgarities, the Eurocentricism of its historical account of the development of capitalism, its status as a metanarrative, its alternating indifference to or reductive absorption of feminist and race-based political agendas – all of this made him, he says, sees Marxism as "a problem, as trouble, as danger, not as a solution" (Hall 1992: 279).

Yet his account of Marxism's *troublesomeness* is inseparable from his account of its *usefulness* – to him and to the collective work of the Birmingham Centre. How could such an irritant also seem so necessary? Hall's essay, "Cultural Studies and its Theoretical Legacies," indirectly attempts to answer that question, and we believe it became urgent for Hall to do so when in the early 1990s he confronted what he says he did not fully understand, but clearly found disquieting: namely, the theoretically fluent but to him insufficiently political nature of

American cultural studies. The existence of that form of cultural work crystalized for him his indebtedness to the Marxist legacy that had enabled him to think of his intellectual work in political terms and had provided a serious if imperfect set of tools and concepts for addressing questions he found urgent.

Like other sophisticated systems of thought, Marxism is the beneficiary of the intellectual labor of many people. It is less a science than an evolving and varied tradition of thought and practice aimed both at understanding the world, and, in its activist dimension, at transforming it. For Hall, the pull of Marxism lay in part in its persistent attention to issues he found pressing, namely:

> the power, the global reach and history-making capacities of capital; the question of class; the complex relationships between power, which is an easier term to establish in the discourses of culture than exploitation, and exploitation; the question of a general theory which could, in a critical way, connect together in a critical reflection different domains of life, politics and theory, theory and practice, economic, political and ideological questions, and so on; the notion of critical knowledge itself and the production of critical knowledge as a practice. These important, central questions are what one meant by working within shouting distance of Marxism, working on Marxism, working against Marxism, working with it, working to try to develop Marxism.
>
> (Hall 1992: 279)

Like most professors in the Humanities, Hall presents himself primarily as a critic of cultural texts, and in that role Marxism played a particular role for him in the theoretical conflicts of the 1980s. In the wake, especially, of the poststructuralist emphasis on textuality and the non-referentiality of language, which Hall took on board, he found in Marxism the irritating imperative to remember the worldliness of the text, its affiliations with what lies outside it, its effects in history. The emphasis within poststructuralism on discursivity, representation, and textuality rendered difficult and complex the passage between the world and the text, challenging residual elements of reflectionism in Marxist thought. Nonetheless, the legacy of Marxism pushed Hall to find tools, such as symptomatic reading, that would enable him to negotiate that passage, however imperfectly, even when working in the area of displacement called culture, where the relation between text and world is never direct. In short, Hall presents his relationship to Marxism as both vexed and productive and as constantly in tension with other political and intellectual developments such as poststructuralism, feminism, and race studies. His description of working on, with, against, and within shouting distance of Marxism captures something of the productive tension he envisioned between it and related knowledge projects. This could mean, for example, letting materialist feminist work on the sexual division of labor and on production and reproduction pressure purely class-based accounts of exploitation; and it could also mean letting Marxist ideas about the interconnections of economics, politics, and culture challenge the adequacy of examining literary texts in isolation from state and economic formations.

We invoke the name of Stuart Hall in the introduction to *Marxist Shakespeares* in part because while he articulates a profound and continuing debt to Marxism, the cultural studies agenda he helped to inaugurate ranges far beyond the topics and modes of analysis associated with traditional Marxism. This volume is produced in the year 2000, at greater remove from the theory wars of the 1980s to which Hall was in part reacting, but it too attempts at once to utilize the analytical and political resources of Marxism and to push the boundaries of Marxist thought by ongoing engagement with feminism, cultural studies, and non-Marxist forms of historicism. In fact, if in the 1980s Marxism recalled the wordiness of texts in the teeth of poststructuralism's emphasis on self-generating and self-sustaining textuality, it has particular usefulness at this moment, at least in early modern studies, in the alternatives it poses to more fragmentary and unanchored forms of historical inquiry. The postmodern critique of master narratives has spawned its own demon fry – forms of criticism that fetishize the local, the particular, and the unmediated materiality of books, objects, and "things" at the expense of considering the "big picture," or at least the bigger picture, that is, arguments about historical change; about the interconnections between past and present or between different spheres of the social formation; about what the local has to do with the national and the national with the transnational; about the social processes that invest mute objects with value, meaning, and exchangeability (Fraser and Nicholson 1988).

In the States, at least, in early modern studies we now find ourselves at one end of a twenty-year explosion of historical and political criticism. But much of it seems an active evasion of Marxist modes of inquiry even when Marxism's conceptual tools could prove of use. The reasons for this have much to do with the red-baiting legacy of American culture and an almost obsessive fear in 1980s and early 1990s criticism that one might fall sway to a "master narrative." Recent work has often aspired to a cultural poetics involving a quasi-Marxist methodology: the discovery of interpretive similarities or homologies between otherwise incongruous materials such as plays and legal documents. Yet frequently there is an evasion of the specifically Marxist roots of these avowedly "materialist" or "political" projects. As Fredric Jameson has argued, recent Shakespeare scholarship seems determined to retain its "discursive conquest of a range of heterogeneous materials while quietly abandoning the theoretical component that once justified that enlargement" (Jameson 1991: 188). Consequently, one frequently reads accounts of the circulation of cultural energy that ironically celebrate the vigor of nascent capitalism even while overtly condemning its social consequences.

Even when contemporary scholars do mention Marxism, it is often to relegate it to the dustbin of the history of ideas. In particular, critics commonly invoke two specific objections to the Marxist project. It is argued, first, that Marx predicted that the economic condition of the working class would steadily decline whereas, in fact, in the century or so that followed Marx's career, the condition of the working class in the West improved. But only a curious collective amnesia about our own history makes it necessary to point out that such improvement came via a century of bitter labor struggle largely inspired by Marxism. It was organized labor and collective bargaining, not the good intentions of corporate capitalism, that gave us safety rules, the eight-hour day, pension plans, and the like. To then cite such social improvements as evidence against the Marxist project is (to adapt the words of Bernard Shaw) really to exceed all limits of impudence and hypocrisy. Marx, moreover, never claimed to be a soothsayer; rather, he argued that capital's inherent "drive" to maximize the surplus value extracted from production would always tend to produce a net increase in human misery. And how far does one have to look to see such misery – in the sweatshops and *maquiladora* factories of borderland "free trade" zones in the developing world, and in new two-tier wage systems, service jobs, and temporary employment arrangements in the developed nations – where capital continues to appear just as it did in Shakespeare's day: "reeking from head to toe, from every pore, with blood and dirt" (Marx 1976: 926).

Second, it is commonly claimed that in *Capital* Marx explicitly grounds the concept of economic exploitation in the labor theory of value, which has been "proven wrong" by subsequent economists in the mainstream or neoclassical tradition. This critique has the virtue of raising issues of theoretical substance; and, indeed, even some Marxists have preferred the more flexible and open-ended exposition of Marx's unfinished *Grundrisse* to the steely logic of *Capital.* But as Richard Halpern (1991) argues with regard to "primitive accumulation," the Marx of *Capital* works in a double register, simultaneously parodying the strategies of conventional economic theory and producing a positive vision of his own. In this case, he appropriated the theory of value employed by Adam Smith and David Ricardo precisely because it was the prevailing orthodoxy of economic thought in the time. He says to the apologists of capital, in effect: I will use your economics, your system of accounting, in order to demonstrate the existence of exploitation. Thus, from a Marxist perspective, to say that the labor theory of value is "wrong" is finally to say little. At most, such an assertion simply means that the so-called "neoclassical synthesis" in economic theory – which adds the consumption-based concept of "marginal utility" to the production-based labor theory of classical economics – is a more accurate predictor of the movement of prices in a market economy. But Marx's goal was precisely to unveil the structures of domination that underlie the supposed freedom and equality of market-based social relations, and to reveal classical economic theory *as* ideology.

Typically, however, in the popular press, the by now reflexive dismissal of Marxism precludes any serious engagement with the tenets of Marxist thought. Instead, it relies on a simplistic equation of the collapse of Soviet-style communism with the "death" of Marxism. Marxism *was* used by repressive regimes; and there is no dodging that part of its complex history. But the sclerotic form of state socialism developed by the Soviet Union is not equivalent to the varied body of Marxist thought, an intellectual tradition that not only provides the most trenchant analysis of the operation of capital that we have, but also a highly developed body of work on issues such as the operation of ideology, the constitution of class societies, nationalism, historical periodization, and the historicity of literary forms and genres. The collapse of authoritarian communist regimes offers a perfect opportunity for a fresh examination of Marxist writings on a host of often neglected topics.

In fact, a decade after the destruction of the Berlin Wall it is time to put aside narratives of Marxism's demise and put its resources to use in new forms of intellectual production. This book attempts to do just that – to use Marx and Marxist-inflected theory to forge fresh narratives about Shakespeare and about the histories and institutions in which his texts have been implicated. In this, we are attempting to make possible new ways of seeing and to produce kinds of knowledge not available within other analytic traditions. This goal seems very much in line with Marx's own project. Consider his writings on political economy. One way to view them – a perspective he himself encouraged – is as an alternative to the readings of the world produced by the bourgeois political economists of his own time. While they accepted private property and wage labor as the natural "facts" from which economic interpretation proceeded, Marx saw these as the unnatural phenomena whose genealogy had to be constructed to produce an alternative understanding of what is natural, good, and desirable. Where others saw a coat for sale in a shop, Marx saw value in the form of congealed labor power. Where others saw profit, he saw the surplus value that had been extracted from alienated wage labor. Such power to "re-see" the world, to challenge the common sense that so often constitutes the dominant ideology of the powerful, is a key element in social struggles, even if its tangible consequences cannot be easily calculated or predicted.

Rather than a natural act, reading, then, is a learned activity and a site of contestation. The essays in this volume undertake acts of re-reading that re-situate, conceptually, the cultural artifacts of early modern England and re-examine their historical afterlives. Collectively, they model the many ways in which contemporary Marxist scholarship can be in productive conversation with feminist, anti-racist, and post-structuralist work. In fact, with the help of postructuralism, we perhaps see more clearly than Marx himself the continuing effects of the unholy alliance between the Enlightenment will to knowledge and the continuing global "drive" of capitalist exploitation even as capitalism's apologists within the Academy now cheerfully attest to such an alliance, defending conservative disciplinary values in the name of the "free market" of ideas.

Richard Halpern, however, in chapter 3, makes the trenchant point that some engagements with Marxism are too attenuated to be productive. For Halpern, this is the case with Derrida's account of his indebtedness to Marxism in *Specters of Marx*. He argues that once Derrida has disavowed the utility of most of Marx's central analytic categories, there is little reason to lay claim to a Marxist genealogy. The editors agree that the tent of historical materialism is not infinitely expandable or Marxism would lose its specificity as a situated knowledge project. The essays in this book explicitly locate themselves in relation to ongoing debates within Marxism and in relation to Marxist categories of analysis while nonetheless opening in a variety of ways to affiliated knowledge-making paradigms. This project of working in interstitial spaces to expand the resources of Marxism is well exemplified in Halpern's own earlier book, *The Poetics of Primitive Accumulation* (Halpern 1991). There he took up the relatively undertheorized concept of primitive accumulation in Marxist thought and did so in full conversation with non-Marxist critics such as Foucault. In the process he showed that the process of primitive accumulation involves *both* the amassing of capital through transformations in the mode of production and the emergence of a broad-based wage-labor class, *and also* the production of certain kinds of skilled subjects with capacities and psyches suited for managing and facilitating the world that was coming into being. Arguing that economic changes need not be completed before the emergence of the political and cultural phenomena we associate with capitalism, Halpern looked at such things as humanist pedagogy or sixteenth-century poetic styles as instruments in the production of differently skilled and socialized subjects. His argument illustrates the continuing capacity of self-identified Marxist criticism to grow beyond its nineteenth-century assumptions and to be transformed by engagement with other knowledge-making paradigms.

It is said Marx himself once irritably stipulated that "I am not a Marxist." The remark must be taken seriously, as a constant reminder that Marxism, across its entire history and in the present volume, cannot be taken as a set of fixed doctrines and beliefs, nor as a simple methodological focus on the analytic category of "class" as opposed to race, gender, or ethnicity. As Fredric Jameson has argued, Marxism is "a problematic: that is to say, it can be identified, not by specific positions . . . but rather by the allegiance to a specific complex of problems, whose formulations are always in movement." Thus the famous metaphor of the economic "base" and the cultural "superstructure" is not "a solution and a concept," but "a problem and a dilemma," and materialism itself is not a "philosophical position" but rather "the general signal for a process (better known as de-idealization), a process that can never be successfully brought to conclusion" (Jameson 1993a: 175).

We thus would argue, as against what some may think of as "orthodox" Marxism, that "class" relations cannot be considered to possess a priority in the colloquial sense, a greater immediacy or practical relevance to any and all human situations. Such a conclusion remains faithful to what Althusser calls the "immense theoretical revolution" of Marxism, which begins by insisting that neither the economic base nor the cultural superstructure, and neither theory nor practice, can serve as the singular and univocal determinant of the other. Marxist theory strives neither to privilege what Althusser mockingly calls the "green leaves of practice over the poverty of gray theory," nor to allow theory itself, even materialist theory, to split itself wholly off from practice, because to do so "necessarily arrives at dividing society into two parts, one of which is superior to society" (Marx 1978: 144). Rejecting the pure gaze of Enlightenment knowledge, Marxism argues for continuing attention to the conditions under which knowledge, including its own, is produced. Therefore, to insist that the category "class" is of more universal importance than other categories such as "race" or "gender" is either to fall into old-fashioned economic determinism in a more or less mechanical sense or into an endless and sterile cycle of subjectivism (more important to whom and for what?). But if economic determinism is typically framed as the characteristic pitfall of Marxism, contemporary cultural studies is more often threatened, by contrast, by a slippage back to idealist formations. Thus a whole range of scholarship tends to privilege some particular instance of culture – religion, nationalism, state power, or especially, the aesthetic itself – as the master key to the whole.

The work assembled in this volume finds new ways to avoid such pitfalls, renewing the resources of Marxism by drawing on categories long central to Marxist analysis and incorporating new ones. The work of Pierre Bourdieu, Negri and Hardt, Heidi Hartmann, Slojak Žižek, Alice Clark, Georges Bataille, Jean-Luc Nancy, Gayatri Spivak, and Fredric Jameson is here absorbed into the ongoing process of working with and against classical Marxism to produce more adequate accounts of past and present worlds. In this volume as in earlier Marxist undertakings, work, labor, and economic processes as they bear on cultural production are given considerable attention. But a number of essays also focus attention on the gendered nature of work, on new definitions of labor, and on emergent forms of cultural production. Traditional Marxist concerns with history and with periodization also thread through this volume, especially in those essays that self-consciously deal with the economic and cultural formations that in the early modern period accompany the transition to capitalism. But this is coupled with a newer insistence on the relative autonomy of superstructural elements and the subsequent move away from a base-driven, bottom-up model of historical development.

Particularly striking is the emphasis in a number of essays on the utopian, future-oriented aspects of Marxist thought. Kiernan Ryan, for example, calls for renewed attention to the utopian writings of thinkers such as Bloch, Benjamin, and Marcuse and invites contemporary critics to take up the task of imagining and enabling less oppressive futures (chapter 11). We find such initiatives in Barbara Bowen's attempts to imagine moments of revolutionary possibility (chapter 6), in Crystal Bartolovich's contemplation of a postnationalist globe (chapter 8), and in Scott Shershow's invocation of a community where the profit calculus of capitalism's economic imaginary will give way to a life lived "in common" (chapter 12). Refusing both teleological determinism and a naive faith in the power of individual agency before historical forces, a number of contributors move from the investigation of past and present culture to innovative mappings of future alternatives.

Indeed, a striking and productive self-consciousness about historical inquiry informs the essays here assembled. Partly in reaction to the relentless historicizing of the last two decades, many contributors articulate an impatience with what Kiernan Ryan calls the regressive nature of a criticism that would tie texts solely to their moments of production or that would refuse to link the study of the past with that of the present or the future. From myriad perspectives this volume addresses a fundamental, but complex question: what is the relationship between the early modern period, when the regimes we have inherited were inaugurated, the moment of nineteenth-century industrial capital when Marx elaborated his analysis, and the moment of late capitalism where we are now negotiating a relationship to both these prior historical moments, a negotiation conducted in this case through a series of texts – Shakespeare's and Marx's – that are being endlessly remade and repositioned in relation to one another and to the political and academic imperatives of the present moment?

It is clear, of course, that Marxist critics are not finished with the task of historicizing the early modern moment. Interestingly, a number of the essays in the volume that attend most acutely to the particularities of early modern culture deal with gender, both with women's labor, women's cultural production, and with new forms of gender ideology emerging with the speeding up of a capitalist market economy. It is as if the traditional Marxist accounts of the transition to capital have not yet provided adequate accounts of how gender hierarchies as well as class hierarchies were reconfigured during that crucial historical process. Moreover, the imperative to undertake these further inquiries stems in nearly every case from an urgent question in the present: Why is the present relationship of Marxism to feminism imagined as an unhappy marriage where the wife loses control of her property? Why have the canons of cultural production been defined in such a way that in modernity women's creative achievements have been trivialized? How do we find ourselves at a point in which the realm of the esthetic, last refuge of a universal humanism, has been cordoned off from history and supposedly cut loose from market values? It is to answer these questions, and so to write a history of the present, that the return to the early modern is enacted in a number of these essays. In such cases, the path to Shakespeare begins insistently in late modernity with a refusal to let the "historical" Shakespeare be separated off from present concerns.

At the same time, many of the contributors simply begin with contemporary Shakespeares, with what he has become in the postmodern moment, as his texts are re-situated by a global film industry, by poststructuralist criticism, by the fluid movement of capital beyond national boundaries, and even by the construction of "national" cultural institutions such as the new Globe Theatre. Shakespeare haunts the present as much as he haunts the past. As if in tacit acknowledgement of that fact, a surprising number of essays meditate on ghosts, especially the ghost of old Hamlet. But what kind of ghost is Shakespeare himself? a harmless apparition late capital can use to sell movie tickets? a resource to be mobilized in struggles for a more just world? a marker of a historical regime sufficiently different from our own to use as a lever to pry apart the iron bars of our common sense? The answer(s) depend, of course, in large part on the purposes for which he is summoned, and the essays that follow demonstrate some of the possibilities.

Peter Stallybrass and Richard Halpern open the volume with pieces that directly address the question of ghosts and of what it can mean to be haunted by the ghosts of old Hamlet, of Shakespeare, or of Marx. In a complex analysis of Marx's reading of Shakespeare and its effects on his writing of *The Eighteenth Brumaire*, Stallybrass suggests that just as Hamlet was haunted by the ghost of his father so the "revolution" of Louis Bonaparte was haunted by the heroic bourgeois revolutions that had gone before. The irony Marx imbibed from Shakespeare and specifically from *Hamlet* makes this haunting particularly complex, however. In the image of Hamlet's father as an old mole grubbing in the earth, Stallybrass reads a hint of prior heroic revolutions as well as overwhelming mockery and contempt for Louis Bonaparte's coup. At the same time, he sees in the undignified ghost the promise of what the proletarian revolution will be: not heroic, but impure, built from what has been borrowed from the past, but transformed, impish, irreverent.

Richard Halpern, by contrast, examines Derrida's claims in *Specters of Marx* to be haunted by his nineteenth-century forerunner. In a stringent critique of this claim, Halpern argues that Derrida will only acknowledge his affiliation to a Marx stripped of everything that makes Marxism an active, dangerous, and material force in the world: namely, a commitment to a transformative practice rooted in actual social relations. Negotiating between the writings of Derrida, Marx, and Shakespeare, Halpern incisively analyzes three positions made available by the text of *Hamlet* which Derrida assumes, at various times, in his reading of Marx – the positions of Prince, Ghost, and Gravedigger. Like Hamlet, Derrida at times wants an idealized, and idealist, father, not one corrupted by gross materiality. Like the Ghost, he wishes to issue ethical imperatives, but in doing so, in Halpern's view, he offers lists of social problems that need redress but no situated place from which to engage with those problems nor a systematic analysis of their causes and interconnections. Like the Gravedigger, he is busy unearthing skulls, here the skull of Marx, but in fetishizing the name and skull of Marx he misunderstands the greatest lesson of Marx, that things are known, not by their ontological status, but by their effects and consequences. To separate the name of Marx from the fully dialectical process of social transformation is, for Halpern, to deliver up a dead Marx indeed, one far removed from the stink and muck of what he dares to call "real history."

The three essays that follow Halpern's summon Marx to answer questions about gender, labor, and cultural production in the early modern period. To do so, they turn as well to feminist theorists and historians and to those working in the areas of performance and performativity. Dympna Callaghan's provocative essay (chapter 4) focuses on early modern women's work with textiles – their role in weaving, embroidering, laundering, mending, and preserving clothing and fabrics. While acknowledging that such work was often enjoined on women as a form of discipline and a remedy for idleness, Callaghan follows Alice Clark in arguing that in the early modern period its productive nature remained visible. It had not yet been reclassified as the private recreation of middling-sort and aristocratic women inhabiting what was constructed as a private sphere of domesticity separate from the public sphere of work, profit, and serious and legitimated forms of cultural production. Arguing against Virginia Woolf's tendency to seek a Judith Shakespeare who had written books to equal William's, Callaghan suggests that one should seek, instead, in the now undervalued products of women's household labor the traces of early modern female creativity.

Natasha Korda (chapter 5) is also interested in what happened to women's labor in the transition to capitalism. Her essay focuses first on the law of coverture and on the gap between theory and practice. Drawing on the work of feminist historians and legal scholars, she shows the kinds of tacit, and in some cases explicit, control that even married women retained over the management, sale, and acquisition of property in the early modern period. She argues, in fact, using *The Merry Wives of Windsor* as an illustrative text, that as middling-sort households acquired more movable property in the early modern period, the role of the housewife was increasingly one of surveillance. She watched over, accounted for, and maintained the material things that defined a class position even as she exercised a gendered self-surveillance grounded in discretion and sexual modesty.

Barbara Bowen (chapter 6) shares with Korda and Callaghan a commitment to rethink the conditions of possibility for women's agency in the early modern period, but she focuses on a specific woman, Aemilia Lanyer, who not only employed her needle creatively, but also wrote texts. Bowen examines Lanyer's *Salve Deus Rex Judaeorum* and the way this poem, in part through its citation of Shakespeare's *Rape of Lucrece*, makes it possible to think about how revolutionary change might occur and about the role of women as a collectivity in inaugurating such change. We should not "under-read" the textual productions of women writers, Bowen argues, by treating them as the precocious but slightly illegitimate and ill-educated stepchildren of the canonical family. In her hands, consequently, Lanyer's account of the passion of Christ is explored as a complex textual site for rewriting received history and imagining a revolutionary challenge to the patriarchal order.

Walter Cohen's essay (chapter 7) takes up another crucial topic: the relation of the early modern theater to developments in the economic sphere, particularly the expansion of trade on a global scale. Arguing that in England the transition to capitalism occurred first in the agrarian sector, Cohen nonetheless urges the importance of international commerce to the full development of capitalist social and economic relations in the sixteenth and seventeenth centuries. By looking comprehensively at shifting geographies of Shakespeare's plays and at the commercial references within them, he suggests how the stage was affected by England's commercial expansion, spearheaded by the joint-stock companies that before 1620 made their greatest profits in ventures to the East. He argues that over the course of his writing career Shakespeare increasingly shifted his focus of attention from northern Europe to the Mediterranean basin while simultaneously increasing his range of reference to the products and the peoples encountered by traders and travelers who ventured to the East and South. Placing the early modern theater in an increasingly global context, Cohen offers a corrective to those accounts of early modern commercial development that focus primarily on England's role in the New World prior to the 1620s.

The next three essays focus, in different ways, on the relationship between "Shakespeare" and the theater itself – as commodity, institution, and shifting marker of national and transnational "culture." Richard Wilson (chapter 8) addresses the transitional nature of the early modern theater, in particular the way Shakespeare mystified the market investments of the commercial stage by imagining the ideal theater as a scene of aristocratic patronage. Drawing on Bourdieu's work on the role of patronage in the development of the ideology of aesthetic autonomy, Wilson argues that the early modern theater at the moment of the transition to capitalism strove to create a space for itself "above" the market by denying its own embroilment in the urban market economy. In its oscillation between the pole of power and the pole of commerce the modern theater found, he asserts, its fable of freedom from both ideology and base lucre.

By contrast, Crystal Bartolovich (chapter 9) shifts to the present moment to examine the consequences of contemporary globalization on attempts to mobilize Shakespeare for nationalist purposes. In the process she mounts a strong critique of attempts, even strategic attempts, to use nationalist ideologies for progressive purposes. Her specific focus is the new Globe Theatre on the south bank in London, an institution which she reads as answering to a national crisis of identity in 1970s Britain and which, in its first season, chose to stage the chauvinistic *Henry V* as part of its celebration of the uniqueness of the English language, English theater, the English essence. Asking who really owns English, Bartolovich, however, questions the very idea of a homogeneous national language or culture. While *Henry V* ostentatiously juxtaposes French and English as discrete tongues, Bartolovich points out that since the Norman Conquest English has been indebted to and informed by the French language. In disavowing and forgetting this debt, the play employs the familiar ruses of a possessive nationalism. As an alternative, Bartolovich calls for a "globality from below" premised on the abandonment of all tendentious nationalisms.

In her turn, Denise Albanese (chapter 10) picks up the volume's preoccupation with processes of globalization as she examines the fissures, in the context of late capital, in the concept of "the Shakespeare film" and the complexities that arise when Shakespeare becomes a commodity in a global market. Contrasting Branagh's reverential film version of *Hamlet* to Luhrmann's *Romeo and Juliet,* Albanese argues that Luhrmann adapts Shakespeare to an international youth market increasingly catered to by the American film industry. Ironically, even Branagh, inheritor of the mantle of Olivier, resorts to an international cast of actors to give his film the box-office appeal that his preoccupation with "the authentic" Shakespearean text would seem to belie. It is Luhrmann's practice, however, that Albanese finds the most complicated since he is able to turn Shakespeare into a popular commodity, but to do so in a way that relies in postmodern fashion on the ironic consumption of racial and cultural difference (here the exotic "Latin" setting of the play's *mise en scène*) and in good capitalist fashion on the cheap labor of film locations south of the US border. Whatever "Shakespeare" once meant as a marker of national culture, his texts now circulate in a global film industry that inadvertently undermines nationalist ideologies.

The final two essays in this collection look beyond the contemporary moment addressed by Bartolovich and Albanese and toward the future. Kiernan Ryan (chapter 11) begins by evoking the utopian and future-oriented aspects of Marxist thought as represented in part by Benjamin, Marcuse, Bloch, and Jameson. Reading strongly against the grain of much contemporary criticism, Ryan argues that a play such as *Measure for Measure* does not simply reveal the workings of a carceral state and regimes of surveillance, but that it also critiques those regimes and opens toward a vision of the future that surpasses the need both for law and for mercy. Refusing the conflation of the Duke and the playwright, Ryan focuses on those formal and narrative elements of *Measure for Measure* that resist the play's hierarchies and its mechanisms of justice. In a deft critique of liberal notions of justice and mercy, he provocatively posits a Shakespeare who taught Marx to anticipate more radical forms of social possibility. His essay offers a deliberate challenge to those who see the end of literary study as an undialectical historicism whose telos is genuflexion before the fleshless skull of the past.

The very last essay begins with a problem in the present, with the question of why Marxism is dismissed as mere "ideology" by proponents of a "universal Shakespeare," who by contrast present the Bard as free, autonomous, unfettered by ideology. Scott Shershow suggests that these two opposed positions have a complex relationship to what Georges Bataille called the "restricted economy" of scarcity and the "general economy" of surplus and plenitude. In a project that shares some ground with Ryan, he suggests that the esthetic was constructed in the early modern period as the domain of a spurious general economy of plenitude that was always in service of the restricted economies of market capitalism. Thus, today, universalizing critics such as Harold Bloom perversely construe Shakespeare as "broad" and theory as "narrow." By contrast, Shershow argues for a model of what Jean-Luc Nancy, building on Bataille, calls "literary communism." "Shakespeare" re-emerges, not as the heroic, autonomous, universal poet – whose words vibrate in tune with the heroic literary interpreter – but instead as what Nancy calls a "singular voice in common."

Marxist Shakespeares is a collective project in many senses. It arose from a special session at a conference of the Shakespeare Association of America. The session's title – "Whither Marxism?" – was the same as that taken by the conference that produced Derrida's *Specters of Marx* and another influential anthology. In both cases, skeptics were quick to turn the title into an imperative: "Wither, Marxism!" But Marxism has not complied. The present volume joins others in suggesting that the fall of communist governments around the world does not signal the ignoble end of Marxist thought, but rather the possibility of its renewal. Marxism continues to provide a compelling framework through which to understand both contemporary texts and events and those of prior periods. If many of us persist in questioning certain aspects of Marx's nineteenth-century project, all of us, in our separate ways, acknowledge that we have not finished thinking through the implications of his immense theoretical revolution. As the essays in this volume suggest, the ghosts of Shakespeare and of Marx continue to work, like old moles, in the cellarage and deep in the soil of the twenty-first century. "Remember me." Of course.

2

"Well grubbed, old mole": Marx, *Hamlet*, and the (un)fixing of representation

PETER STALLYBRASS

In December 1851, Louis Bonaparte staged a coup d'état in Paris and seized control of the state. Marx immediately set to work to write weekly articles for intended publication by his friend, Joseph Weydemeyer, in a German language publication in New York. The publication history of *The Eighteenth Brumaire* (which Marx himself emphasizes) runs counter to Engels's account in his preface to its third German edition of 1885. In his preface, Engels rewrites Marx's journalism within the oeuvre of Marx's earlier theory of the modes of production, outlined in *The German Ideology*. *The Eighteenth Brumaire* merely confirms "the law according to which all historical struggles, whether they proceed in the political, the religious, philosophical or some other domain, are in fact only the more or less clear expression of struggles of social classes" (Marx 1852a: 14).[1] For Engels, what is most striking about Marx's occasional writing of 1851 is that it overrides all contingency to grasp the "ephemeral" aspect of political occasion as the indirect representation of an already known social conjuncture. On Engels's account, the events of 1851 "never took [Marx] by surprise" (Marx 1852a: 14). Engels was, of course, writing after the fall of the Second Empire, and from that perspective, Marx's narrative could be represented as an omniscient analysis of historical teleology.

But there is an extraordinary disparity between Engels's preface in 1885 and Marx's preface to the second edition of 1869. Where Engels claims that Marx was never taken by surprise, Marx's own preface stages the radical contingencies by which his representation of the events of 1851 came (or rather failed to come) to public attention. Marx's essays were intended for what was to be a German language political weekly, published in New York, beginning on January 1, 1852. But Weydemeyer never got sufficient financial backing for his journal, so the weekly never appeared. Instead, Weydemeyer proposed printing a *monthly*, called *Die Revolution*, although this too ran into financial difficulties, and collapsed after the second issue. The first issue of the journal consisted of Marx's *Eighteenth Brumaire*. One thousand copies of the journal were printed, a third of which were sent from the United States back to Europe. But booksellers refused to handle the journal, and those that were distributed at all were distributed by friends and sympathizers (Mehring 1962: 218; Marx and Engels 1982: 216). The work itself, Marx claims, "took shape under the immediate pressure of events" (Marx 1852a: 7) and even the republication in 1869 is due to local circumstances: "in part to the demand of the book trade, in part to the urgent request of my friends in Germany" (Marx 1852a: 7). Marx's text, in other words, far from existing as a stable representation, was itself, as Marx insists, shaped by economic and political contingencies.

One small trace of these contingencies is inscribed in the change to the book's title: when it was printed in 1852 in *Die Revolution*, its title was *Der Achtzehnte Brumaire des Louis Napoleon*; in 1869, it is the 18th Brumaire of Louis *Bonaparte*. The change is a small one but nonetheless striking, and itself suggests Marx's acute attention to historical contingency, the uncertainties which Engels attempted to erase. When Marx first published *The Eighteenth Brumaire*, Louis Bonaparte had not yet assumed the official title of Emperor, which he only did in the December of 1852. As Emperor, he became Napoleon III. To retain the earlier title of the book would be to grant a seeming legitimacy to Louis's claim to the name Napoleon. In this new conjuncture, Marx needed to assert the *illegitimacy* of Louis Bonaparte's assumption of the name, and legacy, of his uncle. He did this by insisting on the family name, Bonaparte, rather than Napoleon.

A conjunctural understanding of history necessarily emphasizes the contingencies which are dressed up as historical inevitability. But in *The Eighteenth Brumaire*, while Marx proposes such a conjunctural interpretation, he also suggests that the present necessarily works through the assumption of the magics of the past: the names (Napoleon), the ideas (empire), the clothes and emblems. Hence, the much quoted opening to *The Eighteenth Brumaire*:

> Hegel remarks somewhere that all facts and all personages of great importance in world history occur, as it were, twice. He forgot to add: the first time as tragedy, the second as farce.
>
> (Marx 1852a: 15)

Any synchronic view of history, in other words, must attend to the ways in which the past haunts the present. Representation itself depends upon *belatedness*, a coming after. We clothe ourselves, whether we want to or not, in the clothes of the past:

> The tradition of all the dead generations weighs like a nightmare on the brain of the living. And just when they seem engaged in revolutionizing themselves and things, in creating something that has never yet existed, precisely in such periods of revolutionary crisis they anxiously conjure up the spirits of the past to their service and borrow from them names, battle cries and costumes in order to present the new scene of world history in this time-honoured disguise and this borrowed language.
>
> (Marx 1852a: 15)

The contingencies of the new are represented through the "borrowed languages" of the past: Luther clothes himself as the Apostle Paul; Cromwell assumes the guise of Old Testament prophet; the Revolution of 1789 to 1814 drapes itself alternately as the Roman republic and the Roman empire.

Marx appears at first to raise the problem of the repetition of the past to distinguish between the "heroic" bourgeois revolutions of the seventeenth and eighteenth centuries and the reactionary coup d'état of Louis Bonaparte. In contrast, the "revolution" of Louis Bonaparte is a farcical repetition, a mere parody of the past, an awakening of the dead only to travesty them. In place of Danton and Robespierre, Caussidière and Louis Blanc; in place of the Montagne of 1793, the Montagne of 1848; in place of the 18th Brumaire of Napoleon I, the coup d'état of his nephew, an adventurer "who hides his commonplace repulsive features under the iron death mask of Napoleon" (Marx 1852a: 17).

But this opposition between the "tragedies" of early bourgeois upheavals and the "farce" of their later simulations is unsettled by Marx's acknowledgement that even those early upheavals only *used* tragedy as one of "the ideals and the art forms, the self deceptions that they needed in order to conceal from themselves the bourgeois limitations of the content of their struggles" (Marx 1852a: 16). "[T]he high plane of the great historical tragedy" is *itself*, then, a repetition in which a society as "unheroic as bourgeois society" dresses itself up (Marx 1852a: 16–17). Only after the revolution can bourgeois society assume its "true" guise: not Habakkuk but Locke. To put it another way, the classical hierarchy of genres, in which tragedy was considered the most elevated and farce the most debased of genres, can no longer retain its unquestioned status within a bourgeois society that pursues the "novel." Tragedy must now itself be understood as farce. From this perspective, Louis Bonaparte is the most appropriate of performers upon the stage of bourgeois society, for he unintentionally unmasks the self-deceptions of the elevated genres through which an earlier bourgeois society imagined itself. In Marx's words, Louis Bonaparte produces "not only a caricature of the old Napoleon," but also "the old Napoleon himself, caricatured as he must appear in the middle of the nineteenth century" (Marx 1852a: 18). And Marx's preface to the second edition makes clear his own desire to submit the cult of the first Napoleon to "the weapons of historical research, of criticism, of satire and of wit" (Marx 1852a: 8).

Marx thus pursues a double strategy in *The Eighteenth Brumaire*. Through the first strategy, history is represented as a catastrophic decline from Napoleon to Louis Bonaparte. But in the second strategy, the effect of this "debased" repetition is to unsettle the status of the origin. Napoleon I can now only be read back through his nephew: his ghost is awakened but as a caricature. Yet caricature, parody, satire, and farce were far from negative forms for Marx. They were indeed the necessary forms of representation in a society where "an epic . . . can no longer be written" (Prawer 1976: 15). Marx, in *The Eighteenth Brumaire*, developed a brilliant if unsystematic account of literary and political representation and of repetition and the settling and unsettling of origins. He did this above all through an indirect re-reading of *Hamlet* as parody or farce.

Let me begin by emphasizing Marx's profound interest both in Shakespeare and in parodic forms. In 1837, as a young man of 19, Marx began work on *Scorpion und Felix*, a comic novel. Its structure and techniques were based not upon the *Bildungsroman* of Goethe but upon Sterne's "anti-novel," *Tristram Shandy*, for which Marx had the highest admiration. Like Sterne, Marx delighted in "sudden, deliberate letdowns" and in "verbal cartoons" (Prawer 1976: 15). Like Sterne, Marx developed a range of parodies: of the Bible, of Ovid, of Goldsmith's *The Vicar of Wakefield*, but above all of Shakespeare. Not only does Marx parody Shakespeare, and in particular *Richard III*, but he also pays particular attention to parody *in* Shakespeare, and to the bitter fool Thersites in *Troilus and Cressida*, a fool whom Marx would continue to quote and to appropriate throughout his life.

Shakespeare was Marx's favorite author, as he was to become his daughters'. Marx had learned his love for Shakespeare in the 1830s from Ludwig von Westphalen, soon to be his father-in-law. Eleanor, Marx's daughter, later wrote that "whereas [Marx's] father read Voltaire and Racine with him, the Baron [von Westphalen] read him Homer and Shakespeare – who remained his favourite authors all his life' (McLellan 1973: 15). But it was particularly when he finally moved to England in 1849 that Marx devoted himself to Shakespeare, whom he read every day. As Franz Mehring wrote in his memoir of Marx:

> After Marx had become permanently domiciled in London, English literature took first place, and the tremendous figure of Shakespeare dominated the field; in fact the whole family practiced what amounted practically to a Shakespearean cult.
>
> (Baxandall and Morawski [eds] 1973: 143; see also Padover 1978: 51, 156, 333, 475, 513, 628)

When they moved to London, the Marxes would frequently take a picnic to Hampstead Heath on Sundays. On the way out, according to their fellow exile, Wilhelm Liebknecht, they would sing African-American spirituals; on their return, Karl and his wife Jenny would recite whole scenes from Shakespeare. Eleanor Marx, in her recollections of her father, wrote: "As to Shakespeare he was the Bible of our house, seldom out of our hands or mouths. By the time I was six I knew scene upon scene of Shakespeare by heart" (Baxandall and Morawski [eds] 1973: 149). Eleanor aspired to become a Shakespearean actor, and later became a keen member of Furnivall's New Shakespeare Society. She and her sister Jenny also wrote a series of articles on Shakespeare for the *Frankfurter Zeitung*. And towards the end of Marx's life, Shakespeare play-readings were held at Marx's house by a group who called themselves the Dogberry Club (Fedoseyev 1973: 518).

But this devotion to Shakespeare scarcely suggests just *what* Marx admired in him, which was precisely the hybridity which had led Voltaire to call Shakespeare a drunken savage. In opposition to Voltaire, Marx praised Shakespearean drama for "its peculiar mixture of the sublime and the base, the terrible and the ridiculous, the heroic and the burlesque" (Prawer 1976: 241). After 1848, according to Paul Lafargue, Marx "sought out . . . all the peculiar expressions used by Shakespeare," and if this was in part to extend his command of

English, it was also because he took particular pleasure in the Shakespearean grotesque: in Falstaff, in Thersites, in the base and the farcical. He was, as Lafargue remarks, interested in "the *peculiar* expressions," as he was interested in the "*peculiar* mixture," of Shakespearean drama. It was, in other words, the very *im*purities of Shakespearean drama, its resistances to a classical theory of representation, which interested Marx. It was a similar fascination with the hybrid which led Marx to call his book in response to the libels of Karl Vogt, "Da-Da Vogt." Da-Da was the name given to a translator of bonapartist pamphlets circulating in Algeria. Although Marx's family and friends persuaded him to discard the title as too obscure, he did so reluctantly. The name "Da-Da," he wrote, "puzzles the philistine and is comical"; it "fits well into my system of mockery and contempt" (Prawer 1976: 265). Marx thus pre-empted the dadaists' subversion of representation by more than half a century.

The farcical in Marx, though, is not only used as part of his "system of mockery and contempt"; it is equally central to his system of celebration. And it is here that Marx works against the pathos of decline ("then, they were giants; now, we are dwarves") which would be one way of reading the opening sentences of *The Eighteenth Brumaire*: history repeats itself, the first time as tragedy, the realm of heroes, the second time as farce, the realm of buffoons and scoundrels. For Marx, though, if Da-Da Vogt can only be represented through the grotesque, proletarian revolution must be represented equally unheroically:

> proletarian revolutions . . . criticize themselves constantly, interrupt themselves continuously in their own course, come back to the apparently accomplished in order to begin it afresh, deride with unmerciful thoroughness the inadequacies, weaknesses and paltrinesses of their first attempts, seem to throw down their adversary only in order that he may draw new strength from the earth and rise again, more gigantic, before them, recoil ever and anon from the indefinite prodigiousness of their own aims, until a situation has been created which makes all turning back impossible, and the conditions themselves cry out:
>
> *Hic Rhodus, hic salta!*
> *Here is the rose, here dance!*
>
> (Marx 1852a: 19)

For Marx, the features of the coming revolution will be hesitancy, an awareness of inadequacy, and revolution is imagined in the realm of fairy tale (the giant who is knocked down only to gain more power) and of Aesop's fables. ("Here is Rhodes, leap here!" is taken from Aesop's tale "The Swaggerer," in which a boaster who claims that he made an enormous leap in Rhodes is mockingly asked to repeat the leap from where he is right now.)

Just as Marx adopts contradictory techniques to represent Louis Bonaparte as simultaneously a shrunken parody of his heroic uncle *and* as the unmasking of the impossibility of *any* heroism (whether Napoeon I's or Napoleon III's) within the categories of bourgeois society, so Marx adopts contradictory techniques to represent revolution. On the one hand, it is, he claims, unrepresentable ("the social revolution of the nineteenth century cannot draw its poetry from the past"; "the content goes beyond the phrase"); on the other, he himself represents it through two odd appropriations of "poetry from the past": the revolution is Puck or Robin Goodfellow from *A Midsummer Night's Dream*; it is the ghost of Hamlet's father. These two latter images are combined by Marx in a speech he delivered on April 14, 1856, on the anniversary of the Chartist *People's Paper*. Here, he stages a curious paradox: what he calls "the new-fangled forces of society" create people who are so novel that they can no longer be grasped through prior systems of representation. The working men and women of the nineteenth century are, Marx declares, "as much the invention of modern times as machinery itself" (Prawer 1976: 246). Yet Marx immediately defines this revolutionary moment through those very past languages which he has implicitly rejected:

> [The new working men] are as much the invention of modern times as machinery itself. In the signs that bewilder the middle class, the aristocracy and the poor prophets of regression, we recognize our brave friend, Robin Goodfellow, the old mole that can work in the earth so fast, that worthy pioneer – the Revolution.
>
> (Marx 1856: 656)

Marx, in other words, imagines revolution *both* as an epistemic break which, having "stripped off all superstition in regard to the past," turns its back upon the past so as to constitute itself in and through the future; *and* as parodic repetition, a repetition presided over by the ghosts of the past.

The Eighteenth Brumaire, indeed, is not only a reworking of *Hamlet* but also a reworking of Marx's own attitude towards ghosts and haunting. Much of his earlier writing had been dedicated to the exorcism of ghosts, whether conjured up by religion or by Hegel. And in the first section of *The Eighteenth Brumaire*, Marx retains a distinction between "mere" ghosts and "true" spirits: the awakening of the dead in earlier revolutions "served the purpose of glorifying the new struggles, not of parodying the old; of magnifying the given task in imagination, not of fleeing from its solution in reality; of finding once more the spirit of revolution, not of making its ghost walk about again" (Marx 1852a: 17). Ghosts are a superstition, a drug (Marx 1852a: 18); the dead must be left to bury the dead. Yet in the final section of *The Eighteenth Brumaire*, as in the opening of *The Communist Manifesto*, the radicalized proletariat *itself* erupts as a ghost: "A spectre is haunting Europe"; "Well grubbed, old mole!" In the imagined proletarian revolution, as in the February Revolution which Marx denounces, a "prophecy" "haunts the subsequent acts of the drama like a ghost" (Marx 1852a: 118).[2]

But the ghosts which Marx invokes are not heroic. Indeed, when he invokes them, they are as parodic as Louis Bonaparte. Marx's prophetic ghosts are Robin Goodfellow or Puck; the ghost of Hamlet's father but in the form of "the old mole that can work in the earth so fast, that worthy pioneer." It is the latter figure upon whom I shall concentrate here. In his speech of 1856, Marx is himself repeating his writing of 1852. In *The Eighteenth Brumaire*, he had written of the seeming defeat of socialism by Louis Bonaparte's coup:

> The struggle seems to be settled in such a way that all classes, equally impotent and equally mute, fall on their knees before the rifle butt.
>
> But the revolution is thoroughgoing. It is still journeying through purgatory. It does its work methodically . . . And when it has done this second half of its preliminary work, Europe will leap from its seat and exultantly exclaim: Well grubbed, old mole! (*Brav gewühlt, alter Maulwurf*!).
>
> (Marx 1852a: 121)[3]

But why does Marx represent the revolution through the ghost of Hamlet's father? And, even more to the point, why does he invoke that ghost (and the revolution) in Hamlet's grotesque and debasing image of his father as a *mole*?

Let me first outline as clearly as possible my major suppositions in my understanding of the relation between Marx's analysis of Louis Bonaparte and his reading of *Hamlet*. To repeat what I have already argued: the period from 1848 to 1852 saw Marx engaged both in a detailed analysis of French politics and the rise of Louis Bonaparte and in intense reading of Shakespeare. These two concerns, I believe, complexly converge in *The Eighteenth Brumaire*, which is, like *Hamlet*, an analysis of *repetition.* While the nephew, Napoleon III-to-be, farcically repeats his uncle, Napoleon I, Hamlet, the son, assumes an "antic disposition" and farcically repeats his father, Hamlet. Both narratives depend upon the repetition of a name (Napoleon, Hamlet); both, at least temporarily, conjure up a previously tragic world which has been displaced by a farcical one. Both texts explore how the past haunts the present.

But if the past haunts the present, it is also *re*-presented, transformed by the remaking of its presence. Nowhere is this more striking than in *Hamlet.* Hamlet, the son, obsessively idealizes his father, comparing him as Hyperion, the sun-god, to the satyr of his uncle, Claudius. And when Hamlet, the father, returns, it is in his most heroic form, dressed in armor. And not just any armor but "the very Armor he had on" when he fought and defeated Fortinbras (1. 1. 60).[4] The father returns, we might say, as the material trace which has survived him: the armor which was a typical legacy from father to son, surviving the father's death to mould, whether literally or ideologically, the son's identity. It was, for instance, "the remainder of two rich armors which were my father's" which Lady Anne Clifford left to her granchildren "to remaine to them and their posterity . . . as a remembrance of him" (Williamson 1922: 467). Such physical remembrances powerfully *fix* representation, and it is precisely such a fixing (of his father's memory, of his own assumption of his father's name) that Hamlet desires, as Napoleon III attempted to fix and appropriate the legacy of his uncle.

What Marx takes from *Hamlet,* though, is not Hamlet's attempt to *be* his father but the radical unsettling of this revenance in the son's (un)naming of the paternal legacy. For Hamlet, as for his friends Marcellus, Barnardo, and Horatio, the Ghost is at first not "he" but "it." The Ghost is only transformed from "it" by Hamlet's own act of naming: "Ile *call* thee *Hamlet,* / King, Father, Royall Dane" (1. 1. 50; my emphasis). And yet, having named his father in the full majesty of his authority, Hamlet proceeds to strip him of those very titles, addressing him with an increasingly mocking familiarity:

> Ha, ha, boy, say'st thou so? art thou there trupenny?
> Come on, you heare this fellowe in the Sellerige.
> (1. 5. 150–1)

"Boy," "trupenny," "fellowe": each word debases the father, dethrones the monarch. "Boy": a male child before puberty; also, in the Renaissance, a servant or slave, and, as a term of contempt, a rogue or knave. "Truepenny": an honest fellow, but a term commonly used patronizingly of an inferior ("Truepenny" is the name of a servant in *Ralph Roister Doister*). "Fellow": a companion or comrade; but also the customary address of a servant, and with the contemptuous sense of a person of no worth. The king and father no longer enthroned but "in the cellarage" – beneath the ground but also, in the technical language of the theater, underneath the stage – literally subordinated, even in his terrifying return.

> The father finally as mole:
> Well sayd olde Mole, can'st worke i'th'earth so fast,
> A worthy Pioner.
>
> (1. 5. 162–3)

Hamlet, the dead father, no longer king and royal Dane but mole and pioneer. In appropriating "old mole" as a figure of revolution, Marx brilliantly illuminates, even as he transforms, the politics of the Renaissance play from which he appropriates. For while *Hamlet* seems to contrast the supposed legitimacy of primogeniture – the chain of father and son, Hamlet and Hamlet – with the illegitimate usurpation of the brother/uncle, Claudius, the play, as Marx's appropriation suggests, stages something more unsettling: the transformation of the principle of legitimacy – the father and king – into the principle of subversion. One should take subversion quite literally here. The modern German for subversive activity – *Maulwurfsarbeit* – means literally the work of the mole. In figuring his father as mole, Hamlet enacts a radical metamorphosis: from human to animal; from omnipotent monarch to blind burrower; from ideological figurehead to a worker in the ground. It is a literal *humbling*, a bringing of the ideological superstructure down to earth (*humus*, the etymological root for "humble," is the Latin for "earth").

The transformation of the father into mole has a further unsettling implication. For the word occurs only one other time in *Hamlet*, and that is in the preceding scene, where Hamlet derides the Danish wassails:

> So oft it chaunces in particuler men,
> That for some vicious mole of nature in them
> As in their birth wherein they are not guilty,
> (Since nature cannot choose his origin)
> By their ore-grow'th of some complexion
> Oft breaking downe the pales and forts of reason,
> Or by some habit, that too much ore-leauens

> The forme of plausiue manners, that these men
> Carrying I say the stamp of one defect
> Being Natures liuery, or Fortunes starre,
> His vertues els be they as pure as grace,
> As infinite as any man may vndergoe,
> Shall in the generall censure take corruption
> From that particuler fault.
>
> (1. 4. 23–36)

The mole, then, not only as burrowing animal, but as defect, taint, a "particular fault" which can corrupt the whole. For "mole" also signifies a discolored spot on linen ("one iron mole defaceth the whole piece of lawn") and a blemish on the skin ("one mole staineth the whole face"). In *King John*, a mother talks of a child who is "sland'rous to [his] Mothers wombe" as one who is "[p]atch'd with foule Moles and eye-offending markes" (3. 1. 47), and when Oberon concludes *A Midsummer Night's Dream* with a blessing upon the betrothed couples, he says:

> So shall all the couples three,
> Euer true in louing be:
> And the blots of Natures hand
> Shall not in their issue stand,
> Neuer mole, harelip, nor scarre,
> Nor marke prodigious, such as are
> Despised in Natiuitie,
> Shall vpon their children be.
>
> (5. 1. 407–14)

In figuring his father as "old mole," Hamlet associates him both with an underground animal and with the "blots of Nature" which subvert legitimacy and unfix the patrilineal bond, and he begins the process by which he will, despite his repeated promises to "remember" his father, reject the suit of armor which would remake him in his father's image.

For if Hamlet takes upon himself the Ghost's demand, if he is buried as a soldier with "[t]he soldier's music, and the rites of war," he never becomes his armored father. Indeed, when Hamlet returns from England, he writes to Claudius in a curiously ambiguous phrase that he is "*set naked on your kingdom*" (4. 7. 43–4). His farcical representation of his father as mole precedes his putting on of an "antic disposition," the disposition of the fool or court jester. And it is the court jester, Yorick, not his father, whom Hamlet most fondly recalls: "he hath bore me on his backe a thousand times, and now how abhorred in my imagination it is: my gorge rises at it. Heere hung those lyppes, that I haue kist I know not howe oft" (5. 1. 185–9). The lips that he has kissed: the lips not of the father but of the jester. Though Yorick is dead, his skull memorializes the legacy he leaves, a legacy which includes the "antic disposition." In striking contrast to *The Spanish Tragedy*, where the ghost returns gloatingly to conclude the plot, the Ghost of *Hamlet* simply disappears after Act 3. One might say that the ghost of the jester displaces the ghost of the soldier-king.

But, if we are to believe the so-called "bad" first quarto of *Hamlet*, the soldier-king had been displaced even before Act 3. In the bed-chamber scene, as Hamlet berates his mother, the stage direction reads "Enter the ghost in his night gowne" (Q1, 3. 4. 101). A king no longer clad in complete steel but in the robes of undress, ready for bed. A supposedly heroic past is subverted by this revelation of domestic vulnerability. It is not clear to whom Hamlet refers when he says "A King of shreds and patches" (3. 4. 102): to his usurping uncle or to his father, stripped of the trappings of power – boy, truepenny, fellow, old mole. Marx himself opens the way for such an absorption of the legitimating father/king into the delegitimating fool and jester in his own reworking of the "old mole" for his speech of 1856, which I quoted before:

> In the signs that bewilder the middle class, the aristocracy and the poor prophets of regression, we recognize our brave friend, Robin Goodfellow, the old mole that can work in the earth so fast, that worthy pioneer – the Revolution.
>
> (Marx 1856: 656)

Hamlet, the father/king, as Puck; Puck, like "Da-Da," as the bewilderer of the bourgeoisie.

In his 1856 speech, Marx extends his previous quotation of *Hamlet*: it is the "old mole," he continues, "that can work in the earth so fast, that worthy pioneer." *This* mole, the "spectre [which] is haunting Europe" of the opening sentence of *The Communist Manifesto*, is "a pioneer," a word which ironically combines *both* the sense of a rupture with the past *and* the sense of the historical conditions "which weigh like a nightmare on the brain of the living." By the 1830s, the metaphorical sense of a pioneer as explorer or initiator had taken on a specific reference in the United States. In 1836, Irving wrote: "As one wave of emigration after another rolls into the vast regions of the waste, the eager eyes of our pioneers will pry beyond." In this sense, the Revolution is imagined as opening up an unforeseen future. But such a future, for Marx, could only be constructed upon the specific labors of the past and the present. A "pioneer" in the older sense is less glamorous, more a mole: "one of a body of foot-soldiers who march with or in advance of an army or regiment, having spades, pickaxes etc. to dig trenches, repair roads, and perform other labours in clearing and preparing the way for the main body"; also, by extension, a miner.

The Eighteenth Brumaire reads *Hamlet* as a staging of the unfixing of representation. Yet that unfixing itself depends upon repetition. Marx's "mole," indeed, repeats not only *Hamlet* but the conclusion of Hegel's *Lectures on the Philosophy of History*, where Hegel argued that "the latest philosophy contains therefore those which went before; . . . it is the product and result of all that preceded it" (Hegel 1955: 552–3; Hegel 1928: 691). "Individuals," though, cannot stand outside that process so as to grasp it; they are themselves "like blind men, who are driven forward by the indwelling spirit of the whole." The Spirit can only emerge "into the light of day" if we "give ear to its urgency – when the mole that is within forces its way on – and we have to make it a reality" (Hegel 1955: 553; Hegel 1928: 691). But Marx's mole, unlike Hegel's, is not working towards the light; it is working in the earth. Its labor is one of uprooting. Indeed, in Marx's rematerialization of the work of the ghost, he *mis*quotes *Hamlet*. In Q2, the lines are:

> Well sayd olde Mole, can'st worke i'th'earth so fast,
> A worthy Pioner.

Or, in the Schlegel/Tieck translation which Marx also knew:

> Brav, alter Maulwurf! Wühlst so hurtig fort?
> O trefflicher Minierer!
>
> (Schlegel 1841: 35)

In *The Eighteenth Brumaire*, though, "Well *said*, old mole" or "*Brav, alter Maulwurf*" becomes "well *grubbed*, old mole" (*Brav gewühlt, alter Maulwurf*), the "*Wühlst*" of the Schlegel/Tieck translation being transferred to the opening phrase ("*Brav gewühlt*"). The mouth as organ of speech in Shakespeare becomes the mouth as organ of eating in Marx. Hamlet, the father, no longer as *paterfamilias*, no longer even as absent/present voice ("well said") but as grubber-up, as delegitimator.

For Marx, the repetition of the name "Hamlet" itself covers a double dislocation: the dislocation of the father from palace to cellarage; the dislocation of the father's legacy and its displacement by that of Yorick and Puck. Yet unfixing itself depends upon repetition, a repetition which can never be totally detached from both fixity and fixation. Fixation cannot be erased; it is itself the site of transformation. Marx stages both fixation and transformation in his own repetitive re-readings of Shakespeare, in his development of the transformation of monarch into mole into miner into Puck. In the unnaming of the patriarch, perhaps Marx found intimations for his radically incomplete interrogation of his own paternal position. When Eleanor, his daughter, wrote her memoir of him, she called it "Recollections of Mohr [the Moor]." Mohr, Challey, Old Nick were the names his family called him, names which dislocate the comic Marx from the tragedy of his frozen legacy. The title "old mole" was reserved not for kings and patriarchs, but for the Revolution – and for a woman, an intimate family friend, named Lina Schöler (E. Marx 1895: 634; McLellan [ed.] 1981: 99–100).

Names, clothes, ghosts, genealogy, and its unfixing: these are the tropes through which *The Eighteenth Brumaire* repeats and rewrites *Hamlet*. They also mark the material crises of Marx from his move to London on September 17, 1849 until two legacies in 1864 brought him financial relief. But the first year and a half, during the end of which Marx wrote *The Eighteenth Brumaire*, were particularly traumatic. On November 5, with the family crowded into a single dismal room in Chelsea, Jenny Marx gave birth to their fourth child. They christened him Henry Edward Guy Marx, but they called him Guido (Kapp 1972: 21).[5] As their friend, Konrad Schramm remarked, "[h]e was born on the anniversary of the Gunpowder Plot and was therefore named Guy Fawkes." Or, as Jenny herself said, he was named after "a great conspirator" (McLellan [ed.] 1981: 22; Kapp 1972: 21).

I conclude with a more recent reworking of the "old mole" – that of Hélène Cixous in *Sorties*:

> So all the history, all the stories would be there to retell differently; the future would be incalculable; the historic forces would and will change hands and change body – another thought which is as yet unthinkable – will transform the functioning of all society. We are living in an age where the conceptual foundations of an ancient culture is in the process of being undermined by millions of a species of mole (Topoi, ground mines) never known before. When they wake up from among the dead, from among words, from among laws.
>
> (Cixous 1986: 65)

The mole itself has changed hands, has changed bodies: from Shakespeare's ungendered "mole" to Marx's masculine *Maulwurf* to Cixous's feminine *taupe* – the French for mole, for landmine, but also, historically, for prostitute and old hag (*vieille taupe*). But the moles which will unfix representation are also, in Cixous's lexicon, *topoi*, commonplaces – like the mole itself, the site simultaneously of cultural repetition and of social dislocation. We make history in the reworking of borrowed names, borrowed words, borrowed costumes.

Notes

1 For a fine account of Marx, *The Eighteenth Brumaire*, and repetition, to which I am deeply indebted, see Mehlman 1977. My debt is even greater to conversations with David Kastan, Andy Parker, and Margreta de Grazia, and also to de Grazia's unpublished paper on the "old mole" in *Hamlet* and in the nineteenth and twentieth centuries.
2 For an extensive analysis of the language of haunting in Marx, which I regret reading only after I had already first delivered this paper, see Derrida 1994. Derrida writes: "haunting is historical, to be sure, but it is not *dated*, it is never given a date in the chain of presents, day after day, according to the instituted order of a calendar" (4).
3 For the German text, see Marx 1952b: 178.
4 All quotations from *Hamlet*, unless otherwise noted, are from Q2 (*The Tragicall Historie of Hamlet, Prince of Denmarke* [London, 1604]) and are followed in the text by act, scene, and line numbers keyed to Shakespeare 1974. On Hamlet Sr.'s armor, see Derrida 1994: 8.
5 On the conditions in which the Marxes were living during this period, see Jenny Marx's letter to J. Weydemeyer in Frankfurt, May 20, 1850 in Marx and Engels 1982.

3

An impure history of ghosts: Derrida, Marx, Shakespeare

RICHARD HALPERN

> Thus, history becomes a mere history of illusory ideas, a history of spirits and ghosts, while the real, empirical history that forms the basis of this ghostly history is only utilized to provide bodies for these ghosts; from it are borrowed the names required to clothe these ghosts with the appearance of reality. In making this experiment, our saint frequently forgets his role and writes an undisguised ghost-story.
>
> (Marx and Engels, *The German Ideology*, 1976: 130)

> I do not argue for mere scholarship, as a Shakespearean might cavil at the reading of *Hamlet*.
>
> (Gayatri Spivak, review of *Specters of Marx*, 1995: 72)

Since its publication in 1993, Jacques Derrida's *Specters of Marx* has elicited responses and commentary from some of the most prestigious figures in Marxist and post-Marxist cultural theory, Fredric Jameson (1995), Gayatri Spivak (1995), Pierre Macherey (1995), Aijaz Ahmad (1994), and Ernesto Laclau (1995) among them.[1] But *Specters of Marx* is not just Derrida's only sustained encounter with Marx and Marxism; it is also a significant, extended meditation on *Hamlet*. This aspect of his work, however, has received far less in the way of response. Perhaps Shakespeare critics fear being lumped in among the scholarly "cavilers" whom Gayatri Spivak dismisses in advance. Derrida scatters about his own apotropaic defenses, declaring early on in his book that "[t]here has never been a scholar who really, and as a scholar, deals with ghosts. A traditional scholar does not believe in ghosts" (1994: 11). I'm not at all sure that I believe in the existence of ghosts *or* of "scholars," as Derrida constructs them. But I do feel that *Specters of Marx* should be taken in the spirit of its letter, meaning that Derrida's reading of *Hamlet* is inextricably bound up with his reading (and misreading) of Marx. Interrogating Derrida's Shakespeare is thus not without political purpose.

"Everyone reads, acts, writes with *his* or *her* ghosts, even when one goes after the ghosts of the other" (Derrida 1994: 139). *Specters of Marx* is largely about failed attempts to control or exorcize ghosts: neoliberal ideologies that hope to banish the spirit of Marx as well as Marx's own supposed obsession with, and fear of, the figure of the ghost. Not surprisingly, Derrida demonstrates that both of these exorcisms fall prey to counter-hauntings. But the above-quoted sentence is primarily an autobiographical admission on Derrida's part that, even as he exposes Marx's demons, he is not exempt from the same logic. Indeed, Derrida goes so far as to stage his own haunting, which is of course just another attempt to control it. In *Specters of Marx*, Derrida self-consciously takes up the role of Hamlet, "haunted" by a paternal ghost which in this case turns out to be the ghost of Marxism.[2] But literary texts do not acquiesce so easily to the practices of conjuration. *Hamlet*, I shall argue, does not passively accept the interpretative limits imposed by Derrida but, in ghostly fashion, returns to haunt his political project.

As Julia Lupton and Kenneth Reinhard observe, "critics neither simply read *Hamlet* objectively, diagnosing its problems, nor project their fantasies onto the play in a purely subjectivist criticism, but rather take up *positions in fantasy* laid out by the play" (1993: 86). My approach to Derrida and *Hamlet* will attempt to bring out the dialectical quality of this dictum: Lupton and Reinhard do not (as I take it) mean simply to displace the first two options with the third but to knot all three together. Readers of *Hamlet* are in some sense allotted fantasy positions by the play, but by a play that they have played a role in constructing. Thus while Jacques Lacan's reading of *Hamlet* is, as I have argued elsewhere (Halpern 1997: 254–68), structured by an identification with the play's protagonist, Lacan's "Hamlet" is very different from Derrida's (though still within a field of possible fantasies mapped out by the play). As a result, Lacan and Derrida exhibit distinctive *styles* of identification. My point in the following essay, then, is not simply to reveal the "symptomatic" nature of Derrida's reading (as if any reading, my own included, might not be symptomatic) but to examine the political coordinates of the particular fantasy positions that Derrida takes up: those of Hamlet, the Ghost, and the Gravedigger.

I An enema of the people: Derrida's purge

Hamlet: Pale or red?
Horatio: Nay, very pale.

(1. 2. 233–4)[3]

Spivak's suspicion that Shakespeare scholars might "cavil" at *Specters of Marx* probably has something to do with Derrida's highly selective use of *Hamlet*, which he pares down to a ghost-story pure and simple. In fact, *Specters of Marx* turns largely on Hamlet's famous line "The time is out of joint," uttered right after his encounter with the ghost. Derrida reads this line to mean, among other things, that the time is awry or unjust, but also that an intrinsic disjointure both afflicts and structures temporality as such, leading to the "non-contemporaneity with itself of the living present" (1994: xix). What Derrida calls the "effectivity . . . of a specter" (10) depends on a time in which the apparent solidity and self-sufficiency of the present is undone by the very real claims of past and future, replacing ontology with what Derrida punningly calls "hauntology" (10). The ghostly disjointedness of time proclaimed by Hamlet not only denotes what is wrong in the present but opens up the possibility of redemption or justice. As we shall see, the effectivity of past and future in Derridean hauntology are not so much material as ethical, a matter of responsibility rather than causality.

Hauntology or "spectropoetics" (as Derrida also calls it) is what allows Hamlet to be sutured onto Marx. Derrida not only traces the well-known references to King Hamlet's ghost (and others) in *The Eighteenth Brumaire* and meditates on Marx's famous phrase about the "specter haunting Europe" at the beginning of *The Communist Manifesto* but traces the rhetoric of ghostliness in Part Three of *The German Ideology* and in the chapter on the commodity in volume 1 of *Capital*. All of these works, Derrida argues, both exhibit and repress a "spectro-poetics" of largely Shakespearean inspiration.

Specters of Marx is an unalloyed celebration of specters but a more ambivalent look at Marx. To be sure, Derrida begins by insisting that the spirit – or rather, spirits – of Marxist critique survive both the collapse of communism and neoliberal proclamations of a New World Order. He employs a supposedly Marxist "hauntology" to analyze the spectralization of politics by the media and to deconstruct Francis

Fukuyama's notorious claims about the "end of history" and the ushering in of an unruffled liberal-capitalist present. But Derrida depicts Marx as being deeply troubled by the same spectropoetics he wields: "Marx loved the figure of the ghost, he detested it, he called it to witness his contestation, he was haunted by it, harassed, besieged, obsessed by it" (106). Ultimately, Derrida argues, "the spectrality whose 'logic' we are going to analyze will have been covered over . . . by Marx's *ontological* response. The response of Marx himself, for whom the ghost must be nothing, nothing period" (30). Hence Marx too must submit to a deconstructive reading which, according to Derrida, will release the most radical aspects of his texts from the constraints of Marxist orthodoxy.

Yet this deconstructive reading does not, at least in the early sections of the book, pose itself as critical of Marx. On the contrary, Derrida insists that deconstruction was always (silently) indebted to Marx and that it "has remained faithful to a certain spirit of Marxism, to at least one of its spirits for, and this can never be repeated too often, there is *more than one of them* and they are heterogeneous" (75; my emphasis). The very title of Derrida's book – *Specters of Marx* – emphasizes his belief that the Marxist inheritance is constitutively plural, hence irreducible to a monolithic world-view or coherent set of political formulae. This part of Derrida's argument relies on Maurice Blanchot's brief essay "Marx's Three Voices," which identifies in Marx's texts three distinct discursive registers – roughly, "philosophical," political, and scientific. These "three voices," which cannot be translated into or reduced to one another, mean that the Marxist inheritance must remain multiple and decentered, and must "submit [it]self to ceaseless recasting" (Blanchot 1986: 19). Derrida eagerly takes up, and makes explicit, Blanchot's merely implied polemic against those (Althusser, in particular) who would reduce Marx's writings to an orthodox, unified, and scientific system; thus he excoriates the "scientistic ideology that often, in the name of Science or Theory of Science, had attempted to unify or purify the 'good' text of Marx" (Derrida 1994: 33). Here Derrida not only tries to protect Marx from ontological reductions but to make him safe for democratic politics.

Yet after citing Blanchot, Derrida silently twists Blanchot's argument in a way that will eventually bring us back to the question of *Hamlet*. While he celebrates Marx's heterogeneity, Derrida also states that this mixed inheritance must be "selected" and "filtered" to separate the still valuable elements from the others (54). The need for such a procedure is self-evident, and yet Derrida applies it with a surprising brusqueness:

> We would distinguish this [filtered and selected] spirit from other spirits of Marxism, those that rivet it to the body of Marxist doctrine, to its supposed systematic, metaphysical, or ontological totality (notably to its "dialectical method" or to "dialectical materialism"), to its fundamental concepts of labor, mode of production, social class, and consequently to the whole history of its apparatuses (projected or real: the Internationals of the labor movement, the dictatorship of the proletariat, the single party, the State, and finally the totalitarian monstrosity).
>
> (88; see also 68)

The appositions of this amazing sentence manage to "rivet" virtually every one of Marx's fundamental categories as well as the history of the workers' movement to the "totalitarian monstrosity" which emerges as their final consequence and truth. Derrida never actually examines such categories as labor and mode of production to show how they are intellectually faulty or imbued with a totalitarian destiny. They are filtered out *prior* to Derrida's argument, not as a consequence of it. What remains of Marx is, as Gayatri Spivak points out, "shorn of all specificity, mark of a messianism without content, carrier of merely the structure of a promise which cancels the difference between democracy and Marxism" (Spivak 1995: 66; see also Macherey 1995: 24). This fact is not lost on Derrida, who admits that "one will observe perhaps with a smile" that the rejected spirits "include *almost everything*" (1994: 89). What remains is indeed a mere "specter" of Marx – and one whose bloodless visage is, like that of Hamlet's father, not "red" but "pale."

Besides revealing his expressions of sympathy with Marxism to be little more than political posturing, Derrida's "filtering" of Marx lands him in several contradictions. His initial celebration of the heterogeneity of Marx's texts now gives way to a wholesale exclusion of at least one of Blanchot's "three voices": the scientific. Moreover, Derrida's attempt to "isolate" one of Marx's spirits through a process that he likens to "chemical analysis" (89) shows him to be just as devoted to textual distillation as are those bad, "scientistic" Marxists who try "to unify or purify the 'good' text of Marx" (33). Derrida takes Marx himself to task for banishing ghosts, "as if he still believed in some decontaminating purification" (122). But Derrida's project of "selecting" and "filtering" Marx reveals the same underlying belief.

It also returns us to the nature of Derrida's identification with

Hamlet, a character who is engaged as well in a purifying mission. Among the relatively few lines from *Hamlet* quoted by Derrida are the following from the ghost:

> I am thy father's spirit,
> Doomed for a certain term to walk the night,
> And for the day confined to fast in fires
> Till the foul crimes done in my days of nature
> Are burnt and purged away.
>
> (1. 5. 9–13)

The ghost of King Hamlet is the only one in Elizabethan or Jacobean drama who seems to come from purgatory (McGee 1987: 23). He later explains his presence there in the account of his murder, when he says that Claudius dispatched him

> even in the blossoms of my sin,
> Unhouseled, dis-appointed, unaneled,
> No reck'ning made, but sent to my account
> With all my imperfections on my head.
>
> (1. 5. 76–9)

Putting aside the theological problems that King Hamlet's account would raise for a Protestant audience, I would like to focus instead on the problem that his father's admission of sin raises for Hamlet. On the one hand, Hamlet seems to absorb the fact of his father's fleshly nature. He later complains of Claudius that "'A took my father grossly, full of bread, / With all his crimes broad blown, as flush as May" (3. 3. 80–1). But this recognition fails to displace another rhetoric in which his father's supposed purity contrasts absolutely with Claudius's (and his mother's) corruption. The father is, in his son's eyes, "So excellent a king, that was to this / Hyperion to a satyr" (1. 2. 139–40). And later, during the scene in his mother's chamber, Hamlet presents her with two pictures, his father's displaying

> Hyperion's curls, the front of Jove himself,
> An eye like Mars, to threaten or command,
> A station like the herald Mercury
> New lighted on a heaven-kissing hill.
>
> (3. 4. 55–58)

Claudius's picture, by contrast, shows like "a mildewed ear / Blasting his wholesome brother" (63–4). Hamlet's description of these two images as "the counterfeit presentment of two brothers" (53) speaks unwittingly to the fact that he has falsified both in rendering their differences absolute.

When contrasting him with Claudius, Hamlet canonizes his father. Burning away the sins of the dead king's fleshly existence, Hamlet's imagination thus becomes the psychic counterpart to the purgatory in which his father's spirit is being painfully cleansed. But the son's obsessive insistence on the father's purity simply registers the strength of the disavowal needed to produce it. Putting this in Lacanian terms: Hamlet attempts to separate King Hamlet as Symbolic father – ghostly, disembodied bearer of the law – from Claudius as Real father, subject of an obscene enjoyment. Hamlet wants to purge the ghost so as to convert it from an inconsistent to a consistent Other, one whose injunctions are ethically coherent and may thus confer an acceptable symbolic mandate. To put this less abstractly, Hamlet must contrive a pure father whose orders come from a place absolutely *elsewhere* from the "rotten" state of Denmark. Otherwise, they might simply be another instance of, rather than an ethically clear rebuke to, the corruption of the royal court.

I would argue that Hamlet's purgatorial imagination provides the first of the three points of fantasy through which Derrida is inducted by the play. That is to say, Derrida's identification with Hamlet, self-conscious up to a point, here takes on the qualities of a symptom as Derrida engages in an obsessive cleansing or purgation of the "spirit" of Marxism, detaching it from the "crimes of its days of nature." Just as Hamlet desperately attempts to isolate the Symbolic from the Real father, Derrida hopes that a process of "filtering," "selecting," and "chemical analysis" will separate the acceptable "spirit" of Marx from the real history of socialism and the workers' movement, a history construed not as a mixture of heroism and stupidity, triumph and defeat, but as absolute, "totalitarian" idea.

Yet to put things this way is unnecessarily crude. For what Hamlet represents is not a kind of pure symptom but rather an "aporetic" point at which the lines between intellectual scrupulousness and obsessive ritual become hopelessly fuzzy. It is not only perfectly reasonable but even imperative that Hamlet should attempt to discover whether the Ghost is an "honest ghost" (1. 5. 142) or a demon before carrying out its command. From one perspective, his own process of "filtering" spirits is thus completely justified. And yet, even he begins to suspect that his doubts may serve to delay and fend off, rather than secure, his role as avenger. Likewise, it would be intellectually irresponsible for Derrida, as it would be for anyone else, to accept the Marxist legacy (or any other legacy) whole hog, without scrutinizing, judging, and therefore filtering or selecting it. But there is also a point where the ceaseless hunting down of onto-theological remnants becomes mere repetition compulsion, an attempt to avoid an encounter with the traumatic Real. Or as Slavoj Žižek puts it: "The fear of error which conceals its opposite, the fear of Truth: this Hegelian formula encapsulated perfectly the subjective position of the obsessional neurotic: the incessant procrastination, the endless precautions, which characterize his approach" (Žižek 1989: 191). As we shall see, Derrida also shares with Hamlet a sense of urgency which conflicts with a tendency to delay.

Among the many objections that might be raised against my argument thus far, the most obvious would seem to be that I have gotten Derrida's argument exactly backwards. Instead of purifying Marx's texts, Derrida not only demonstrates but extols their necessary impurity, which he depicts as inherent to the logic of the specter.[4] Indeed, one of his chapter subtitles is "(impure 'impure impure history of ghosts')" (95) and here he criticizes Marx's hunting down of the specter, "as if he still believed in some decontaminating purification in this regard" (123). While Hamlet wants to reduce the ambiguities of the father's ghost to an unambiguous truth, Derrida wants to maintain the internal heterogeneity of the Marxist specter, even against Marx's own attempts to impose an ontological consistency.

To this I would make two answers. First, Derrida's rhetoric of impurity contradicts his use of terms such as "filter" and "chemical analysis" to describe his own critical labors. Second, while the difference between purity and impurity seems crucial at a conceptual level, it proves less important at a performative one. That is to say, the obsessive-compulsive "fear of error" is defined more by form than by content, more by the logic of gesture than by the particular ideal in whose name the gesture is performed. At this level, the substitution of "impure" for "pure" makes no difference whatsoever. For what Derrida demands is "pure" impurity, impurity with no admixture of the pure. That is why he hunts down ontological elements in Marx's texts with far more zeal than Marx ever pursues the specter.

Derrida makes an interesting and symptomatic omission when summarizing the structure of Marx's arguments against Stirner in Part Three of *The German Ideology*. It is Stirner who, in his book *The Ego and its Properties*, introduces the language of spirits, specters, and spooks which Marx and Engels ridicule (though hardly "obsessively," *pace* Derrida). Stirner (Derrida claims that Marx claims) recounts "the whole history of spirits, ghosts, or *revenants*: first the pure history of spirits (*reine Geistergeschichte*), then the history of the possessed (*die Bessessenen*) as impure history of phantoms (*unreine Geistergeschichte*), then the impure impure history of spirits (*unreine unreine Geistergeschichte*)" (120). In fact, Marx and Engels first divide Stirner's history of ghosts into two parts, not three: a "pure" history and an "impure" one. The impure history is in turn divided into two sub-parts: an "impurely impure history," but before this, a "purely impure history of ghosts" (*reine unreine Geistergeschichte*)" (Marx and Engels 1976: 132; 1958: 115). Now admittedly, the manuscript is inconsistent (impure?) in this regard, for the "purely impure history" noted in the schematic summary of Stirner's argument falls away in the analysis that follows. But its role in the schema is important. Marx and Engels identify the "impurely impure history" as "historical" (*historische*), suggesting that the impurity is supplied by this very element, whereas the "purely impure history" is non-historical or philosophical.[5] But Derrida's own *Specters of Marx* is just such a non-historical or philosophical account. It is, moreover, a *purely* impure history in precisely the sense that I have described above: a scrupulous/obsessive purging of all purities. Derrida's omission of this term from his analysis, though surely accidental, is nonetheless telling, since it exactly denotes his own position.

"Deconstruction has never had any sense or interest, in my view at least," claims Derrida, "except as a radicalization, which is also to say *in the tradition* of a certain Marxism, in a certain *spirit of Marxism*. There has been, then, this attempted radicalization of Marxism called deconstruction . . ." (1994: 92). Derrida's claim that Marxism has always served as an (unacknowledged) stimulus for deconstruction, while hardly credible in itself, does at least prepare for the immediate reversal, in which deconstruction becomes the radicalized inheritor (hence only legitimate trajectory) of Marxism. The "this" in "this attempted radicalization," which suggests that it may be only one among others, should not mislead, for Derrida mentions no others. His purgatorial cleansing of Marx's texts, his filtering of their *internal* heterogeneity, thus aims at eliminating their difference from deconstruction. Derrida is quite clear on this point: the only acceptable (i.e. truly "radical" and democratic) Marxism is indistinguishable from deconstruction. Difference will not be tolerated.

And here, at last, the logic of purgation meets up with its etymological and political neighbor: that old war horse of Stalinist policy, the *purge*. Since Derrida, like the Pope, has no divisions to command, the purges that constitute the "New International" are, naturally, bloodless.

But they are still decisive. Althusser, for instance, is excommunicated without any evidence, or even clear charges, being produced against him. His guilt is simply self-evident. More striking still is the legion of apostates and revisionists who sought to radicalize Marxism without adopting a specifically deconstructive apparatus to do so – thinkers from Trotsky to Adorno to Negri – whose names are never even mentioned. Like those ghostly or "spectral" figures whose images were simply airbrushed out of official photographs, these names persist only as empty spaces. Derrida does, however, issue a list of *approved* radicalizers (185, n. 9).

While any comparison of Derrida and Stalin is obviously facetious, it is meant to show how the logic of his procedures can betray their stated aims. There is no doubt that a careful deconstructive reading of Marx's texts can be both intellectually and politically fruitful. The question is how and why, in the case of Marx and Marxism, Derrida's painstaking intellectual conscientiousness can co-exist with the most cavalier dismissals of entire intellectual traditions and political movements. As with Hamlet, Derrida's scruples do not prevent him from thrusting blindly through the arras without bothering to determine who, exactly, hides behind it.

To his credit, Derrida acknowledges the symbolic violence that his method entails: "And of course, we must never hide from the fact that the principle of selectivity which will have to guide and hierarchize among the 'spirits' will fatally exclude in its turn. It will even annihilate . . . Which is why what we are saying here will not please anyone" (87–8). What Derrida does not explain, however, is why his exclusions are preferable to or more justified than the ones he sets them against – or even why the heterogeneity he seemed to celebrate should not be allowed to persist without filtering. Nor, in the end, can rhetorical gestures suggesting relentless self-criticism and self-scrutiny justify the sweeping exclusions he has engaged in.

II "*Exit Ghost*": Derrida as academic specter

> The hand of little employment hath the daintier sense.
>
> (*Hamlet* 5. 1. 70–1)

Derrida's self-conscious (though still in some ways wayward) identification with Hamlet is complicated and overwritten by a second, more nebulous one with the Ghost. Since Hamlet himself identifies with and eventually incorporates his father's spirit, these two positions are by no means at odds. But Derrida's ancillary role as ghost will reveal other facets of his book's politics.

"There is no inheritance," writes Derrida, "without a call to responsibility" (1994: 91). This sentence, which delineates Derrida's ethical response to the spirit of Marxism, is also clearly informed by Hamlet's relation to his father's ghost, who saddles his son with a series of injunctions. Part of taking responsibility seriously means not idealizing its conditions. Hamlet's father does not return as a comforting spirit; he *haunts* his son, unnerves him, returns at unexpected and ominous intervals. He thus serves Derrida well as symbol of what it means to inherit.

"[G]host or revenant, sensuous-non-sensuous, visible-invisible, the specter first of all sees *us*. From the other side of the eye, *visor effect*, it looks at us even before we see it or even before we see period. We feel ourselves observed, sometimes under surveillance by it even before any apparition" (101). Responsibility, the ethical covenant, arises within the visual field of a specter whose regard contains us without itself being seen. The ethical subject is constituted under the gaze of an Other which is at once Lacanian and Levinasian – brutal, implacable superego and fragile neighbor for whom we are primordially responsible. King Hamlet's ghost, alternately imperious and pathetic, perfectly (dis)-embodies this alarming duplicity. Hence he delivers what is at once entreaty and malediction, a plea for assistance and a murderous law. No wonder his apparition disorients Hamlet.

Derrida employs the ghost of King Hamlet to meditate on the dilemmas of inheritance, responsibility, and decision. In so doing, he engages themes – such as the aporia of the decision, the violence of law, the logic of the gift – that have marked his more recent, more politically oriented writings. The responsibility that Derrida addresses pertains not only to the Marxist inheritance but to the state of the world in general, a world in which "the time is out of joint," twisted awry with injustices but also open to unpredictable events charged with a messianic force. *Specters of Marx* attempts, in its way, to give an account of the sorry state of the world, partly as a riposte to Fukuyama and other cheerleaders of the New World Order, partly to impress the reader with Derrida's seriousness. The book echoes repeatedly with a rhetoric of moral and political urgency whose earnestness, genuine enough in some respects, is nevertheless shadowed by mere political posturing.

In the book's ethical register, Derrida once again adopts the role of Hamlet, harried by a specter, in order to act out the predicaments of responsibility. His project of selecting among the spirits of Marxism is, for instance, received as a kind of ghostly injunction: "'One must' means *one must* filter, sift, criticize, one must sort out several different possibles that inhabit the same injunction" ("*Il faut* veut dire *il faut* filtrer, cribler," [etc.]) (1994: 16; 1993: 40).[6] Now the imperative is an explicit subject of inquiry in this book, as when Derrida interrogates Kojève's use of "doit": "'Doit' what? Is 'doit' to be translated here as 'must' or 'should'?" (1994: 73).[7] One might similarly ask, then: what is the logic of Derrida's "il faut"? The impersonal form indicates a kind of abstract neccesity to which Derrida is, along with the rest of us, subject. We are *all*, that is to say, obligated to sift through the internal multiplicity of whatever intellectual tradition we are in the position of inheriting. And yet, does not Derrida's self-positioning as subject of/to this impersonal law perhaps obscure the fact that he is actually issuing it? A prominent critic of Derrida has pointed out how, "in making the law unknowable," he "legislates without admitting that he is legislating."[8] As such, Derrida is not Hamlet, the recipient of a commandment, but rather the Ghost as commanding or imperative subject.[9] Moreover, by casting these orders into an impersonal form, Derrida spectralizes his own authority.

The dislocated quality of his commandments is complemented by a moral and political elusiveness on the part of Derrida as writing subject. *Specters of Marx* spends considerable time cataloging and bewailing the world's problems, culminating in the list of ten "plagues" visited upon the New World Order (81–4). Yet it is never clear what position Derrida occupies with respect to these ills, other than that of "concerned intellectual." Indeed, his sense of moral responsiblity seems to depend precisely on the absence of any other, more material form of implication – either as victim or perpetrator – of the ills he lists. That is to say, Derrida's ghostly elusiveness results from a determined failure to locate himself materially in the web of social relations and practices from which these ills arise. Gayatri Spivak describes Derrida quite accurately as a "well-placed migrant" (1995: 71). Jetting from conference to conference, unencumbered by the conditions of production that shape the lives even of most of his academic audience, Derrida becomes ungraspable. He does not abide our questions:

Barnardo: 'Tis here!
Horatio: 'Tis here!
Marcellus: 'Tis gone. *Exit Ghost.*
(1. 1. 141–2)

This unlocatability on Derrida's part is not entirely unconscious, however. He openly celebrates the demise of traditional forms of Marxist organization based on class interests, including parties and unions (1994: 13), and calls instead for the formation of what he calls a "New International": "without coordination, without party, without country, without common belonging to a class. The name of the New International is given here to what calls to the friendship of an alliance without institution" (85–6). A "vulgar Marxist" might respond that Derrida simply universalizes his own conditions of class existence, fantasizing a world of "concerned" but otherwise unfettered individuals. In the New International one feels the tug of conscience but no material constraints.

Which is not to say that "class interest" can simply be substituted for "responsibility" as a motive force for social change. One's political sympathies and commitments must (and I will happily take responsibility for this "must"), for various reasons, extend beyond the boundaries of one's own interests. And Derrida is right to imply that "class interest" can operate harmful forms of exclusion (though, it must also be said, helpful ones as well). But one of Marx's great insights was to recognize the political inefficacy, as well as the hypocrisy and disguised forms of domination, that mark most ethical preaching of this sort.

The disarticulated quality of the "New International," sign of its apparitional status, answers, moreover, to Derrida's way of constructing the very situation this International is meant to redress. This he does by listing the ten "plagues" that afflict the New World Order: unemployment, exclusion of homeless citizens, international economic war, the contradictions of the free market, foreign debt, the arms industry and trade, nuclear war, inter-ethnic wars, mafia and drug cartels, and "the present state of international law and of its institutions" (81–4). Less interesting than Derrida's particular canon of woes is the formal device of the list. Derrida himself points out, and criticizes, both Fukuyama's and Marx's uses of lists (57, 139), so it is a little strange to find him resorting to this mechanism. To be sure, it has its rhetorical point. Derrida recalls the ten plagues of Egypt as a way of countering Francis Fukuyama's "Hegelian neo-evangelism" (100). These Old Testament plagues bespeak the persistence of the bad, old world behind the Christianizing sublations mouthed by defenders of the New World Order. But the form of the list seems equally directed against the Marxist tendency to organize these phenomena as symptoms of a totality known as late capital. Derrida would oppose such a totalization, for predictable reasons. Yet his list of plagues cries out for some attempt at articulation; lacking that, it offers nothing more than atomized political "causes" which lack even a relative ranking of urgency. Is it really so difficult, or so reductive, to seek for economic determinations that might at least construct a meaningful grouping of these "plagues"? Or does this menu of disasters simply reflect the interests of the concerned but nomadic or "ghostly" intellectual who would prefer to drift at will from cause to cause, topic to topic?

III Skulldiggery; or, the phrenology of spirit

> A variety of ideas may well occur to us in connection with a skull, like those of Hamlet over Yorick's skull; but the skull-bone just by itself is such an indifferent, natural thing that nothing else is to be directly seen in it, or fancied about it, than simply the bone itself.
>
> (G. W. F. Hegel, *Phenomenology of Spirit*, 1977: 201)

> Here's fine revolution, an we had the trick to see't.
>
> (*Hamlet* 5.1.82–3)

There is little point in mounting a conceptual defense of Marxism against Derrida, since Derrida does not, for his part, offer a conceptual critique of it. What he offers instead is a figural critique of the rhetoric of spectrality, focusing mostly on *The German Ideology* (an early, unpublished work) and issuing in general accusations of onto-theology but no detailed demonstrations of how this afflicts concepts such as mode of production or surplus value.[10] What I shall do in this final section, then, is to return the favor by isolating a moment of hastiness in Derrida's figural argument and, from there, locating a figural register in Marx's work that resists or falls outside of Derridean spectropoetics. I shall do this by pondering the place of the skull in both *Hamlet* and *The German Ideology*.

Skulls pop up here and there in the course of Derrida's argument, via Shakespeare and Valéry. At one point Derrida even compares his own meticulous labor of reading Marx, word by word, to the work of the Gravediggers in *Hamlet* as they dig up and identify skulls (1994: 114). Yet for Derrida, the skull is often completely assimilated to the specter; thus he can speak indifferently of "skulls or spirits" (9). In *Hamlet*, skulls do indeed participate in the logic of the spectral – up to a point. But in neglecting the limits of this identity, Derrida fails to "do justice" to the skull, and simultaneously forsakes his identification with *Hamlet*'s Gravediggers.

In what sense do the skulls in *Hamlet*'s graveyard scene resemble ghosts or spirits? They are, to begin with, revenants that escape their supposed resting place to haunt the present. That Yorick was a kind of supplementary father to the child Hamlet, bearing him playfully on his back, makes the return of his skull a striking counterpart to the return of King Hamlet's ghost. Skulls are, moreover, bearers of memory and prophecy – Yorick's skull confronts Hamlet both with remembered scenes of childhood and with the mortality that awaits him. Bombarding the present with past and future, skulls drive the time out of joint. More exactly, they drive the *Prince's* time out of joint. For the Gravediggers, by contrast, these skulls possess no spectral or uncanny qualities but are simply natural things (as they are to Hegel in the epigraph above) or, rather, objects of labor. Hamlet is horrified by the unfeeling manner in which the Gravediggers cast skulls about, violating both spiritual decorum and (surprise!) distinctions of social rank. While Hamlet views the skulls as charged with ghostly qualities, the Gravediggers can grasp them as brutely material things. It may well be that the salutary or therapeutic effect of the graveyard scene on Hamlet results from his gaining access, through the Gravediggers, to a "dead" material stratum which has thus far eluded him.

The return of Yorick's skull, in any case, does not so much parallel as it parodies the return of King Hamlet's ghost. For there is nothing spooky about this later return. Yorick's spirit does not ascend from the torments of purgatory; rather, his bone is simply cast up, in a perfectly natural and ordinary fashion, by the hand of the Gravedigger. Indeed, the skull inverts the Ghost in any number of respects. In place of what Derrida calls the Ghost's "visor effect" – seeing without being seen – the eyeless skull is seen without seeing. Unlike King Hamlet's ghost, moreover, it cannot speak for itself but must be identified by the Gravedigger. And in this case, the stated identity of the skull is simply accepted at face value by Hamlet, though it is in fact as unprovable and dubious as that of the Ghost.

But what most profoundly distinguishes skull and specter are their respective modes of materiality. Derrida states that "the specter is a paradoxical incorporation, the becoming-body, a certain phenomenal and carnal form of the spirit" (6). This is, however, "a supernatural and paradoxical phenomenality, the furtive and ungraspable visibility of the invisible" (7). Thus, for instance, we cannot say whether the Ghost's armor is "part of the spectral apparition" or "the body of a real artifact, a kind of technical prosthesis" (8), and this uncertainty represents for Derrida the irreducible spectrality of the material as such.[11] And yet, the Ghost's armor and its spectral body collude so nicely because each is, in its way, uncorruptible. The very materiality of the Ghost is cleansed and scoured – spiritualized – thus instantiating the pure or purged body that Hamlet's sublimating imagination wishes all bodies to be.

Yorick's skull, by contrast, is the rotting or putrescence of that part of the body – bone – which otherwise seems most incorruptible or permanent. If the skull represents a seemingly more solid and less paradoxical materiality than does the Ghost, it is nevertheless in the slow process of disappearing once and for all – in a way that will preclude future ghostly returns. But the skull does not lack all relation to the spiritual; indeed, it produces a parody of spirit in the malodorous gas or smell it gives off.[12] This stink of the real causes the fastidious Hamlet to thrust the skull from him, much as Derrida does with the unsavory corpse of real socialism.

But if Yorick's skull is in the process of rotting away, this process is a slow one – so slow, in fact, that it is still going on at the opening of *The German Ideology*, where Marx and Engels, descendents of Shakespeare's Gravediggers, cast the skull up once more. The relevant passage, which occurs near the beginning of Part One, mocks the conflicts in German philosophy since Hegel:

> Certainly it is an interesting event we are dealing with: the putrescence of the absolute spirit. When the last spark of its life had failed, the various components of this *caput mortuum* began to decompose, entered into new combinations and formed new substances. The industrialists of philosophy, who till then had lived on the exploitation of the absolute spirit, now seized upon the new combinations. Each with all possible zeal set about retailing his apportioned share. This was bound to give rise to competition, which, to start with, was carried on in moderately civil and staid fashion. Later, when the German market was glutted, and the commodity in spite of all efforts was not favourably received in the world market, the business was spoiled in the usual German manner by cheap and spurious production, deterioration in quality, adulteration of the raw materials, falsification of labels, fictitious purchases, bill-jobbing and a credit system devoid of any real basis. The competition turned into a bitter struggle, which is now being extolled and interpreted to us as an upheaval of world significance, the begetter of the most prodigious results and achievements.
>
> (1976: 27–8)

As employed here by Marx and Engels, the figure of the *caput mortuum* is richly overdetermined. It derives in part from the language of chemistry, where it refers to the residue left over from a process of purification or sublimation. But a more proximate and pertinent source is the *Phenomenology of Spirit*, where the skull or *caput mortuum* occupies the center of Hegel's reflections on materialism. Appreciating Marx's and Engels's allusion will thus require a brief excursus on Hegel.

The *caput mortuum* appears in the section of the *Phenomenology* entitled "Observing Reason." In a subsection on phrenology, Hegel examines and critiques the notion that mental faculties – character, intelligence, and so forth – can be read from the shape of the human skull. More generally, he rejects the idea that "inner" qualities of Spirit are made immediately legible through sensuous, natural things. Rejecting the pseudoscience of phrenology, Hegel points out that the skull is not an organ (whereby Spirit might express itself in action) or even a sign, however arbitrary, of what lies concealed "inside" the head. It is, rather, simply a Thing – a meaningless, natural object (Hegel 1977: 200–1). Hence, as he points out in the epigraph quoted above, even Hamlet's remarks on Yorick's skull do not derive their content from the skull itself. The skull as Thing is a cause of Hamlet's discourse but not a meaningful element in it. Though this skull once "had a tongue in it" (5. 1. 76),[13] it can no longer speak – not even to say that it was Yorick's skull. Nor can it say anything to phrenologists, whose failed attempts rely on the bizarre presupposition that "the *being of Spirit is a bone*" (208, emphasis in the original).

Hegel invokes the absurdities of the phrenologists in order to bring to a head (as it were) the contradictions inherent in *observing* reason, which expects simply to discover Spirit in pre-existing, material objects instead of externalizing it by means of its own activity (see Hyppolite 1974: 275). In reducing the phrenologists' stance to "the being of Spirit is a bone," Hegel is criticizing not materialism as such, but rather the debased and vulgar materialism which focuses on objects rather than on human activity or practice. Hence his stance here is actually quite close to that taken by Marx in the first of the "Theses on Feuerbach": "The chief defect of all previous materialism – that of Feuerbach included – is that things, reality, sensuousness are conceived only in the form of the *object* or of *contemplation*, but not as *human sensuous activity, practice*, not subjectively" (Marx and Engels 1976: 6). As a thing usurping the place of practice, Hegel's skull is a primordial instance of reification. In the end, then, it does become a sign – not, to be sure, of the human capacities it supposedly exteriorizes but of the temporary ossification of dialectic itself. Having reached the dead end of the skull, observing reason thus passes over into practical reason, and thence from individual to collective forms of practice (see Hyppolite 1974: 261–2).

Marx's and Engels's citation of Hegel does not merely evoke the general context of Hegelian phrenology; by depicting the "absolute spirit" as having degenerated into a *caput mortuum*, they playfully re-enact the phrenological axiom that "the being of spirit is a bone." The point here is not to return to a vulgar, Feuerbachian, or object-based materialism; rather, the skull activates a carnivalesque rhetoric that will degrade the heaven of reason into the humus of real history. Just as the Gravediggers in *Hamlet* indirectly mock the Prince's spiritual pretensions, so Marx and Engels laughingly bring the rarified discourse of German philosophy to ground level.[14]

And they do this not only through the figure of the *caput mortuum* but also through the witty description of the "industrialists of philosophy" and their commercial practices. By revealing philosophy itself to be a form of cultural production subject to the laws of production in general, this latter conceit (which is only half-joking) jarringly retrieves the economic realities that German philosophy has blissfully ignored. The *caput mortuum* which provides the industrialists of philosophy with their raw materials is, moreover, not just any skull but *Hegel's* skull; Marx and Engels thereby convert Hegelian *Geist* into Hegelian *Geist* © – not an abstract concept but a brand-name commodity, as of course it had become. Paradoxically, they also foreshadow the process through which later industrialists of philosophy, at future conferences on the defunction of Marxism, will traffic in the remainders of Marx's *caput mortuum*.

Derrida might well complain that this materialist rhetoric of the skull simply confirms, rather than exceeds, his critique of Marx. Speaking of Marx and Hamlet in their respective graveyards, he notes that mourning "consists always in attempting to ontologize remains, to make them present, in the first instance by *identifying* the bodily remains and by *localizing* the dead" (1994: 9). Making Spirit into a skull – Hegel's skull – would seem to conform to this process of ontologizing and identifying the dead (Marx's and Engels's manner of mourning is jocular, but it is mourning still). Yet Derrida's bugbear of ontology (his own unconjurable ghost) seems to miss Marx's radical turn from philosophy. For the solidity of the real in Marx is pragmatically, not ontologically defined, as in the following passage:

> This sum of productive forces, capital funds and social forms of intercourse, which every individual and every generation finds in

> existence as something given, is the real basis of what the philosophers have conceived as "substance" and "essence of man", and what they have deified and attacked: a basis which is not in the least disturbed, in its effect and influence on the development of men, by the fact that these philosophers revolt against it as "self-consciousness" and the "unique."
>
> (Marx and Engels 1976: 54)

For Marx, the "real" is defined, on the one hand, by "its effect and influence on the development of men," that is, by its social effectivity and not by an ontological determination which would ally it with "substance" or "essence." But it is defined on the other hand (and in a complementary fashion) by its practical imperviousness to the philosopher's discourse. The real, for Marx, is that which is not perturbed by critique. It is a Thing whose place is not jostled by our symbolizations of it, one of the "things between heaven and earth" which are not "accounted for in your philosophy." The skull or *caput mortuum* which calmly and blankly returns the philosopher's gaze embodies the solidity of a real which maddeningly persists beyond our attempts to think away its contradictions.

But if the skull thus chastizes the neo-Hegelian thinkers – Feuerbach, Bauer, and Stirner – whom Marx and Engels critique, it also grimaces at Derrida, whose philosophical project reproduces the limits encountered by the young Hegelians when they tried to tackle social reality. That Derrida takes up the cudgels for Stirner in his struggle with Marx bespeaks the fact that Derrida feels himself proleptically critiqued by *The German Ideology*. The uncanniness of this effect is multiplied by the fact that Marx and Engels occasionally refer to Stirner as "the profound Jacques" (241) or "Saint-Jacques le bonhomme" (327), as when they speak of "Jacques le bonhomme accepting in good faith the illusions of philosophy" (282). Indeed, with some minor alterations, their judgement of Stirner's *The Ego and its Properties* will serve nicely as a rejoinder to *Specters of Marx*:

> We shall point out only that "deconstruction" is characterized by Saint-Jacques' getting the onto-theological out of his head for the nine-hundredth time, whereby, as we in our turn are compelled to point out for the nine-hundredth time, everything remains as before, not to mention the fact that it is no more than a pious wish.
>
> (Marx and Engels 1976: 433, slightly amended[15])

The *caput mortuum* embodies reality's tendency to "remain as before" in the face of philosophical critique. But this inertness is also the *product* of philosophy insofar as the latter unconsciously adopts the stance of what Hegel calls observing reason. For Marx, the *caput mortuum* is precisely such an undialectical materiality, a dead or object-like materiality which results from abstracting things from the social relations in which alone their "life" subsists. In a passsage from *The Critique of Political Economy* which Derrida briefly discusses, Marx writes: "If the hoard were not constantly in tension with circulation, it would now simply be a heap of useless metal, its monetary soul would have disappeared and nothing but burnt-out ashes of circulation, its *caput mortuum* would remain" (Marx 1970: 131; cf. Derrida 1994: 46). In other words, the exchange value of gold depends on its use in circulation; if gold stopped being so used, the "value" of hoarded gold would disappear, leaving a physical lump of metal behind, a purely object-like materiality but not a social one. The hoarder's merely contemplative relation to wealth is thus the economic counterpart to the phrenologist's merely contemplative relation to spirit.

The German Ideology takes up a similar problem when it critiques Stirner's idea that people can overcome the "alienated character" of the banker's wealth simply by seizing it. As Marx and Engels point out, this would result merely in the possession of "useless paper" or the "corpse" of wealth, for "the wealth of the banker is wealth only in the framework of the existing relations of production and intercourse and can be 'conquered' only in the conditions of these relations and with the means which are valid for them" (Marx and Engels 1976: 383–4). Once again the figure of the dead body signifies the objectival remainder of a social process. Stirner, unlike the phrenologist and the hoarder, seems to abandon a merely contemplative stance and endorse a radical form of practice (seizing wealth). But as Marx and Engels show, this undialectical practice is the efflux of his philosophical detachment, not the transcendence of it. Revolutionary practice is not simply a matter of "doing something" as opposed to sitting still; it arises in conjunction with a theory that grasps the dialectical nature of social process and of its own place within it. While Derrida does not advocate seizing the banker's wealth, his division of global crisis into discrete "plagues" or social "causes" converts each into a corpse or *caput mortuum*, much as Stirner does. Each provides the double advantage of remaining insoluble and of thereby insuring that the "concerned" intellectual will always have something to fret about. Derrida-as-Hamlet has a whole row of skulls to stimulate his unfocused political urgency.

If the *caput mortuum* serves Marx in general as a kind of ossified remainder of social practice, the inert materiality of the dialectical leftover, the one at the beginning of *The German Ideology* complicates this function by *not* remaining inert. Instead, it decomposes and thereby re-enters the cycle of production and exchange. In this instance, then, Marx and Engels delve past Hegel to Shakespeare, for their skull is not the petrified object of observing reason but rather the rotting or putrifying skull encountered in *Hamlet.* For Marx and Engels, the absolute spirit of Hegel is both recycled and debased in the pages of the young Hegelians, much as for Hamlet the remains of Alexander can be traced until they are found stopping a bunghole. Thus the very language used to ridicule the philosophy-industry at the opening of *The German Ideology* also points a way beyond it by figuring an earth-bound and dialectical process as opposed to the idealized abstractions of German philosophical criticism.

I do not claim that the figure of the skull or *caput mortuum* is completely "other" to Derrida's concerns in *Specters of Marx*, although it points to a more recalcitrant, a thicker, and a more genuinely "impure" materiality than the one that Derrida considers there. Nor, despite my own facetious tone, do I wish to suggest that Derrida's political project is frivolous or worthy of ridicule. But there is something undialectical, and, as a result, self-congratulatory, in the way that Derrida interrogates Marxism at the hands of deconstruction without really bothering to interrogate deconstruction at the hands of Marxism – or, for that matter, without bothering even to engage with Marxism in a serious way. If Derrida really wants to play the Gravedigger in *Hamlet*, as he claims, it is necessary to put off his princely fastidiousness, curtail his project of endless "filtering" and purgation, and delve in the sometimes unpleasant muck of real history.

Notes

1 Some of these listed responses, along with others and a response from Derrida, have since been collected in a volume entitled *Ghostly Demarcations* (Sprinker [ed.] 1999).
2 Both Ahmad (1994: 91–2) and Spivak (1995: 66) note Derrida's identification with Hamlet.
3 All quotations of *Hamlet* are taken from Shakespeare (1997c).
4 For instance, Derrida writes of "the essential contamination of spirit (*Geist*) by specter (*Gespenst*)" (113).
5 This distinction is, admittedly, a bit murky. For one thing, Marx and Engels claim that Stirner never really addresses (or even bothers to learn anything about) history, so the difference is at best relative. In addition, the "purely

impure" history focuses on what Stirner identifies as "negroid" and "mongoloid" elements in so-called "caucasian" history. Since Stirner describes both of the former cultures as static, Marx's distinction may well apply to content rather than method. The two are not entirely unrelated, however.

6 This particular command is repeated in 1994: 54, and 1993: 93.

7 See also Derrida 1998: 14 on Freud's use of *mussen*.

8 Gillian Rose, paraphrased in Beardsworth 1996: 58.

9 Ahmad (1994: 105) has also pointed out Derrida's identification with the Ghost, though on different grounds.

10 The only Marxist categories which Derrida treats in more than passing are the commodity, use value, and exchange value (148–64). But not only is Derrida's critique of use value as ontological misplaced, as Gayatri Spivak has shown (1995: 74–5); it also repeats, in a rather pale fashion, the more rigorous analysis done by Baudrillard twenty years before (see "Beyond Use Value", in Baudrillard 1981: 130–42).

Derrida would rightly criticize any hard-and-fast distinction between the conceptual and the figural; but this does not mean that his figural reading obviates the need for a careful look at Marxism's central conceptual apparatus.

11 Compare Derrida's critique of Marx's (supposed) attempt to isolate a self-identical use value as simple materiality from a relational and irreducibly spectral exchange value.

12 Derrida himself points out that Hegelian *Geist* is a gas, "the sublime effluvium of a fermentation" that "rises up or rises up again above the decomposing dead, to interiorize itself in the *Aufhebung*" (1989: 99).

13 Hamlet says this of one of the other skulls, but of course it applies to Yorick's as well.

14 Of course, it is part of Derrida's complaint against Marx that he is too quick to scoff in the face of ghosts and of Max Stirner's pneumatology (Derrida 1994: 121, 174). I don't have the space here to investigate the very interesting question of Marx's laughter, but I would like to record my dissent from Derrida's claim that it is primarily an anxious, apotropaic laughter designed to guard Marx's ontological presuppositions from the corroding effect of a spectropoetics.

15 I have substituted "deconstruction" for "the 'unique'", "Saint Jacques'" for "his", and "onto-theological" for "holy."

4

Looking well to linens: women and cultural production in *Othello* and Shakespeare's England

DYMPNA CALLAGHAN

Mary Lamb is best known as the co-author with her brother, Charles, of *Tales From Shakespear* [sic] (1807). But she achieved a different kind of notoriety in her lifetime. In 1789 armed with a sewing scissors, and in a rage apparently induced by needlework, she savagely attacked and murdered her own mother (Anthony 1945: 93–4; Wolfson 1990: 24).[1] In light of this murderous frenzy, her declaration in 1815 that: "Needlework and intellectual improvement are naturally in a state of warfare" is surely something of an understatement. Nor did this put an end to Lamb's sewing career, and in a letter to Sarah Stoddart she reports (ominously) that she is "busy making waistcoats and plotting new work to succeed the *Tales*" (Wolfson 1990: 16). Nonetheless, for Lamb, like her nineteenth-century contemporaries, writing was accorded creative and aesthetic value while sewing was either a labor of economic necessity or part of "that train of female garniture which passeth by the name of accomplishments" (Wolfson 1990: 99).

Mary Lamb's labors, both in ink and in thread, are known to us at all only because of their conjunction with Shakespeare and with the Romantic luminaries of her brother's circle. I begin with Lamb not because she committed matricide (though that does lend a certain color to her remarks about the antipathy between writing and sewing) but because she offers an example (albeit a sensational one) of what this essay is about, namely, the far from straightforward relation between women's production – both material and cultural – and canonical writing, especially Shakespeare's. Lamb's waistcoats signal the way in which production in general – that is the manufacture of objects for use in the everyday world – is palpably connected with cultural production, a connection that is ideologically occluded in the instance of canonical writing. Indeed, women's work in the sphere of textiles is the place where the continuity between writing and other forms of production becomes uniquely visible. The historically feminine activities related to fabric production are culturally contiguous with male-defined literary practice: the needle, for example, is both the analog and the antithesis of the pen as weaving is the antithesis and analog of writing. Textiles constitute the feminine mirror or photo negative of male textuality, what we might call the other side of representation. Certainly, in the early modern context, much women's "writing" includes ditties, rhymes, and prayers that have specific and practical uses in the everyday world and as such probably have more in common with material artifacts than with literature *per se*.

Mary Lamb also represents the culmination of a friction between needlework and literary production that had been building at least since the Renaissance when women began to exchange the needle for the pen: "Many gentlewoman to please their lovers which were Poets, left the socke and the needle, & took in hand pens and bookes" (Robert Greene, quoted in Camden 1972: 46). Yet, the devaluation of women's labor that makes the superiority of a woman's writing to her sewing self-evident both for Mary Lamb and for us had not been fully accomplished in the Renaissance. For Martin Billingsley, in *The Pen's Excellencie*, for example, writing, while a typically masculine activity, is not inherently superior to sewing: "And if any Art be commendable in a woman, (I speake not of their ordinary workes wrought with a needle, wherein they excell) it is this of *Writing*" (Billingsley 1618: B5). While all activities engaged in by men appear to have been given greater cultural importance (not to mention greater remuneration) from time immemorial, the precapitalist gender division of labor situates the work of men and the work of women as analogous rather than simply antithetical activities. The *Declaration of the Estate of Clothing in 1613*, for example, situates spinning and tillage as loosely equivalent activities: "Like men that would lay no hand to the plough, and women that would set no hand to the wheele, deserving the censure of wise Solomon, Hee that would not labour should not eat" (quoted in Clark 1982: 94).

The gendered division of labor as well as the heavily gender-coded conceptual categories which began to subtend it (work/leisure, production/consumption) intensified with the advent of capitalism. Both literate and illiterate women of all classes were engaged in sewing, embroidery, spinning, or cloth making. For well-to-do women, the embroidery needle, like the spindle and the loom for lower classes, was an implement of women's cultural and material production. Yet many such activities, merely because they were engaged in by women, in the course of the seventeenth century ceased to be defined as work at all.[2] Crucially, over the long haul of capitalist development (between the inception of capitalism and the industrial revolution), women's labor became subject to intense reorganization as a minority of privileged women were increasingly relegated to the sphere of consumption and reproduction, while a growing body of poor women barely received remuneration sufficient for the maintenance of life.[3] These changes were nowhere more evident in the seventeenth century than in the field of textiles.[4] It was here that the most exponential capitalist developments occurred, especially in the creation of a pool of pauperized female labor that would eventually fuel the industrial revolution in the cotton mills of England.[5]

In this essay, I propose to follow my intuition that the various, vexed, and complex relations that obtain between women and cultural production might ultimately be illuminated in those literary moments where women are palpably embedded in the material dimensions of non-literary practice (see Fleming 1994: 199–204). I will focus, therefore, on those literally material objects (that is those that were made, used, or owned by women) that are also, famously, the key stage properties of *Othello* – sheets and a handkerchief.[6] That there are, even within the most monumental of canonical objects, vestiges of those items "spun, woven, sewn, embroidered by female hands" (King 1999: 22) uncovers, I propose, precisely what the canonical construct we have inherited occludes, namely women's material and cultural production.

In what follows, I fill out the material dimensions of Desdemona's "handkerchief / Spotted with strawberries" (3. 3. 440)[7] and her wedding sheets by turning my attention to the female labor which produced and (crucially) maintained them. In doing so, I will argue that, even as the play anticipates the gender-coded taxonomies of private and public, work and leisure, art and artifact, which constitute the framework of full-blown capitalism, women's labor in *Othello* was far more visible to Shakespeare's audience than it is to us. For if "history" and "canonicity" as ideological constructs have obscured, erased, and devalued women's labor, Shakespeare's play emphatically does not. Instead, *Othello* is uncannily preoccupied with artifacts wrought by female hands, both esthetically prized and mundane. This represents an important contrast to the historically subsequent occlusion of female labor that continues to enable a considerable portion of the exploitation on which capitalism depends. Crucially too, both the handkerchief and the wedding sheets are potentially the carefully wrought and heavily ornamented objects of "cultural" rather than simply productive labor. This latter point bears some significance for feminist cultural studies, which even as it now entertains a possibility Virginia Woolf never considered, namely that, had she existed, Judith Shakespeare might have used the needle rather than the pen, unquestioningly accepts the distinction between sewing, say, a sheet and the Bayeux tapestry. It is precisely this distinction between women's aesthetic and productive labor that I aim to address. I hope both to recover historical forms of women's labor, and crucially, to show how such labor came to be inscribed in a system of valuation which opposed women's aesthetic and productive labor within the field of textiles (for example, embroidering love tokens versus sewing seams), and opposed all forms of textile labor, both aesthetic and non-aesthetic, to an ostensibly "higher" and ultimately "canonical" or aesthetic value in the realm outside it, namely that of writing and of texts. To clarify, the distinction between esthetic and productive labor pertains not only in the distinction between writing and needlework, but also to the numerous practices involved in various forms of textile production.

My purpose here, in short, is to take seriously and with fully feminist intent Thomas Rymer's parodic injunction to "all good wives" that they "look well to their Linnen."

"This may be a warning to all good Wives, that they look well to their Linnen," was, of course, Rymer's infamous summary of the moral of *Othello* in *A Short View of Tragedy* (1693). A long way from A. C. Bradley's understanding of *Othello* as "great man" tragedy, Rymer found the play embarrassingly domestic and an affront to the idea of tragedy. He offers instead an alternative plot that would comport with his own ideas of poetic justice:

> *Desdemona* dropt the Handkerchief, and missed it that very day after her Marriage, it might have been rumpl'd up with her Wedding sheets: And this Night that she lay in her Wedding sheets, the *Fairey* Napkin (whilst *Othello* was stifling her) might have started up to disarm his fury, and stop his ungracious mouth.
>
> (Rymer 1693: 138)

The suggestion that the handkerchief "might have been rumpl'd up with her Wedding sheets" (perhaps in the post-consummation laundry) reminds us that the play itself, and not just Rymer, is excessively preoccupied with linens, with domestic objects, with the "house affairs" that have concerned Desdemona since Othello first wooed her in her father's house.

Shakespeare as much as Rymer forges a connection, both actual and symbolic, between the handkerchief and the wedding sheets in the fabric of his tragedy. Desdemona's napkin, after all, constitutes a miniature of the nuptial linens, bearing as berries the blood stains of marital defloration. Indeed, the terms "sheet" and "napkin" were sometimes used interchangeably. In *The Anatomy of Melancholy* for example, Robert Burton refers to the nuptial undersheet as "the bloody napkin," which, he informs readers, precisely because it bore the visual evidence, the ocular proof of consummation, was preserved unlaundered by Greeks, Jews, and Africans.[8] There was, then, a ritual consciousness of a tradition, albeit one probably little practiced in England, that wedding sheets were *not* washed and were sometimes even objects of communal display. Further, the notion that blood on a cloth constitutes a mystical representation irreducibly attached to femininity dates back at least to St. Veronica who is also associated with the biblical account of the woman with flux of blood (Kuryluk 1991). For Othello the handkerchief becomes the reified emblem, not of chaste consummation, but rather of Desdemona's specifically sexual guilt: "To lose't or give't away were such perdition / As nothing else could match" (3. 4. 68–9). Shades of Othello (albeit very mundane ones) are suggested by the second earl of Clare who in 1689 produced a lengthy tirade about his wife's insistence on sending the linen out to careless laundresses rather than doing it herself, thereby shredding the work of his female ancestors (Mendelson and Crawford 1998: 307, 309). Giovanni Michele Bruto in *The Necessarie, Fit, and Convenient Education of a Young Gentlewoman* (1598) had similarly argued that no gentlewoman should be "so proud that she shold disdaine to be present when they lay their bucks [steep their laundry in lye] . . . but to be present at all household works" (quoted in Camden 1972: 44).

Female labor produced, preserved, and accumulated over generations sheets, pillow covers, bed hangings, cushions, towels, napkins, and table cloths – the indispensable material accoutrements of everyday life. The truly diligent housewife would manufacture these linens as well as launder them. Torquato Tasso in *The Householders Philosophy* (1588) declared:

> Neither ought a good Huswife to dysdaine or scorne, to let her hand now and then to some work. I mean not in the kitchen, or other soyled places, which may spoile or ray her garments, because such busines are not to be manedged and handled by noble Matrons (yet to be seene unto by such whose state may tollerate such thrift) but in those onlely that without noysommes or filthines they may be bolde to touch, and such are properly the wheeles, lombes, & other instruments that appertaine to weaving, wherewith a good Huswife may furnish any sifficie[n]t house or dwelling . . . and not without reason was this arte first attributed to Minerua goddess of wysedome, in so much as it was derived first from her.
>
> (20)

Importantly, the most compelling reason that Tasso contrives for the lady of the house to avoid the filth of certain forms of manual labor is that it may "spoile or ray her garments"; that is, it is in the interests of fabric preservation. Furthermore, those activities that are deemed suitable are again in the realm of cloth: spinning and sewing. Household "stuff," then, whose etymology, interestingly, means "material" and matter but especially textiles, is dependent on women's labor, highly prized, and essential to the conduct of domestic life.

John Taylor's *The Praise of Cleane Linnen* (1624) suggests that civilization itself is unthinkable without the products of women's work:

> We should without our Bibs an Biggins bee;
> No shirts or Smockes, our nakednesse to hide . . .
> No kerchiefs, Quayfes, Chin-clouts, or Marry-Muffes,
> No Cros-cloaths, Apron, Hand-kerchiefes, or Falls,
> No Table-cloaths, for Parlours or for Halls.
> No Sheets, no Towels, Napkins, Pillow-beares
>
> (Taylor 1624: A1v)

The humor in this itinerary of household comforts depends on the interplay of stark necessity – the covering of nakedness – and the ostentation of the purely decorative and the merely ornamental. Perhaps because the world of cloth was, despite the laws of coverture, the world of women, tailors (i.e. men who plied the needle) were typically regarded as effeminate (Shepherd 1992). Moseby in *Arden of Feversham*, for example, is equipped with a bodkin rather than a sword, a diminished implement of his masculinity, and Gammer Gurton's lost needle belongs to her even though it is finally located in her husband's trousers. In contrast to the likes of Moseby and Gammer's husband,

Othello, who in the play's denouement makes a point of the fact that the weapon on his thigh is a dagger, disparages the cushioned existence of effeminate men. More than merely accustomed to Spartan conditions of a warrior's life, in his terror about being effeminized, he actually prefers them:

> The tyrant custom, most grave senators,
> Hath made the flinty and steel couch of war
> My thrice driven bed of down. I do agnize
> A natural and prompt alacrity
> I find in hardness
>
> (1. 3. 234–8)

The cushioned existence of emasculated "chamberers" whose "soft parts" (3. 3. 268–9) are the rationale behind his anxieties about housewives and domestic space and are the object of soldierly scorn: "I would not my unhoused free condition / Put into circumscription and confine" (1. 2. 26–7); "Let housewives make a skillet of my helm" (1. 3. 273). Othello insists that the female realm is a thing apart – quite distinct from his own existence, an erroneous belief that the play demonstrates to be at the root of his downfall. Thus, the "bed of down" ("thrice driven" refers to the sifting process employed to obtain the softest, lightest feathers) constitutes the feminized antithesis of "hardness" as well as being the place of "feathered cupid" (1. 3. 270) and of tragic conclusion.

Crucially, featherbeds, linens, and other household stuff were the primary form of property owned by women, what was, as Martha Howell puts it, "most . . . fully her own" (Howell 1996: 35). Elizabeth Busby went to law with her brother over a feather bolster in 1633 having inherited "one christening sheet," "One waistcoat," "one facecloth whereof she made an apron, one tablecloth [with] which she made smocks, and two ruffs, part whereof she cut for herself . . . as also a biggin[hood] which she converted to a coif, and another piece of linen which she made a neckcloth of" (Mendelson and Crawford 1998: 222). Because textiles could be recycled and refashioned, they were a medium of exchange, almost as fluid as money. When an Elizabethan widow in Manchester, for example, left thirty-four pairs of sheets, her bequest signified a considerable accumulation of wealth (Mendelson and Crawford 1998: 222, 225). Such artifacts have a further significance when we recall that Shakespeare himself infamously bequeathed Anne Hathaway his second-best bed and its linens: "Itm I gyve vnto my weif my second best bed with the furniture [sheets]" (McDonald 1996: 38).

The tragic potential of the handkerchief, then, lies not only in its being freighted with socio-cultural value as a love token, but in part also in its specifically economic value. The handkerchief is an object in a world where attachment to objects was to become the dominating theme in the capitalistic circulation of increasingly libidinized goods (see Mukerji 1983: 28; Agnew 1993: 24). "Where should I lose that handkerchief . . . /Believe me, I had rather lost my purse / Full of crusadoes" (3. 4. 23–6).

Taylor (1624) demonstrates some familiarity with the lost object – the love token – as a common predicament:

> A *Handkercheife* is quickly found, and lost.
> Like love where true affection hath no ground,
> So is slightly lost and lightly found;
> But be it tentimes lost, this right Ile doe it,
> The fault is his or hers that should looke to it.
>
> (B3)

Even though it is in fact Othello who thrusts the handkerchief away in the process of rejecting Desdemona's ministrations for his headache, Desdemona bears the blame as the supervisor of "house affairs," for dwelling in the realm of linens. Though the ultimate responsibility for the handkerchief's loss must lie with Iago, the immediate fault is Emilia's:

> I am glad I have found this napkin,
> This was her first remembrance from the Moor.
> My wayward husband hath a hundred times
> Wooed me to steal it
>
> (3. 3. 294–7)

Shakespeare's audience would have known the symbolic and economic value of linen as people who use Kleenex and buy their sheets at the whites sale at Penney's or Selfridges do not. Because of this, linens were particularly vulnerable to theft. Iago may have Emilia steal the handkerchief for its symbolic rather than its cash value, but in *A Winter's Tale*, when Autolycus declares: "My traffic is sheets; when the kite builds, look to lesser linen . . . a snapper-up of unconsidered trifles" (4. 3. 23–5), his motives are clearly pecuniary. His language is echoed both in *Othello* itself and in Rymer: "Yet we find it entered into our Poet's head, to make a Tragedy of this *Trifle*" (Rymer 1693: 145). In quarter-session records, most linen thieves are not men but poor women, and sheet stealing was known as a particularly feminine form of theft. For example, on March 4, 1612, Christiana Johnson and Margaret Richardson of Hornsey, both designated as "spinsters", were whipped and gaoled for stealing a sheet worth 10 pence and five shirts worth 5 shillings (Le Hardy 1935: 66).[9] Linen theft was a feminine mode of pilfery because sheets were a form of specifically feminine property: "The world of stolen clothes, linen and household goods was populated by women: Women stealing, women receiving, women disposing, women searching, and women passing on information, as well as goods, to other women" (Walker 1994: 97). These were not the diligent housewives of the manuals but the indigent poor who fell afoul of both sexual and social regulation. Evident here in social reality is the slippage, represented in the play in terms of Emilia's theft of the handkerchief, between the ideological promulgation of orderly domesticity from the household manuals to the disorderly improvisations routinely made by working women.

The handkerchief itself was, more than just a symbol of Othello's love for Desdemona, a sign of luxury (rather than necessary) consumption since most early moderns did not think it inappropriate to wipe their noses on their sleeves. When Emilia avers that while she might betray her husband for the infinite political power, "the whole world," to which women singularly did not have access, she would not betray him "for measures of lawn, nor for gowns, petticoats, nor caps, nor any petty exhibition" (4. 3. 72–3). Emilia thus articulates a position on marital infidelity in terms of a model of female consumption. She implicitly distances herself from those women who, like Bianca, exchange sexual favors for desirable material objects – sheets, shirts, handkerchiefs, lingerie, and trimmings.

Consumption is a key aspect of women's problematic relation to every sphere of production. Consumption necessarily inheres in the dynamics of production. (Raw materials are "consumed"). No matter how labor-intensive, however, consumption cannot be conflated with production. Nonetheless it can constitute work. Certainly, in the early modern period the use and supervision of linens in which Desdemona has been found negligent by her husband required highly labor-intensive maintenance (repair, laundry, preservation from moths, etc.) (Mendelson and Crawford 1998: 309) which does not comport with the model of consumption invoked by Emilia as one of frivolous, effortless waste.

Thomas Tusser's *A Hundred Good Points of Housewifery* (demonstrating, incidentally, if evidence were needed, that metrical infelicities and stylistic deficiencies are an issue for men's as much as for women's writing) contrasts the thrifty housewife with the idle consumerism of the lady:

> Good sempsters be sowing of fine pretty knacks,
> Good housewives be mending and piecing their sacks.
> Though making and mending be housewifely ways,
> Yet mending in time is the housewife to praise.
> Though ladies may rend and buy new every day,
> Good housewives must mend and buy new as they may.
> (quoted in Aughterson 1995: 202)

The productive woman is praiseworthy because she makes and mends whereas the morally suspect lady, the consumer, rends (or even perhaps loses) and buys. As linguistically trite as Tusser and rather more bawdy, Iago insists in the dockside scene that women in general are negligent housewives. He claims that their domestic and sexual function variously erodes and intensifies the distinction between work and sexual pleasure: "Players in your housewifery, and housewives in . . . / Your beds . . . You rise to play and go to bed to work" (2. 1. 112–15) (Callaghan 1989: 125–6). (There is perhaps an Ovidian echo here: Ovid laments that women think about their needlework while having sex.) Iago's critique of housewives is a culturally compelling one and his damaging assessment comes to replace Othello's chaste vision of Desdemona as a housewife in Brabantio's house.

Philip Stubbes's excoriating attack on female leisure and consumption in *The Anatomy of Abuses* [1597] 1877–9 uses no humor to disguise its misogynist venom:

> Some of them lye in bed . . . till nine or tenne of the clocke every mornyng; then beyng roused from their dennes, thei are two or three howers in puttyng on their Robes, which beeyng doen, thei go to dinner, where no delicates either of wines or meates are wanting. Then their bodies beeyng satisfied, and theur heades pretely mizzeled with wine, thei walke abrode for a time, or els confer with their familiars (as women you know are talkative enough, & can chat like Pies) all the world knoweth it. Thus spende the daie till supper tyme, and then the night, as before. Other some spende the greatest parte of the daie in sittyng at the doore, to shewe their braveries, to make knowen their beauties, to beholde the passengers by, to viewe the coast, to see fashions, and to acquainte themselves with the bravest fellowes: for if not for these causes, I see no other causes why thei should sitt at their doores, from Mornyng till Noon (as many

doe) from Noone till Night, this vainly spending their golden daies in filthie idlenesse and sinne.

(Stubbes 1877–9: 87)

These are well-worn diatribes against female sloth, sexuality, and ostentation. Indeed the association of women with the pejorative "lying in" both in the morning and in childbed is pervasive. Even Mary Wollstonecraft some two hundred years later inveighs against women who are still in their dressing gowns in late morning. Whereas men are understood to be engaged in a productive wrestling with nature, femininity, by contrast, was conceived as "a kind of natural idleness," corrupting the ability and will to work. The heraldic device symbolising labour and industry was a masculine arm, 'fortified . . . with strong arteries, nerves, muscles and sinews'" (Charles and Duffin [eds] 1985: 133). Even women's reproductive labor was contested by one commentator who claimed that it could be considered no more arduous than "a goose laying a great egg" (quoted in Roberts 1985: 166, from *The XV Comforts of Rash and Inconsiderate Marriage*, 1682). Stubbes describes a model of womanhood which is nothing less than a model of decadent female consumption that gained momentum in the course of the seventeenth century. In James Shirley's *The Lady of Pleasure* (1637), for example, Lord Bornwell continually upbraids his wife for "[c]hange of gaudy furniture, and pictures / Of this Italian master, and that Dutchman" (I. i).

In an ideological manipulation concurrent with the advent of capitalism, men are associated with virtuous production and women with wasteful consumption, leisure and idleness. The effect is to render the idleness of some women hyper-visible, while barely registering the pauperized labor of the rest. Also erased is the historical fact that women's consumption as much as women's work, both productive and reproductive, were indispensable components of economic growth. Marx, of course, emphasized production at the expense of consumption, and since women's labor has not historically been defined as productive, the effect is to further occlude women's *relation to production* in its totality – which encompasses both output and use. So for example while bedmaking, laundering, storing, and repairing sheet fabric is not "productive" in the narrow sense of being an aspect of manufacture, the fabric lacks all productive value apart from such uses (Appleby 1993: 172; Shammas 1993: 177).

There is a pervasive sense in the period that unemployed labor – whether destitute or otherwise – was a wasting economic asset

(Clarkson 1971: 170), and that women of the middling sort and above, in particular, should be kept at all costs from idleness, even as they were not permitted (actually and ideologically) to be productive. This posed something of a dilemma, and it was one to which needlework offered some solution. As Lena Orlin has suggested, especially in the manufacture of aristocratic woman's embroideries, it is the process and not the product that really mattered (Orlin 1999: 91). In a letter of 1521 to the French humanist Budé, Erasmus, reporting the erudition of the More household, both anticipates the Protestant work ethic and the association of women's work with consumption, frivolity, and waste: "There you never see one of the girls idle, or busied with the trifles that women enjoy; they have a Livy in their hands" (cited in Lamb [forthcoming, in Donawerth, ed.], from R. A. B. Mynors [trans.], *Collected Works of Erasmus*). "Trifles" (the very designation Iago uses to refer to the handkerchief), then, are the objects and activities that belong to women and are especially disconcerting if there is some suspicion that women may enjoy them. And reading, the consumption of books as objects, when properly supervised by men, was socially acceptable because it is reframed as productive labor comparable (though superior to) the conventional textile labors of women. Robert Burton approvingly juxtaposed/opposed intellectual pursuits with the manual occupations of women, which are explicitly figured not as labor but as leisure: "Now for women, instead of laborious studies, they have curious needle-works, cut works, spinning, bone-lace, and many pretty devices of their own making, to adorn their houses" (Burton 1982: Part 2, sec. 2, mem. 4).

Although Bianca is associated with production, she is singularly devoid of virtue. Lynda Boose has pointed out that the embroidery on the handkerchief is most frequently referred to in *Othello* as "work" (Boose 1975: 369). Cassio orders: "I like the work well. Ere it be demanded – / As like enough it will – I would have it copied / Take it, and do't" (3. 3. 184–6). Needlework, too is often shortened just to "work" (Orlin 1999: 91; Mendelson and Crawford 1998: 309), connoting both sexual activity (as in Iago's pun about going to bed to "work") and labor.

That the handkerchief is taken to Bianca to be copied suggests that prostitution is not her only, or even her primary trade and that it may supplement needlework. Crucially, though both are "housewives," this signals Bianca's different class position from Desdemona. Bianca we are told is "a huswife that by selling her desires / Buys herself bread and Cloath" (4. 1. 95–6). "Cloath" is "cloathes" in Q1, and it is not clear whether Bianca uses her revenue from prostitution to make clothes or to buy the finished product. In this case, it may be raw material she works up for customers just as much as the means of appareling herself. For it is possible that her career as a courtesan supplements her work as an embroiderer, rather than vice versa. Bianca may well fit the profile of those unmarried women from respectable families who were in fact particularly vulnerable to prostitution because few needle trades were considered proper, creating an abundant pool of labor and thence the lowest of wages (Duplessis 1997: 293).

Largely because textile industries did not pay women even subsistence wages, women combined spinning and needletrades with prostitution. A disproportionately high number of women accused of prostitution in sixteenth-century Augsburg, for example, were spinsters and needlewomen. Like Bianca, Anna Linmaer was engaged in skilled needlecraft making veils and fine handkerchiefs, work she combined with prostitution when necessity prevailed. Olwen Hufton points out: "The integration of prostitution within a general economy of work – if one could get it – and the recourse to commercial sex in times of difficulty or after a day's consignment of sewing or other labour, continued to be common throughout the period" (Hufton 1998: 332).

There were a few ways to avoid dependence on a man's labor with the advent of a wage economy: going out "to wash, to nurse, or take in needlework" (Clark 1982: 13). Since it is Iago who designates Bianca as a woman for sale, we should not, perhaps, take her status as a prostitute at face value. While the character list indeed categorizes Bianca as a "courtesan," Valerie Wayne argues that this was the only descriptive epithet available in early modern England for a woman who had lost her virginity to a man not her husband (see Wayne 1999). Regular sexual relations with a man to whom she was not married but to whom she was in some measure economically dependent, might make a woman a courtesan, but it would not necessarily make the conditions of her sexual service synonymous with, say, a brothel in Southwark.

For all that Bianca may not share the conditions of her employment with the likes of Mistress Quickly, both characters ply the needle. Quickly declares bawdily that she is one who lodges "a dozen or fourteen gentlewomen that live honestly by the prick of their needles" (*Henry V* 2. 1. 32). She is, of course, a seamstress, someone who makes workaday garments rather than the fine, decorative stitching which employs Bianca. In *1 Henry IV*, she demands repayment from Falstaff:

You owe me money, Sir John, and now you pick a quarrel to beguile me of it. I bought you a dowzin of shirts to your back.

Falstaff: Dowlas, filthy dowlas. I have given them away to bakers' wives: they have made bolters of them.

Hostess: Now as I am a true woman, holland of eight shillings an ell.

(*1 Henry IV* 3. 3. 58–64)

Mistress Quickly appears to have bought the material – whether coarse cloth ("dowlas") as Sir John claims, fit only to be made into sieves by bakers' wives or fine linen ("holland") as she counters.

Like Bianca in *The Taming of the Shrew*, virtuous women are, of course, repeatedly enjoined, "Go ply thy needle" (2. 1. 23–5). The *prima facie* association is with virtuous activity, but given Bianca's clandestine lover/tutor, a less chaste association remains. In fact, while being the mark of female industry, sewing, merely because it was a female activity, had, to use Derrida's phrase, "always already" dubious sexual connotations. The lexical parallel between the prick of the needle and the male member had its counterpart in social reality all over Europe. Sewing offered a range of bawdy puns in which the needle became, depending on the context, dangerous or comic phallic implement. On the one hand, of course, needlework was appropriate employment for dutifully chaste, silent, and obedient woman, on the other it is a figure for female licentiousness. These contradictions come to the fore in John Taylor's pattern book, *The Needles Excellency* (1634), which advertises itself as being "A New Booke wherein are divers Admirable Workes wrought with the Needle. Newly invented and cut in Copper for the pleasure of the industrious", over a frontispiece which depicts three women of which the central figure sits sewing under a tree to represent the figure of "Industrie," while Wisdome is a woman reading, and Follie is engaged in no occupation whatsoever other than that of trying to distract her industrious sister (Figure 1). Follie is a fascinating figure of the woman who neither sews nor reads – the very epitome of Stubbes's female consumer.

Despite Taylor's list of noble needlewomen, (including that needlewoman of "vertuous industry, and studious learning" Lady Mary Wroth) and his primarily female audience, Taylor begins with a surprisingly scurrilous prefatory poem. In "The Praise of the Needle," the needle becomes the emblem of phallic resilience in the face of extraordinarily vigorous copulation which leads even to venereal disease

Figure 1 Frontispiece from John Taylor's *The Needles Excellency* (1634). Reproduced by permission of *The Huntington Library, San Marino, California.*

("Frenchefyde with heat"). Furthermore, there is specific reference to the rigors of embroidery, commonly known as "colours":

> Hee's true as steele, and mettle to the backe . . .
> As a stout Captaine, bravely he leads on,
> (Not fearing colours) till the work be done.
> Through thicke and thinne he is most sharply set,
> With speed through stitch, he will the Conquest get
> And as a Soldier (Frenchefyde with heat)
> Maim'd, from the warres is forced to make retreat:
> So when a Needles point is broke, and gone,
> No point Monsieur, he's maim'd, his werke is done
> And more the Needles honour to advance,
> Is Taylors Javelin, or his Launce.
> And for my Countries quiet, I should like,
> That Women-kinde should use no other Pike.
> It will increase their peace, enlarge their store,
> To use their tongues lesse, and their Needles more,
> The Needles sharpnesse, profit yeelds, and pleasure,
> But sharpenesse of the tongue, bites out of measure.
> A needle (though it be but small and slender)
> Yet it is both a maker and a mender.
>
> (n.p.)

Taylor's book is usually quoted as unambiguous evidence of the injunction to be chaste, silent, and obedient, apparently verified by the selective use of the quotation "It will increase their peace, enlarge their store, / To use their tongues lesse, and their Needles more" (Hull 1982: 47). In context, however, the lines are humorously scandalous, with the author asking his female readers to take up his own enlarged phallus, which in comparison to their everyday "needles" is a "Javelin," "Launce," or "Pike." Possibly, Taylor had a wider audience in mind than aristocratic embroiderers, one that may conceivably have encompassed women like both of Shakespeare's Biancas.

Sir Anthony Fitzherbert, in his *Book of Husbandrye* (1555), explained the apparent contradiction that characterizes descriptions of early modern women's textile work:

> It nedeth not for me to shewe for they be wyse ynough, and thereof may they make shetes, bord clothes, towels, shertes, smockes, and suche other necessaryes, and therfore lette thy dystaff be alwaye redy for a pastyme, that thoug be not ydell. And undoubted a woman

> cannot get her livinge honestly with spinning on the dystaffe, but it stoppeth a gap and myst nedes be had.
>
> (quoted in Clark 1982: 48)

Fitzherbert acknowledges that women's labor for sewing and spinning is indispensable, but also that "a woman cannot get her livinge honestly with spinning on the dystaffe." All she can do is supplement the family income or, like Bianca, the prostitutes of Augsburg, and many more, augment her own "dishonesty" by selling her sexual services. There is, then, little or no social space, even as early as the 1550s, and well before capitalism had taken hold, for either a woman's sexual or her economic independence from men.

In the tormented throes of his jealousy Othello acknowledges, perhaps euphemistically: "Hang her, I do but say what she is: so delicate with her needle" (4. 1. 188). However, in context, Othello seems to ponder his wife's skill as evidence of her virtue in order to counter the accusations of Iago. It is, nonetheless, an interjection as remarkable as Marcus's commentary on Lavinia's dexterity with a needle in *Titus Andronicus*. Discovering his raped, mutilated niece (whose literacy, incidentally, is not only explicit but also pivotal in the play), he especially laments the loss of her ability to sew:

> Fair Philomela, why she but lost her tongue,
> And in a tedious sampler sewed her mind;
> But, lovely niece, that mean is cut from thee.
> A craftier Tereus, cousin, hast thou met,
> And he hath cut those pretty fingers off,
> That could have better sewed than Philomel.
>
> (2. 4. 38–43)

We have here the familiar topos of needlework executed in a frenzy, which presumably is why Philomel elected sewing over writing as a means to discover the identity of her rapist. "Tedious" in this passage means laboriously executed or labor-intensive, precisely the sense in which as keen a needlewoman as Mary Queen of Scotts described her work to her gaolers (Orlin 1999: 189). There is a sense here in which the loss of both speech and writing is less significant than Lavinia's loss of the capacity to sew.[10] Marcus's speech is reminiscent of the value system evident in James I's riposte to the information that a young lady presented to him knew Latin, Greek, and Hebrew: "Ay, but can she spin?" (Camden 1972: 43). On the other hand, Marcus's speech may imply that needles and pens are parallel implements. This is certainly the case in F. Vaughan's injunction in 1651 to "Lay by your Needles

Ladies, Take the pen," enjoining aristocratic women to privilege a male model of creativity over a female one not in indispensable social production but of gender-differentiated cultural production among the privileged classes (Trill et al. [eds] 1997: 1). Similarly, Edmind Coote's literacy manual, *The English Schoole-Master* (1614; 1624), advises that when stuck with a hard word, "If thou canst not find out the meaning, and true vse of any rule or word, and hauing none present to help thee, make a marke thereat with thy Pen or Pin, vntill thou meetest with your Minster, or other learned Scholler" (A3). Pin and pen become interchangeable here in the activities, not of artistic, but of manual labor.

Especially given his admiration for her sewing, Othello might have done well to heed the marital advice offered husbands by Nicholas Breton in *Pasquils Mistresse: Or The Worthie and Unworthie Woman* [1600] 1875–9:

> Cherish al good humors in her: let her lacke no silk, cruell, threed, nor flaxe, to worke on at her pleasure, force her to nothing, rather prettily chide her from her labour, but in any wise commend what she doeth: if she be learned and studious, perswade her to translation, it will keepe her from Idlenes, & it is a cunning kinde taske: if she be unlearned, commend her huswifery, and make much of her carefulness . . . let her use thy purse but be not privie to thy state . . . At boord be merrie with her, abroad kind to her, alwaies loving to her, and never bitter to her, for patient Grizell is dead long agoe, and women are flesh and blood, though some have little wit & reason.
>
> (Breton, II. 1, 14 ws)

Breton's argument is contradictory – simultaneously forward-thinking (women should be permitted freedom) and retrograde (they have little wit or reason). Further, it is far from clear in the discursive context of the Renaissance that "Grizell is dead." Rather she seems all too alive and well and reincarnated as Desdemona. As well as being publicly rebuked (Othello strikes her in front of the deputation from Venice), Desdemona is infantilized by marriage, which here and pervasively in the culture is envisaged as a means of both discipline and pedagogy whereby the inferior moral and mental capacities of the woman are dealt with to the point that she can become socially useful:

> Those that do teach young babes
> Do it with gentle means and easy tasks.
> He might have chid me so, for in good faith,
> I am a child to chiding.
>
> (4. 2. 128)[11]

Already skilled in the arts of housewifery under Brabantio's tutelage, Desdemona seems to expect further instruction and discipline – it is merely the degree of severity with which it is administered that troubles her.

A prominent model of the gentle education of women to which Desdemona refers was, of course, humanist pedagogy, which produced learned women albeit as ornaments to the men who taught them.[12] Lady Jane Grey found that being taught by Mr. Elmer "who teacheth me so gently, so pleasantly, with such fair allurements to learning" was a reprieve from abusive parental discipline:

> One of the greatest benefits that ever God gave me, is, that he sent me so harsh and severe parents, and so gentle a schoolmaster. For when I am in the presence either of father or mother . . . I am so sharply taunted, so cruelly threatened, yea presently sometimes with pinches, nips, and bobs, and other ways (which I will not name for the honour I bear them . . .) whatsoever I do else but learning, is full of grief, trouble, fear, and whole misliking unto me.
>
> (quoted in Bradford 1956: 39)

Humanist indoctrination might have been more lenient but its end was the same: the inculcation of female discipline. Women's occupations – whether with the needle, distaff, or pen – were forms of discipline whereby female energy, both libidinal and intellectual, was contained and kept under surveillance.

The danger of sewing, and therefore the justification for female literacy, according to humanist Richard Hyrde, was that it gave women the dangerous opportunity for thinking independently of men:

> Also reading and studying of books so occupieth the mind, that it can have no leisure to muse or delight in other fantasies, when in all handy works that men say be more meet for a woman, the body may be busy in one place and the mind walking in another: and while they sit sewing and spinning with their fingers, may takest and compass many peevish fantasies in their minds.
>
> (Aughterson 1995: 174)

Here again we find the ubiquitous fear that women might have "leisure" that they might "muse" or experience "delight." While much sewing probably was wearisome and laborious, the Renaissance reworkings of the classical story of the weaving competition between the goddess Athena and the mortal Arachne (Arachne is just too good and so Athena has her turned into a spider) offer clear cultural recognition of the working of textiles as a highly estheticized form of cultural production. That these female weavers are understood to be artists implies that the products of their labors might have involved precisely the "fantasies" and "delight" that were commended when they were found in men's writing (Jones 1996).

The culturally proximate nature of the textual and the textile becomes visible in *Othello* in that the handkerchief serves as a visual text which is treated like a printed book – and as we have seen is repeatedly described with the scribal term "copy," which renders needlework as especially analogous to writing as the physical activity that produces a manuscript. Indeed, there were those in the period who defended penmanship as more than merely a mechanical art against those who "thinke writing to be onely a hand-labour" (Billingsley 1618: C). As a piece of needlework, the handkerchief can serve the same cultural function as writing, namely, patronage and exchange. Young Princess Elizabeth, for example, gave her father and Catherine Parr calligraphic manuscript translations of Protestant authors (including Calvin) covered with embroidery, thus combining the arts of needlework and writing as appropriate adornments of female virtue (Frye 1999: 167).

Although as we have seen, Othello acknowledges Desdemona's sewing as a sign of her productive labor, she herself becomes an object – a sheet – when she's literally positioned as a text: "Was this fair paper, this most goodly book / Made to write 'whore' upon?" (4. 2. 72–3). Desdemona is the "fair paper," the *sheet* that had been blotted with inscription analogous to the culturally commonplace "fowling of fair linnen". The play thus extrapolates the pervasive pun on linen sheets and paper sheets. "Bed" and "sheet" were, for example, the "technical" terms used at the print shop for the paper and the press upon which it lay (de Grazia 1996: 63–94). Similarly, in a joke on reading in *Much Ado*, Beatrice and Benedick are said to be found "between the sheet" (2. 3. 133) (Williams 1994: 1231). Othello's "goodly book" also refers back to Iago's pivotal and profane deployment of the handkerchief as scriptural confirmation of Desdemona's guilt: "Trifles light as air / Are to the jealous confirmations strong / As proofs of holy writ" (3. 3. 325–7).

Having lost her handkerchief, Desdemona requests of Emilia: "Prithee, tonight / Lay on my bed my wedding sheets; remember" (4. 2. 106–7). The sheets are about tragic premonition, which evokes the association between wedding and winding sheets, the "shaking of sheets" in both copulation and the *danse macabre*, and they seem to be a psychological compensation as much as a physical substitute for the loss of the love token (see Neill 1997: 75):

> *Emilia*: I have laid those sheets you bade me on the bed
> *Desdemona*: If I do die before thee, prithee shroud me
> In one of these same sheets.
>
> (4. 3. 20–3)

Act 4 scene 3 is a boudoir scene, the epitome of the private world, the realm of women. It is not only a moment of bed linen, it is also an undressing scene, for Desdemona has refused her "night-gown" (i.e. dressing gown) with "Unpin me here" (4. 3. 33). Like the dressing-table scene in John Webster's *The Duchess of Malfi*, it serves as a counterpoint to male-defined public space and especially to the world of state power. In lieu of such private moments perhaps, male characters have soliloquies. For all that Ophelia reports that while sewing in her closet she saw Hamlet "doublet all unbraced, / No hat upon his head, his stockings fouled, / Ungartered, and down-gyved to his ankle" (2. 1. 75–8) and that in Q1 the Ghost too visits Gertrude's chamber in his nightshirt, one can't begin to imagine "To be or not to be" pronounced while Hamlet is in his nightshift. At least that was the sentiment of outraged critics who attended Mark Rylance's production of the play in which Hamlet delivered the most famous soliloquy in the English language in his pyjamas.

Desdemona, however, is now attired in only the most intimate apparel – a linen undergarment (chemise or shirt for men, smocks for women) worn by all classes. The condition of this linen is also an indication to the audience of Desdemona's virtue. In an important essay on this scene, Peter Stallybrass has asked what the audience *saw* when Desdemona undressed, and assumes that what is revealed is the boy actor's male, breastless body (Stallybrass 1992; Callaghan 1999: 99). However, the dramatic construction of feminine chastity may rely more on Desdemona's underwear, that is on the clothes rather than on the body of the actor. That such garments were regularly subject to some degree of public scrutiny is apparent in George Whetstone's *Heptameron of Civil Discourses* (1582): "[T]hough her Gownes be plaine, in her lynnen she must be curious and fine: for otherwise were she attyred all in Silke: if her sleeves, Partlet and other Linnen be coarse, torne, or sluttishly washed, she shall neither be praysed of straungers, nor delight her Husband" (Y.y.) (quoted in Sim 1996: 50). Wives, urged Whetstone, should wear clean lingerie: "[C]leane lynnen [is] commendable in a wife." Nor was his an isolated view. Torquato Tasso, too, like a detergent salesman *avant la lettre*, thought that women should attend not only to their own underwear, but also to that belonging to everyone else in the household:

> Ovr English Houswife after her knowledge of preseruing, and feeding her family, must learne also how out of her owne endeauours, she ought to cloath them outwardly & inwardly for defence from the cold and comlinesse to the person; and inwardly, for the cleanlinesse and neatnesse of the skin, whereby it may be kept from the filth of sweat, or vermine; the first consisting of woollen cloth, the latter of linnen.
>
> (Tasso 1588: 167)

Linens have contact with the flesh, and in the layers of garments that construct the early modern subject's sartorial identity, underwear serves as quasi-moral protection from filth. The conscientious housewife thus becomes responsible for the physical and moral hygiene of her household. Nor was this a trivial task: rat fleas which harbored the plague liked to nestle in white rather than colored fabrics before emerging in warmer weather to infect the populace (Honan 1998: 148). Writing while on tour to his wife Joan who remained at home in the plague-ridden Bankside, the actor Edward Alleyn urged: "My good sweet mouse, kepe your house fayr and clean which I knowe you will and every evening throwe water before your dore and in your backside and have in your windowes good store of rwe [rue] and herbe of grace" (Honan 1998: 152). Desdemona's nightshift, like her wedding sheets, is the symbolic obverse of "the stinking clothes that fretted in their own grease" (3. 5. 113–14) in the buck-basket of dirty laundry in which Sir John Falstaff is dispatched in *The Merry Wives of Windsor* (Helgerson 1999: 159).

Perhaps the definitive text on early modern underwear is John Taylor's *The Praise of Cleane Linnen* (1624). He avers in blunt mock-heroic strains what the willow scene in *Othello* confirms in more nuanced terms, that the smock is nothing less than "the Robe of maryed chastitie" (B1). The smock is also the destination of male desire and the fulcrum of the private and public worlds:

> For what so ere men toyle for, farre and nere
> By sea or land, with danger, cost, and feare,
> Warres wrinkled brow, & the smooth face of peace
> Are both to serve the *Smocke* and its encrease.
>
> (B1)

The preservation of lineage and property depends not quite on women's chastity – because the humor here is dependent upon seeing the garment as distinct from the woman who wears it – but on the undergarment itself. The image is reminiscent of Enobarbus's remark on the death of Fulvia in *Antony and Cleopatra*: "your old smock brings forth a new petticoat" (1. 2. 192). Taylor's language of war also echoes *Richard III*:

> Grim-visag'd War hath smooth'd his wrinkled front:
> And now, instead of mounting barbed steeds
> To fright the souls of fearful adversaries,
> He capers nimbly in a lady's chamber
>
> (1. 1. 9–12)

This is precisely the transition that Othello is unable to make between the deepest recesses of intimacy (the bedchamber is *the* location in the world of linen) and the world of war. So while 4. 3 seems to be a reprieve from tragic tension, it also demonstrates that far from being set apart from things of state, private matters, like jealousies and linens, are intimately – and even causally – related to them:

> *Emilia*: Pray heaven it be
> State matters, as you think, and no conception
> Nor no jealous toy, concerning you.
>
> (3. 4. 155–7)

Emilia rightly understands that sexual jealousy is far more momentous than the squabble between the Venetians and the Turks about Cyprus. It is, after all, this "private" passion that will render Othello unfit for "public" office.

Again, on the same ideological register as *Othello*, if on an entirely different esthetic one, Taylor incontrovertibly demonstrates that apparently trivial properties of household management are more than obliquely connected with the fate of Christian statehood:

> By Linnen in your beds, you are embrac'd
> Then, twixt the sheetes refreshing rest you take,
> And turne from side to side, and sleepe, and wake:
> And sure the sheetes in every Christian Nation
> Are walles and limites of our generation etc.

The sense here is that household management is a species of statehood. Bed linen represents the reprieve from the public world, "refreshing rest", but also the ultimate location of the topography of nation and empire – "walles and limites" – the place of legitimacy where the most fundamental kind of "building" – conception – takes place. Certainly this was the case in dynastic families. In divorce deliberations of 1529, Catherine of Aragon's supporters sought to produce her wedding sheets as evidence that her marriage to Henry VIII had been consummated.

Such literally material and symbolic boundaries were vulnerable on several fronts. Lear, for example, invokes the pointless legitimacy of his fiendish daughters "Got 'tween the lawful sheets" (4. 6. 117). Illicit consummation likewise threatened the "walles and limites" of generation, a threat represented onomastically in the Henriad by Doll Tearsheet, a professional despoiler of marital linen. Taylor's verse further conveys the contradiction inherent in the ultimately arbitrary division between the public world and the private one, the world of women's linen and the world of walls, citadels, a world of men. Linens represent the flimsy and permeable nature not just of private boundaries, but crucially also those public structures that the material culture of women precariously underpins.[13] Sheets, both clean and dirty, demonstrate, then, "the effectively public character of even the most private spaces" (Jankowski 2000: 300).

The public realm depends upon a domestic sphere that far from being protected and secluded from the outside world (i.e. "private") is ever subject to the punitive pressures of surveillance and voyeurism. Placed in this sphere, which allows patriarchal intrusion more often than female escape, women are effectively barred from crossing the threshold into the fully political world of men. Desdemona, for example, is not only discouraged, but murdered for attempting to participate in her husband's affairs by petitioning Othello on Cassio's behalf. And there is little evidence that early modern culture as a whole welcomed women's intervention in matters of public moment. For example, Elizabeth Cary was clearly less trouble to her husband, and possibly to society, when she was engaged in literary activities like *The Tragedy of Mariam* than in her attempts to participate in public affairs, which included an unsuccessful attempt to establish textile production in Ireland. Her husband observed to Lord Conway in a letter from Dublin of July 1625:

> I conceive women to be no fit solicitors of state affairs for though it sometimes happen that they have good wits, it commonly falls out that they have over-busy natures withal. For my part I should take much more comfort to hear that she were quietly retired to her

> mother's in the country than that she has obtained a great suit in the court.
>
> (quoted in Clark 1982: 20)

In Act 3 scene 4 Desdemona repeatly presses her suit on behalf of Cassio, to which Othello responds over and over again "Fetch me the handkerchief," "The handkerchief!" an iteration which successfully confines her within "the walles and limites" of domestic space.

Othello, however, seems more than usually appreciative of – even mesmerized by – the arts of needlecraft. Shakespeare gives to Othello what is probably the most beautiful account ever written of women's ubiquitous labor in the field of textiles:

> There's magic in the web of it.
> A sibyl that had numbered in the world
> The sun to course two hundred compasses
> In her prophetic fury sewed the work.
> The worms were hallowed that did breed the silk,
> And it was dyed in mummy, which the skilful
> Conserved of maidens' hearts
>
> (3. 4. 68–73)

Not only has foreign female labor produced this fetish, women have invested their creative labors, their emotions – literally, their hearts. (There is no hint of alienated labor here.) We are also told that the handkerchief, prior to Othello's possession of it, has circulated in an all-female circuit of exchange: "That handkerchief / Did an Egyptian to my mother give. / She was a charmer, and could almost read / The thoughts of people" (53–6). It is inappropriate to apply the Marxist category, commodity fetishism, here. This is the term Marx uses to describe the erasure of the human energy that has wrought an object so that it seems to have an entirely independent existence. The female labor that produces the object is "mystified," however, in that it involves intense pyschic rather than manual labor; the literally mysterious inspiration inherent in the creative rather than mechanical processes of production. However, the handkerchief is clearly a fetish in the psychological sense: Desdemona "reserves it evermore about her / To kiss and talk to" (3. 3. 299–300). The charmer knows the power of the handkerchief as an object because she partakes of not only the physical but, crucially, also the psychic energy which has produced it – an energy that is palpable in Othello's history of the object.

That needlework constitutes art is a notion made explicit in Taylor's pattern book, where embroidery is posited as imitation endowed with the creative capacities of Nature itself:

> The Needles worke hath still bin in regard,
> For it doth ART, so like to NATVRE frame,
> As if IT were HER Sister, or the SAME.
> Flowers, Plants, and Fishes, Beasts, Birds, Flyes, and Bees,
> Hils, Dales, Plaines, Pastures, Skies, Seas, Rivers, Trees;
> There's nothing neare at hand, or farthest sought,
> But with the Needle may be shap'd and wrought.
>
> (Taylor 1634: n.p.)

This passage is reminiscent of Hermia and Helena's collaborative labors in *A Midsummer Night's Dream* where they "like two artificial gods / Have with our needles both created one flower, / Both on one sampler, sitting on one cushion" (3. 2. 204–6). Indeed, the plurality of labor suggests its difference from ostensibly single-handed male cultural production.

Although even some of the most proficient women may not have been able to read Taylor's prefatory poem and may have used the book only to consult the patterns, the text engages in a remarkable maneuver which reverses the hierarchy of the cultural analogy between letters and needlework. Taylor writes of the patterns contained in his book:

> And as this book some cunning workes doth teach,
> Too hard for meane capacities to reach
> So for weake learners, other workes here be,
> As plaine and easie as are A B C.
>
> (Taylor 1634: A2)

Taylor's implication is that those skilled in literacy are also skilled in embroidery, and that if anything, writing is an art more readily acquired than needlework.

The handkerchief passage in *Othello*, then, is notable not only as an account of needlework, but as one of the most compelling accounts of creative inspiration in the canon of English literature. That the artist is a woman, and an African one at that, is surely a spanner in the works of patriarchal precept. The handkerchief demonstrates, at the very least, that the invisibility of women's work as well as the creation of an absolute distinction between aesthetic and productive labor is a relatively new phenomenon, and one which certainly postdates the Renaissance.[14]

While literature may not "reflect" social reality, literary discourse traverses the conceptual chasm between its own aesthetic practices and that unwieldy range of material, social, and discursive productions and practices formerly known as "life." Historically, it is with "life" rather than with letters that women have been identified.[15] Highlighting the material objects of women's labor in Shakespeare's play demonstrates that canonical writing, just as much as non-canonical ditties about bedlinen and housewifery, occupies the zone between the transparently literary – that is, those discourses and practices whose aesthetic and rhetorical coherence render them self-evidently part of the realm of letters – and its obscure, opaque others – including the subliterary, the domestic, and the gross materiality of labor in the workaday world. The handkerchief in *Othello* figures the borderland between writing and all that is not writing, the sphere of the counter-discursive and of materiality itself.

Notes

I am grateful for a fellowship at the Huntington Library, and to Scott Shershow, Jean Howard, Laurie Maguire, and Fiona McNeill for their comments on this essay.

1 There are early modern instances of women murdering their husbands with scissors. In *A Warning for Bad Wives: or, the Manner of the Burning of Sarah Elston* (Anon. 1678), Sarah claims she was holding out the "Sizzars" to defend herself and doesn't think she intentionally stabbed her husband. In a 1629 ballad, "A Warning For Wives," Katherine Francis "tooke . . . / her Sisers from her side, / And hit him therewith such a stroake / Ith necke, that (some thinke) he nere spoke" (stanza 10, 11. 3–6) (Rollins 1922: 299–304).

2 In a historic development, which arguably propelled the aesthetic efflorations of the Renaissance, labor became recognized as the fundamental economic factor in production (Clarkson 1971: 12 and Fox-Genovese and Fox-Genovese 1983: vii).

3 Robert S. Duplessis cautions: "Economic history can be a difficult, even a frustrating, field to study. It is characterized less by dramatic events and famous individuals than by processes that take place over extended periods of time, begin and end at dates that are almost impossible to pinpoint, and involve the efforts of people who mostly remain anonymous" (Duplessis 1997: xi).

4 This case was first adumbrated by Alice Clark's pathbreaking *The Working Life of Women in the Seventeenth Century* (1982) and though there is considerable disagreement about its details, even the most recent feminist historians

concur on its broad outlines. Catherine Stimpson summarizes the situation for women as a whole: "As men gained authority, women forfeited more and more of theirs . . . after women's labor status slipped, so did their legal rights" (Stimpson 1986: x).

Stephen Orgel remarks of women's declining presence in the guilds: "The fact that the presence of women in the guild system declined markedly (it dropped, in Southampton, during the course of the seventeenth century to 9 percent) was, like the fact that there were no English actresses on the Elizabethan and early Stuart stage, a matter of social convention, not statute. Presumably, as long as the labor force was small enough for women to be needed in it, the guild system accommodated them. When they started to represent competition to men (when, for example, in the seventeenth century the crafts and guilds became a viable professional option for the younger sons of gentry) women were gradually either eased out, or eased into such clearly gender-linked crafts as the needle trades" (Orgel 1996: 73).

5 Clark summarized these developments as follows: "[T]he wife of the prosperous capitalist tended to become idle, the wife of the skilled journeyman lost her economic independence and became his unpaid domestic servant, while the wives of other wage earners were driven into the sweated industries of that period" (Clark 1982: 235; see also 94, 97).

Critics fault, among other things, Clark's idealization of precapitalist society, her premature placing of the change from household to capitalist production in the seventeenth century, and her conflation of capitalism with industrialization. For critiques of Clark, see Charles and Duffin (eds) 1985: 8; Roberts 1985: 122–60, esp. 156; and Middleton 1985: 181–206, esp. 182. See also Chaytor and Lewis 1982: xxix–xl; Howell 1986: 30–3; Hufton 1998: 25; Hanawalt (ed.) 1986: xv–xvii.

6 This is what Patricia Fumerton (1991) calls that uniquely "intimate association between the everyday and domestic space, which increasingly in the sixteenth and seventeenth centuries was seen to be the arena of women" (9).

7 All quotations from *Othello* are taken from Shakespeare (1997a). Quotations from the other plays are from Shakespeare (1997b).

8 See Honigmann's notes (Shakespeare 1997a: 237) and Ross 1960: 225–40. Lynda Boose (1975), in the definitive essay on every aspect of the handkerchief, notes that while in Cinthio, Shakespeare's source, Othello and Desdemona have been married for some time, Shakespeare makes the play emphatically about a bridal couple (361).

9 On sheet theft as a feminine crime, see Walker and Kermode (eds) 1994.

10 In one of Shakespeare's few and unusually explicit stage directions, in *Coriolanus*, Volumnia and her two companions are to "set down on three low stools and sew" (1. 3. 55). See also Shakespeare's *Henry VIII* 3.1 for which the stage direction reads: "*Enter Queen Katharine and her women, as at work.*"

11 On the public nature of Othello's violence, see Dolan 1999: 215–16.
12 In his introduction to the Arden edition of *The Taming of the Shrew*, Brian Morris points out that both Bianca and Kate are disciplined by their prospective husbands. Although Bianca is trained by the humanist method and Kate the old-fashioned way, the result is the same – docility and submissiveness (Shakespeare 1981: 129–33).
13 On the problem of the public/private dichotomy, see McNeill 1999: 234 and Warnicke 1993: 123–40. Warnicke argues: "That their lives were private does not mean that women never entered the public arena or never pursued family business outside the home. It did mean that they could only affect [sic] public policy in indirect ways through the manipulation of their male relatives who actually held community or royal office" (140).
14 For example, Susan Frye points out, needles very often became pens in the hands of women who deprived of ink were well equipped with thread (1999: 166).
15 In a comprehensive account of needlework scenes in early modern English drama, Lena Cowen Orlin writes: "Admittedly, it [needlework] is a practice *represented* on the English stage, but we will beg the issue of representation for the moment, to investigate the evidence that stage plays provide in the matter of the ideology of needlework." These dramatic instances, she argues, outline "less historical practice than cultural myth about the role of stitchery in gender construction, patriarchy, and domestic ideology" (1999: 192).

5

"Judicious oeillades": supervising marital property in *The Merry Wives of Windsor*

NATASHA KORDA

"The 'marriage' of marxism and feminism," Heidi Hartmann famously argued in an essay written several decades ago, "has been like the marriage of husband and wife depicted in Engish common law: marxism and feminism are one, and that one is marxism" (Hartmann 1981: 2). Given that Hartmann's highly influential essay continues to be cited as a conceptual watershed by materialist feminist critics, it is curious that no one has commented on the oblique historical analogy she uses to characterize materialist feminist criticism. What is at stake in her reference to the English common law doctrine of "coverture"?[1] Hartmann glosses her comparison as follows: just as coverture held that a woman's legal identity and right to own property were "veiled . . . clouded and overshadowed" by her husband during marriage (E. [Edgar?] 1632: sig. I7), so the coupling of Marxism and feminism has "subsume[d] the feminist struggle into the 'larger' struggle against capital" (Hartmann 1981: 2). Yet one might suspect that there is more behind this analogy, whose longevity suggests that it has captured something that runs quite deep in feminism's political unconscious. Hartmann's invocation of the doctrine of coverture in this context, I would suggest, conjures up (however unwittingly) a specter that has long haunted feminist theory, namely, the trope of women as objects, rather than subjects, of property. Feminist criticism has not so much suffered a loss of identity or theoretical propriety through its marriage to Marxism, I would argue; rather, it has participated in the eclipsing of women's complex property relations under capitalism. While I agree wholeheartedly with Hartmann's assertion that materialist feminist criticism must account for both "the development of western capitalist societies and the predicament of women within them" (2–3), I would nevertheless suggest that as a crucial first step in this process we need to subject the all too familiar trope of women as property to historical and theoretical scrutiny. The law of coverture, which has come to stand as an exemplary example of this trope, is a good place to begin.

Coverture's looming, yet adumbrated, presence within feminist discourse is problematic in that it uncritically reflects the rhetoric of the doctrine itself: that of a monolithic, all-encompassing, obscuring, legal entity. Hartmann's evocation of the term is no exception; it presupposes a reductive conception of the law as a totalizing, unified system that mirrors and serves to protect the interests of the dominant class – here, ironically, represented by the totalizing tendency of Marxism itself, which in Hartmann's view, leaves feminism in its shadow. In defense of the former, one might point out that Marxist legal theorists have themselves abandoned this instrumentalist view of law in favor of a more complex analysis of legal systems as (in Althusser's terms) "relatively autonomous," or determined by relations of production "in the last instance" (see Cain and Hunt 1979: 62; Collins 1982: 22–30, 47–52). Thus, Maureen Cain and Alan Hunt suggest that the law, far from being a mere reflection of dominant ideology, may incorporate "contradictory features and effects," functioning as "both an active agency in historical processes" and one that "records and encapsulates the balance between social forces at particular historical moments and the ideological forms in which these struggles are fought out" (Cain and Hunt 1979: 64–5). This notion of law as a dynamic site of struggle has recently been taken up by feminist legal theorists and historians, who emphasize the heterogeneity of legal systems as including not only "the rules that constitute the formal body of law," but "the discourses in which those rules are situated, and through which they are articulated and elaborated; the institutions by means of which they are constantly subverted and modified in their implementation and administration . . . and the various actors whose participation . . . sustains the enterprise" (Dalton 1995: 4). This new emphasis on the discourses, institutions and actors who variously support or subvert the law's application has led in turn to a far more nuanced account of women's property relations under capitalism.

Recent scholarship on women's property rights in early modern England suggests that there was far greater complexity and less rigidity in the legal systems governing marital property, and a wider discrepancy between legal theory and actual practice, than was previously imagined (see Erickson 1993; Salmon 1986; Staves 1990; Brewer and Staves [eds] 1996). Analyses of documents such as conveyancing manuals and probate accounts and of legal records of litigation over marriage settlements have begun to reveal faultlines in the purported hegemony of the doctrine of coverture (see Erickson 1993; Staves 1990; Bonfield 1983). Such scholarship has been instrumental in documenting what property actually passed through the hands of both elite and ordinary women in the period. For example, we now know that in spite of the legal fiction of coverture, many wives retained various forms of separate property, secured through marriage settlements that were defensible in equity courts. Though it is difficult to say how widespread the practice of "separate estate" was, Amy Erickson has found evidence of women at all social levels establishing various forms of separate property during coverture, whether through formal settlements, simple bonds, or more informal arrangements between spouses. While the origins of "separate estate" remain obscure, it is generally agreed that it was a well-established practice by the end of the sixteenth century when the feudal doctrine of coverture began to conflict with the shifting exigencies of a rapidly expanding market economy (Kenny 1879: 9).[2] Legal historians have suggested that the vast increase in the nation's moveable wealth and increasing value and importance of personal property or "moveables" – the form of capital most often owned and inherited by women – relative to real property, may have contributed to the rise of separate estate (Erickson 1993: 61–82).

However, Erickson cautions that it would be a mistake to read the emergence of married women's separate property in the period as straightforward evidence of women's increasing independence or economic emancipation, for the institution of separate estate did not "improve women's economic position steadily or consistently" (Erickson 1993: 107). Nonetheless, her study of long-neglected aspects of women's property rights highlights the disjuncture between legal theory and actual practice in ways that make visible "the ingenuity of many ordinary women in working within a massively restrictive system" (20). A variety of factors – none of them aimed at promoting women's economic independence *per se* – probably contributed to the increasing popularity of marriage settlements, such as the desire of the bride's natal family to secure property descent through her to her children, or to relieve themselves of financial responsibility for her in the event she should be widowed, separated, or her husband prove a spendthrift or golddigger. Moreover, most settlements dealt only with women's rights to certain property in their widowhood, and not during coverture. Nevertheless, Erickson provides compelling evidence that women with such settlements generally took out of their marriages what they brought in, and thus, she argues, were unlikely to have "stopped thinking of certain property as theirs simply for the duration of the marriage" (122, 150). She provides poignant anecdotal evidence of this in the case of certain women who actually inscribed their personal property, prior to marriage, with an identifying signature or mark. Such was the case with Janevive Deane, who, before her second marriage to one Charles Pressye of Wiltshire, Esq. in 1600, demarcated her personalty "that soe shee might still keep hir owne stock and goods whole, in apparancie to the worlde" (Erickson 1993: 123, 137). Deane's demarcation of her moveables, which insists upon maintaining the visibility or "apparancie" of her proprietary interest in them during marriage, may be read as a small act of resistance to the legal shroud of coverture. It suggests, moreover, as Garthine Walker has claimed, that "although in legal terms the ownership of property was weighted towards men, popular perceptions of ownership did not strictly adhere to legal definitions" (Walker 1994: 83). Citing evidence of disputes over inheritance in which women "physically fought bailiffs and constables who attempted to serve warrants on their goods and chattels," Walker maintains that women "felt uninhibited in claiming the right to protect goods and chattels which they deemed to be theirs" (83). This rift between legal theory and actual practice with respect to married women's property rights did not go unnoticed in legal treatises of the period, such as *The Lawes Resolutions of Womens Rights*, which noted that while it could offer "no remedy" to the law of coverture, nevertheless "some women can shift it well enough" (E. [Edgar?] 1632: 6).

Such forms of resistance to the law of coverture are occluded, however, by the black-and-white conception of women's property rights that has hitherto governed our thinking about women's economic status in the period, and suggest that we need to rethink their historical relation to and control over property in a way that will allow us to account for these gray areas of ownership, while being careful not to romanticize them. "It is not enough," Carol Rose has argued, for a "property claimant to say simply, 'It's mine,' through some act or gesture; in order for the statement to have any force, some relevant world must understand the claim it makes and take that claim seriously" (cited in Dickenson 1997: 39). The variety of claims that have been taken seriously by traditional jurisprudence, however, indicate how complex and ambiguous the legal concept of ownership itself is. The jurist, A. M. Honoré, outlines eleven different rights and incidents of ownership, each representing the ground of a potential claim, but also a different type of ambiguity inherent in the concept of "owning" (Honoré 1961: 112–13; see also Dickenson 1997: 2–3).[3] Even the right or claim to outright possession, he points out, may not entitle an owner to exclude everyone from her property. Another common incident of ownership, the claim to "use," contains its own ambiguities as well: it may include the right to management and income, or, in a narrower interpretation, only the right to personal use and enjoyment. Ownership may or may not also include or be limited to the right to manage, which itself confers the power to determine access and use. While managerial control and the right to use is certainly not always tied to legal ownership, Honoré points out that sometimes an owner's rights are even more restricted than those of a manager or tenant (114–25). The ambiguities inherent in the legal concept of ownership, and in particular those surrounding the right to management or use, may help to clarify the predicament of wives living under coverture. For while the law of coverture ostensibly relegates the housewife to the status of a merely "vicarious" owner – a non-proprietary, custodial manager – formal and informal agreements and disagreements between spouses over married women's property suggest that women's custodianship of marital property could become a site of negotiation and contestation as well.

Janevive Deane's insistence upon maintaining the visibility of her proprietary interest in her marital property exposes the contradictions inherent in the legal fiction of coverture, which defines the housewife as a non-proprietary manager of goods which she may herself have brought into the marriage. While the law of coverture attempts to set a limit (which was itself unstable and shifting) to women's custodial relation to marital property, however, it is insufficient in itself to account for the historical exigency of this custodial role. For whether or not the goods over which married women had custodial care were their own prior to or (in the case of some separate trusts) during coverture, domestic ideology demanded that wives care for them *as if* they were their own. The housewife's managerial role with respect to household property took on crucial importance with the increasing value and proliferation of consumer goods in the period; the birth of consumer culture in early modern England turned housewifery among the middling sort into a task centered on the care, safekeeping, and display of "household-stuff" (see Korda 1996). In the words of the anonymous author of *The Ladies Dictionary*, a late seventeenth-century compendium of commonplace wisdom for women: "there is no Woman in the World can show her House-wifery, and her ingenuity in an House where there is nothing but bare Walls." Rather, "the brightness of the Bosses of her Fire-Irons, and the glaring Lustre of her Pewter, and Preserving-pan," came to distinguish the diligent housewife (H. 1694: 184). The proliferation of status objects lent increasing importance to the household's function as a "hold," a place where goods of value were held, kept safe, watched over, and maintained. The term "hold" derives from the Gothic *haldan*, which carries the senses "to watch over, guard, defend; to keep possession of, contain." This constellation of terms precisely defined the housewife's managerial function in a nascent consumer society: to watch over, or vigilantly *behold*, her household stuff.

Domestic manuals and marriage sermons of the period were notably emphatic about the specifically *visual* dimension of this supervisory role, exhorting the housewife to "often tymes *over looke* her house & householde stuffe" (Vives c. 1553: sig. U3; my emphasis), and to "busie herselfe in *viewing* and *surveighing* such things, as she charged to be kept" (Tasso 1588: sig. E4v; my emphasis). One of the earliest of such treatises, Gentian Hervet's translation of Xenophon's *Treatise of Householde* of 1532, compares the housewife's supervisory role to that of a military commander: she must "*overse* the stuffe, vessell & implements of [the] house, none other wise than the captaine of a garison *overseeth* and proveth the soudiours" (Xenophon 1532: fol. 33v; my emphasis). The latter passage illustrates a primary preoccupation of all of these treatises, namely, that of disciplining the housewife's gaze. The most elaborate description of the housewife's duties as a domestic overseer and the dangers attendant upon her insufficient vigilance appears in John Dodd and Robert Cleaver's popular treatise, *A Godlie Forme of Householde Government* of 1598:

> She must lay a *diligent eye* to her household-stuffe in every Roome, that nothing be embezeled away, nothing spoyled or lost for want of *looking to*, nothing mard by ill usage, nor nothing worne out by using more then is needfull, nothing out of place, for things cast aside, are deemed to be stolen, and then there followeth uncharitable suspicions, which breedeth much disquietnesse.
>
> (Dodd and Cleaver 1598: 93)

The housewife's diligent eye is charged with guarding the household objects in every room, with insuring their assiduous safekeeping, meticulous maintenance, and rigorous organization. It is her task to order her household-stuff in such a way that it is entirely visible to her gaze at all times, for anything that slips from her view may give rise to "uncharitable suspicions." The precise nature of the "disquietnesse" that might arise from the housewife's insufficient vigilance, however, is not entirely clear. The threat is vaguely defined as one of theft; yet the identities of the proprietor and the culprit in this imaginary crime scene remain obscure. Indeed, the criminality of the scene is itself open to doubt, for the things cast aside are only uncharitably *deemed* to be stolen, implying that they may not be stolen at all, but merely "lost for want of looking to" – temporarily misplaced or hidden to view due to the housewife's lack of diligent scrutiny, her careless neglect of her supervisory duties. If the goods in question are not in fact stolen, however, what is motivating the uncharitable suspicions that seem inexorably to follow their disappearance? The passage effectively mobilizes anxieties surrounding the housewife's managerial control over household property by invoking a scene of domestic disorder that results in an unmanageable, yet unnamed, "disquietnesse." For an early modern reader, this "disquietnesse" would probably have evoked the clamor of a public hue and cry, and the summoning of a local constable, events that would have typically followed a scene of domestic theft. Or perhaps even the turmoil and humiliation of a public shaming ritual, commonly used to punish disorderly households and undisciplined housewives in the period. Yet these specters of public punishment are only briefly and implicitly conjured up so that they may be warded off by the disciplinary regime of female domestic supervision that the treatise aims to institute. All that is needed to protect the domestic sphere from the interventions of law or community, the passage suggests, is the diligent eye of a disciplined housewife.

Insofar as this discourse of domestic discipline positions the housewife as a non-proprietary, custodial manager of marital property, it clearly works to buttress a political economy based on patrilineal property relations and the sexual division of labor that lent it support; it works to define the bourgeois household as a sphere of emergent privacy whose property and propriety are presided over by women. Yet the relationship between discipline, law, and political economy is perhaps not as straightforward as the preceding claim would suggest. Disciplinary regimes, Foucault argues, "do not merely reproduce . . . the general form of the law or government . . . they are not univocal," but rather "define innumerable points of confrontation, focuses of instability, each of which has its own risks of conflict, of struggles, and of an at least temporary inversion of the power relations." Unlike juridical regimes, he argues, they do not "obey the law of all or nothing" (Foucault 1979: 27). Taking the relationship between the housewife's disciplined surveillance of household property and the law of coverture as an example, we can see these instabilities and points of confrontation surface. For the housewife's contrafactual ("as if") proprietorship over marital property resides in a gray area of ownership somewhere between coverture's purported "all or nothing," and as such represents innumerable potential sites of conflict. Foucault's description of the slow disappearance of spectacles of punishment and their gradual replacement by more discrete mechanisms of control and discipline presents a compelling framework within which to understand emergent forms of domestic discipline aimed at averting residual (yet still quite popular) rituals of public shaming. I here follow Richard Halpern's suggestion that Foucauldian and Marxist histories of discipline and capital might profitably supplement one another in a relation of "mutually critical complementarity," particularly in attempting to account for "mechanisms of power which are latent rather than patent, and invisible, rather than spectacular," that is, for the subtle, coercive forms of power (what Foucault terms the principle of "mildness-production-profit") operative under capitalism (Halpern 1991: 5–6). The "wedding" of these two discourses provides an apt framework within which to account for the complex forms of coercive self-discipline governing women's property relations with the rise of capitalism, while allowing for diverse forms of female agency, appropriation, and resistance. In so doing, it may provide us with the historical ground on which to rewrite the "unhappy" marriage of Marxism and feminism.

In what follows, I will examine the workings of this discourse of domestic discipline in Shakespeare's *The Merry Wives of Windsor*, a domestic comedy which fully explores, if only to dispel, "disquietnesse" surrounding the housewife's management of household property. At the start of the play, as Rosemary Kegl has argued, Shakespeare depicts the "elaborate legal machinery" that formed the interface between state, local, and domestic governance in early modern England as "ludicrously ineffective" (Kegl 1994a: 261). A representative of this machinery, Justice Shallow, famously threatens to "make a Star Chamber matter" (1. 1. 1–2) of Falstaff's riotous behavior.[4] Had he succeeded in this, Kegl argues, Shallow would only "have announced that Windsor's magistrates were incapable of controlling disorder and thus required the direct intervention of the crown in their local affairs"

(266). Yet Shallow does not succeed, because the community seems bent on settling the matter discreetly. To this end, Parson Hugh Evans offers "to make atonements and compromises between [Falstaff and Shallow]" (1. 1. 31). Evans comes up with a plan in which he, Page, and the Host of the Garter Inn will act as "umpires" who will "hear [the matter] and end it with as great discreetly as we can" (1. 1. 131–2), as Evans puts it in his frittered English. Yet his plan never materializes; for in the end, it is not the three "umpires" who give Falstaff his just desserts, but rather the merry wives themselves. They do so, I shall argue, not by publicly shaming Falstaff (as Kegl maintains), but rather by rendering any outside intervention superfluous; they protect the property and propriety of their households by demonstrating their competence as disciplined, yet discreet, domestic supervisors.

When we first observe the merry wives' observational skills they are trained on their not-so-illustrious guest, Sir John Falstaff, who, in the aftermath of several visits to their respective households, has sent the two wives identical love letters. Appalled by the fat knight's untoward behavior, Mrs. Ford vows:

> I shall think the worse of fat men as long as I have an eye to make difference of men's liking; and yet he would not swear, praised women's modesty, and gave such orderly and well-behaved reproof to all uncomeliness that I would have sworn his disposition would have gone to the truth of his words.
>
> (2. 1. 53–9)

Though she resolves henceforth to make better use of her discriminating gaze, Mrs. Ford demonstrates that she has *already* thoroughly scrutinized Falstaff's demeanor. She seems reluctant to believe that a knight, a member of the court, who "praised women's modesty," and gave "orderly and well-behaved reproof to all uncomeliness," could himself act in so "uncomely" a manner. Mrs. Ford's speech exemplifies the way in which, as Norbert Elias has argued, the adoption of an aristocratic code of conduct by the upwardly mobile "middling sort" in the early modern period was "very closely bound up" with a new "manner of seeing" (Elias 1978: 78). For the "civilizing process," in Elias's view, necessitated an "increased tendency of people to observe" the behavior of others to ensure that it conformed to a new standard of civility (79). The canon of civility thereby instituted a newly discriminating or differentiating gaze – or in Mrs. Ford's terms, an eye that "make[s] difference."

Ironically, it turns out to be the very scrupulousness with which the wives observe their guest that renders them vulnerable to his advances and consequently to the threat of "disquietnesse" and "uncharitable suspicions." For when Falstaff confesses his own designs on the wives, he makes clear that he has translated their scrutiny of his behavior and physique into his own lascivious terms:

> I do mean to make love to Ford's wife. I *spy* entertainment in her: she discourses, she carves, she gives the *leer* of invitation; I can construe the action of her familiar style, and the hardest voice of her behavior, to be Englished rightly, is "I am Sir John Falstaff's" . . . I have writ me here a letter to her; and here another to Page's wife, who even now gave me *good eyes* too, examined my parts with most *judicious oeillades*; sometimes the *beam of her view* gilded my foot, sometimes my portly belly . . . O, she did so course o'er my exteriors with such a greedy intention that the *appetite of her eye* did seem to scorch me up like a burning-glass!
>
> (1. 3. 40–63; my emphasis)

In effect, Falstaff espies the wives espying him, examining his parts under the magnifying lens of civility. The speech repeatedly underscores the boldness of their looks, the intensity and rigor with which they scrutinize their guest, leaving no inch of his vast exterior unexamined. In this episode, the potential dangers attendant upon the housewife's role as supervisor of the domestic sphere begin to surface. The assertive manner of looking necessitated by this role, a mode of looking that is dangerously at odds with the shy, retiring gaze traditionally associated with feminine modesty, renders the housewife vulnerable to allegations of impropriety. Falstaff construes the forwardness or "greediness" with which their eyes course over him in licentious terms, describing their looks as "leer[s] of invitation" and "judicious oeillades." According to the *Oxford English Dictionary*, the term "oeillades" (pronounced "iliads" in the period) designates "a significant look (especially an amorous one), an ogle." In calling the merry wives' surveying of his exterior "judicious," Falstaff flatters himself by implying that they are discriminating admirers. He also suggests, however, that they do not simply gawk at him, but that their scrutiny, however thorough, is tempered with a furtive discretion. Although their judicious observation of the lewd knight is aimed at protecting the propriety of their households, and ultimately, as we shall see, at warding off other forms of judicial intervention, much to the merry wives' chagrin Falstaff interprets their furtiveness not as a sign of civility, but of a lascivious intent that must be concealed or dissimulated.

The civilizing process, which in Elias's view profoundly altered the way in which subjects regarded one another, was equally profound in its influence on the way in which subjects regarded objects. The "civilized" household in this period, as we have seen, could not have "bare walls," but was replete with status objects that manifested social distinction through their proper order, maintenance, and display. Housewifery among the middling sort was no longer concerned merely with the management of subjects (children, servants, apprentices, etc.) but with the management of objects. From this perspective, the gaze through which the merry wives "gild" Sir John's foot or "portly belly" does not seem fundamentally different from the gaze which lights with satisfaction on the "brightness of . . . [their] Fire-Irons, and the glaring Lustre of [their] Pewter" – except, of course, that the former gaze is not nearly as satisfied with Falstaff's "exteriors" as he would have us believe. This dissatisfaction results in the merry wives quite literally scouring him clean in Act III, when Falstaff is "carried in a basket, like a barrow of butcher's offal" (3. 5. 4–5), "rammed . . . in with foul shirts and smocks, socks, foul stockings, greasy napkins" and "the rankest compound of villainous smell that ever offended nostril" (3. 5. 80–4) to be "washed" in the Thames.

That the wives' scouring of the filthy-minded knight should take the particular form of a housekeeping project follows from the play's repeated identification of the threat of sexual impropriety with the housewife's undisciplined supervision of household property. From the very beginning, Falstaff makes clear that his interest in the merry wives is primarily pecuniary: "I am almost out at heels," he confides to his followers. "There is no remedy: I must cony-catch; I must shift" (1. 3. 29–32). His choice of Mistresses Ford and Page is specifically attributed to their access to their husbands' wealth. "Hang him, poor cuckoldly knave," Falstaff says of Ford, adding: "Yet I wrong him to call him poor: they say the jealous wittolly knave hath masses of money, for the which his wife seems to me well-favoured. I will use her as the key of the cuckoldly rogue's coffer, and there's my harvest-home" (2. 2. 259–64). The dangers associated with the housewife's management of household property, whether they take the form of insufficient vigilance or an actively appetitive gaze, give rise to the threat of sexual infidelity, and not vice versa. Warning Ford of Falstaff's designs on his wife, Pistol describes adultery as a form of theft: "Take heed," he says, "have open eye; for thieves do foot by night" (2. 1. 108, 117–20). As in the case of the Dodd and Cleaver passage cited above, the identification of the purported thieves in this imaginary crime scene remains ambiguous: it may refer to Sir John and his cohorts or to the merry wives themselves. That the merry wives may be the true subjects of uncharitable suspicions in this play is supported later by the terms Ford uses to describe his own suspicions regarding the wives' sexual infidelity:

> My bed shall be abused, my coffers ransacked . . . Page is an ass, a secure ass: he will trust his wife, he will not be jealous. I will rather trust a Fleming with my butter, Parson Hugh the Welshman with my cheese, an Irishman with my aqua-vitae bottle, or a thief to walk my ambling gelding, than my wife with herself.
>
> (2. 2. 281–94)

The wives' supposed sexual impropriety is here specifically identified with their untrustworthiness with household property. Yet, in spite of Sir John's insistence on the wives' greedy intentions, on their playing fast and loose with property and propriety, the play works very hard to ward off this interpretation. While the ostensible aim of the wives' schemes of revenge is to punish Falstaff for his wantonness, it becomes clear that the greater ideological burden of their task is to prove that their gaze is sufficiently disciplined. They do so by quite literally conveying the stain of impropriety, embodied by the fat, "greasy" knight, out of their households with their dirty linens to have them "bucked" or bleached until they are cleansed.

To understand how the play works to cleanse or discipline the housewife's gaze we must begin with the way they respond to Falstaff's lewd invitation. Alarmed at his advances, and unable to explain the "mystery of [his] ill opinions" (2. 1. 69), Mrs. Page begins to scrutinize her own conduct:

> What an unweighed behavior hath this Flemish drunkard picked – with the devil's name – out of my conversation, that he dares in this manner assay me? Why, he hath not been thrice in my company! What should I say to him? I was then frugal of my mirth. Heaven forgive me!
>
> (2. 1. 22–8)

The demands of civility in early modern society, according to Elias, necessitated not only a careful observation of others; it gave rise to a powerful "compulsion to check one's own behavior" (Elias 1978: 82). In a similar vein, the play appears to caution that the housewife's gaze must be focused not only on her house and its hold, but with equal if not greater intensity and rigor on herself. Mrs. Page feels compelled to canvass her prior conduct with the knight in search of some "unweighed behavior," some slight indiscretion that may have escaped her vigilant self-scrutiny and account for Falstaff's unsolicited solicitation of her. As we watch her doing so, we see her certainty that she has played the part of the good housewife with him (having been "frugal" with her mirth) give way to a fear that she should have acted otherwise ("What should I say to him?"), prompting her to beg heaven's forgiveness.

The reflexive turning of the discriminating gaze upon the gazing subject, which Elias maintains is characteristic of the self-scrutinizing consciousness that "civilized society demands of its members" (Elias 1978: 190), may be glimpsed in Mrs. Page's plan for a thorough self-scouring:

> it makes me almost ready to wrangle with mine own honesty. I'll entertain myself like one that I am not acquainted withal; for, sure, unless he know some strain in me that I know not myself, he would not have boarded me in this fury.
>
> (2. 1. 81–6)

Mrs. Page's use of the term "entertain" here contrasts with Falstaff's earlier use of the term ("I spy entertainment in her"). Whereas Falstaff fancies that his scrutiny of the merry wives has uncovered concealed opportunities for entertainment, Mrs. Page's entertainment is itself a form of scrutiny. In promising to entertain herself as she would another, she is vowing to scrutinize her own conduct as rigorously as she would that of an unknown other, a task requiring a splitting of the simultaneously scrutinized and scrutinizing subject. The split in Mrs. Page's subjectivity is in a sense even more radical, however, in that she vows not simply to observe herself as she would another, but to observe herself as another would observe her. Her self-scrutiny is thus not merely reflexive, but entails an identification with the gaze of a stranger, who, however undeserving, represents a code of civility to which she herself aspires. What is of particular interest in Mrs. Page's planned self-scrutiny in the present context is its assumption that she is *not entirely visible to herself*. Falstaff, she fears, knows something about her, is able to see something in her, that she is herself unable to see, something that is imperceptible to or concealed from her own vigilant gaze. In order to make this opacity visible, to see the unclean thing she fears is hidden within her, she must exit herself and look at herself from the outside, from the perspective of a stranger. It is precisely this concern that the housewife may not be entirely visible to herself, that there is a limit to her powers of self-observation, that appears to motivate, while effectively rationalizing, the play's expressed concerns over her role as an unsupervised domestic supervisor. For how can the housewife be sure that there is nothing amiss within or missing from her household, that nothing within it has escaped her vision, if she is not entirely visible to herself? The ideological ruse of this internalized, disciplinary regime, of course, is that a higher degree of scrutiny will alleviate the housewife's alienation or self-estrangement (*Entfremdung*); for it is produced not by her imagined self-opacity, but rather by the contradictions inherent in her structural position as a contrafactual proprietor of household property.

Within the play, the fear that the housewife will leave some part or corner of her home unsupervised, the potential failure of her gaze to monitor every subject and object within her household, exposes the domestic sphere to the public gaze of the community, and consequently, to the threat of public humiliation. Uncharitably suspicious of his wife's domestic supervision, Ford is not content to inspect his home with his own eyes, but insists upon bringing along a posse of "all the officers in Windsor" (3. 3. 108) to search with him. Arriving at his home with "half Windsor at his heels" (3. 3. 105), he cries out, "Here, here, here be my keys; ascend my chambers; search, seek, find out" (149–51). In her book, *Private Matters and Public Culture in Post-Reformation England*, Lena Orlin identifies this kind of communal surveillance, and the cultural impetus that lent it support, as modes of resistance to emergent forms of privacy (Orlin 1994). In a discussion of communal shaming rituals she cites Philip Julius, a foreign visitor to England in 1602, who claimed: "In England every citizen is bound by oath to keep a sharp eye at his neighbor's house, as to whether the married people live in harmony" (Julius 1892: 65, cited in Orlin 1994: 7). This "mandate for public vigilance," Orlin argues, reflected a deep-seated "suspicion of the private." Domestic drama, in Orlin's view, like public shaming rituals, aimed to assuage suspicions of the private by allowing Elizabethan audiences to "see through walls, to discover the intimate secrets of conjugal relationships, to identify disorder, and to imagine that in this way it is mastered, to participate in a communal restoration of the preferred order of domestic things." Such plays, she argues, alleviate anxieties about the privatization of the domestic sphere by depicting "a house yielding up its secrets to observers" (7–9). In *The Merry Wives of Windsor*, this suspicion of the private would appear to be displaced onto the figure of the housewife. Mistrustful of his wife's ability to supervise their household, Ford seeks a communal restoration of domestic order. His communal search of his "chambers . . . coffers, and . . . presses" (3. 3. 195) effects an opening up of the private, of places that are closed off, shut or secured within the home. Ford voluntarily yields up the supposed secrets of his home to outside observers, and vicariously, as Orlin suggests, to the play's audience.

It would be difficult, however, for an audience to identify with the group of spectators that accompanies Ford on his search, not least because the search party does not turn up anything – their prying eyes do not find what they are looking for. "If there be anypody in the house, and in the chambers, and in the coffers, and in the presses," Parson Evans reports back to Ford, "heaven forgive my sins at the day of judgement!" (3. 3. 194–6). It is crucial, I would argue, that Ford's anxiety about his wife's domestic management is publicly revealed to be misplaced, and he is humiliated for it: "Fie, fie, Master Ford, are you not ashamed?" Page chides his friend. "What spirit, what devil suggests this imagination? I would not ha' your distemper in this kind for the wealth of Windsor Castle" (3. 3. 198–201). The excess of Ford's "distemper" is later described by Mrs. Page: "Why, woman, your husband . . . so buffets himself on the forehead, crying 'Peer out, peer out!' that any madness I ever yet beheld seemed but tameness, civility, and patience to this distemper" (4. 2. 18–23). Ford is cast as uncharitably suspicious of the hidden recesses of his home, and what they may conceal; he obsessively turns the nooks and crannies of his household inside out to bring to light what may be hidden within them. When he comes to search his house for the second time, Mrs. Ford warns Falstaff wearily: "Neither press, coffer, chest, trunk, well, vault, but he hath an abstract for the remembrance of such places, and goes to them by his note. There is no hiding you in the house" (4. 2. 53–7). Mrs. Ford's long list of potential hiding places habitually inspected by her husband underscores the excessive nature of his domestic surveillance. Ford is publicly shamed for his suspicions, an outcome he himself unwittingly predicts: "Help to search my house this one time. If I find not what I seek, show no color for my extremity; let me for ever be your table-sport; let them say of me, 'As jealous as Ford, that searched a hollow walnut for his wife's leman'" (4. 2. 147–51). The play thus sets up a cry-wolf scenario in which all future, spousal suspicions will themselves be treated with suspicion by the community: "If I cry out thus upon no trail," he says, "never trust me when I open again" (182–5).

That Ford's uncharitable suspicions center not only on his wife's purported sexual impropriety, but on her inability to be trusted with household property, is borne out by the specific form of his lunacy. Taking to heart Pistol's advice to "have open eye," Ford develops a kind of paranoia about the commodities that fill his home: "Awake, Master Ford," he says to himself, "there's a hole made in your best coat, Master Ford. This 'tis to have linen and buck-baskets!" (3. 5. 130–3). Mistrustful of the very valuables upon which his status depends (his fine linens and costly apparel), he repeatedly searches his household looking for the gargantuan Falstaff in the smallest of objects. "He cannot 'scape me," he cries, " 'tis impossible he should; he cannot creep into a halfpenny purse, nor into a pepper-box . . . I will search impossible places" (3. 5. 135–8). Ford's obsessive searching of his household thus arises not so much from a generalized suspicion of the "private," I would maintain, however, but rather from a suspicion that seems more particularly concerned with private property: it focuses on those hidden places or holds in which things of value are kept, from his smallest, halfpenny purse and pepper-box,[5] to his chests, trunks, "coffers, and . . . presses" (3. 3. 195). His overscrupulous surveillance clearly seeks to compensate for his wife's presumed lack of vigilance. "I will find out this" (2. 1. 124), he promises, "I will look further into't" (2. 1. 224–5). Yet Ford does not find what he is looking for; his household goods do not "yield up" any secrets to him.

Insofar as the play castigates the husband's excessive supervision of his wife, mocks it, by ridiculing Ford, it functions to restore confidence in the housewife's ability to supervise herself. "Pardon me, wife," Ford apologizes at the end of the play, and pledges, "Henceforth do what thou wilt" (4. 4. 6). The play works to ward off suspicions of the housewife's role as an overseer of household property not by allowing the audience to identify with the prying gaze of the community, however, but rather by vindicating the vigilance of the merry wives themselves, a vigilance that renders public scrutiny unnecessary or superfluous. It does so, as we have seen, by depicting the gaze that defines housewifery turning in upon itself. Yet the creation of this perfectly self-reflexive female gaze, a gaze that is entirely visible to itself, in the end works to render itself hidden to public view, and therefore, in a sense, culturally invisible or self-effacing. For what distinguishes the merry wives' domestic surveillance from that of Ford is that it is performed, to use a term that is repeated throughout the play, discreetly. The merry wives do not yield up their domestic secrets to observers. Rather, the play emphasizes the discretion with which they execute their punishment of Falstaff: they hide his love letters (2. 1. 98–9), plan their revenge in private (2. 1. 159–60), and reward those who help them carry out their plan in secrecy (Mrs. Ford thus promises Robin, Falstaff's page, "this secrecy of thine shall be a tailor to thee" [3. 3.

29–30]). The discretion of the merry wives' domestic surveillance, however, involves a great deal more than mere secrecy. According to the *OED*, the term "discretion" signifies as well the fundamental "action of separating or distinguishing." The housewife's discretion requires, as we have seen, a differentiating gaze, or to borrow Mrs. Ford's apt phrase, an "eye to make difference." The definition of discretion likewise reflects the reflexivity of the housewife's judicious gaze, insofar as it entails the "ability to discern what is right, befitting or advisable, especially with regard to one's own conduct or action." The discretion of the merry wives works prophylactically to protect the privacy of the household; they scrutinize themselves in order to ward off the probing eyes of others, by ensuring that any external scrutiny will not detect anything unforeseen, anything hidden to their own gaze. If the merry wives are able to protect themselves in the end from the threat of public scrutiny and exposure, it is because they identify with the gaze of the public, in effect incorporating the prying eyes of the community into their own reflexive gaze.

Ironically, the merry wives prove that they are diligent and discreet housewives by pretending to be the very opposite. Mrs. Ford thus repeatedly invites Falstaff into her home while her husband is out, pretending "to take an ill advantage of his absence" (3. 3. 100–1). In so doing, their revenge schemes mobilize, in order to dispel, cultural anxieties surrounding the housewife's unsupervised supervision of the household. When Mrs. Page arrives, Mrs. Ford tells Falstaff to hide, claiming that her friend is "a very tattling woman" (3. 3. 84). Mrs. Page answers in kind, accusing her friend of sexual impropriety: "O Mistress Ford, what have you done? You're shamed, you're overthrown, you're undone for ever! . . . O well-a-day, Mistress Ford, having an honest man to your husband, to give him such cause of suspicion!" (86–92). By facetiously enacting the role of untrustworthy ("suspicious") and indiscreet ("tattling") housewives, they effectively demonstrate that such suspicions are unfounded, and in so doing restore confidence in their managerial function. Their schemes thus work to dissuade absent husbands from falsely suspecting their wives, and from unjustifiably meddling in their wives' household affairs.

The disciplinary regime of self-supervision instilled in the housewife thus works to reinforce the emergent privatization of the household, and its differentiation as a specifically feminine sphere. Ford's search for Falstaff in his wife's buck-basket comes to stand as a symbol of his inappropriate meddling. When Ford arrives and asks whither the buck-basket is being taken, he is thus scolded by his wife: "Why, what have you to do whither they bear it? You were best meddle with buck-washing!" (143–4). Later, when he comes to search his house a second time, having discovered the way the wives had earlier concealed and conveyed Falstaff out of it, he decides to search the buck-basket himself. It is Page this time who seeks to draw the gendered line of division between masculine and feminine spheres of labor: "Why, this passes, Master Ford; you are not to go loose any longer, you must be pinioned" (113–14). Evans likewise cautions, "Why, this is lunatics; this is mad as a mad dog" (115), to which Shallow adds, "Indeed, Master Ford, this is not well, indeed" (116). When Ford stubbornly continues to ransack the laundry basket, crying "I shall find you anon" (127), his wife seeks to shame him into relinquishing it to her: "Are you not ashamed? Let the clothes alone" (127). Evans likewise cautions him to stay away from it: "'Tis unreasonable; will you take up your wife's clothes?" (129) he asks, punning on Ford's literal taking up of the laundry for which his wife is responsible, but also on his figurative crossing of the gendered line of division between masculine and feminine spheres, as if his meddling interference in his wife's domestic management has effeminized him. "Come away" (130), Evans nervously insists.

Domestic manuals of the period similarly insist that husbands should not meddle in their wives' supervision of the house and its hold. Thus, Xenophon's *Treatise of Householde* cautions men against spending too much time at home and encroaching upon their wives' domestic duties: "And it is more shame for a man to byde slouggynge at home than to applie his mynde to suche thynges as must be done abrode . . . [God] will punisshe hym outher for bicause he is negligent in that that he shulde do or elles *bycause he takethe upon hym that that belongeth to the wyfe*" (Xenophon 1532: fol. 24r, 25r; my emphasis). Defining the household as a sphere that is "proper to the wife," a discrete domain whose property she properly presides over,[6] Dodd and Cleaver's treatise, *A Godlie Forme of Householde Government*, likewise insists upon mutual spousal discretion in crossing this gendered line of division:

> the husband is not to deale, but soberly and in great discretion with affaires, that are proper to the wife . . . Wherefore, as the husband cannot well abide, that his wife should shew her selfe more skilfull and wise in his businesse then himselfe: so cannot the wife suffer, that her husband should despise and account her a foole, by meddling with her small household affaires.
>
> (Dodd and Cleaver 1598: 186–7)

What is significant about this doctrine of domestic discretion is its mutuality. For while the idea that the wife should not attempt to interfere in her husband's affairs was commonplace in the period, the notion that the husband should refrain from supervising his wife's domestic supervision, that he should relinquish to her the daily management of the household economy, was only beginning to emerge. The devaluation of housewifery consequent upon this ideological definition of the household as a feminine sphere is apparent in the assertion that the housewife's affairs are unimportant or "small," and by implication, not worth the meddling. In the late seventeenth century, *The Ladies Dictionary* similarly trivializes the housewife's supervision of house and hold in order to ward off excessive spousal supervision: "they must be accounted over-curious, or rather mean spirited," it cautions husbands, "that cannot let a Woman alone with Pipkins, Pyes and Puddings, but must be peeping, prying, and finding fault with the Feminine Jurisdiction" (H. 1694: 203). The alliterative repetitions of the passage disparage the husband's "over-curious" surveillance, his "peeping" and "prying" into what is now comfortably labeled "the Feminine Jurisdiction." Any potential anxiety surrounding the housewife's supervisory role with respect to household property, however, is once again tamed by the triviality of the objects ostensibly at stake in her perusal ("Pipkins, Pyes and Puddings").

What is particularly ingenious about the way in which the merry wives restore confidence in their ability to govern the "Feminine Jurisdiction" is the weapons they use to do so: a buck-basket, a cowl-staff, and dirty linens – all household objects that were commonly used in public shaming rituals in the period to punish unruly or wayward housewives and their hapless husbands. The cowl-staff, for example, was commonly used in "ridings," a spectacle in which whores, adulteresses, cuckolds and wife-beaten husbands were "ridden" through town, hoisted on a cowl-staff, accompanied by a boisterous procession of jeering neighbors.[7] Falstaff's ride on the cowl-staff (which is used to hoist the buck-basket in which he is carried to and then summarily dumped in the Thames) resembles other public shaming rituals as well, such as charivari, in which victims were "dragged out of the house, thrown in a wet hole, trampled, beaten and covered with mud and filth, then washed" in a lake or river in a "cucking stool" (Ingram 1984: 81). This appropriation and dramatic transformation of the tools of communal shaming, here used not to punish wayward wives but rather to vindicate the wives' honesty by punishing their would-be seducer, may likewise be found in the merry wives' second scheme of revenge, when Falstaff is lured to Mrs. Ford's house, and coerced into disguising himself in the "gown" (4. 2. 75), "thrummed hat" (70), "muffler" (70), and "linen" kerchief (73) of the "fat woman of Brainford" to escape Ford's search party undetected. As an interloper in the "Feminine Jurisdiction," Falstaff, like Ford, finds himself effeminized, forced not merely to "take up" but to wear women's clothes. The scheme parodies a common form of public shaming ritual called Skimmington, in which husbands who had been beaten or cuckolded by their wives were made to dress up in their wives' clothing and to ride the cowl-staff while being beaten by a neighbor (see Ingram 1984: 86; Underdown 1985: 131). The merry wives effectively transform the tools of such public spectacles into a discreet form of punishment which succeeds in hiding the transvestite giant's identity from the search party.

While one member of this party, Parson Hugh Evans, demonstrates that his powers of observation are quite keen – "I spy a great peard under his muffler" (4. 2. 181), he says suspiciously – his prying gaze is not sharp enough to penetrate the merry wives' prank. When he later realizes his error, Evans describes Falstaff's disguise as "one of the best discretions of a 'oman as ever I did look upon" (4. 4. 1–2). Evans's rather eccentric, plural use of the term "discretion" refers at once to the success of the disguise, which was able to hide the hulking knight, and more generally to the powers of female discretion, which Falstaff here appropriates in order to protect himself, like a woman, from public view. It also seems to suggest that a woman's "discretions" are something that one may "look upon," rather than an invisible, abstract quality. In a sense, Evans here gives voice to the ideological work performed by the play, which serves to make the housewife's discretion visible. As I have suggested, however, this ideological work cuts both ways: it brings to light the housewife's *de facto* management of household property, while at the same time suggesting that her managerial skills are so impeccable, her gaze so watchful, so vigilant, so visible to itself, as to render her management once again invisible, because not worth the watching, not in need of spousal supervision. The comedy thus functions to assuage male anxiety surrounding the housewife's supervisory role with respect to the goods of the household by bringing this role into visibility – or in Janevive Deane's terms, "apparancie to the worlde" – only to be eclipsed once more by the housewife's consummate discretion.

Notes

This paper has benefitted from the insight of several generous readers. Most especially, I would like to thank John Guillory and Jean Howard, who have each had a profound influence on my thinking about these issues. I would also like to thank auditors at the Harvard University Renaissance Seminar and the Columbia University Shakespeare Seminar for their helpful feedback on earlier drafts presented there. Finally, I am extremely grateful to Wesleyan University for supporting my research through a fellowship at its Center for the Humanities, to its Director Elizabeth Traub, and to my fellow CHUM fellows, in particular Claire Potter, Gay Smith, Cameron McFarlane, and Cameron Anderson, who provided daily intellectual support and inspiration during my semester in their delightful company.

1 As formulated by William Blackstone's *Commentaries on the Laws of England*, this doctrine dictated: "the husband and wife are one person in law: that is, the very being or legal existence of the woman is suspended during the marriage, or at least incorporated and consolidated into that of the husband: under whose wing, protection, and *cover* she performs every thing; and is therefore called . . . a *feme-covert* . . . and her condition during her marriage is called her *coverture*" (Blackstone 1979: 430). See also the anonymous treatises, *Baron and Feme: A Treatise of the Common Laww Concerning Husbands and Wives* and *A Treatise of Feme Coverts: Or, the Lady's Law*.

2 Kenny's study, like that of Basil Edwin Lawrence (1884), bear testimony to an emerging interest in the complex history of married women's property rights that followed upon the passage of the Married Women's Property Acts 1870 and 1880.

3 The rights and incidents of ownership, according to Honoré, include: the right to possess, the right to use, the right to manage, the right to the income of the thing, the right to the capital, the right to security, the right or incidents of transmissibility (to give or bequeath) and absence of term, the prohibition of harmful use, the liability to execution (e.g. debt), and the incident of the residuary (the right to the residue or remainder of an estate).

4 All references to *The Merry Wives of Windsor*, unless otherwise indicated, are to the Arden edition (Shakespeare 1971).

5 Pepper was still a relatively expensive, imported commodity in the late sixteenth century. Ford's search of his pepper-box is thus akin to that of his buck-basket of fine linens; it signals a mistrust of the luxury goods upon which his status depends, goods which he entrusts his wife to "keep," but which render his household vulnerable to the threat of theft (the penetration of his "hold") and sexual impropriety (the penetration of his wife) (Shammas 1993: 179).

6 "As properly the husband is to get [goods] . . . the wife is to order and dispose [them] . . . The dutie of the husband is, to travell abroad to seeke living: and the wives dutie is to keep the house . . . The dutie of the husband is, to be a giver: and of the wife, to bee a saver . . . The dutie of the husband is, to dispatch all things without doore: and of the wife, to

oversee and give order for all things within the house" (Dodd and Cleaver 1598: 170–1).

7 "To ride on a cowl-staff," according to the *OED*, is "to be set astride a pole and carried in derision about in the streets; a rough form of popular punishment, inflicted especially on a husband who allowed himself to be beaten or abused by his wife." (See also Underdown 1985: 131; Ingram 1984: 86.)

6

The rape of Jesus: Aemilia Lanyer's *Lucrece*

BARBARA E. BOWEN

The terms of the national debate have subtly, insidiously shifted. What used to be called liberal is now called radical; what used to be called radical is now called insane.

(Tony Kushner, "American Things", in *Thinking about the Longstanding Problems of Virtue and Happiness: Essays, A Play, Two Poems, and a Prayer*. 1995)

My question is how to recognize moments in early modern writing when revolutionary change is imagined. Without assuming that we know in advance what form that change would take or that its understanding of class, gender and other social relations would be automatically recognizable, I am struck by how difficult it has become to ask that question, particularly about women's writing. Everything from the supposed discrediting of communism in 1989 to the right-wing attacks on political correctness to the formation of Renaissance studies itself contributes to the inhibition we may feel in approaching the outlines of utopian desire or the possibility of collective struggle in early literature. It is significant that both cultural materialism and new historicism are more clear-sighted about the limits than the possibilities of radicalism in cultural texts: along with the bracing focus on the individual's encounter with ideology has come a shift of attention away from collective social movements and how they may be made thinkable by the deep grammar of literary texts. At the same time, Shakespeare studies, like other disciplines, has been deformed in the last decade by the restructuring of American higher education along neoliberal lines. Early modernists have yet to register how neoliberalism's substitution of a reified "market" for all other measures of value has left its imprint on the intellectual map of our field. We pay a price in loss of forward momentum for the collapse of the academic job system, which has removed a whole generation of young scholars from full-time work just at the moment when the field was being remade by feminism, queer studies and historicist scholarship. One casualty is the full critical attention that should be given to early women writers; another is the integration of the growing knowledge about women in the period into the study of canonical male authors, above all Shakespeare. As the traditional university melts into air, we face deepening epistemological loss: fewer and fewer questions about radical possibility will be asked if half a century of expansion in higher education is reversed and the university excludes the populations of students who have historically demanded and produced new knowledge.[1]

This essay is an attempt to concentrate attention on a radical political imaginary in early modern literature, recognizing that such a discussion is enabled by the work of the past two decades that it hopes in some ways to challenge. I want to start by taking seriously the proposition that the literature produced at the period of transition to capitalism would bear, in addition to the deep scars of consciousness that capitalism still delivers, some openings for resistance to its already visible oppressions, some imagining of collective agency.[2] Important work on this subject has already been done by Rosemary Kegl and Richard Halpern, in very different books on the relation of Renaissance literature to the early formation of capitalism. My aim is to work, as they do, in the tradition of Lukács and Jameson, on the deepest reaches of literary form, but to extend the discussion to texts by women.

Women's writing is critical to such an inquiry, though not because it is automatically progressive or because it occupies a transparent political position. As is well known, women in early modern England were enjoined specifically from public speech, with the authority for the prohibition located in Genesis by Paul: "Let the woman learn in silence with all subjection. I permit not a woman to teache, nether to usurp autoritie over the man, but to be in silence. For Adam was first formed, then Eve. And Adam was not deceived, but the woman was deceived, & was in the transgression" (Geneva Bible, 1969: 1 Tim. 2: 12–14). Thus even a woman who wrote "of divinest things," as Aemilia Lanyer described herself (1993: 3), to some extent threatened a cornerstone of a system of subjugation based on the premise of women's inferiority to men. Whether violating one major tenet of an obscenely hierarchical society would have made women writers more likely to question others, or to understand their individual acts of resistance in relation to a larger system of oppression, are questions with which feminist criticism continues to wrestle.[3] Kim Hall reminds us that the acquisition of what Elizabeth Cary called "public voice" fostered contradictory drives for English Protestant women: on the one hand, to consolidate one's own power at the expense of even more marginalized groups – such as servants, laborers, Turks, Africans or Jews – and on the other, to understand related structures of oppression more fully (1995: 178–82). Other recent feminist work has also stressed how carefully we need to theorize our assertions of the political in these texts: Margaret Ferguson's review essay (1994) is a seminal discussion of women's agency; critical also is the work of scholars of the Civil War period, who have argued that Renaissance women's writing might best be understood in a trajectory that looks beyond 1625 to the pre-Civil War escalation of publishing by women (Hinds 1996: 2–3).[4] Thus while early women wrote from a variety of sometimes contradictory political positions, their writing remains a vital site for an inquiry into utopian expression or oppositional consciousness in the period. Positioned as radically speechless, these writers necessarily violated the prohibition that rendered them non-subjects, even when their class, religious or political affiliations dictated that they not understand their writing as a challenge to larger structures of oppression. And it seems likely that women's writing from the 1590s to the 1640s would bear especially vivid traces of epistemic violence and the will to overcome it, for this half-century formed a pressured interval during which the prohibition against public speech was still strongly in force but was increasingly being flouted. The decades of the emergence of a women's print culture in England – and I would argue that such a culture did begin to exist in the early seventeenth century[5] – make a claim on us as a locus of subjugated knowledge, if only because they gave women intellectual access to each other for the first time in spaces beyond the domestic and religious.

In *The Rhetoric of Concealment*, Rosemary Kegl studies four male authors and traces the power of rhetorical gesture to "make unimaginable any sort of collective struggle for social change" (1994b: 9). I want to ask what sort of rhetorical gestures might make collective struggle imaginable, or at least disrupt a political imaginary that actively engaged in preventing organized resistance to subordination by women of any social position and by the new sector of wage workers, who were both women and men. How could literary texts by women, for instance, allow women readers to understand their subordination as the result of a political structure in which they might have agency? Could literature offer a subject-position from which the shape of the emerging political economy was visible? Richard Strier, who also examines the space for radical politics in Renaissance literature but from a "post-Marxist" position, is nevertheless surely right when he says that accusations of ahistoricism are used to limit the political potential of literary readings (1995: 6); in a sense this essay courts the charge of ahistoricism in order to open up a more usable reading of women's writing within history, one that attempts, as Walter Mignolo writes, "to speak the present by theorizing the past" (1995: xiii).

My hope in this essay is to bring together the feminist impulse to clarify and enlarge our reading of early women with the Marxists' attention to literary form. I have argued elsewhere that despite the groundbreaking work on early modern women writers produced in the past few years (especially on Aemilia Lanyer, where the scholarship is very rich[6]), women's writing still tends to be read as if it were less complex, smaller, than it is. A more useful sense of the political work of these writings might follow from an expansion of the literary claims we are willing to make for them. What if we restored to women's writing the real drama of their reading? Imagine an analysis that assumed the woman writer's overdetermined encounter with the male-authored literary tradition, her full engagement with the debates of her time, her knowledge of male writers like Shakespeare but also Nashe, Christine de Pizan and Augustine, her curiosity about visual and musical traditions. Would an expanded sense of women writers' political thought emerge? This essay is a kind of thought-experiment in response to such questions: I am not interested at this stage in arguing in detail for Lanyer's knowledge of any one of the sources I shall cite, nor do I want to suggest that it would be simple to determine exactly what editions of earlier writers she might have had access to, even as a woman on the periphery of the court who was mistress to Elizabeth's Lord Chamberlain. My aim is rather to discover whether another kind of reading of women writers is possible if we were to lift what I see as a form of self-censorship in our readings of their work.

The focus of my discussion will be a single line in Aemilia Lanyer's 1611 religious narrative poem, *Salve Deus Rex Judaeorum*, in which is embedded a quotation from Shakespeare's *Rape of Lucrece*. I shall assume in approaching this passage that Lanyer had read every account of the Lucretia story available in seventeenth-century England – from Livy to Ovid to Salutati to Machiavelli to Christine de Pizan to Chaucer to Edward More; that she was aware of the history of controversy about Lucretia's suicide – a debate initiated by Augustine and vigorously taken up by Tyndale and other English Reformers – that she could offer a critique not only of Shakespeare's poem but of the tradition of representations of rape to which it belongs; that she might have known of the visual tradition of depictions of Lucretia; that she had read widely and deeply in the Calvinist passion narratives with which her poem is in dialogue; that she has a reason for invoking the story of the Roman matron who was raped and then committed suicide in the context both of the crucifixion and of her own volume's preoccupation with female solidarity and the arbitrariness of class; and that her poem has something to say about rape in early capitalist England, about the gendered body in pain, about the link between the crucifixion and rape, and about the connection between wounds to women's bodies and the possibility of female agency in transforming public, political life.

The reference to Shakespeare occurs at a pivotal moment in the account of Christ's passion that forms the center of *Salve Deus*; it marks the threshold of Lanyer's most transgressive revision of Christianity's master narrative.[7] As a writer of Christianity's central mystery, and especially as a woman writer, Lanyer does not have the freedom to alter the story; instead she creates a counter-discourse, weaving in and out of the evangelical text a rich mix of addresses to women either biblical or contemporary, an undersong of allusion and quotation, and an explosion of female voice. Pilate's wife, mentioned only in Matthew, has to be a central character for such a project, for unlike the other women present at the passion, whose mute witness serves to validate male suffering, the wife of Pilate claims suffering as her own and transforms it into speech: "Have thou nothing to do with that juste man: for I have suffered many things this day in a dreame by reason of him" (Geneva Bible, 1560: Matt. 27: 19). Achsah Guibbory describes the speech Lanyer invents for Pilate's wife as an act of literary recovery, as if Lanyer were retrieving the words that "went unrecorded in Matthew . . . [and correcting] the silencing of women's words by the men who wrote the Gospels" (1998: 199). The appearance of *Salve Deus* in the same year as the King James Bible has led several critics, including Guibbory, to speculate on whether the poem is a conscious attempt to write a new Bible, undertaken as the Authorized Version was in progress – a deliberately unauthorized version, perhaps, dedicated pointedly to Queen Anne rather than overseen by the King. The "recovered" speech by Pilate's wife is famously a defense of Eve. As several readers of the poem have shown, the outline of the defense follows other contributions to the contemporary print debate about the virtue of women (Richey 1997: 106–28; Jordan 1990: 22–6, 122–7), but Lanyer's innovation is to put pressure on the meaning of the crucifixion through a re-reading of the Fall. The link between the two events is patriarchy: Pilate's wife names the Fall, at least as it is interpreted within Christian doctrine, as the source for the ideology of patriarchal oppression. With considerable psychological subtlety, she urges her husband not to condemn Jesus because it would mean the end of male supremacy: the crucifixion, she warns, will be the Fall of men.

> Condemne not him that must thy Saviour be;
> But view his holy Life, his good desert.
> Let not us Women glory in Mens fall,
> Who had power given to over-rule us all.
>
> Till now your indiscretion sets us free,
> And makes our former fault much lesse appeare.
> (Lanyer 1993: 84)

Pilate is being asked to save male sovereignty, not to save Jesus: the wife's argument is that men will no longer be able to "over-rule us all" if one man commits an "indiscretion" so much greater than Eve's. The slippage in tense and voice here is critical – "Till *now* your indiscretion sets *us* free." A certain fluidity of syntax is not unusual in Lanyer, but the apparent illogic of this passage bears close investigation. Readers of the poem have argued over whether the voice here is Pilate's wife's or the poet's own, whether the time period jumps into the present or remains in the biblical past. For if the condemnation of Jesus leads to the freedom of women, then the liberation should already have happened: "the fact that [Lanyer] is also writing in seventeenth-century England and protesting the continued subjection of women suggests that Christ's redemption . . . has yet to be enacted on earth," as Guibbory writes (1998: 201). She explains the paradox by suggesting that Lanyer anticipates some of the radicalism of the Civil War Protestants; this seems clearly right, especially when we see in a few lines that Lanyer, like the Quakers, envisions sexual equality as the prelapsarian condition ("let us have our Libertie *againe*"). But Guibbory attributes Lanyer's radicalism finally to Christianity's own "revolutionary spirit" (1998: 201). I would argue instead that the paradox of the liberation in the past that remains in the future points to something like Juliet Mitchell's "longest revolution": the knowledge of defeat that accompanies this expression of utopian desire is part of the story *Salve Deus* wants to tell.

Although provocative and even facetious defenses of Eve had been a feature of gender controversy writing since the 1540s,[8] there is nothing playful in *Salve Deus*'s assertion that Adam, not Eve, "was most too blame" (85). In the first dedication to the poem, Lanyer draws attention to "faire *Eves* apologie" and challenges the reader "To judge if it agree not with the Text" (6). Her poem is a serious exercise in exegesis. Sara Mendelson and Patricia Crawford's history of early modern women reminds us of what was at stake: "The Genesis narrative was understood not only as a symbolic representation of gender roles in marriage and the family, but as a concrete event in the past which accounted for women's loss of power and independence in the secular world" (1998: 33): to revise it was to rewrite history and challenge the text that supported an immense architecture of subordination. The argument in Matthew for Christ's innocence here becomes an argument for Eve's, with the substitution of a woman for a man presaging the more radical substitution to come. Heretically and spectacularly, Pilate's wife compares the excusable transgression of Eve – committed out of "ignorance," desire for "knowledge" and "too much love" for Adam (84–6) – to the unforgivable sin about to be committed by Pilate:

> Her weaknesse did the Serpents words obay;
> But you in malice Gods deare Sonne betray.
>
> Whom, if unjustly you condemne to die,
> Her sinne was small, to what you doe commit;
> All mortall sinnes that doe for vengeance crie,
> Are not to be compared unto it:
> If many worlds would altogether trie,
> By all their sinnes the wrath of God to get;
> This sinne of yours, surmounts them all as farre
> As doth the Sunne, another little starre.
>
> Then let us have our Libertie againe,
> And challendge to your selves no Sov'raigntie;
> You came not in the world without our paine,
> Make that a barre against your crueltie;
> Your fault beeing greater, why should you disdaine
> Our beeing your equals, free from tyranny?

> If one weake woman simply did offend,
> This sinne of yours, hath no excuse, nor end.

With the claim that the crucifixion is a gendered crime, committed by men, and a greater crime than Eve's, Lanyer's poem repudiates the entire exegetical tradition. Yet the poem's revisionary project extends further. The pace of allusion quickens as *Salve Deus* reaches its central moment, and Lanyer's text not only reads Scripture against itself but rewrites the language of secular verse. That the two literary traditions share a masculinist rhetoric and support each other in undergirding what Lanyer calls "tyranny" is one of the poem's most far-reaching insights. The connection emerges in the final couplet of the passage, which includes a quotation from Shakespeare's *Rape of Lucrece.* In Shakespeare the phrase occurs as Tarquin argues with himself about whether to go through with the rape of Lucrece, the wife of his fellow soldier and friend, Collatinus:

> 'Had Collatinus killed my son or sire,
> Or lain in ambush to betray my life,
> Or were he not my dear friend, this desire
> Might have excuse to work upon his wife
> As in revenge or quittal of such strife.
> But as he is my kinsman, my dear friend,
> The shame and fault finds no excuse nor end.'
> (Shakespeare 1997b: ll. 232–8)

No excuse nor end: the phrase sounds as if it might be proverbial, but extensive inquiry has not been able to find any reference to it as a proverb. Even if the expression were found to be proverbial, however, Lanyer's positioning of the phrase makes it clear that her poem is remembering Shakespeare's, which was widely circulated after 1594 and had been reprinted four times before the publication of *Salve Deus* in 1611.[9] She places the phrase in exactly the same position Shakespeare does – at the end of a couplet that concludes a stanza – and within a line whose rhythm and pattern of monosyllables precisely mirrors his.[10] Her *ottava rima* stanzas simultaneously veer away from and recall Shakespeare's seven-line rhyme royal in *Lucrece.* Quotation in Lanyer is never casual; *Salve Deus* is a profoundly citational text, as self-conscious an appropriation of Scripture as *Paradise Lost.* The whole project of the poem is revisionary, thus every allusion, especially one at this extraordinary break in exegetical orthodoxy, demands attention. The turn in Lanyer's line away from *The Rape of Lucrece*, enacted in the substitution of second-person plural address ("This sinne of *yours*" rather than "The shame and fault") marks a distance from Shakespeare and creates the space for a new political imaginary.

The moment Lanyer quotes from *Lucrece* depicts the male rapist hesitating to commit the crime not because of its effect on Lucrece but because of his political and affiliative ties to another man. As Nancy Vickers has shown (1985: 95–115), rape in Shakespeare's poem, like the crucifixion in Lanyer, is a negotiation between men: rape is the punishment women incur for being praised by men; its result and its goal is women's silence.[11] Lanyer is in a sense the anti-Lucrece; she breaks the silence and speaks Lucrece's part, which is drowned out in Shakespeare by Lucrece's concern with the pollution of her husband and then displaced in the long meditation on Hecuba. That Lanyer borrows the voice of the rapist, however, for her condemnation of the crucifixion suggests the delicate negotiation in her text with the rhetorical traditions for the representation of violence. Debora Shuger's analysis of the contemporary passion sermons shows how these texts interpellate the (male) reader to identify with the torturers as well as the tortured Christ (1994: 89–127); by inviting the reader here to identify with the voice of Tarquin, as spoken by Lanyer's female character, *Salve Deus* reveals a similar process at work in narratives of rape. Through what Lorna Hutson calls "the incriminating display of the female body" (1992: 168), fictions of rape present the female victim as erotic object even as the reader is asked to condemn the rapist: Lucretia, in Stephanie Jed's phrase, "has returned innumerable times to the witness stand to describe, to a jury of humanistic readers and writers, the experience of things a man did to her body" (1989: 4). Lanyer's double-voiced character – at once the rapist Tarquin and the feminist wife of Pilate – exposes the contradictions in the subject-position offered by traditional narratives of rape and suggests that the same position may be offered to the male reader of the passion. If one project of the poem is to free the discourse of rape from the masculinist rhetoric of display, another – equally urgent – is to reimagine the passion for women.

The stanza in which the line from *Lucrece* is embedded starts with a call for the end of female subordination and ends with a reference to rape; not only does it insinuate that the violation of Lucretia is a crime of the same magnitude as the crucifixion, it connects women's loss of liberty to their inscription in a rape culture. If male "Sov'raigntie" is maintained ideologically by reliance on the story of Eve, it is maintained physically and institutionally by rape. The buried narrative of

Lucretia, surfacing at the one moment in the poem where the speaker directly names women's subordination and men's agency in perpetuating it, allows *Salve Deus* to connect a political economy that subordinates women to the apparently individual act of sexualized violence. Now, twenty-five years after Susan Brownmiller's *Against our Will*, the relation between rape and patriarchy as a political system may seem obvious, but it was deeply occluded in early modern English culture. Other early women writers, notably Christine de Pizan, Marguerite de Navarre and Gaspara Stampa, had developed resistant readings of the patriarchal discourse of rape,[12] and as we shall see, the legal definition of the crime was beginning to shift in ways that suggested an awareness of the systematic oppression of women, but Lanyer is aiming for something different here: the passage both implicates rape within patriarchy and moves toward a political imaginary in which resistance to patriarchy is possible.

For the rape of Lucretia, as Stephanie Jed's work has made us aware, is a political story as much as a sexual one. In her book *Chaste Thinking* Jed shows that the story of Lucretia was "a founding myth of liberty" for Renaissance humanism: just as the murder of Jesus allowed for the establishment of Christianity, so Lucretia's rape and subsequent suicide were understood to have prompted the expulsion of the Tarquins from Rome and enabled the establishment of the Roman republic (1989: 5). Lucretia was constructed as the sacrificial victim whose willingly accepted death ushers in a new order; her violation became for Florentine humanists the Benjaminian document of barbarism that made Roman, and later, their own culture possible. In versions that came down to the Renaissance from Livy and Ovid, the legend unravels the mystery of how political change is possible: the overthrow of tyrants by citizens can occur only in the aftermath of sexual violence. Like the story of the Fall, the rape of Lucretia is an attempt to explain the inexplicable through domestic narrative. Rome had been under Etruscan occupation and was ruled by Tarquin, who, as Shakespeare writes in the *Argument* to his poem, "had possessed himself of the kingdom . . . contrary to the Roman laws and customs, not requiring or staying for the people's suffrages." Shakespeare drops almost all interest in the political meaning of the events in the poem itself, but the *Argument* makes the key connection between the woman and the city. Raped by the son of the king, Lucretia becomes a figure for Rome under occupation; her "liberation" through suicide presages and enables the liberation of Rome.

It is Jed's purpose to show how deeply the liberationist reading of the legend of Lucretia is entwined in the consolidation of absolutist patriarchal power in Renaissance Florence. When I suggest that the liberatory meanings of the story are in play for Lanyer, I do not mean to imply that the historical transition to a slave republic in Rome was anything like a revolution in the Marxist sense. But I would argue that the tradition of reading this story as a prologue to a liberatory political change, available to an early modern English reader in versions from Machiavelli, Salutati and others, was a critical part of its appeal for Lanyer. It is significant that *Salve Deus* voices an indictment of rape culture through a narrative that has historically been read to mean that oppressive political systems can be challenged by violent collective struggle. Consider again how Pilate's wife ends her defense of Eve: "If one weake woman simply did offend, / This sinne of yours, hath no excuse, nor end." But the speech does not stop there; the next two lines are for me the political hinge of the poem:

> To which (poore soules) we never gave consent,
> Witnesse thy wife (O *Pilate*) speakes for all.
>
> (87)

This is the most radical expression of female solidarity in *Salve Deus*, and significantly it is the point where the poet's own voice has most often been heard within or above the wife's. Who is telling Pilate to "witness"? Is it the wife's own voice that speaks of herself in the third person and calls for her husband to occupy the traditionally female role of witness while she seizes the role of speaker? Or is it the poet's voice, calling to her character to be more attentive and to her audience to focus on this central moment of the poem? Answers to these questions are less important than the claim to speak for all. The passage argues that while women never consented to the crucifixion they have a collective interest in voicing their dissent. Without being a blueprint for social struggle, the lines plant an image of female collectivity in the center of the poem and at the height of its engagement with a narrative of political change. Perhaps what we hear in the urgency of the plea to Pilate is the desire for rather than the achievement of collectivity; even so, the importance of this passage, coming where it does after a call for freedom, is its suggestion that gender functions as a political identity and that it can form the basis for collective action.[13]

But what would it have meant in the early years of the seventeenth century to imagine political action in the name of women or even to think about rape? These are questions that obviously need longer discussion than I can provide here, but recent scholarship suggests that the truism about women's lack of agency in the political sphere needs to be re-examined. Mendelson and Crawford remind us "that women's expressions of political consciousness were unlikely to be noted in official documents unless such women were considered unusually threatening by authorities"; they discuss a range of forms women's political action did take: claiming participatory rights such as voting; proselytizing as some Leveller women did for separatist congregations; engaging in "mass political movements," during the 1640s and 1650s; conducting and sometimes leading public protests as both women and workers (1998: 146–7). Displaced from the land by enclosure and starved by the spiraling inflation of the sixteenth and seventeenth centuries, women were particularly active in the series of enclosure and grain "riots" that accompanied England's entrance into capitalist modernity. Women were present, as John Walter has established, "in almost every food riot in the period, and some riots were exclusively feminine affairs" (1980: 62). The largest recorded participation of women in popular protest in the period was in 1629 in Essex, where they responded to famine by drawing on their own informal networks and shared knowledge – as well as their ambiguous position under the law – to effect political change. Enraged by the government's refusal to protect local grain markets and the freedom of foreign merchants to buy up English grain for export, a hundred women from several local towns convened with their children on a Flemish ship and forced its crew to fill the women's caps and aprons with the grain intended for export. The authorities responded by arranging for some distribution of grain and imposing only mild punishment on the women. Three months later one of the participants, Ann Carter, had begun to call herself Captain Carter and was touring the local clothmaking towns to gather support from unemployed male workers for another assault on a mercantilist grain ship. This time there was a crowd of three hundred, men as well as women, and the reaction was different: Carter and three men were hanged (Walter 1980: 52–64). That women from different towns could act together, however, and that they understood famine not as a natural condition but as a result of political policy suggests both a broader definition of politics than has traditionally been assumed and a stronger possibility that gender was being mobilized as a public identity. Dorothy Berry, one of the protestors, when asked by local authorities who had incited her to riot, replied, "the Crie of the Countrey and hir owne want" (Essex ROD/B3/208, no.14, quoted in Walter 1980: 54).

Whether rape was normally understood in terms of gender identity is less clear: *Salve Deus* is ahead of the period's emerging discourse on women's legal rights in its examination of rape in the context of patriarchy. The closest analog is probably *The Lawes Resolutions of Womens Rights*, a 1632 guide to the law for women, which begins with a list of the consequences of what it calls "Adams sinne" ("that Women have no voyse in Parliament, They make no Lawes, they consent to none"), and ends with an analysis of rape. The discussion centers on the distinction between "rape" – what we would call abduction – and "ravishment," a crime of sexual violation but not theft. It defines ravishment as "a hideous hatefull kinde of whoredome in him which committeth it, when a woman is enforced violently to sustaine the furie of brutish concupiscence: but she is left where she is found, as in her owne house or bed, as *Lucrece* was" ([Edgar?] 1632: 377–8).[14] The distinction between rape and ravishment began to appear in English law only in 1555; until then the rape statutes recognized little difference between the abduction of property and the abduction of a woman. The severity of the punishments for rape (still a capital offense in the seventeenth century) was the result of a need to protect the property of the ruling class, not to safeguard women; as late as 1487 the law on rape articulated that women were "like Goods, oftentimes taken by Misdoers," and served to protect families in which the daughters chose to marry men not sanctioned by their fathers.[15] The tension expressed in *The Lawes Resolutions* between women's status as property and their status as persons points to a deeper fissure in the conception of female subjectivity, one that is at issue both in the legal text and in *Salve Deus*. As a crime that depends on the acknowledgement of a woman's "capacity to give consent or exercise will" (Hartman 1997: 79), rape produces a legal and ontological crisis in a culture that grants agency to women only selectively. Lanyer's invocation of rape in the same breath as her call to restore women's "Libertie" suggests a reconceptualization of female agency, one that does not depend on women's consent being violated in order to assert that it exists.

During Lanyer's lifetime rape as a crime of non-consensual sexual intercourse was nearly invisible in the legal system, except for the spectacular case of the Earl of Castlehaven in the 1630s: during the entire reign of Elizabeth, for example, the Sussex assize courts handled only 14 rapes, compared to 1,000 cases of larceny and 100 of murder. The conviction rate for rape was also extremely low, especially when the victim was not a child: whereas 80 per cent of people tried for burglary in Kent in the second half of the sixteenth century were found guilty, only 20 per cent of the rape trials resulted in convictions. Rape is not absent from the legal record, however, but it most often appears as the hidden narrative in other cases – frequently when a woman is sued for defaming a man's character – and most often in cases involving women in domestic service.[16] Richard Halpern writes that "the capitalist state secures and reproduces political dominion precisely by *not* exercising violence or class power, save in exceptional circumstances, and by limiting the right of others to do so. If this is a form of power, it nevertheless lacks points of application or surfaces of transmission" (1991: 7). Rape may be the exception to this theory of relative autonomy, because at least in this period it did provide a surface for transmission of power, as the class of women displaced from the land and forced to work as servants was policed both by the threat of sexual violence from their "masters," and by sexual violence itself. We are just beginning to understand the routine use of sexual violence within relations of domestic service: Miranda Chaytor's research has shown how frequently women's rape narratives cite the interruption of their work rather than the harm to their bodies or psyches as the damage done by rape. Women's honor, Chaytor writes, was "metaphorically transposed from the sexual body to the body that worked" (1995: 404). How visible this history would have been to a woman of Lanyer's class is difficult to determine, but Lanyer's own experience as the public mistress of a powerful man might well have sensitized her to the sexual abuses of service.

If the social history of rape in early modern England, as one historian has recently argued, "could be described as a non-history, a history of absence" (Walker 1998: 1), the literary history, though extensive, exhibits its own form of silence and displacement. Lucretia was a signal figure in the discursive and visual traditions of rape, but the rape itself is often occluded – as it is in Shakespeare – and replaced by meditations on chastity or suicide. That Lucretia's story could be told as an example of heroic female suffering rather than sexual violation is a key to its appeal as the canonical account of rape, and at the same time to its reappearance as a tale of sainthood or even crucifixion. Lanyer was not the first to see in Lucretia's rape/suicide an image of the crucifixion, and while she may not have been aware of all the developments that preceded her – though I don't want to foreclose that possibility yet – it is clear that her invocation of Lucretia within the passion is part of a hermeneutic tradition. One starting point might be Augustine's acid question: "If she is an adulteress, why is she praised? If chaste, why was she put to death?" (quoted in Donaldson 1982: 28, from *City of God*, Bk. 1, chap. 26). Augustine's unwillingness to accept as heroic a woman who survived a rape lies behind one of the two competing interpretive traditions around her legend; as Ian Donaldson shows in *The Rapes of Lucretia*, the tradition that venerated Lucretia as an emblem of chastity was countered by an almost equally vigorous one that derided her as an example of immorality. Tyndale wrote in 1528 that Lucretia's death was attributable not to chastity but to pride – which "God more abhoreth than the whoredom of any whore" – while writers of legends of good women debated whether her death might have been a holy sacrifice. The interpretive conflict is made explicit in George Rivers's 1639 book *The Heroinae:* in a section entitled "Contra Lucrecia" he wonders whether "in the nick of the act" she yielded "to some secret enticement [that] might staine her thought"; while in "Pro Lucrecia" he writes that at the moment of her death, "her soule too pure for her bodie, diclogg'd it self of clay, and broke the vault of all mortalitie" (56–7). The elevation of Lucretia continues in the work of the Jesuit Pierre Le Moyne: in his 1647 poem "Lucrece parle" Lucretia offers the Christ-like explanation that she has to die many times in paintings to convince unbelievers of her death (1647: 169). More suggestively, Le Moyne meditates on Lucretia's wound in terms that are instantly evocative of Christ's passion (1647: 165): "son innocence et la pureté de son coeur se voyent par la playe: et sa playe luy est comme une nouvelle bouche, qui crie aux yeux, et persuade en silence" ("her innocence and the purity of her heart are revealed by the wound, and the wound itself is like a new mouth, that cries out to the eye and silently persuades"). Compare this to a poem like Crashaw's "On the wounds of our crucified lord," where the trope is used, more conventionally, for Jesus.

> O these wakefull wounds of thine!
> Are they Mouthes? or are they eyes?
> Be they Mouthes, or be they eyne,
> Each bleeding part some one supplies.
>
> (Crashaw 1972: 11, 1–4)[17]

The terror and beauty of Christ's wound – which renders his body open, expressive, penetrable, generative – supplies one of the links between his death and Lucretia's. The need for a female sacrificial figure, an analog to the rich portrayals of St. Sebastian and even to Christ, supplies another. The parallel is developed most explicitly in the visual tradition, where male Renaissance and Baroque artists exhibit the same double vision of Lucretia as the Rivers *Heroinae,* but with the added urgency of finding a visual language for rape. "The actual portrayal of rape can best be understood as a form of visual taboo," writes

Brigitte Beuttner in a study of illustrations of Boccaccio's *De claris mulieribus*: "as such, it is bound up with cultural thresholds that established what was acceptable, or not, for representation" (1996: 40).[18] Although there are important sixteenth-century depictions of Lucretia that focus on the rape itself, such as Titian's of 1551, even these portray the moment just before the sexual violation, as Lucretia struggles to resist Tarquin's advances. In the "monologic" treatments of the subject that followed the discovery of a Roman statue of Lucretia in the early sixteenth century, suicide and rape tend to be collapsed into a single moment, and Lucretia is regularly represented in the nude (Hults 1991: 215). The nudity, however, makes her available as both object of desire and symbol of heroic Christian martyrdom. Lucas Cranach's thirty-five versions of the subject in the mid-sixteenth century test the limits of the voyeuristic approach; in his paintings of a seductive, nearly-nude Lucretia, rape and suicide are suggested simultaneously, the knife blade poised at Lucretia's breast standing in for the rapist. In Cranach's Lucretia paintings rape becomes seduction, even masturbation, and the viewer, imagined as heterosexual and male, is invited to understand the female body as penetrable. While Cranach's fascination with the image gave rise to some of its most startling, compressed depictions, the more somber versions by Dürer and Raphael were influential throughout early modern Europe. Linda Hults's important article on Dürer's 1518 *Suicide of Lucretia* shows that his depiction of a solitary, unseductive female figure, strangely unmoved by the blade she is about to insert in her side, recalls the image of the virgin saint (1991: 224). Hults also speculates that Dürer may have known and been influenced by Cornelius Agrippa's *De nobilitate et praecellentia sexus foeminei*, a strong candidate for the source for Lanyer's defense of Eve, which was circulating in manuscript in the same circles in which Dürer was working on his panel (1991: 230).

Probably the most widely known version in the period, however, was Raphael's, which was based on the Roman statue and achieved currency throughout Europe in the form of Raimondi's much copied 1510 engraving (Shoemaker and Brown 1981). Donaldson, Hults and others have argued convincingly for the reference to the crucifixion in this beautiful image; "As odd as it seems," Hults remarks, "Lucretia was often compared to Christ" (1991: 224). For Donaldson, the engraving "daringly summons up a central Christian image," its outstretched arms reminiscent of arms in the crucifixion, its expression of "surrender rather than self-destruction" evocative of Christ's death (1982: 27). The paired woodcuts produced the following year by Hans

Baldung Grien, Dürer's star pupil, may represent a reading of the Raimondi engraving. Baldung makes the Lucretia/Christ parallel inescapable: Lucretia is given an inscription above her head to match the "Ecce Homo" of Christ; her eyes, like his, focus away from her body, as if she had no part in her own stabbing; her halo of hair echoes his crown of thorns. The strangest detail is the binding of her wrist, for which there is no support in the narrative; it must be designed to link her to Christ, but also perhaps to imply that she was restrained during the rape and thus innocent of adultery.

In all of these representations, the key passage is the wound, which in Dürer's 1518 panel is placed exactly in the traditional position of Christ's, on the right side. Completely gratuitous in the story of the crucifixion and inflicted after Christ had already died, the wound renders the body of Jesus, like Lucretia's, radically open *in extremis*. "But when they came to Jesus, and sawe that he was dead alreadie, they brake not his legges. But one of the souldiers with a speare perced his side, & forthwith came ther out blood and water . . . For these things were done, that the Scripture shulde be fulfilled . . . Scripture saith, Thei shal se him whome thei have thrust through" (Geneva Bible, 1560: John 19: 32–4). The mysterious image of blood and water may well lie behind Shakespeare's puzzling account of the blood flowing from Lucrece's body after death: "And bubbling from her breast, it doth divide / In two slow rivers" (1736–7). Lanyer's allusion to *Lucrece* may thus represent a subtle reading of Shakespeare, even a tribute to *The Rape of Lucrece*, at the same time as it registers opposition to Shakespeare's poetics of rape.[19] For Lucrece, the wound in the side takes the place of the unrepresentable wound of rape, for Christ it suggests the abjection and the power of his body under torture.

If *Salve Deus* expands the meaning of the passion – in part through troubling the issue of Christ's gender, in part through reading the crucifixion as a scene of sexual violation – it joins deep currents within Christian devotion and contemporary spirituality. As Caroline Walker Bynum's work has shown, Christian thought had long included the idea of a feminized, nurturing Christ – the Jesus as mother who appears frequently in late medieval affective spirituality (1982). A hybridity of gender also surfaces in medieval and early modern understandings of the crucifixion, as the disturbing openness of the body on the cross suggests both male and female, both strength and vulnerability. The eroticism of this expressive masculine body for a male reader had also been explored in the devotional literature, especially in the ecstatic poetry of Lanyer's male contemporaries: Donne,

Herbert, Crashaw, Vaughan and Traherne. Reading Lanyer as part of the "experimental expressive project" (Rambuss 1998: 1) of seventeenth-century religious poetry, rather than within the category "woman writer," has the immediate effect of liberating our analysis: it becomes clear that her invocation of rape contributes to and extends an existing dialogue on the eroticism of the passion. For male writers of Reformation passion narratives, as Debra Shuger has brilliantly argued, the crucifixion's terrifying spectacle of "the destruction of manhood" (1994: 96) prompted a discursive crisis of masculinity which it was the project of the passion narrative to manage. That the story of Christ's death was a primary site for the invention of subjectivity is a central insight of recent work on medieval and Renaissance passions; Shuger illustrates how male subjectivity is at stake in the work of Calvinist writers such as Joseph Hall, Nicholas Breton and Thomas Nashe, who emphasize simultaneously the degradation of Christ's body and the power of his oppressors.

Lanyer's occupation of a different narrative position in *Salve Deus*, one that insistently identifies with the crucified Christ and never with the torturer, represents an effort to reconceive the crisis of subjectivity in the passion for a female readership. Her volume is emphatically addressed to women in a series of eleven dedicatory epistles, and the idealized female reader Margaret Clifford, Countess of Cumberland, is figured throughout the poem. As many of Lanyer's critics have stressed, female readership is inscribed throughout *Salve Deus.* The immediate occasion for the poem is a property battle over a woman's right to inherit land in which Clifford and her daughter notoriously engaged for over forty years: the passion is offered as consolation for her loss and mirror of her suffering at the hands of an evil world.[20] If the male passion narratives of the seventeenth century attempt to recover from the contemplation of "this figure of abject vulnerability" (Shuger 1994: 99) by offering consoling visions of Christ as knight or as the Bridegroom of Canticles, *Salve Deus* presents wholeness and heroism in a contemporary woman alongside rich images of female collectivity: the community of women readers, an allegorical vision of the Countess of Pembroke surrounded by nymphs and enshrined with Art and Nature, the closing lyric on Clifford's country house, an all-female world of learning and virtue. In *Salve Deus* there is none of the attraction to violence that characterizes the Reformation passion narratives by men; Lanyer's poem refuses to dwell on the brutality of the crucifixion because it locates power elsewhere – in the repudiation of patriarchal hermeneutics, in the existence of alternative forms of social organization, in the possibility of collective oppositional voice. (Pilate's wife "speakes for all" women; Dorothy Berry hears "the Crie of the Countrey.") *Salve Deus* is among other things a passion for women: it finds in the crucifixion a model for female heroism and suffering, an epic whose hero assumes the traditional feminine role and where passion rather than action constitutes the heroic.[21] But it is also part of an early feminist imaginary that hopes to find something beyond suffering as the space of female agency: *Salve Deus* unlocks a deep discourse of struggle as well as critique when it allows the woman's raped body to irrupt into the sacred scene of the crucifixion.

Lanyer's own site of struggle, and one that she imagines as a radically collective project, may be expressive culture. Her poem is as much engaged with the traditions of representing rape as it is with rape itself; its angriest moments occur when it takes on the masculinist literary tradition in which rape has been articulated. There is a second allusion to *The Rape of Lucrece* in *Salve Deus*, and it directs us toward what Saidiya Hartman calls "the discourse of seduction": the institutions of culture that protect male violence against women under the name "seduction," and that locate women's value in a "beauty" that makes them rapable (1997: 81). For Lanyer the sign of this discourse is the obsessive poetics of red and white: she enunciates her own poetic ambitions by attacking the conventional praise for women's complexions and arguing for an alternative, inner quality, for which she can find only the name "virtue." The passage in which she cites Shakespeare's red and white is also the only moment in her poem that directly names Lucrece; both references are part of an assertion of what her poem is *not* that allows her finally to express what it is.

The reference to Shakespeare summons up the opening moments of *The Rape of Lucrece*, as a blazoning contest leaves Tarquin inflamed with lust for "Lucrece the chaste." Collatinus, the husband of Lucrece, makes the mistake of boasting that his wife possesses the impossible combination of beauty and virtue:

> Haply that name of "chaste" unhaply set
> This bateless edge on his keen appetite,
> When Collatine unwisely did not let
> To praise the clear unmatched red and white
> Which triumphed in that sky of his delight.
>
> (Shakespeare 1997b: ll 8–12)

Lanyer directly answers this opening passage before she allows us to read her account of the passion. In a passage described in the marginal gloss as "*An Invective against outward beuty unaccompanied with virtue*," the poet announces:

> That outward Beautie which the world commends,
> Is not the subject I will write upon,
> [. . .]
> As for those matchlesse colors Red and White,
> Or perfit features in a fading face,
> Or due proportion pleasing to the sight,
> All these doe draw but dangers and disgrace.
>
> (59)

Given her poem's interest in *The Rape of Lucrece*, the sharp phrase, "As for those matchlesse colors Red and White," appears to be an answer to Shakespeare's "unmatched red and white," the words that introduce one of the organizing tropes of his poem. Red and white are woven in and out of the fabric of *Lucrece*, personified as beauty and virtue in the "heraldry" of Lucrece's blushing face, and invoked in the metaphor of the "white fleece" that stands in for the action of the rape itself. By quoting – and contesting – the first appearance of the colors in *Lucrece*, Lanyer signals her oppositional reading of Shakespeare's poem and its project of displaying the woman's raped body.[22] The blazoning of Lucrece's red and white, Lanyer suggests, leads directly to her rape ("All these do draw but dangers and disgrace"); her project is to find a language for beauty that delinks it from violence.

Immediately afterwards, Lucrece herself appears:

> Twas Beautie bred in *Troy* the ten yeares strife,
> And carried *Hellen* from her lawfull Lord;
> Twas Beautie made chaste *Lucrece* loose her life,
> For which prowd *Tarquins* fact was so abhorr'd.
>
> (60)

Helen, Lucrece and then Cleopatra – three of the primary classical female *exempla* – are followed in the next few stanzas by the two women from English history, Rosamund and Matilda, and finally by Christ. Both of the English historical figures had been the subject of male literary works in the 1590s – Samuel Daniel's *Complaint of Rosamund* in 1592, and Michael Drayton's *Matilda* in 1594 – and all three of the classical women had appeared in numerous plays and poems in the preceding years – Heywood's *Lucrece* as well as Shakespeare's poem,

Mary Sidney's *Tragedy of Antonie*, Chapman's Homer and others. These are women whose lives were ruined by beauty as it is defined in the masculinist rhetoric of Petrarch and of Shakespeare's *Lucrece*. Now it becomes clear why Lanyer quoted the lines in Shakespeare's poem where the rapist names the reason he will *not* rape Lucrece; in part her aim is to stop the action before it can go forward to its Shakespearean conclusion, to write another ending for the story. Lanyer's own literary project is voiced in the lines that follow the list of women represented in men's writing: "His Death and Passion I desire to write." Her "taske of Beauty" (108), as she calls it near the end of the poem, is to discover a way to write womanhood outside of the discourse that has positioned male readers with the rapist; she seeks to disrupt what Jed describes as "our own agency in making this rape occur over and over again" (1989: 6). Lanyer's Muse is Icarus, whose "poore Infant Verse must soare aloft," where it will no doubt fly too close to the sun, "Where thou wilt perish in thine own desire" (63). If the Muse does not perish, however, *Salve Deus* will have succeeded in finding a language in which women can be loved without being objectified, and the only language for that she knows is the celebration of Christ's body on the cross.

Rape in literary texts, write the editors of *Rape and Representation*, appears over and over "as an absence or gap that is both product and source of textual anxiety, contradiction, or censorship" (Higgins and Silver 1991: 3). Elaine Scarry has argued that pain is both unsharable and inexpressible because it is "resistant to language" (1987: 4). What if Lanyer were inventing a language for pain, specifically for the female body in pain and subject to the invisible wound of rape? "His joynts dis-joynted, and his legges hang down, / His alabaster breast, his bloody side, / . . . Anguish and Pain doe all his Sences drowne" (101). I am proposing that *Salve Deus Rex Judaeorum* is a work about rape and the historical representation of rape at as deep a level as it is a work about the crucifixion. But I would also suggest that the articulation of pain and the projection of bodily disintegration onto a *male* sacrificial victim enables the female subject to imagine political agency. The legal theorist Drucilla Cornell claims in *The Imaginary Domain* that the first necessary condition for "the chance to transform ourselves into individuated beings who can participate in public and political life as equal citizens is bodily integrity" (1995: 4).[23] *Salve Deus* is an imaginative restoration of bodily integrity to women and others who are dispossessed – as a precondition for entrance into public life, political struggle.

Notes

I am grateful for the responses of colleagues and of feminists in early modern studies who heard earlier versions of this essay: Theodora Jankowski and Susan O'Malley; Shari Zimmerman, Joan Hartman and Cristina Malcolmson; Jennifer Summit, James Saslow and Eileen Krest. Jean Howard and Scott Shershow have been exemplary editors.

1 I am indebted to Anthony O'Brien's invocation of Marx in a discussion of university restructuring that "is being made to seem like capitalist modernity itself" in *The New Caucus Response to the Schmidt Report* (1999).
2 See Halpern for a provocative discussion of the way "the absolutist state anticipated the forms of a more advanced capitalist state and thus created many of the juridical, political, and even economic presuppositions of capital" (1991: 10). Without entering into the debate on transition here, I refer to what Rosemary Kegl, thinking of Marx, calls "the long tradition of understanding sixteenth- and seventeenth-century England as, in some way, a transitional period" (1994b: 179).
3 I am drawing here on Kegl's sense of what is *missing* from "pro-women" writers of the period: "they argue that Renaissance women's subordination tended not to be experienced as oppression, and that gender tended not to serve as a political identity – particularly as an identity that might organize any sort of collective politics" (1994b: 9).
4 Among the many important commentaries on the political valences of Renaissance women's writing are the comprehensive studies by Lamb (1990), Krontiris (1992), Hobby (1988) and Lewalski (1993).
5 For discussions of the emergence of a women's print culture, see Sanders (1998) and Wall (1993).
6 For a comprehensive listing of this scholarship, see Nelson (1998). My understanding of Lanyer is indebted to the whole range of work cited by Nelson, although the discussion that follows will be able to make only some of these debts explicit.
7 In an earlier article on Lanyer I mention the reference to *The Rape of Lucrece* but focus on other issues in her work (Bowen 1999: 278–9).
8 The most playful and original of the defenses of Eve in the gender controversy is Cornelius Agrippa's *De nobilitate et praecellentia sexus foeminei* (1509). For a range of other defenses, see Woodbridge (1984: 18–48).
9 *Lucrece*, as the first edition was titled, was first printed in 1594. Other editions quickly followed: one in 1598, two in 1600 and one in 1607. Not until the 1616 edition, however, did the title-page read *The Rape of Lucrece*, although the phrase had appeared as the running-title as early as the first edition. For a discussion of early editions, see F. T. Prince in Shakespeare (1976: xii–xiii). *Salve Deus Rex Judaeorum* was entered in the Stationers' Register on October 2, 1610, and, as Susanne Woods argues (Lanyer 1993:

xlvii), probably printed that year, even though the first edition is dated 1611. Internal evidence suggests that the final, pastoral section of Lanyer's poem was written after February 1609, although there is no firm date for the composition of the passion narrative.

10 I am not, of course, suggesting any particular *agon* on Lanyer's part with Shakespeare, certainly not a biographical connection, nor am I arguing that she singled him out for contestation among the other numerous contemporary writers she quotes. Lanyer's most spectacular revision is not of Shakespeare but of the Gospels. On the canard of Lanyer as the Dark Lady of the Sonnets, see Woods in Lanyer (1993: xxx) and Bevington (1998: 10–28).

11 For other important feminist readings of the poem, see Kahn (1976, 1991). Throughout, I am working with Diane Wolfthal's definition of rape as "a crime in which one person forces another to engage in sexual intercourse" (1999: 2), although it will be important to my argument that men as well as women can be raped.

12 On transformations of the Ovidian myth of Philomela as a site for rethinking the representation of rape, see Jones (1991: 263–77). For Marguerite de Navarre's sustained attention to rape in the *Heptaméron*, see Cholakian (1991) and Freccero (1991). Christine de Pizan's commentary on rape occurs in the course of her discussion of Lucretia; for a discussion, see Gravdal (1991).

13 See Jean Howard (1991: 305–11) for an argument that in the early modern period gender could provide a basis for women's affiliation, alliance and sometimes political action.

14 On the history and authorship of this work, see Prest (1991). Many other contemporary legal treatises include discussions of rape; see, for instance, Dalton, *The Countrey Justice* (1635): "to ravish a woman where shee doth neither consent before nor after; or to ravish any woman with force, though she do consent after, it is a felony . . . Now Ravishment is here taken in one and the same signification with Rape, which is a violent deflowring of a woman, or a carnall knowledge had of the body of a woman, against her will" (281). Despite the sophistication of this discussion of women's sexual consent, Dalton also includes the commonplace that "[i]f a woman . . . do conceive with childe by the Ravisher, this is no Rape, for a woman cannot conceive with childe except she do consent" (281).

15 The most sustained treatment of the subject is Bashar (1983). See also Post (1978).

16 See Gowing's discussion of the suit against Susan Turton for defamation, brought by her master in 1624: "she was sometymes out of breath to resiste him and [he] did throwe her upon a bed and strived with her by pulling up of her Cloathes" (1994: 37). In 1630 a landlord, William Garrad, sued his tenant Dorcas Newton when she accused him of "lying with her against her will in ye malt room at her dwelling house" (ibid).

17 Rambuss discusses this epigraph as one of Crashaw's "persistently surrealist figurations of Christ's wounds as dilated eyes and kissing mouths" (1998: 30). Woods cites Crashaw as an analog to some of Lanyer's "richly sensuous biblical poetics," but argues that the two poets have little in common (Lanyer 1993: xxxix).

18 But see Wolfthal for examples of depictions of rape, which was not entirely unrepresentable, especially in illustrations of war, in the seventeenth century. Wolfthal argues that there was a greater production of "heroic," sanitized rape scenes in the Renaissance than in earlier or later periods (1999: 180–1).

19 Shuger comes close to suggesting that Lucrece is a Christ figure in her discussion of the closet drama *Iphigenia in Israel*, in which she also sees an analog to Christ: "as in Shakespeare's *Lucrece*, it is the female victim who grasps the sacrificial law of the father" (1994: 148). Shuger also argues that the rhetoric of Shakespeare's poem is similar to that of the Calvinist passion narratives (1994: 230, n. 55), but she does not include Lanyer in her discussion of passion narratives.

20 On female collectivity and its connection to the image of the mirror, see especially McGrath (1991).

21 The idea of the importance of heroic suffering in *Salve Deus* was suggested to me by Mary Ellen Lamb; I am grateful to conversations with her. See also Lamb (forthcoming in Donawerth [ed.]).

22 More specifically, Lanyer enters into conversation with the fetishizing of whiteness so prominent in Shakespeare's poem: Margo Hendricks (1998) has written about the ways the multiple meanings of "race," still an unstable term in the 1590s, are being explored in *The Rape of Lucrece*.

23 I am grateful to Ann Wallace for suggesting the connection between Scarry and Cornell. See Wall for an important discussion of the way both Lanyer and Sidney deflect "corporality onto a male figure who cannot be reprimanded for public display" (1993: 329).

7

The undiscovered country: Shakespeare and mercantile geography

WALTER COHEN

The concern with imperialism in Renaissance studies over the past quarter-century seems initially to have been inspired by the specter of genocide. From Vietnam it was not an implausible step back to the early modern extermination of Americans and the enslavement – and mass killing – of Africans, demographic catastrophes in which the Renaissance as an esthetic category in various ways seemed implicated. Such a reckoning was long overdue. Gradually, however, a more appropriately global picture of west European expansion has come into view (e.g. Loomba 1996; Bartels 1997; Loomba and Orkin [eds] 1998). On the other hand, even many distinguished accounts of colonialism and Renaissance literature have not yet come to terms with the probably decisive role of economics in overseas expansion (e.g. Todorov 1987; Greenblatt 1993; Mignolo 1995). The problem here is not the pursuit of original lines of inquiry. Emphasis on, for example, the imperial role of writing and discourse has introduced an important new perspective that might well seem in addition the distinctive province of literary criticism. The difficulty thus arises beyond the level of the individual text, in the collective underestimation of economics by contemporary criticism.

In reaction, it is tempting to accord enormous explanatory power to the profits of empire. European economic expansion, however, depended primarily on the emergence of capitalist agriculture – in England, through the landlord–tenant system (Fox-Genovese and

Genovese 1983: 3–25). Indigenous economic transformation and growth, which increased the possibility of acquiring goods from abroad and hence provoked a rising demand for imports, galvanized overseas enterprise in pursuit especially but not exclusively of luxury items for the rich. Shortly before Shakespeare's birth, England initiated its modern imperial adventure by embarking on the oceans of global trade under the leadership of London's merchant elite. During Shakespeare's lifetime, its greatest international successes came in Europe and western Asia, rather than across the Atlantic.[1] Despite the importance of state policy, economic interests, and especially mercantile ones, drove Europe's – and England's – quest for global dominance in the Renaissance (Andrews 1984; Brenner 1993; Blackburn 1997).[2] This point has been missed even in socio-economic discussions of Renaissance literature and theater, which, in emphasizing either popular or monarchical and aristocratic culture, have often underestimated the impact of intermediate social groups and classes (e.g. Cohen 1985).[3] Yet as we will see, both the character and the agents of innovation inform Shakespeare's plays not only by lending them a distinctive subject matter but also and more importantly – if more speculatively – by opening up new conceptual possibilities.

I

From the late fifteenth century on, the royal-chartered, London-based Merchant Adventurers Company controlled English international trade, exporting cloth to northwest Europe and especially to Antwerp. To the end of Shakespeare's life, this company and its heavy woolen textiles known as the "old draperies" remained the center of the national merchant community.

But two not entirely separable new departures mark the second half of the sixteenth century. First, and at the time less important, the privateering expeditions of Drake and others siphoned off some of the Iberian peninsula's New World wealth. Such marauding was both a cause and an effect of the sea war between England and Spain from 1585 to 1603. The primary means by which the English conducted the war – the pursuit of plunder – overlapped not only with state power but also with outright piracy and ordinary overseas mercantile trade. Though the war was militarily inconclusive, it weakened Spain's economy and shipping while strengthening England's. At the same time, it symbolically heightened nationalist fervor, which took the form of maritime imperial aspirations.

Second, in London groups of merchants organized a series of new royal-chartered companies dedicated to imports (above all silk, currants, and spices, but many other products as well) rather than exports and aimed in new geographical directions – toward Spain, Portugal, and west Africa; toward Russia; toward Venice and the Levant; and toward Persia and the East Indies. The novelty lay partly in the expanded range of products, partly in the increased volume, and partly in the fact that they arrived in English rather than foreign merchant ships. Like the Merchant Adventurers, the innovative merchants behind these new trade routes belonged to the City elite. Yet their companies, whose membership had a high degree of overlap, remained separate from the Merchant Adventurers. Their greatest profits came from the Turkish empire. In the early 1570s, English merchants returned to the Mediterranean, initially for Italian commerce, after decades of absence. Their re-entry may have been eased by the Venetian-Turkish war for Cyprus (1570–3) and by a new surge of piracy (1569–72), both of which weakened England's European trading competitors and the latter of which English shipping (including its military capability) and commercial organization were unusually well equipped to resist. The Turkey trade was opened at the end of the 1570s and beginning of the 1580s. During the 1580s, England established consuls in leading cities of the Ottoman empire, including Aleppo, Alexandria, Algiers, Damascus, Tunis, Tripoli in Syria, and Tripoli in Barbary. A further important step was the merger of the Venice and Turkey Companies in 1592.

Nonetheless, the last fifteen years of the century produced relatively few initiatives. But amid the fits and starts of English expansion, the next decade witnessed an enhanced level of activity that, despite its lack of immediate economic payoff and the difficulties of subsequent decades, was never really reversed. The East India Company was formed in 1600, and redwood was imported from Sierra Leone beginning in 1607. The West Indies contraband trade was expanded beginning in 1602, and a colony was established in Guiana in 1604. The Virginia Company was founded in 1606 and Jamestown settled immediately thereafter. In 1602 and especially beginning in 1606, New England reconnaissance and trade picked up; for enterprise farther north, the Newfoundland Company was chartered in 1610. To the far north the search for the northwest passage was renewed in 1602. Sailing for the Muscovy Company in 1607 with the aim of finding a passage to the South Seas via the North Pole, Henry Hudson sighted the west coast of the Spitsbergen island group, between 76° and 81° N, far north of the Arctic Circle. Three years later, sponsored on what proved his final voyage by the East India and Muscovy Companies as well as leading aristocrats and London merchants, he entered Hudson's Bay in search of the northwest passage.

All of the American initiatives had either failed or faltered badly by 1620. But they prepared the way for a new surge almost immediately thereafter, when a third body of merchants began to take charge of the American trade (fur, provisions for the colonists, tobacco, and later sugar and slaves as well). Of provincial or humbler London stock, often experienced as tradesmen, colonists, or sea captains, they operated without royal charters. America was open to them because initially it was riskier, more arduous, and less lucrative than trade with Europe and points farther east. Ultimately, of course, it was the grand prize. But leading aristocrats, gentry, and London merchants had tried – and failed – to turn a quick profit in the New World. These new, upwardly mobile merchants succeeded where their betters before them had not, increasingly forging ties in the American trade with the more purely capitalist aristocrats, who also lacked royal protection for their economic ventures. In short, one can distinguish three successive but overlapping orientations of Tudor and early Stuart trade – the export of "old draperies" to northwest Europe; the import of silk, currants, and spices from points south and east; and the import of the new products of colonial expansion in the New World.

II

In charting this sea-change in relation to Shakespearean theater, the following account moves from a very brief look at biographical clues, through a geographical and mercantile inventory of the plays, to the artistic and ideological forces behind that geography, before concentrating on the appropriation of maritime enterprise in Shakespearean drama, particularly as that appropriation changes over the course of more than two decades in the theater roughly along the lines of the tripartite chronological model sketched above. The conclusion attempts to draw out the implications of the preceding discussion, in part by reference to the economic character of the theater industry as it relates to empire and revolution in seventeenth-century England.

Shakespeare read about his country's international economic expansion. Beginning in the 1580s, English overseas aspiration shifted from anti-French militarism aimed at continental conquest to mercantile initiative. Richard Hakluyt's *Principal Navigations* (1589, 1598–1600) proved the most important intellectual agent of this transformation (Helgerson 1992). Shakespeare could also have gotten information from some of the leading courtiers and merchants who were active supporters of maritime enterprise and were possibly connected to his poetic and theatrical career or his private affairs – Walsingham, Burghley, Leicester, Essex, Southampton, Salisbury, Ralegh, Sir Dudley Digges, William Leveson, and Henry Rainsford. The evidence is perhaps strongest with regard to Southampton (but only through 1594), Digges, and Leveson (Andrews 1984: passim; Schoenbaum 1977: 103, 106, 115–16, 124, 131, 145–6, 155, 167, 170–4, 177–9, 186, 187, 194, 210, 217–19, 249, 250, 259, 269, 288, 300, 303; Bullough 1975: vol. 8, 239).[4] But Shakespeare surely saw the ever-increasing number of merchant vessels on the Thames, and he could simply have looked at the food on his table and the goods in his lodging.

Whatever the mechanisms, the plays register the rise of England's international trade, not least geographically. Shakespearean geography may be thought of along at least three axes – setting, character, and allusion. With the exception of *The Merry Wives of Windsor*, all of the plays are distanced from contemporary England in space, time, or both. They are almost all set in western Europe or the Mediterranean: in England (primarily during the later Middle Ages); in antiquity; in Renaissance Italy, the Italian Mediterranean, and Italianate states; and in medieval or Renaissance France, in descending order of frequency. *Hamlet* is an outlier. Since classical antiquity extends to north Africa and western Asia, however, there is potential for a certain exoticism, from a Renaissance English perspective, in the invocation of Egypt, Antioch, or Tyre, for example. The characters who make their way to west European and classical locales further extend the geographical range. Shakespeare brings on stage Goths and Moors, Spaniards and Amazons, the Irish and the Jewish, a Moroccan and, it seems, an American Indian.

Finally, the pattern of allusion produces almost a global feel. The frequency of citation conforms to the choice of setting, with references above all to modern England, Italy, and France, and to ancient Greece and Rome. But if references to towns, regions, rivers, landmarks, products, and peoples are included, one comes across Iceland, Ireland, England, Scotland, Lapland, the North Pole, Norway, Denmark, the Low Countries (Holland, Belgium, Flanders, Brabant), France (Navarre, Burgundy, Brittany, Normandy, and many others), Germany, Italy, Rome, and Europe; Russia, Poland, Bohemia, Austria, Hungary, Pannonia, Transylvania, Thrace, Macedon, Illyria, Dalmatia,

Epidamnum, and Greece; Sardinia, Sicily, the Ionian (Adriatic) Sea, the Adriatic, the Mediterranean, Crete, Thasos, Lesbos, Rhodes, and Cyprus; Turkey (Constantinople/Byzantium, the Hellespont, the Propontic, Ionia, Lydia, Phrygia, Cilicia, Cappadocia, Paphlagonia, the Cimmerians, Pontus) and the Pontic (Black) Sea; the Scythians, the Tartars, Colchis, Armenia, the Caucasus, Media, Parthia, Persia, and Hyrcania; Assyria, Mesopotamia, Babylon, Syria, Aleppo, Damascus, Phoenicia, Tyre, Jordan, Israel, Palestine, Arabia, the Ottoman Empire, Asia, and the East; Ethiopia, Egypt, Alexandria, Libya, Tripoli, Tunis, Carthage, Algiers, Morocco, the Barbary coast, Mauritania, and Africa; the Canary Islands, Madeira, Portugal, and Spain; Bermuda, the West Indies, Guiana, Mexico, Virginia, America, and the New World; the Antipodes, the South Sea, the East Indies, India, Cathay, and Mongolia (through the Great Cham: Kublai Khan); and, more fancifully, the anthropophagi, the Pygmies, and the Amazons. This list is not at all exhaustive; neither does it capture the evocativeness of invoking Lisbon, Jerusalem, the Nile, or the Saxons.

Nearly all Shakespearean drama includes a political or military conflict, most often between sovereign states and thus with imperial aspirations at stake. In the majority of the works, that conflict has a maritime dimension; and the sea (including its fish and storms), ships, voyaging, and sailing have a role in several other plays as well – literally, metaphorically, or both. There are frequent references to traveling, venturing, and trading, as well as to the merchants and pirates who undertake these activities and to the galleys and argosies at their disposal. The prizes of such activities are also well represented – linen, satin, jewels, and perfumes; gems, drugs, dyes, and medicines from the East; silk from China and Persia; spices such as mace, ginger, nutmeg, and pepper from the East Indies; furs, hemp, flax, tallow, and wax from Russia; fish from Newfoundland and New England; carpets from the Middle East; currants, oil, and sweet wines from Venice and its island possessions; ivory, wine, sugar, and dyes from Portuguese west Africa and the Atlantic Islands; oil, raisins, almonds, lemons, oranges, and wine (above all, sack) from Spain; gold, silver, gems, pearls, sugar, spices, dyes, and silk from Spanish America; and the cloth the English exported to help pay for these goods.

But correlations are not causations. The correspondences between the language, characters, and plots of the plays and the locales and commodities of English maritime expansion might seem fortuitous, insignificant, or both. The literary and theatrical heritage apparently generates much of Shakespearean geography. A particular source or influence – Holinshed's *Chronicles* (1587), Plutarch, the Italian *novella* or drama, Marlowe – may determine not only a setting but also a perspective on neighboring territories and even a mercantile outlook. The persistence of Marlowe in Shakespeare is particularly striking. Though Shakespeare generally responds to his unorthodox contemporary swiftly and – many would argue – conservatively, Marlovian iconoclasm obliquely reappears years later, sometimes in geographical form. *Dr. Faustus*'s psychological and metaphysical scrutiny of the European tradition's impressive worldly achievements returns, so to speak, with a vengeance in *Hamlet.* The contempt for religion in *The Jew of Malta* is partly put to rest in *The Merchant of Venice*, but the disquieting doubts remain, and the culturally and racially liminal status, the confrontation between European and non-European of Marlowe's Mediterranean island, resurfaces with undiminished force in the maritime no-man's-land of *Othello* and again of *The Tempest.* The heroic vaunting of *Tamburlaine,* though arguably put at the service of the nation in the first *Henriad* (1591–2), re-emerges abroad in *Coriolanus* and *Antony and Cleopatra,* in the latter of which Marlowe's vast terrestrial range finds both its maritime analog and its allusive central Asian echo.[5] We will return to each of these instances at some length. Here, however, the point is simply to acknowledge the danger of attributing excessive explanatory power to trade or any other single cause when multiple forces – prominent among them, sources – shape the plays.

Yet recourse to Shakespeare's heritage partly begs the question. It may not always be possible to choose between literary and economic explanations because the two options, far from being mutually exclusive, operate at different levels of abstraction. Even if it could be shown that Shakespeare unreflectively followed theatrical fashion, one would need to know if standard stage practice somehow responded to a collective interest in a mercantile national destiny. When one of his plays stays close to its sources, it is worth asking why a certain kind of material seemed congenial at a particular time. And even if the representation of maritime enterprise in Shakespearean drama is an inadvertent consequence of other purposes, only a narrowly intentionalist model of art and of culture is thereby undermined: international trade remains present in the plays. But of course Shakespeare did not have to set his plays where he did. He could have located his action in central Asia as Marlowe initially did or in contemporary London as Jonson, Middleton, and others frequently did. Similarly, he did not have to devote so much of his career to the national history play: no one else did. Related considerations apply to the classical and Italian plays.

Thus Shakespearean settings should be understood as theatrical and thematic choices. Where Shakespeare deviates from his sources, as he often does – by emphasizing the products of trade and the process of empire, cross-cultural contact and exotic detail, nautical terminology and maritime experience – he is that much more likely to be responding to overseas economic expansion. The Shakespearean catalog of commodities often matches more closely with mercantile enterprise than with literary heritage. Particularly when representing characters from the periphery of European civilization or beyond – Moors (*Titus Andronicus*, *Othello*), a Jew (*The Merchant of Venice*), Egyptians (*Antony and Cleopatra*), or an American (*The Tempest*) – Shakespeare tends to play up alterity, to increase the distance from European norms (Gillies 1994: passim). The relocation of landlocked Verona, Milan, Padua, Bergamo, and Bohemia to the shore (Schoenbaum 1977: 170) – though sometimes based in literary or ephemeral historical precedent – seems to indicate a maritime sensibility at work. A comparison of the place-names found in Shakespeare with both his literary sources and the trade routes pursued by English merchants reveals the considerable extent to which the former has been supplemented by the latter, especially at the level of allusion. Particularly noteworthy is the range of reference to the Ottoman empire. Every one of its cities in which England opened a consulate in the 1580s is mentioned in both the plays and Hakluyt's *Principal Navigations* (Hakluyt 1927: vol. 3, 101–17, 126–9). Yet of these only ancient Alexandria can be found in a source (Plutarch) for the Shakespearean work (*Antony and Cleopatra*) in which it appears, and the reference to Aleppo in *Macbeth* (1606), which alludes to both sailor and ship (1. 3. 3–6), is almost certainly inspired by a voyage to the east from 1604 to 1606.[6] In short, though the precise impact of international trade on the plays may be difficult to measure, there can be little doubt that it carries a specific weight of its own.

III

The patterns just outlined obscure the extent to which Shakespearean geography shifts over time: the late plays reveal a more global range than the early ones. An initial emphasis on England and on Renaissance Italy increasingly gives way to the ancient Mediterranean, which Shakespeare had abandoned years earlier and returns to in part for its panoramic possibilities. The widening spatial, temporal, and religious vistas coincide with both a shift in genre – from national history play and romantic comedy to tragedy and tragicomedy (ultimately, tragicomic romance) – and in some instances with an apparent desire for greater ideological freedom. No early classical play has the spatial breadth of *Antony and Cleopatra* or *Pericles*. None of the early Italian plays with the possible exception of *The Merchant of Venice* combines geographical restriction with the questioning of physical and cultural boundaries characteristic of the last two Italian(ate) works, *Othello* and *The Tempest*. The changes in Shakespeare's outlook can be attributed to personal and familial experience, theatrical fashion, and a deepening sense of crisis at the start of a new century and, soon after, a new reign. Like the relative frequency of foreign setting, character, and allusion in the plays, these shifts may also be related to the changes in English overseas expansion after 1550. Because those changes were both gradual and overlapping, one characteristically finds the co-presence of multiple tendencies in almost every play. The chronological correspondence is nonetheless clear. Not surprisingly, Shakespearean geography conforms more closely to the first two phases of mercantile leadership than to the third, with the first dominant before the turn of the century and the third emergent toward the end of his career.

In a sense Shakespeare might seem behind the times in the 1590s. The English history plays almost inevitably focus their attention on war with France – the very perspective that Hakluyt was already beginning to leave behind. This outlook is particularly evident in *1 Henry VI* (1592), *King John* (1596), and *Henry V* (1599), all of which play upon late sixteenth-century English desires to expand the nation's continental holdings beyond the single remaining outpost of Calais. Yet *King John* and *Henry V* are both ambivalent about imperial adventure. Even earlier, however, there are specifically economic echoes of the traditional northwest European orientation of English international relations – via references to the cloth industry in the representation of Cade's Rebellion in *The First Part of the Contention* (*2 Henry VI*; 1591). Cade, who has royal aspirations, dismisses his captives as "silken-coated slaves" and one of them, Sir Humphrey Stafford, retorts that Cade is himself "a shearman" involved in cloth manufacturing (4. 2. 115, 120). Cade takes evident verbal pleasure in punningly and metaphorically dressing down another prisoner, Lord Saye. "Ah, thou say, thou serge, thou buckram lord!" (4. 7. 20–1) – where the fabrics are listed in order of increasing coarseness.

Paradoxically, England's traditional geographical stance receives its fullest representation in one of Shakespeare's most original, introspective, even claustrophobic works – *Hamlet* (1600). The play recalls the victories of Hamlet's father over Norway and Poland; dramatizes Fortinbras crossing Denmark from Norway to fight the same Poles; sends Laertes back to Paris, center of courtly refinement, before returning him to Denmark; testifies to his skill in fencing by invoking at length the testimony of "a gentleman of Normandy" (4. 7. 67); briefly calls for the King's Swiss mercenaries (4. 5. 93); singles out Rhine wine amidst the general carousing (1. 4. 11, 5. 1. 166); denies Hamlet's request to go "back to school in Wittenberg" (1. 1. 113), home of the Reformation, but brings his schoolmate Horatio, "more an antique Roman than a Dane" (5. 2. 283), to Elsinore from there; ships Hamlet to the tributary state of England but cuts short his journey by an encounter with pirates; summons Rosencrantz and Guildenstern to the Castle before dispatching them to England and to their deaths; belatedly trots out the Ambassadors from England to see the results of the concluding carnage; and simultaneously but more consequentially deposits the newly triumphant Fortinbras in Elsinore to claim the kingdom. All of these events and allusions point to northern – mainly northwestern – Europe.

But the pirates, who are initially reported on by a Sailor, additionally evoke the privateering heyday of the time and thus also the mercantile expansion of which it was part. This larger field of play, primarily to the south and east, is represented in *Hamlet* by the Viennese setting (replacing the Guiana of the problematic first quarto), the Italian (and Latin) characters, and the Italian authorship of *The Mousetrap* (3. 2. 217–19, 240); the passing mentions of the "Turk," "Provençal," and "Barbary" (3. 2. 254, 5. 2. 108 and 118); the borrowings from Seneca and Tacitus; and the various constellations of references to the ancient Mediterranean – to classical mythology and especially to Hyperion and Hercules, to Carthage and the fall of Troy in the players' first appearance, to Rome and especially to Julius Caesar, and to classical culture more generally through the characters' names (1. 2. 140, 153; 1. 4. 60; 2. 2. 345; 3. 4. 55; 5. 1. 276; 3. 1. 426–98, 535–7; 2. 2. 373–84; 3. 2. 363–4; 1. 1. 106.5–13; 3. 2. 93; 5. 1. 196). Some of this international material derives from the tragedy's sources – Saxo Grammaticus, François de Belleforest, and perhaps Kyd's (?) lost *Ur-Hamlet*. Some was introduced by Shakespeare himself. Events from the late 1580s on and especially from near the end of the century involving Anglo-Danish diplomacy, piracy, and Poland – the likely origin of the name Polonius, called Corambis in the first quarto – provide numerous parallels to *Hamlet*. These include narrowly political matters but generally concern trade (Danish and Polish export of grain to the Spanish Netherlands, English seizure of Danish shipping, Danish demands of tolls and licenses from English merchants and fishermen). In short, a medieval revenge tale is reimagined through a wide-ranging appropriation of the legacy of antiquity and the early modern period. The resulting geographical, political, and cultural range of *Hamlet* has led Geoffrey Bullough to argue that "of all Shakespeare's tragedies it is the richest in incidents, in the variety of extraneous matter not essentially connected with the one plot running through the whole piece." Shakespeare's aim was "to include a whole courtly society with international connections" (Bullough 1973: vol. 7, 50, 59).

Why does this claim seem descriptively true but affectively false? Why does that "whole courtly society with international connections" carry relatively little weight with audiences and readers alike or, more precisely and paradoxically, why does it arguably assume its greatest importance in its ultimate unimportance? Neither the opening nor the close of the play apparently justifies such questions. Both are devoted to affairs of state in an unsettled international political and military setting. Yet the insubstantiality of those affairs and that setting may be registered by considering what Hamlet has accomplished by the end of the play. Though he has honored the Ghost's injunction to kill his murderous, usurping uncle, he has undone the military victories of his father, victories that Claudius proves quite capable of defending, and delivered over the Danish state and Danish independence to Norway. Indeed, with his dying words Hamlet demonstrates his sense of political responsibility by urging Fortinbras's succession to the throne. The concluding collapse of Danish sovereignty has no real parallel elsewhere in Shakespeare, for whom the fate of the nation routinely looms large. Here, though one recognizes that Fortinbras is no Hamlet, the political catastrophe goes virtually unnoticed. This combined assertion and depreciation of international affairs conforms to a fundamental logic of the tragedy. *Hamlet* dramatizes the full political, military, social, economic, cultural, religious, intellectual, literary, and theatrical heritage of European civilization in order to create a powerful sense of its attractiveness and genuine achievements. That heritage is then rejected on the grounds that it is nonetheless degraded, meaningless, and evanescent. The rejection is carried out in the name of an interiority whose content is simultaneously ineffable and authoritative (Barker 1984: 31–3). Finally and most problematically, however, the threat that the world will be absorbed into the black hole of Hamlet's consciousness is partly transcended by the positing of a connection between inwardness, action, and providence.

The full range of the European past and present is available not just to the playwright but also to his protagonist. Hamlet is its heir, in all its contradictoriness. From this perspective the play's notorious religious inconsistencies can be explained, if not explained away (Greenblatt 1997). What counts is that the full scope of Christianity is there for the hero. Similarly, Hamlet deploys humanist learning that extends from knowledge of antique authors and history to philosophical stance: "What a piece of work is a man!" (3. 1. 293–4). Cultural access is combined with social and political pre-eminence: he is "The courtier's, soldier's, scholar's eye, tongue, sword" (3. 1. 150). In short, Hamlet's denunciation of the world carries conviction in part because he has it all.

That denunciation famously encompasses misogynistic rage, suicidal self-loathing, and a more general preoccupation with death rooted in the conviction of the ultimate spiritual and physical corruption of all humanity. Hamlet's witty comments to Claudius on the last of these topics threateningly combine social and religious leveling while alluding to the crucial conflict between Luther and Catholicism at the Diet of Worms in 1521 (4. 3. 17–31). In a similar passage extending the motif of social reversal from earlier in the Gravedigger scene and of the reduction of the body to dust from earlier in the play (1. 2. 71, 2. 2. 298, 4. 2. 5), Hamlet implicates the heroic grandeur of Europe's classical heritage. His arch meditation inspired by Yorick's skull leads him to wonder: "Why may not imagination trace the noble dust of Alexander till a find it stopping a bung hole? . . . Imperial Caesar, dead and turned to clay, / Might stop a hole to keep the wind away" (5. 1. 187–97). Hamlet is usually linked with the popular cause in a fashion consistent with this metaphysical leveling (2. 2. 255–7, 3. 1. 72–6, 3. 2. 50–5, 4. 3. 4, 4. 7. 18, 5. 2. 87–9). In viewing "Th'oppressor's wrong" (3. 1. 73) as a spur to suicide, he seems to be speaking out of character. Yet precisely his position of privilege lends conviction to his negativity, to the critique of social hierarchy. The play also rejects various worldly alternatives through a series of contrasts between Hamlet and other characters – the mindless imperialism of Fortinbras (4. 4. 9.15, 50, 8–9); the similarly thoughtless vengeance of Laertes; the actual rather than contemplated madness and possible suicide of Ophelia; and even the idealized moderation of Horatio, compromised from the start by Gertrude's and especially Claudius's criticisms of Hamlet for his immoderate grief.

Hamlet's extremist repudiation of the social world is carried out in terms of a surface-depth model. The unreliability of appearances encompasses cosmetics; the sycophantic flattery he finds so insufferable; the spying and betrayal of Polonius, Rosencrantz and Guildenstern, and even Ophelia; and of course the more profound hypocrisy of Claudius. In opposition Hamlet deploys (pretended) madness, the feigning of the theater, and the doubleness of wordplay, while insisting on something still deeper that is simply inaccessible: "that within which passeth show," "the heart of my mystery" (1. 2. 85, 3. 2. 336). He concludes that "[t]here are more things in heaven and earth, Horatio, / Than are dreamt of in our philosophy" (1. 5. 168–9). It is this unspecifiable essence that comes close to replacing the external world as a locus of meaning. Yet the homology between the hidden meaning of heaven and earth and that of Hamlet's own soul makes possible the apparent transformation near the end of the play. Though Hamlet remains unwilling or unable to pursue the revenge to which he is sworn, he seems to accept his reactiveness, to be willing to let events take their course. "There's a divinity that shapes our ends," he tells Horatio, "Rough-hew them how we will" (5. 2. 10–11); "There's a special providence in the fall of a sparrow . . . The readiness is all" (157–60). Though this trust in providence arguably costs Hamlet his life, it saves his soul. He complies with the Ghost's demand for a vengeance prohibited by Christianity, but he honors the letter rather than the spirit of that demand – retaliating on the spur of the moment for Claudius's murder of himself and his mother rather than cold-bloodedly avenging his father's earlier death. And as noted earlier, his new sensibility enables him to turn his dying thoughts back to the future of his country.

How does Hamlet reacquire metaphysical confidence and an accompanying national and international perspective? Aquatic, maritime, and nautical language is more insistent in *Hamlet* than the plot requires. After Laertes obtains royal permission to return to Paris, his mode of transportation is mentioned twice (1. 3. 1, 55–6). The plan to send Hamlet to England comes up at least five times (3. 1. 168–74, 184–6; 3. 3. 1–27; 3. 4. 183–5.9; 4. 1. 28–9; 4. 3. 43–69). Consistent with Claudius's treachery as well as with the general pattern of romance, the sea generally carries ominous connotations. Marcellus asks why there is "foreign mart for implements of war, / Why such impress of shipwrights, whose sore task / Does not divide the Sunday from the week?" (1. 1. 73–5). Horatio warns Hamlet that the Ghost might "tempt you toward the flood" (1. 4. 50 ff.). Hamlet considers whether he should "take arms against a sea of troubles, / And, by opposing, end them," and Gertrude calls him "Mad as the sea and wind when both contend / Which is the mightier" (3. 1. 61–2, 4. 1.

6–7). The impetuous Laertes is like an unruly “ocean” (4. 5. 95); Rosencrantz predicts that “The cease of majesty / . . . like a gulf doth draw / What’s near it with it” (3. 3. 15–17). Ophelia’s death by drowning is reported at length and with pathos by Gertrude before becoming comic social and metaphysical grist for the two gravedigger Clowns.

Yet there are also occasional hints of the sea’s redemptive power. When Claudius determines to send Hamlet to England, he prophetically hopes, “Haply the seas and countries different, / . . . shall expel / This something-settled matter in his heart” (3. 1. 170–2). He later informs Hamlet:

Hamlet: For England?
King Claudius: Ay, Hamlet.
Hamlet: Good.
King Claudius: So is it if thou knew’st our purposes.
Hamlet: I see a cherub that sees them.

(4.3.46–50)

Beyond the insincerity and veiled threats of this exchange lies the truth of Hamlet’s concluding statement. Aboard ship, Hamlet does believe he has benefitted from heavenly aid in replacing Rosencrantz and Guildenstern’s letter and thus thwarting Claudius’s plan (4. 6. 16–17; 5. 2. 4, 7, 8, 31–2, 54–5). Both his suffering and his salvation are then adumbrated by an allusion to Christ’s crucifixion: “They have dealt with me like thieves of mercy; but they knew what they did” (4. 6. 17–18). Thus, at the end of the play Hamlet can inwardly feel that divine providence is ordering his affairs and can concern himself with England, Norway, and Denmark because he has undergone the sea-change of romance. What is less clear, however, is whether this restorative pattern really aligns the soul of Europe with the soul of Hamlet, rescuing it from the negativity of Hamlet’s earlier inwardness and preserving it despite the death of its profoundest exemplar. In this way, the radical subjectivity of Hamlet leaves *Hamlet* poised between devastating critique and painful reaffirmation of England’s and Shakespeare’s traditional northwest European heritage.

IV

Plays of the 1590s and of course thereafter are also responsive to the later phases of mercantile activity outlined above and especially to the second phase – the shift from the export-driven trade with northwest Europe to the import-driven commerce with the south and east.

Despite a considerable range of geographical reference, *1* and *2 Henry IV* (1596, 1598) and *The Merry Wives of Windsor* (1597) register this expansion primarily at the level of the commodity. Though Falstaff's Spanish sack occupies pride of place in the *Henry IV* plays, there is still room for "a cup of Madeira," "a pint of bastard" (another Spanish wine also available "In Barbary"), and "a whole merchant's venture of Bordeaux stuff" (*1*: 1. 2. 102; 2. 5. 23, 68, 70; *2*: 2. 4. 54–5). The plays present "the honey of Hybla" (Sicily); "two races [roots] of ginger," "pepper gingerbread," and "a peppercorn"; and a "pennyworth of sugar" (*1*: 1. 2. 37; 2. 1. 23–4; 3. 1. 251; 3. 3. 7; 2. 5. 19–20; see also 2. 5. 26, 53, 428; 3. 3. 147). There are likewise fancy imported goods – a "Spanish-pouch"; a lord "perfumèd like a milliner" (so called because the goods often came from Milan), and holding a "pouncet-box" (perfume box) and praising "parmacity" (spermaceti from the sperm whale but associated with Parma) – and, metaphorically, a lord "as bountiful / As mines of India" (*1*: 2. 5. 66; 1. 3. 35, 37, 57; 3. 1. 164–5). According to Falstaff, who dines at the shop of the "silkman," Hal repents striking the Lord Chief Justice "not in ashes and sackcloth, but in new silk and old sack" (*2*: 2. 1. 25; 1. 2. 179–80). When the Hostess protests that she has bought Falstaff "a dozen of shirts," he dismisses them as "Dowlas, filthy dowlas" (coarse linen) and she retorts by insisting they were "holland [fine linen] of eight shillings an ell" (*1*: 3. 3. 59–64). In a complex sexual, geographical, and economic pun, Hal notes Poins's "low ebb of linen . . . because the rest of thy low countries have made a shift to eat up thy holland" ("low countries" = Holland, the Netherlands, sexual organs, brothels; "shift" = expedient, dress; "holland" = [the money needed to buy] linen; *2*: 2. 2. 18–20). Similarly, when Doll Tearsheet accuses Falstaff of stealing "our chains and our jewels," he launches a sexual pun by evoking "Your brooches, pearls, and ouches" (clasp or setting for a precious stone; the jewelry was slang for venereal disease sores; *2*: 2. 4. 42–3).

These are very much like the riches the Falstaff of *The Merry Wives* imagines in Mistress Page, whom he plans to seduce and then fleece:

> She bears the purse too. She is a region in Guiana, all gold and bounty. I will be cheaters [treasury officers; robbers] to them both, and they shall be exchequers to me. They shall be my East and West Indies, and I will trade to them both. . . . Sail like my pinnace to these golden shores.
>
> (1. 3. 58–62, 70; Kegl 1994b: 105)

Though most of the many sexualized references to the East and West Indies in Shakespeare's plays metaphorically invoke the wealth of the Indies to praise a woman and hence implicitly, if unintentionally, to commodify her as an object of exchange on the international market,[7] Falstaff here literalizes the metaphor to indicate a primary interest in the woman's wealth. In the same play Mistress Quickly tells Falstaff that "The best courtier . . . could not have brought [Mistress Ford] to such a canary [quandary]" as he has (2. 2. 59–60). The Host announces that he and Falstaff will "drink canary," a wine from the Canary Islands (3. 2. 74). Mistress Quickly argues that even the luxury imports offered by aristocrats cannot sway Mistress Ford: "all musk; and so rustling, I warrant you, in silk and gold, . . . and in such wine and sugar of the best and fairest, that would have won any woman's heart; and, I warrant you, they could never get an eyewink of her" (2. 2. 63–7). Most of this language centers on Falstaff. What is extraordinary about such material is, paradoxically, how ordinary it is. Though absent from Shakespeare's sources, the densely populated world of commodities from abroad is simply taken for granted as part of English life. It contributes to the well-known counter-courtly tavern settings and hence the social range of the *Henry IV* plays and to the class hierarchies of *The Merry Wives*. Though access to expensive goods correlates with rank, the fruits of the import business – even some luxury items – cross class lines, reaching to lower class as well as upper.

The logic of mercantile exchange is still more tellingly realized in *The Winter's Tale* (1610). As the Clown prepares for the country festival, he says to himself,

> Let me see. Every 'leven wether tods, every tod yields pound and odd shilling. Fifteen hundred shorn, what comes the wool to? . . . Let me see, what am I to buy for our sheep-shearing feast? Three pound of sugar, five pound of currants, rice – what will this sister of mine do with rice? . . . I must have saffron to colour the warden pies; mace; dates, none – that's out of my note; nutmegs, seven; a race or two of ginger – but that I may beg; four pounds of prunes, and as many of raisins o'th' sun.
>
> (4. 3. 30–45)

Much of the list is familiar – sugar, currants, saffron, mace, nutmeg, ginger – though it is not to be found in the play's sources. The passage also explains how the Clown will be able to afford these imported foods: he will sell wool. At 1 pound, 1 shilling per "tod" (28 pounds), 11 rams producing 1 "tod," and 1,500 rams in all, the Clown will receive over

140 pounds (currency, not wool). And he will get that sum by providing the traditional raw material that, in various finished forms, English merchants sold abroad in order to finance the imports for the growing home market. As in the *Henry IV* plays, that market has a significant popular dimension. *Et in Arcadia ego*! The timeless, bucolic green world of the romance, apparently set against the sophistication and modernity of the court, is in fact fully integrated into the international economy. In this respect, Autolycus and Polixenes are hardly alien intruders into a pristine pastoral world.

V

Other plays, mainly from the 1590s, focus more on the process and agents of international trade than on the products. Here too emphasis is on the second, southeastern phase of mercantile expansion. *The Comedy of Errors* (1592), *The Taming of the Shrew* (1593), and especially *The Merchant of Venice* (1596) dramatize the world of the Mediterranean merchants. *The Comedy of Errors* is framed by what seems like a trade war between Ephesus and Syracuse, which leads in the opening lines to a death sentence for Egeon, a merchant of Syracuse. His son Antipholus of Syracuse is aided by a Merchant of Ephesus and is mistaken for Egeon's other son, Antipholus's long-lost twin, Antipholus of Ephesus, who is also a merchant. The play achieves its effects by then making that familiar world of goods and trade into an exceedingly strange and unsettling place, a combination of farcical mistaken identity and implicitly providential transcendence.

In *The Taming of the Shrew* the trade war of *The Comedy of Errors* is merely a ruse. Lucentio, who secretly woos and wins Bianca, is the son of Vincentio, "A merchant of great traffic through the world"(1. 1. 12). After Petruccio and Baptista quickly reach agreement on the financial terms of Petruccio's surprising offer to marry Baptista's shrewish daughter Kate, Baptista explains that he will "play a merchant's part, / And venture madly on a desperate mart." For Tranio, Kate was "a commodity lay fretting [losing value] by you. / 'Twill bring you gain or perish on the seas" (2. 1. 318–21). The bidding war, with its invocation of luxury commodities, then begins for Bianca, Baptista's younger daughter. Old Gremio invokes his house, which "Is richly furnishèd with plate and gold, / . . . My hangings all of Tyrian tapestry. / In ivory coffers I have stuffed my crowns, / . . . Fine linen, Turkey cushions bossed with pearl, / Valance [bed drapery fringe] of Venice gold in needlework" (339–46). But he quickly returns to his means of acquiring still more wealth, "an argosy / That now is lying in Marseilles road," only to be bested by Tranio: "my father hath no less / Than three great argosies, besides two galliasses / And twelve tight galleys" (366–71). As in *The Comedy of Errors*, however, the play is headed elsewhere – here toward an inquiry into the proper relationship between husbands and wives. Yet when Petruccio arrives for his marriage on a crazily attired horse, he is accompanied by "his lackey, for all the world caparisoned like the horse, with a linen stock on one leg and a kersey boothose on the other" (3. 2. 59–61). Social absurdity is rendered through the class distinctions of the cloth trade.

The Merchant of Venice also uses its mercantile setting as a springboard for diving into other issues, including religious and marital ones, but it differs from the earlier comedies – and indeed from virtually all of Shakespeare's other drama except *Timon of Athens* – in retaining a focus on economics. The high valuation of merchants is achieved through an ahistorical splitting off of merchants from usurers, Christians from Jews. But both the detailed representation of Shylock and the unsettling ambiguities generated by his presence and treatment entail a deeper exploitation than in the earlier plays of the enhanced cultural opportunities made available by Mediterranean trade.

That process is still further extended by *Othello* (1604) in at least two respects. The ethnically alien character is accorded more sympathetic treatment, even though in the end Othello commits the murder that Shylock is prevented from carrying out. The contrast with Aaron the Moor in *Titus Andronicus* (1593) is still more striking. Relatedly, though the play's setting, plot, and theme depend on the mercantile background, explicit concern with economics recedes toward the vanishing point. Shakespeare took pains to develop the potential of his material in the direction of inter-cultural contact. The threat to the island of Cyprus by the Turkish fleet recalls the war between Venice and the Ottoman Empire of the early 1570s that, as noted earlier, helped the English re-enter and, by century's end, dominate Mediterranean trade. The Ottoman menace is not in the play's main source, Decade Three, Story Seven of Giraldi Cinthio's *Gli Hecatommithi* (1565). For the tense military background, Shakespeare looked to Richard Knolles's *Generall Historie of The Turkes* (1603)[8] as well as other historical and fictional materials. As a youth James I had written an epic poem called *Lepanto* that appeared in a new edition in 1603. The play projects the Spanish-led naval defeat of the Turks at Lepanto in 1571 back in time so as to convert the Turkish conquest of Cyprus into a Venetian victory. The storm that accomplishes this imaginary feat by destroying the Turkish fleet echoes the role of the weather in dispersing the Armada and subsequent Spanish maritime threats. In short, Shakespeare relocates Cinthio's domestic drama within an international rivalry of great interest throughout Christendom, dramatizes a moment important to English merchants and monarch alike, and encourages identification with Venice by generating resonances with England's own recent naval history. He then focuses that identification and indeed the protection of Christendom from the forces of Islam on a figure who would routinely be thought of as a religious and political ally of the Turks. These opening moves challenge and expand the cultural range of the audience: Othello is both exotic and exemplary.

The plot exploits this duality even though it concentrates on private concerns seemingly of small consequence for affairs of state. The dominating theme of sexual jealousy is developed in disturbing racial terms.[9] Iago informs Brabanzio that "an old black ram [Othello] / Is tupping your white ewe [Desdemona]" (1. 1. 88–9). Roderigo evokes "the gross clasps of a lascivious Moor" (1. 1. 127), Brabanzio Othello's "sooty bosom" and "foul charms" (1. 2. 71, 73). Brabanzio's conjuring up of black magic dovetails with the aspersions on skin color and nationality to underscore Othello's potentially threatening exoticism. Yet the play is also indebted to a minority, heterodox, pro-Moorish outlook. Othello's nobility and marriage are officially approved and unofficially applauded. The play then provides a double view of his degeneration into the crazed murderer of Desdemona. Its well-known double time allows enough time for Desdemona to have committed adultery but at the expense of turning Othello into a fool; alternately, it so compresses events as to render Othello's charge literally absurd but psychologically plausible. Similarly, Iago, the agent of Othello's transformation, is both a merely duplicitous young man who easily deludes a guilty fool, and a supernatural devil who inevitably bests his relatively innocent religious victim. Othello's destruction is also linked to Christian secular mores. Under Iago's tutelage, Othello reconceives himself according to the very racial degradation that the play itself has already repudiated. From this perspective he explains Desdemona's supposed waywardness – "Haply for I am black" (3. 3. 267) – and laments that his "name . . . / is now begrimed and black / As mine own face" (3. 3. 391–3). Iago thus succeeds in part because he voices Othello's own socially induced, unacknowledged racial anxieties. Here the duality of Cyprus helps. Though it is a military outpost where a professional soldier ought to feel comfortable, the early dispersal of the Turks partly converts it into a morally ambiguous peacetime world analogous to Venetian society.

Sympathy and exoticism sometimes seem to merge. Othello's mother gets the fateful handkerchief from "an Egyptian . . . charmer" who promises that it will "subdue my father / Entirely to her love" (3. 4. 54–8). But at the end of the play, it becomes just "a handkerchief, an antique token / My father gave my mother" (5. 2. 223–4). In her grief Desdemona remembers the analogous experience of her mother's "maid called Barbary" (4. 3. 25), who died singing a willow song. Desdemona has "much to do / But to . . . sing it, like poor Barbary" (4. 3. 30–2).

And sing it she does. The reference to Barbary lends a surprising non-European aura to Desdemona in her victimization that links her to Othello and valorizes the alien as a repository of pathos. In his final long speech, Othello compares himself to "the base Indian" who "threw a pearl away / Richer than all his tribe" (5. 2. 356–7). This reading from the quarto links him to an uncivilized "Indian" unaware of the value of a pearl. The folio's "Judean" may suggest malice rather than ignorance by alluding to Judas, betrayer of Christ, or perhaps Herod, who killed his wife Mariamne out of jealousy. "Judean" also anticipates "circumcisèd" (364) and hence an identification of Othello with Semitic peoples.[10]

Othello "[d]rops tears as fast as the Arabian trees / Their medicinable gum" (5. 2. 359–60). He notes

> that in Aleppo once,
> Where a malignant and a turbaned Turk
> Beat a Venetian and traduced the state,
> I took by th' throat the circumcisèd dog
> And smote him thus.
>
> *He stabs himself*
>
> (5. 2. 361–5)

Unmentioned in the play's sources, Aleppo, it will be recalled, was one of the consular outposts of the English Levant Company. This memory enforces Othello's self-division at the point of death. He both administers justice and suffers punishment, both defends and attacks the Christian state. He is at once Venetian and Turk. Exoticism allows the acknowledgement and expiation of guilt. Though Christian Europe gets off the hook rather too easily by the export of blame, this is the means by which Othello nobly takes responsibility and memorably takes his leave. As in *Hamlet*, Shakespeare elaborately constructs an international crisis only to efface its explanatory significance before reasserting its importance at the conclusion. And just as *Hamlet* plumbs the depths of England's traditional northwest European mercantile orientation, *Othello* abstracts from the economic reorientation to the southeast to investigate the broad significance of intercultural contact in the Mediterranean.

VI

Of the five or six plays Shakespeare probably composed immediately after *Macbeth* between 1606 and 1610 – *Antony and Cleopatra*, *Pericles*, *Coriolanus*, *Cymbeline*, *The Winter's Tale*, and perhaps *Timon of Athens* – all have classical settings. Of the six or seven plays probably written through 1611 – the above group plus *The Tempest* – five are located partly or wholly in the Mediterranean. Of the very last, collaborative plays, *The Two Noble Kinsmen* returns to the classical Mediterranean. In early 1606 James decided to commit England to the national enterprise of colonizing Virginia. Only *The Tempest* seems to dramatize that enterprise directly, though the concluding prophetic praise in *All Is True* alludes to Virginia and Jamestown, to Elizabeth and her successor (5. 4. 50–2, 60). But considering the accelerated tempo of English activity in America during the first decade of the seventeenth century – from Guiana through Virginia to New England, Newfoundland, and the northwest passage – Shakespeare's last period may be seen as an extended meditation on the nation's engagement with the New World, overseas colonization and empire, and what proved to be the preconditions for the third, American stage of English mercantile expansion in the early modern period. Antiquity's maritime and imperial legacy, including its reflection on contact with the culturally exotic, probably encouraged Shakespeare's recourse to the distant past during these years.

Despite the enthusiasm of the passage from *All Is True*, Shakespeare's evaluation of the English overseas adventure is by no means clear. The doubts harbored by *King John* and *Henry V* are trumped by the misogynistic, cynical deromanticizing of imperial war in *Troilus and Cressida* (1602). Hector's charge that "Every tithe-soul, 'mongst many thousand dimes [souls], / Hath been as dear as Helen" (2. 2. 17–19) is echoed by Diomedes's evocation of "such a hell of pain and world of charge" that Helen brings, "such a costly loss of wealth and friends" (4. 1. 58, 62). Shakespeare may simply have shared with his monarchs a distrust of the grandiose international aspirations of Ralegh and others. Such skepticism, though in the end undermined by England's astounding imperial success, would have found ample pragmatic and moral support in the spotty record during the early years of the century and for a couple of decades thereafter. Even *All Is True* (1613) presents conflicting evidence. Providence enters the play partly through the metaphorical evocation of the standard sea journeys of Shakespearean romance. The play is laced with the language of watery disaster (1. 1. 113; 1. 2. 80–1; 2. 1. 129–32; 2. 4. 196–7; 3. 2. 38–40, 198, 362–5, 384, 437–8; 4. 2. 21). Romance's providential counter-tendencies, linked to aquatic expansion and maritime peril, are more subdued (1. 1. 21; 4. 1. 45; 2. 3. 87; 4. 1. 73–4). These hints become explicit when the preceding nautical dangers are made good by Elizabeth's baptism and the accompanying vision of transatlantic English colonialism noted above. It is uncertain, however, whether the concluding assertion carries sufficient weight to outbalance all that has gone before.

For many readers and audiences, *The Tempest* (1611) takes, as it were, a different tack, presciently celebrating and perhaps unwittingly revealing the mechanisms behind the English and European conquest of the world. One might cite the dependence on overseas experience of the conclusion's socially inclusive construction of national unity or the violently hierarchical relationship between Prospero and Caliban, a relationship that flatteringly confirms the master's own opinion of his superior rationality. Yet the play ignores the justifications of colonialism offered at the time – religious conversion, economic gain, and relief of overpopulation. Settled on the island out of necessity, Prospero brings his occupation of it to an end at the first opportunity. Caliban is allowed to express anti-imperial sentiments, and his possible – and Ariel's definite – freedom at the end also points away from colonialism. Finally, the unceremonious dismissal of Gonzalo's utopian speculation may reflect the dismay at the progress of the Virginia colony that had set in by the time of *The Tempest*.

A similar ambivalence characterizes other late plays. *Cymbeline* (1609) stages Britain's successful military resistance to the forces of the Roman empire, who resonantly invade from Gallia (France, 4. 2. 335), only to have Cymbeline reverse course and "submit to Caesar" (5. 6. 460–2). The British victory perhaps looks back to *King Lear* (1605), where the invading French forces, though led by Cordelia, must fall because they are foreign and the British defenders, though led by Goneril and Regan, must triumph because they are British. The submission may recall both the Roman conquest of Britain and Octavius Caesar's assertion in *Antony and Cleopatra* that "[t]he time of universal peace is near" (4. 6. 4) – a prediction of the *pax Romana* the historical Caesar actually established and a parallel to the roughly contemporaneous Nativity in a distant Roman province. This order is reversed in *Coriolanus* (1608): after initial celebration of the protagonist's military prowess, emphasis falls on the destructive and, for Coriolanus, self-destructive conflict between Rome and Antium. As Coriolanus confesses to the enemy city, "'Tis I that made thy widows. Many an heir / Of these fair edifices fore my wars / Have I heard groan and drop" (4. 4. 2–4; see also 5. 6. 151–4). And in the unusually somber *Two Noble Kinsmen* (1613), though chivalric military norms give a touching nobility to the action and war is praised because it "cur'st the world / O'th plurisy of people" (5. 1. 64–5; see also 1. 2. 20–4), combat generates less the salvation of society than the loss of life.

Antony and Cleopatra and *Pericles*, probably the earliest of the final plays and certainly the most restless from a geographical point of view, both turn on maritime and imperial experience. In *Pericles* (1607) a princess is captured by pirates, a queen survives burial at sea, and a ship's crew is sent to a watery grave. Though all of these catastrophes contribute to the providential romance resolution, Pericles's – and *Pericles*'s – sufferings retain a contingent feel, an unexplained character. The doubts about maritime experience are complemented by the play's anti-commercial outlook, an outlook that links it especially with *Timon of Athens* (1607). In Tarsus before famine struck, "All poverty was scorned, and pride so great/ The name of help grew odious to repeat" (4. 30–1). The Master fisherman who helps rescue Pericles at Pentapolis denounces "our rich misers" (5. 68). Commerce enters the play only in the brothel scenes, with predictably negative connotations. As the Bawd advises Marina, "You have fortunes coming upon you . . . despise profit where you have most gain . . . pity begets you a good opinion, and that opinion a mere profit" (16. 111–17). Partly as a result, the play concludes with a purely aristocratic and royal circle whose political efficacy is uncertain, whether one looks to Antioch, Tarsus, Ephesus, Mytilene, or even Pentapolis and Tyre.

What is not questionable is the hostile view of empire (Johnson 1997: chap. 4). When the ruler of beleaguered Tarsus first learns of approaching ships, he draws the obvious, though in the event incorrect, inference – that "Some neighbour nation / Taking advantage of our misery, / . . . [will] make a conquest of unhappy men" (4. 64–8). Pericles has come in relief of Tarsus only because he fears the vengeance of the tyrant Antiochus. Having fled Antioch to save his life, Pericles realizes that he has simply invited an invasion of Tyre, a small state like England that is always endangered by larger powers (2. 16–98). This jaundiced view of the eastern Mediterranean Greek city-states of late antiquity perhaps derives from the classical period itself, with its suspicion of Oriental tyranny, luxury, and decadence. That view may have been intensified by the continued Muslim domination in the early seventeenth century of the entire region, including its Christian holy sites. In varying degrees, then, maritime adventure, trade, and empire all carry negative connotations, connotations rooted in the multilayered symbolic – ultimately providential – geography of the play.

Mediterranean geography is also symbolic, though not providential, in *Antony and Cleopatra* (1606). Its spatial expansiveness breaks with the primarily Roman focus of *Julius Caesar* (1599), its predecessor in Shakespeare's narrative of the decline and fall of the Roman republic. This territorial range enables the play to counterpose Eastern sexuality to Roman imperial domination. That opposition – between restrained masculine political nobility and sybaritic feminine opulence – is present in many classical writers including Plutarch, the main source for the tragedy. This ancient ideology once again proved serviceable in the Renaissance as the West began a fresh round of subjugation of distant peoples. In *Antony and Cleopatra* Antony must choose either the world or the flesh; public life or private existence; Rome or Egypt; Octavius Caesar or Cleopatra; fidelity to a chaste white wife, Caesar's sister Octavia, or adultery with a promiscuous, "tawny," "black" seductress, Cleopatra (1. 1. 6, 1. 5. 28). These contrasts are accentuated through rapid shifts of scene across enormous distances that help impart an epic feel to the struggle for Mediterranean supremacy. But in a manner reminiscent of *Hamlet* and *Othello*, the play then drains war and politics of significance – not as in the earlier tragedies by valorizing a private interiority or by confining conflict to the domestic sphere but instead by investigating the possibility of heroic action in a post-heroic world and asking whether epic meaning can be transplanted to the ostensibly private terrain of love.

It does so partly by destabilizing its own foundational antinomies (Harris 1994: 408–25). The political struggle pits neither republic against empire nor Western freedom against Oriental autocracy; it just brings into collision two men who are unable to share power with each other. Though Antony makes much of his own battlefield accomplishments at the expense of Caesar's bureaucratic management of war, in reality both "Caesar and Antony have ever won / More in their officer than person" (3. 1. 14–17). Similarly, for all of the association of sexuality with Egypt, love looks like a Roman preserve. Shakespeare fills out Antony's retinue by supplementing Plutarch's Eros (love) with Philo (love), who opens the play. Cleopatra's considerable charms are registered exclusively by men from the West – Antony, of course, but also Enorbarbus, Dolabella, and earlier, we are told, both Julius Caesar and Pompey (1. 5. 29, 31). The relationship between Antony and Cleopatra accordingly does not turn on the inner transformations of earlier Shakespearean lovers or on efforts to secure moments alone together. Their affair seems to eschew privacy, thriving only in a quasi-exhibitionist public world where an expansive eroticism can mimic and pretend to supplant an expansive Roman militarism.

In the wake of the disastrous battle of Actium, however, the play closes in geographically on the protagonists, confining their movements to Alexandria and our attention, following Antony's suicide, to Egypt and Cleopatra. What kind of alternative to Rome and Caesar do they finally represent? Metaphorically, they stand for a rejection of solid land in favor of water. Antony's "dotage . . . / O'erflows the measure" (1. 1. 1–2); it could bring down the state, as he readily acknowledges: "Let Rome in Tiber melt, and the wide arch / Of the ranged empire fall" (1. 1. 35–6). Cleopatra is equally willing to dispense with her country when she learns of Antony's marriage to Octavia: "Melt Egypt into Nile, and kindly creatures / Turn all to serpents!" (2. 5. 78–9). The flooding here recalls not only the Nile's rising to bring life to the surrounding land but its queen's salvational skills as well. Shakespeare's probable recourse to Plutarch's *Of Isis and Osiris* may stand behind the play's allusions to the goddess Isis (e.g. 3. 6. 16–18), the sister–wife of Osiris, who revives her brother–husband Osiris after Typhon, his brother–rival, kills him. At the end of the play, the same task falls to Cleopatra.

Yet as one would expect from other Shakespearean plays and especially, as we've seen, from *Hamlet* and *Othello*, the conclusion opts not for choice but for the very synthesis toward which the blurred distinctions between Rome and Egypt seem to point. Cleopatra dies the death of a Roman hero:

> My resolution's placed, and I have nothing
> Of woman in me. Now from head to foot
> I am marble-constant. Now the fleeting moon
> No planet is of mine.
>
> (5. 2. 234–7)

Isis, goddess of the moon, is here implicitly repudiated on the grounds of inconstancy. Cleopatra will instead die a loyal Roman wife – "Husband, I come. / Now to that name my courage prove my title" (282–3) – and a virtuous Roman matron:

> Peace, peace.
> Dost thou not see my baby at my breast,
> That sucks the nurse asleep?
> [. . .]
> As sweet as balm, as soft as air, as gentle.
> O Antony!
> [*She puts another aspic to her arm*]
> Nay, I will take thee too.
> (5. 2. 303–7)

The stage direction is a modern editorial suggestion, and "thee" in the last line may refer to Antony, whom Cleopatra maternally comforts at her breast, after applying the poisonous asp, as if he were her baby. But "O Antony" also expresses the sexual ecstasy associated throughout the play with the Orient, and by means of the asp Cleopatra dies an Egyptian death. East and West, love and war, and – not least – Cleopatra and Antony come together in the heroine's suicide. Thus the play both is and is not imperialistic.[11] But even if one glosses over Cleopatra's obvious opportunism to the very end, the soaring strains of her final scene look like an effort to make the best of a disastrous situation. The grand style of Antony and Cleopatra has no place in the political domain. Does the stress in her "Immortal longings" (5. 2. 276) fall on "immortal" or on "longings?" Even an affirmative interpretation points away from the third stage of mercantile enterprise during the English Renaissance, away from the New World, and toward a kingdom – and an empire – not of this world.

VII

The evidence and arguments presented here suggest neither that Shakespearean drama would look radically different if only one adequately registered the impact of mercantile expansion nor that this expansion is the fundamental force behind the plays. Both hyperbolic claims would cut against the delimited understanding of trade and empire in relation to domestic economic transformation outlined at the outset; the relative accessibility of the plays, which renders suspect hermetic and previously unimaginable interpretations; and, relatedly, the cumulative heritage of centuries of Shakespearean criticism, a heritage that deeply informs the work of even those critics seemingly in full rebellion against their predecessors. On the other hand, overseas economic enterprise influenced Shakespeare far more than is routinely recognized: one sees its impact everywhere from local detail to the shape of the career. In *The Merchant of Venice*, Bassanio asks with alarm about Antonio's fortunes:

> Hath all his ventures failed? What, not one hit
> From Tripolis, from Mexico, and England,
> From Lisbon, Barbary, and India?
>
> (3. 2. 266–8)

None of these locales appears in the play's sources, most are not even hinted at, and some – Mexico, India, and, in a different way, England – seem more appropriate to London than to Venice. In *Antony and Cleopatra*, Caesar complains that the titular characters

> Now are levying
> The kings o'th' earth for war. He hath assembled
> Bocchus, the King of Libya; Archelaus
> Of Cappadocia; Philadelphos, King
> Of Paphlagonia; the Thracian King Adallas;
> King Malchus of Arabia; King of Pont;
> Herod of Jewry; Mithridates, King
> Of Comagene; Polemon and Amyntas,
> The Kings of Mede and Lycaonia.
>
> (3. 6. 69–75)

These lists produce both quantitative and ideological effects in part through their power as sheer sound. In a theater short on scenery, evocative language must have helped deliver to the audience, in the etymological sense, what filming on location provides for the modern movie-viewer.

Because the processes, products, and purposes of maritime initiative interact with a vast array of other materials in Shakespearean drama, perhaps their greatest interest lies not in instances of direct representation of international trade but in the new opportunities they open up, in a broadened range of cultural reference and reflection. This line of argument places one on a slippery slope, however: anything can be seen as metaphorically or allegorically related to mercantile expansion. The perspective adopted here is an intermediate one that tries to steer a course between a widely practiced kind of *Zeitgeist* criticism that would swallow up everything into the thematic preoccupation at hand

– in this case trade – and a conservative scholarly approach that would confine the impact of economic imperialism to indisputable representations and allusions. Overseas trade does not provide the hidden key to Shakespearean interpretation. Yet it lent a distinctive feel to the plays through a far greater range of specific references than it has been possible to detail here, and it more generally offered new perspectives that would otherwise have been unavailable on a broad range of issues.

This seems true whether the focus is on northwestern Europe, the Mediterranean, or America. Shakespearean geography suggests an interest in the nation complemented by a concern with the relation between the exotic and the domestic. Though it is tempting to posit increasing otherness as the distance from England grows, the potentially allegorical character of setting produces counter-tendencies. When England is the primary locale, foreign peoples stand for themselves and the plays reveal a straightforward pattern of conflict combined with attempts at resolution or assimilation. The history plays often pit England against France and sometimes against the Papacy as well. In a more comic mode, *Henry V* seeks the incorporation of the Welshman, the Irishman, and the Scot into an expanded vision of nationhood, and *The Merry Wives of Windsor* brings the Welshman and the Frenchman into the local community as figures of fun but as members of the community nonetheless. On the other hand, when a play is set in another country, that land represents both itself and England. Though the portrayals of Denmark, Venice, republican Rome, and the France of *Love's Labour's Lost* (1594), for example, attempt in varying degrees to render a foreign culture, they are never merely ethnographic; they are always meant to overlap significantly with the world of the audience. Thus, even when Shakespeare accentuates the exoticism of his source, there is a limit to the procedure. The ostensibly alien is never meant to represent pure otherness. The spatial analog of anachronism, it always reveals an actual or potential dimension of English behavior; it always enlarges the cultural repertoire, sometimes in disquieting ways.

Like the merchants who in this fashion inadvertently enhanced the capaciousness of his theater, Shakespeare worked in a profit-making industry that enjoyed monopolistic privileges granted by the crown. Both lines of work benefitted from the restraint of trade; neither had to sail on the open sea of the free market. The new merchants who developed American commerce beginning in the 1620s lacked these protections. But they increasingly depended on slavery, on the restraint of labor. Here too, then, fully capitalist enterprise lies beyond the horizon. Yet one cannot afford to overlook the internal political differentiation among these mercantile initiatives. The revolution of the 1640s revealed the conflicting allegiances. Despite earlier periods of (occasionally sharp) antagonism toward the monarchy, the chartered London merchants understood that their interests ultimately lined up with those of the crown, which they accordingly supported during the civil-war era. The chartered London acting companies saw things in the same light as their mercantile contemporaries. By contrast, the unchartered American merchants played a crucial role in linking the more radical gentry in Parliament to the London population who needed to be mobilized in support of the revolutionary cause. In addition these merchants were close to the radical officers of the New Model Army who eventually took power. One result was that, beginning in the Commonwealth era, England adopted an aggressively imperial foreign policy, not least toward America, of a sort that had never been fully embraced by the monarchy. Structural dependence on the crown notwithstanding, however, even monopolistic overseas economic endeavor contributed to the innovative, modernizing dynamic that eventually undermined the old order. The same is true for elements of Shakespearean theater, in part because of the sheer novelty that maritime aspiration helped inspire.

Yet Shakespeare's mercantile debt also provokes a more disturbing inference, this one rooted in what is often the very routineness, even banality of its representation in the plays. Emphasis on the role of English overseas expansion in Shakespearean drama and theater tends to inflect emphasis away from the state and toward private economic agents. Robin Blackburn has argued that the New World slave economies were the first junk-food industries, servicing an insatiably growing consumer demand especially in England that in part entailed the absorption of an ever-increasing percentage of the population into the economy of commodity exchange (Blackburn 1997: 561). It is tempting to project this model of junk-food imperialism backwards – and forwards. A focus on European and especially Spanish murderous, even genocidal, policies in the New World fits well with a sensibility shaped by the American invasion of Vietnam, where the moral issues were clear and the conflict was fundamentally with state power. In the post Cold War global economy, things are experientially muddier. United States dominance of the international political system may be greater than ever, and that dominance includes frequent displays of wholesale military violence. Yet the importance of the political system seems to be declining at the expense of an economic regimen to which all must adapt. Ordinary private consumption helps fuel the international engine of accumulation and thus the expanding demand for governments capable of delivering cheap, disciplined labor. Because this regimen is the only game in town, daily life implicates one in its reproduction. It is relatively easy to understand – and oppose – a national leadership determined to rain death from the sky on a distant peasant society. It is harder to challenge the far more dispersed practices of the makers of the commodities we consume – the US and foreign corporations operating abroad that employ work forces in ways that are appalling by American standards but may be above average by the norms of the host country. The argument I have made for Shakespearean drama's ambivalence toward European and English imperialism functions primarily at the level of the state. It does not extend to the less spectacular but arguably more profound economic transformation of the world over the last half millennium, a process that shows no signs of abatement. In Shakespeare, as today, that process is usually just taken for granted. Where Shakespeare could not see, we too remain blind. The plays are thus an early but unwitting witness to a continuing dilemma.

Notes

1 Brotton's (1998) emphasis on mapping the Old World seems to encourage an attention to economics that appears less common in accounts of the New World.
2 The historical summaries in this essay draw primarily on these works.
3 The brief discussions of *The Merchant of Venice* and *The Tempest* below are drawn from this study.
4 All discussion of Shakespeare's sources is based on Bullough's eight-volume work.
5 Bloom (1973: 7) exempts Shakespeare from any anxiety about Marlowe's influence on him, arguing instead that Shakespeare completely absorbed and hence transcended his predecessor. The movie *Shakespeare in Love* (1998) seems to me preferable, however, in imagining an early Shakespeare jealously competitive with his more prominent fellow playwright. I would go further than the film in positing the continued pressure of Marlowe throughout Shakespeare's career.
6 All dates of probable first performance and quotations of Shakespeare's plays are from Greenblatt et al. (eds) (1997). Many of the discussions of individual plays below are adapted from my introductions for this edition: Adapted from *The Norton Shakespeare: Based on the Oxford Edition*, edited by

Stephen Greenblatt, et al. Copyright © 1997 by W. W. Norton & Company, Inc. Used by permission of W. W. Norton & Company, Inc.

7 See *As You Like It* (1599), 3. 2. 77–8; *Twelfth Night* (1601), 2. 5. 11–12; *Troilus and Cressida*, 1. 1. 96–100; and *All Is True*, 4. 1. 45. In *Troilus and Cressida* the woman literally does become an object of exchange. Less typical is the use of the metaphor to criticize female appearance in *The Comedy of Errors*, 3. 2. 131–5, and *The Merchant of Venice*, 3. 2. 97–101. A more idealizing approach occurs when the lover projects himself or herself as the Indian, in *Love's Labour's Lost*, 4. 3. 219–20 and 5. 2. 200–1, and *All's Well That Ends Well* (1605), 1. 3. 197–200.

8 Compare *Othello*, 1. 3. 14–16, with Knolles, in Bullough (1973: vol. 7, 262).

9 On the racial and imperial dimensions of *Othello*, I am particularly indebted to Greenblatt (1980: 222–54) and Newman (1991: 71–93). Also valuable in this regard are Hunter (1967), Fiedler (1972: 139–96), Orkin (1987: 59–129), Parker (1994), and Bartels (1997).

10 Several of the passages quoted here from *Othello* actually come from the folio version, which is probably Shakespeare's reworking of the earlier quarto text.

11 It is ultimately imperial for Archer (1994: 24–5).

8

The management of mirth: Shakespeare via Bourdieu

RICHARD WILSON

The Elizabethan playhouse at Knowsley, near Liverpool, remains one of the dark secrets of Shakespearean England. Very few commentators are aware of even the existence of this theatre, built by the Stewards of Henry Stanley, Earl of Derby, on the site of his cockpit, some time in the 1580s. Though the records of the Lancashire playhouse were collated from county archives in 1951 (Bailey 1951), the Shakespeare industry has ignored this building, which survived as late as 1902 as Flatiron House, so called from its shape, 60 foot deep and with a stage about 30 foot wide: almost exactly the dimensions of an auditorium such as the Cockpit-in-Court. Like the Yorkshire troupe which toured the Dales with *King Lear* and *Pericles* in 1609, the purpose-built theatre that operated until that year on the estate of a northern territorial magnate does not fit the dominant narrative of the Shakespearean stage, with its fixation on the bourgeois city and the commercial amphitheatre. Provincial stages are supposed to have been improvised in halls, inn yards or barns; but the Earl of Derby's Lancastrian theatre was a permanent structure expensively equipped for professional performance, and its quarter-century history offers a glimpse of an alternative itinerary to that of Stratford and Southwark, and a route not taken by the critics: away from Bankside, along with the diaspora to which, according to Peter Burke, early modern "European popular culture owed its unity . . . the mass of the acting profession . . . who spent their lives on the move from town to town, and were no respecters of political frontiers" (Burke 1978: 97). And facilities created for the players at petty courts like that of the so-called "King of Lancashire" might also help to explain one outstanding mystery of Shakespearean drama: which is that London's most successful commercial entertainment occludes its actual locale, by consistently staging scenes of aristocratic patronage, rather than holding a realistic mirror up to its "barren spectators" (*Hamlet* 3. 2. 41[1]) in the metropolitan playhouse.

On September 20, 1589 the Governor of Carlisle notified the English embassy in Edinburgh that on learning of King James's "earnest desire to have Her Majesty's players repair unto Scotland to His Grace, I did forthwith despatch a servant unto them where they were in furthest Lancashire." The Queen's Men were at Knowsley, where they acted in Derby's playhouse on September 12 and 13; but a month later they were being "used with great kindness and all courtesy" by the Earl of Bothwell in Edinburgh, while James escorted his bride, Anne of Denmark, from Elsinore. There her father had become the first continental monarch to host English actors, a band of Derby's stars, whom the Danish King passed on to the Elector of Saxony. So, whether or not Bothwell enticed the Queen's Men to Scotland to rehabilitate himself after an abortive coup (Wentersdorf 1980: 33–6), these journeys north all beg the question posed by Hamlet when "the tragedians of the city" likewise beat a path to Elsinore: "How chances it they travel," when "Their residence, both in reputation and profit, was better both ways" in the metropolis? The surprising answer supplied by Jerzy Limon in his revelatory survey of "English players in Central and Eastern Europe," *Gentlemen of a Company*, is not, as Rosencrantz complains, that performers were forced from the city by competition, when rival troupes, like the "little eyases," were "tyrannically clapped"; nor that plague or prohibition drove them; but that "The best actors in the world" found the grandiose production values in aristocratic courts so superior to those of "the common stages" in London (*Hamlet* 2. 2. 326–92). The Europe of principalities described by Limon was a paradise for players, not because livery protected them from politics, but because it transported their productions out of the bearpit of economic necessity. As the composer John Dowland testified, continental patronage was embraced by performers because its extravagance defied the mercenary logic of the marketplace:

> When I came to the Duke of Brunswick he gave me a rich chain of gold, £23 in money, with velvet and satin and gold lace to make

> apparel, and a promise that if I would serve him he would reward me with as much as any prince in the world. From whence I went to the Landgrave of Hesse, who gave me the greatest welcome that might be for one of my quality, who sent a ring to my wife valued at £20, and gave me a great cup with a gilt cover, full of dollars, with many great offers for my service.
>
> (Limon 1985: 8)

"Motley's the only wear . . . O that I were a fool! I am ambitious for a motley coat": though it is "a charter as the wind, / To blow on whom I please," which attracts Jacques to ducal livery (*As You Like It* 2. 7. 34–49), the liberty aristocratic service offered the performers, Limon believes, was as much from commerce as from censorship. For as Stephen Greenblatt argues, when they accepted old clothes from new rulers in post-Reformation Europe, theatrical companies "received more than an atttractive, cut-rate wardrobe; they acquired the charisma that clung to the old vestments" (Greenblatt 1990a: 162). What this aura involved, when, for example, the Landgrave of Hesse "ordered old apparel, weapons, armour and clothes in our possession despatched for the performance of a comedy about ancient potentates," had more to do with fantasy than profit. As Limon suggests, by loading them with "silk suits for the entire company of nineteen players and sixteen musicians," coaches, banquets, painted clouds, and multiple changes of scenery, these princelings elevated "the English comedians" who "strut in collars set with pearls," onto an aesthetic plane where they became living signifiers of the arbitrariness of state consumption (Limon 1985: 20). Thus, at the very time when, as Kathleen McLuskie records, English dramatists were lamenting "the shift from patronage to commerce," and the decline of a feudal economy where "every man's house was a commonwealth in itself" (McLuskie 1991: 126), their continental passports secured them entry into the new cultural order which would supplant the old patronage system and reach its apex at Versailles. The court theatre named the "Ottoneum" built by the Landgrave at Kassel in 1604; or the Royal Theatre designed by Italian architects in Warsaw in 1637, were the arenas where a select few English actors came closest to the system Burke has termed the "bureaucratization" of art (Burke 1992: 58); but it is a central paradox of Shakespeare's drama that, despite the small numbers employed, it is this absolutist regime of warrants, subsidies, annuities, committees and intendants, supervised by some enlightened Duke, which haunts the plays he wrote for his London public as the imaginary matrix of their own production:

> Come now, what masques, what dances shall we have,
> To wear away this long age of three hours
> Between our after-supper and bed-time?
> Where is our usual manager of mirth?
> What revels are in hand? Is there no play
> To ease the anguish of a torturing hour?
> Call Philostrate.
>
> (*A Midsummer Night's Dream* 5. 1. 32–8)

In Shakespeare's ideal theatre it is a noble patron who welcomes the troupers, chooses the play to be "preferred" (*Dream* 4. 2. 34), provides the "rabble" with "glistering apparel" (*The Tempest* 4. 1. 37, 193 SD), and underwrites the production by commanding his "usual manager of mirth" to "[s]tir up the youth . . . to merriments" (*Dream* 1. 1. 12). It is then his master of ceremonies who counts the words of the script, edits its "abridgement" and keeps the "revels in hand" by overseeing rehearsals (5. 1. 39–70). Meanwhile, if his court chamberlain censors "the argument" to ensure there is "no offence in it," it is this officer who is also charged with seeing the players "well bestowed" and housed after his "own honour and dignity" (*Hamlet* 3. 2. 242; 2. 2. 520–30). In Shakespearean fantasy, the lord will even "give instructions" about stage-business, such as how to provoke tears with "an onion . . . in a napkin" (*The Taming of the Shrew*, Induction 1. 122–7); or direct a run-through, to the extent of inserting "some dozen or sixteen lines" of his own into the play-text (*Hamlet* 22. 2. 538); and during the action it is the aristocrat who ordains "No tongue! All eyes! Be silent!" (*Tempest* 4. 1. 59); warns the audience to "stay themselves from laughter" (*Shrew*, Induction 1. 132); instructs the stage-manager when to "draw aside the curtain and discover" the scene (*The Merchant of Venice* 2. 7. 1); prompts when lines dry (*Love's Labour's Lost* 5. 2. 663); is "as good as a chorus" glossing the plot (*Hamlet* 3. 2. 254); and may act a part himself to ensure "we will not have our audience disappointed" (*The Book of Sir Thomas More* 4. 1. 257). It is the prince who defends even "the worst" actors from the critics (*Dream* 5. 1. 210); pretends that "That sport best pleases that doth least know how" (*Love's* 5. 2. 514); and promises that "if art fail, we'll inch it out with love" (*More* 4. 1. 117). And it is the great man who cues the comedians when to "play on" or repeat "That old and antique song" (*Twelfth Night* 1. 1. 1; 2. 4. 3); who tells them, "Well done! Avoid! No more!" (*Tempest* 4. 1. 142); announces whether to hear an epilogue (*Dream* 5. 1. 345); and at the end gives the order to "Play, music" (*As You Like It* 5. 4. 175), or to "Strike up pipers" (*Much Ado About Nothing* 5. 4. 125). Finally, it is the nobleman who decides whether to award the players pensions, like the "sixpence a day for playing Pyramus" anticipated for Bottom (*Dream* 4. 2. 20). As Alvin Kernan comments, Shakespeare's dream of patronage is as far as possible from "the rough actualities of production on Bankside," for his imaginary theatre is monopolized by a "ruler as the source of all benefits and the wielder of all powers" (Kernan 1995: 161).

Shakespeare's monarchical theatre projects the cultural bureaucracy that was developing in the absolutist courts of Europe and was perhaps envisaged for England with the accession of the Stuarts. Thus, Richard Dutton has described the jockeying to upgrade the haphazard Elizabethan role of Master of the Revels into an authoritative post "along lines of a Master of Ceremonies who would supervise grand occasions"; yet he goes on to relate how, even when the court was modernized in 1603, "Stuart autocratic ambitions (at least in theatrical matters) were matched by incompetence" (Dutton 1991: 312). For what is striking about Shakespeare's wishful thinking on princely orchestration of "triumphs, mirth, and rare solemnity" (*The Two Gentlemen of Verona* 5. 4. 162) is its inconsistency with English practice. Though "The actors entered wholeheartedly into the fiction" that they existed "to serve the King and Crown," as Kernan argues, he concedes that the reality was that "court theatre was shaped by professionals working in public theatres," and that "the official court view was that the king, and not the play, was the thing" at centre-stage (Kernan 1995: 5. 14. 190). Elizabethan and Jacobean government was clearly neither as coercive nor as conducive to players as Shakespeare's artistic dictators imply. Elizabeth's parsimony and James's attention span militated against the royal involvement in theatricals assumed by new historicism; while, as Dutton concludes, "the Masters of the Revels, though ostensibly representing an absolute authority . . . were products of a factional system . . . and likely to foster the relatively free expression that went with it" (Dutton 1991: 145). Such was Shakespeare's disillusion with the poverty of patronage, Kernan believes, that he wrote his sonnets as "a description of a failed patronage relationship," and never forgot how his real income derived from "public means which public manners breeds" (Sonnet 111). That he shared contemporary cynicism towards actors who "pretend to have a royal master," when "their wages prove them to be the servants of the people" (Chambers 1923: 256); and impatience with a patronage system that supplied, at most, a mere 10 percent of his company's income, only highlights the anomaly, therefore, that "When Shakespeare portrayed a theatre, he did not imagine a public theatre," but always a stage in "a court or noble house," where "the players are as base as the audience is noble" (Kernan 1995: 178, 180, 195).

The discrepancy between Shakespeare's ideal patrician audience and his real plebeian one seems so structural and self-evident – once it is pointed out – that what is surprising is that it has scarcely ever been discussed. The aberration that "The great house dominated the representation of players in Shakespeare's plays, even as it disappeared from their lives," and that the dramatist who created more fictional players than any other confined them to "a series of 'great house plays;' neither established in the city, nor travelling independently . . . (but) dependent on aristocratic hospitality," has recently been diagnosed by Meredith Anne Skura, however, as symptomatic of a profound insecurity. Unfortunately, it is the thesis of *Shakespeare the Actor and the Purposes of Playing* that the reason why "Shakespeare's players all conform to the outdated image of the player as a beggar living on alms," even though "his own experience lay on the up-to-date public stage," is that he was thereby expressing stage-fright as a performer abreacting "the narcissistic pleasure of exhibiting himself" for approval or rejection by his parents. Thus, rather than staging his actual conditions, "Shakespeare accentuated the inferiority implied by patronage," and portrayed actors as "childlike dependents" of noblemen, Skura infers, in a compulsive repetition of "the infant's narcissistic wound . . . an annihilating terror of deprivation" (Skura 1993: 18, 30, 85). What such vulgar Freudianism proves, of course, is the need for a true sociology of Shakespearean production, and one which takes account of evidence that players did not merely evade economics, but actually "increased their touring activities as they achieved pre-eminence in London." A simple explanation proposed by Alan Somerset for this conflict between deference and self-interest is that touring under patronage was one of "the expected duties, as was entertaining the monarch" (Somerset 1994: 54). This is a suggestion that helps to situate Shakespeare, not as some psychotic genius, but as originator of a project defined precisely by its relations to power and profit. *Putting Shakespeare in his place* in this way involves reconstructing the author's intentions through a methodology that, unlike naive biographical criticism, locates his position within his entire universe of creative production. And it is just such an analysis that has been made possible by the theory of the literary field developed by Pierre Bourdieu.

For Bourdieu the literary field is a space "in which one discusses what it means to be a writer," in the way that all social practices are organized as spaces of objective relationships endowed with greater or lesser autonomy in interaction with other fields, and crucially those of power and money (Bourdieu 1971). It is the *relational* mode of this critique which distinguishes Bourdieu's concept of the field from both internal methods of analysis, such as formalism or deconstructionism, and external methods, such as "old" historicism or Marxism. In particular, such a theory allows criticism to go beyond the reflection model of Marxists such as Lukács and Goldmann, which by reducing works to the expression of class interests, and the writer to the medium of a mental structure or world-view, neglected the *relative autonomy* of the literary field and so obliterated its literary specificity. By contrast, Bourdieu's crucial insight – "that there are immaterial forms of capital, as well as an economic form, and that it is possible to convert one of these into another" (Calhoun 1993: 68) – offers what some see as "not only the best, but the only . . . tool for analysis of production, text, and audience in culture studies" (Lash 1993: 193). What Bourdieu adds to Marxism is the recognition that "a much wider range of labour is productive of capital than Marx suggested," though what he has been slow to develop is any explanation of the historical determinants of the convertibility of different kinds of value. Yet, as his commentators remark, it is the very convertibility of capital that distinguishes different historical epochs, as "A high level of convertibility is characteristic of complex, market-based, and above-all capitalist societies," which are driven by "a logic of increasing convertibility" (Calhoun 1993: 68). So, though he has rarely written about it, Bourdieu implicitly affirms the importance assigned the Renaissance by new historicism, as the age when art starts to be differentiated from money and prestige, as much as from prayer or propaganda. Greenblatt's dictum that Shakespeare's playhouse "escapes from the network of social practices that govern" it, because the stage "would seem to be of no *use* to its audience," derives, in fact (as he acknowledges), directly from a reading of Bourdieu:

> The triumphant cunning of this theatre is to make its spectators forget that they are participating in a practical activity. Shakespeare's theatre is powerful and effective precisely to the extent that the audience believes it to be nonuseful and hence nonpractical.
>
> (Greenblatt 1990b: 18)

Like new historicism, Bourdieu's sociology of culture has been simultaneously branded by detractors "a kind of Marxism" and a form of "postmodern relativism" (Wacquant 1993: 237), and it is easy to see why a theory of the disinterestedness of art, that yet insists on the interest of the disinterested, should seem confusing to American and British readers. Such post-Marxist evasion of all "false antinomies" of agency and society, culture and economy, or text and context, looks to Anglo-Saxon eyes very much a genuflection to the *grandes écoles* that inculcated not only the triangulating mentality of de Gaulle's *enarques* but also of Barthes, Derrida or Piaget (Brubaker 1993: 227). None the less, it is Bourdieu's axiom that "the work of art is a product of a negotiation between a creator or class of creators, equipped with a communally shared repertoire of conventions, and the institutions and practices of society," which is adopted by Greenblatt to explain the primacy of the Shakespearean theatre as the prototypical site of this "mutually profitable exchange" (Greenblatt 1989: 12). Likewise, though never quoted, it is Bourdieu's concept of symbolic capital that informs Svetlana Alpers's interpretation, in *Rembrandt's Enterprise: The Studio and the Market,* of the one painter who, along with the dramatist, became most identified with the pricelessness of art, and whose lust for gold had less to do with accumulation of wealth than with the aesthetic liberties he took at the expense of patrons and public (Alpers 1988: 94, 100). Thus, if autonomization of art is for Bourdieu a condition of capitalism, it is the Shakespearean era, his admirers infer, which is the threshold of modernity. And though he pays lip service to the structuralist taboo against "the idol of origins," Bourdieu is happy to go along with this periodization, conceding how it was in the seventeenth century that the cultural field "began to define itself in opposition to the economic, political and religious powers" (Bourdieu 1971: 162). Autonomization turns out, for Bourdieu, to be highly historically specific.

For one who is accused of treating all interests as if they were transhistorical and invariant, Bourdieu offers a surprisingly definite account of the Renaissance as the period when art "gradually came to be organized into a field as creative artists began to liberate themselves economically from the patronage of the aristocracy and the Church and their ethical and aesthetic values" (Bourdieu 1971:162). The relevance of this analysis to Shakespearean culture has been demonstrated, moreover, by Alain Viala in his 1985 study, *Naissance de l'écrivain*, a "sociology of literature in the classical age," which traces the emergence of a literary field in France to the rule of Richelieu, when the autonomy of art was first instituted in foundations such as the Académie Française (Viala 1985). And Bourdieu himself notes that freedom of expression and liberation from the external legitimizing authority of the nobility were accelerated in the case of Elizabethan drama due to "the demands of theatre managers and, through them, to entrance fees paid by a public of increasingly diverse origin" (Bourdieu 1971: 162). But, as he also points out, "for a long time this process remained ambiguous, to the extent that artists paid with a statutory dependence on the state for the recognition it accorded them" (Bourdieu 1996: 367, n.1). It is this solidarity between art and power which concerns Christian Jouhard, who is intrigued that "If there is autonomy . . . it does not establish itself at the expense of power, which, on the contrary, sustains it." To Jouhard, then, what is striking about the literary field is that it was initiated not in defiance but in deference to patronage; and it is his identification of an "association between power and literature, profitable to both," that supplies a solution to the puzzle of Shakespeare's self-subjection. For on this view, early modern patronage was just as much an operation of mutual exchange as the capitalist art market, and never a relationship of crude appropriation:

> The new values of purism from which the profession of writer began to define itself, were produced in the context of a dependence on power . . . which became the initial condition of the construction of the first literary field.
>
> (Jouhard 1994: 34)

In his solitary comment on the dramatist, Bourdieu observes that the character of Shakespeare's who seems to argue most adamantly for the autonomy of art, when he "instructs the actors like an experienced director," is in fact a royal patron and arts administrator. *Hamlet*, Bourdieu remarks, is a play that reminds us that "the artist did not always display towards external restraints the impatience which for us appears to define the creative project," and that the playwright himself addressed his own patron as one who "In other's works dost but mend the style . . . / But dost advance / As high as learning my rude ignorance" (Sonnet 78). Thus, in an era when "the writer for the stage was no longer dependent on the goodwill of a single patron," Shakespeare deferred to the aristocracy not from nostalgia, but as "the group most anxious to distinguish itself" from the bourgeois (Bourdieu 1971: 163). This is the context, according to Bourdieu, of the Prince's notes to the Players to "speak the speech . . . as I pronounced it to you, trippingly," and to "suit the action to the word," in respect of the "necessary question of the play." For what emerges from this rehearsal is that the integrity of the artistic project will be contingent on the freedom from any "pitiful ambition" to please "the groundlings" that is a privilege of "the judicious" (3. 2. 1–45). Already, then, at the dawn of absolutism, the contract struck by an enlightened despotism will be to "make the market disappear" by liberating art from consumer expectations. Thus, what Bourdieu calls "The symbolic revolution through which artists free themselves from bourgeois demand by refusing any master except their art," commences in the Shakespearean text as a strategy to exchange the economic capital earned in the public playhouse for the cultural capital awarded by the princely patron. Hamlet's neoclassical decree, when itemizing the Players' crowd-pleasing, to "reform it altogether" (37), marks the aesthetic price demanded, on this view, of Europe's state academicians, whose emancipation from economics is made conditional on their submission to the esotericism and humanistic ideals of those who clothe them in their "motley" costume (Bourdieu 1996: 61, 81).

"Like iron filings," shaken between power and the public, Bourdieu remarks, those committed to the construction of the literary field were forced to "slide towards whichever pole" seemed, from their position, to be momentarily strong (Bourdieu 1996: 58). Thus, in the Elizabethan theatre, as McLuskie shows, a utopian solution might be that afforded by the Universities, according to the Parnassus plays, where the true artist could "scorn each Midas of this age, / Each earthly peasant and each drossy clown" (Macray [ed.] 1886: 54); but a writer such as Jonson, torn "between the need to earn a living and refusal to compromise the poet's vocation," was forced by abhorrence of the bourgeois and attraction to the pole of power to "divide his public into tiers, with the theatre audience at the bottom, and at the height, the enlightened aristocrat who had the status to make him an appropriate patron." Trapped within this "contradiction between the material need for employment and an ideology in which art and money were opposed," dramatists like Middleton and Marston either dedicated works insultingly or to the "most honourably renowned Nobody," as though "they had no language with which to address" their customers; while, by contrast, it was the market that magnetized Dekker, who savaged Jonson for prostration to his patrons (Marston 1965: 3; McLuskie 1991: 130–3). Between a political pole of attraction and economic pole of repulsion, the force field of Elizabethan drama corresponded closely, therefore, in this analysis, to the literary field of nineteenth-century France that is the subject of Bourdieu's *The Rules of Art* (1996). There he recounts how the autonomization of literature that began in the time of Shakespeare was finalized by Flaubert as the project of "art for art's sake" in resistance to "a bourgeois world that had never before asserted so bluntly its pretension to control the domain of culture." Thus, just as Jonson protested how it was impossible "in these Times, and to such Auditors, to observe the splendour of Dramatic Poems with preservation of any popular delight" (Jonson 1966: 5); so "Everything was false," Flaubert declared. "The moment was disastrous for verse. Imagination was flattened by a public that was not disposed to permit independence of mind" (Bourdieu 1996: 58). From the instant of the Renaissance inception to the nineteenth-century completion of the process, then, the rupture with the bourgeois was accomplished by cultural producers negating the economic pole with the pole of power:

> a challenge to all economism, the literary order presents itself as an inverted economic world: those who enter it have an interest in disinterestedness. But this does not mean there is no economic logic in this charismatic economy founded on the sort of social miracle which is an act free of any determination other than aesthetic intention . . . Because of relations among different kinds of capital, the field of cultural production occupies a dominated position within the field of power.
>
> (Bourdieu 1996: 215)

"The economic world turned upside down" might be the title of Shakespeare's first intervention in this process, the Induction to *The Taming of the Shrew*, where a "charismatic economy founded upon a social miracle" is instituted by the Lord with all the scorn for plebeian reality that distinguishes Limon's nobility. It would be possible to connect the structure of this play with the takeover that occurred after the probable assassination in April 1594 of Shakespeare's theatre patron, Ferdinando, Lord Derby, when his players, based at Knowsley and the Rose, were reincorporated under the control of the Lord Chamberlain, Lord Hunsdon. Derby's (or Strange's) Company had been unique, Scott McMillin claims, for its ruinous size and subversiveness (McMillan 1987: 57, 71): luxuries it owed to Ferdinando; and the on-stage audience for *The Shrew*, dropped half-way through, looks like a relic of his unsustainable standards of sponsorship. "Struggles in the political field may best serve the interest of writers most concerned about literary independence," Bourdieu remarks (1996: 52), and whether devised before or after his death, the Induction to this comedy is itself a display of the exorbitance the Earl funded and that is its subject. When the Lord orders the drunken tinker, Sly, to be "convey'd to bed, / wrapp'd in sweet clothes, rings put upon his fingers, / A most delicious banquet by his bed, / And brave attendants near him when he wakes," this "flattering dream or worthless fancy" (1. 35–42) therefore literalizes what Bourdieu takes to be a founding principle of the world of art, which is its denegation of commerce, since "[t]he game of art is, from the point of view of business, a game of 'loser takes all'." Viewed in this way, the evanescence of Sly's "dream" cruelly obeys the dictate that "In this economic world turned upside down, one cannot conquer money, honours, women," since "The law of this *paradoxical* game is that the love of art is a crazed love" (Bourdieu 1996: 21): like the love of Kate and Petruchio acted to amuse the beggar. We can only guess how this loser will react when he finds his "lady" is a boy; but meanwhile the Players succeed, according to the rules of the game, precisely to the extent that they efface his real plebeian presence:

> There is a lord will hear your play tonight;
> But I am doubtful of your modesties,
> Lest over-eyeing of his odd behaviour –
> For yet his honour never heard a play –
> You break into some merry passion
> And so offend him; for I tell you, sirs,
> If you should smile, he grows impatient.
>
> *First Player*: Fear not, my Lord, we can contain ourselves,
> Were he the veriest antic in the world.
>
> (Induction 1. 91–9)

With its dense references to the Stratford locality, the Induction to *The Shrew* is usually interpreted as Shakespeare's rite of passage from his social origins. As the Arden editor comments, "The whole atmosphere is redolent of Warwickshire, which he left for London in the 1580s. No other play refers so specifically to the county of his birth. It may be that he was making dramatic capital out of personal nostalgia" (Shakespeare 1981: 63). It is important, however, to recognize what is involved in this production of "dramatic capital" out of social marginality, as it typifies not only the ruse by which, as Bourdieu proposes, intellectuals or artists, such as actors, acquire cultural capital by becoming "dominated dominators within the field of dominant power"; but also the way in which Shakespeare, like Flaubert, inscribes the dynamics of his own social trajectory into his artistic project (Bourdieu 1993: 37). Robert Greene notoriously reviled him as an "upstart crow beautified with our feathers"; but seen in the light of Bourdieu's theory, it was Shakespeare's self-awareness of his *arriviste* status, as a provincial glover's son, without elite education, who became a "gentleman born" (*The Winter's Tale* 5. 2. 132) only by gatecrashing the field of cultural production, which determined both his famous capacity to "contain himself" in his creative work – the "habitus," in Bourdieu's terms, which Henry Chettle praised as "his demeanour no less civil than he excellent in the quality he professes" – and his representation of those of the petite bourgeoisie, commencing with Sly, who "beautify" themselves in borrowed feathers (Schoenbaum 1975: 115–19). For while "old Sly's son of Burton-heath" enters the art world with meagre cultural capital, being "by birth a pedlar, by education a card-maker, by transmutation a bear-herd, and by present profession a tinker" (2. 18), its rules dictate that so long as he submits with *goodwill* to the "dream" (which Bourdieu calls the *illusio*) of its legitimacy and autonomy, he will be exalted as "the lord indeed" (73) for whom it is produced. Nothing could be further, therefore, from the Parnassian contempt for "each earthly peasant" than the *distinction* condescendingly conferred by his cultural consumption on "this simple peasant" (1. 133), who (as Bourdieu notes of the middlebrow) struggles with such a mixture of "anxiety and avidity" to close "the gap between his knowledge and recognition" (Bourdieu 1984: 315, 327):

> *Sly*: Is not a comonty
> A Christmas gambol or a tumbling trick?
> *Page*: No, my good lord, it is more pleasing stuff.
> *Sly*: What, household stuff?
> *Page*: It is a kind of history.
> *Sly*: Well, we'll see't. Come, madam wife, sit by my side
> And let the world slip; we shall ne'er be younger.
> (2. 137–42)

Sly's question about its household utility leads editors to suspect that he takes comedy not for a "comonty" but a *commodity*; and the emendment is appealing since the commodification of art is confronted by Shakespeare with a self-reflexivity alien to other Elizabethan dramatists, who, as McLuskie notes, unanimously despise those who buy their culture like clothes: "haunting theatres, to sit there like a popinjay, only to learn speeches which afterward they furnish to maintain table talk"; or spouting "nothing but pure Shakespeare and shreds of poetry gathered at theatres" (Dekker 1967: 167, 73; Macray [ed.] 1886: 56; McLuskie 1991: 128). By contrast, from the moment when Sly lets his world slip into theatrical illusion, Shakespearean culture will advertise itself as a product that transforms the paying public into private patrons, dignifying the playhouse spectators, in the words of the Prologue to *Henry V*, as "gentles all" (8). As Louis Montrose concurs, throughout the plays "the status of the popular audience is elevated in acknowledgement of the imaginative authority theatre confers upon them . . . gentility is conferred upon those empowered to judge the play . . . and in each play power to confer such gentility resides in the players themselves" (Montrose 1996: 202). So, when, at the beginning of his career, Puck invites the audience to "Give me your hands, if we be friends" (*Dream* 5. 1. 23); or when, at the end, the Prologue of *Henry VIII* pledges that "The first and happiest hearers of the town" will "see away their shilling" as intimates of "the very persons of our noble story" (12, 26), Shakespeare's strategy is to gentrify his playgoers as interlopers at exclusive celebrations in houses of nobility, like the Lord who commissions the comedy for Sly. Thus, in an era when theatre entrepreneurs were accruing huge fortunes from the modern world's first mass medium, Shakespearean drama inverted its economic conditions by representing itself to both its producers and consumers as a disinterested benefaction of some Maecenas, such as a Prince of Wales, King of France or Navarre, or Duke of Milan, Vienna, Illyria, Messina, Verona, Ephesus or Athens:

> All I will tell you is, that the Duke hath dined. Get your apparel together, good strings to your beards, new ribbons to your pumps; meet presently at the palace. Every man look to his part: for the short and the long of it is, our play is preferred.
>
> (*Dream* 4. 2. 32–7)

Mediating between the egalitarian playhouse, where professional entertainers purvey their cultural product, as Montrose says, according to a commercial contract "freely entered into by the parties," and "a royal court or noble hall, where the retainers perform in homage to their betters" (Montrose 1996: 201), Shakespearean theatre invites its consumers to insinuate themselves with the actors on their entry to the palace. For David Wiles, there is something literally *patronizing* about this inducement of the paying public to intrude themselves "as fellow commoners alongside the players, granted through their visit to the playhouse vicarious access to an elite gathering to which they would not normally be admitted," which he interprets as proof of how intimately Shakespearean drama is "integrated with upper-class celebration" (Wiles 1998: 67, 78). Yet this adoption of what Bourdieu characterizes as "Thersites' viewpoint" risks missing what he insists is the function of the art game, which is as the field in which the upwardly-mobile "cash-in" economic capital to obtain cultural capital for themselves and their descendants (Bourdieu 1996: 191; 1984: 125). It overlooks, in this sense, how Shakespeare's theatre was shaped by the very rules of the field his plays helped to produce, when they metadramatized themselves not as consecrations of nobility, but as opportunities for social struggle and advancement. In nineteenth-century Paris, according to Bourdieu, "art for art's sake" was the creed of those who wore their culture, like a dandy's costume, in denial of all sordid commercialism, asserting, with Flaubert, that "Nobody is rich enough to pay us. A work of art has no commercial value" (Bourdieu 1996: 81). Likewise in Elizabethan London, Shakespeare's difference, it seems, was to ironize his labour as "No more yielding than a dream" to those "Gentles" who did "not reprehend" its "weak and idle theme" as their commercial loss (*Dream* 5. 1. 413–15). Thus, art was autonomized by this dramatist as a priceless "court cloak" on that journey from the province to the palace of which his own career was the prototype and pattern:

> See you these clothes? Say you see them not and think me no gentleman born: you were best say these robes were not gentlemen born: give me the lie; do; and try whether I am not now a gentleman born . . . and have been so any time these four hours.
>
> (*The Winter's Tale* 5. 2. 131–7)

Meeting a troupe of actors twice on the same road, Ratsey, the highwayman hero of a 1605 pamphlet, is scandalized that they purport to "serve such an honourable Personage" one day and another the next. Taking back the 40 shillings he paid them, the gangster therefore lectures them to give up their deceit of patronage and make an "honest profession" of themselves in town, where they will become good businessmen playing roles like Hamlet, "for I have heard of some that have gone to London very meanly, and have come to be exceedingly wealthy." "Rise up, Sir Simon Two Shares and a Half," Ratsey therefore jokes, as he dubs their leader "the first Knight that ever was Player in England" (Munro 1909: 154). The gibe is thought to be aimed at managers like Edward Alleyn as much as shareholders like Shakespeare; yet Ratsey's advice to renounce the figment of patronage betrays a classic *misrecognition* of the inverted economics of Shakespearean theatre, which would, of course, actually carry so many Hamlets to their knighthoods. Licensed under the flag of convenience of some "Baron or other honourable personage," Shakespeare's drama was legitimated precisely by pretending to the gratuitousness of an aristocratic gift, oblivious of its routine dependence on groundlings "capable of nothing but inexplicable dumb-shows and noise" (*Hamlet* 3. 2. 11). As Fredric Jameson writes, the moment of Shakespearean theatre was when "nostalgia for an organic social order opposed the phantasmagoria of 'imagination' to the bustling commercial activity all around it" (Jameson 1981: 148). It was when profits began to pile up from the Globe after 1600 that the contradiction became acute between this pretense of *noblesse oblige* and a reality where, in Andrew Gurr's words, "companies were not doing what pleasure-loving lord commanded, but what brought most money" (Gurr 1980: 29). Then, Shakespeare's staging of the ruin of the nobility in *King Lear, Coriolanus* and *Antony and Cleopatra* provoked revulsion from those "mechanic slaves / With greasy aprons" (*Antony and Cleopatra* 5. 2. 208–9) before whom the crisis was displayed; while in *Timon of Athens* the actual bankruptcy of the patronage system cued a curse on the "slaves and peasants" of the "detestable town" who had feasted on the show (2. 2. 165; 4. 1. 33). But until Prospero at last untied the "art to enchant" from the field of power, the fiction was maintained that Shakespearean theatre was indeed what this Duke asserts: some arbitrary "provision" or "vanity of mine art," which, having been created *ex nihilo* by princely fiat, would as soon be withdrawn from its tantalized consumers – like the "great globe itself" – to "Leave not a rack behind" (*Tempest*, Epilogue 14; 1. 2. 28; 4. 1. 41, 156).

"Graves at my command / Have wak'd their sleepers," boasts Prospero, "By my so potent Art" (5. 1. 47–8); and, as Stephen Orgel claims, it does seem that *The Tempest* brings to a climax the Renaissance idea of an art, not for art, still less for its audience, but for aristocracy, and that the masque within the play is "Shakespeare's essay on the power of the royal imagination, unique in that its creator is the monarch at its centre." Shakespeare's depiction of Prospero as a royal illusionist "derives from profound understanding of court theatre," Orgel states (Orgel 1975: 45); yet it is exactly at this moment, when "the last of the great house lords" attains absolute control of the stage (Skura 1993: 201), that the play envisages an art freed from power as much as economics. For if Ariel is indeed, as critics suppose, "a celebration of the boy player," and his "rabble" of "meaner fellows" (4. 1. 35–6) Shakespeare's fantasy of the "quality" of the acting profession (1. 2. 193), it is the end of patronage when the actor who has played a nymph and harpy and "presented Ceres" (4. 1. 167) is set free, "like an apprentice bound in indentures and chafing to be released" (Mann 1991: 41). Prospero's abjuration of his "rough magic" (5. 1. 50) – the "courtly aesthetic" that hinged, as Gary Schmidgall (1981) writes, on scenery, lighting, dance and music – can only be read, in this light, as the renunciation by power of its claim on art as homage. For while "the King remained the patron of his acting troupe," and his plays "fitted smoothly into court life," even Kernan admits that "Shakespeare's patronage art always transcended his immediate occasion," and that "Nowhere does Renaissance art speak of its powers with more confidence" than here, where it is implied that "art is now at least as interesting as the political power it is paid to serve." By releasing Ariel, then, "Shakespeare claims a value for his theatrical art" beyond its service to the mighty, like the value attached to "the 'absolute' work of art" by painters such as Vasari (Kernan 1995: 159, 181, 185, 201). Yet that this enfranchisement occurs only with Prospero's consent, underlines the paradox that it is in the courts of princes that the autonomy of art is first conceived, and that even as Shakespeare writes, it is power which both licenses the literary field and renders it fraught with fragility and contradiction.

"Gentle breath of yours my sails / Must fill, or else my project fails" (Epilogue 11–12): conventionally interpreted as "the supreme moment of balance, when art can protest its own right to exist, immune to the sceptical challenge of the world" (Edwards 1968: 153), the ending of *The Tempest* in fact situates this project of autonomization historically as a compact between power and the public within the early modern market for symbolic goods. Shakespeare's "prime duke" will be relieved of his responsibility for legitimating the "liberal arts," of which he has been guarantor during their Renaissance development (1. 2. 72), in return for their future liberation from those mercenary bonds that chain them to consumer demand and expectation. Thus, Prospero begs the new commercial public to prove its gentility, and "release me from my bands / With the help of your good hands" (Epilogue 9–10), in a negotiation that exactly foretells the process outlined by Bourdieu, when with "the ending of dependence on a patron . . . artists and writers notice that this liberty is no more than submission to the laws of the market," and so affirm "the irreducibility of a work of art to the status of merchandise" (Bourdieu 1993: 112). This is a transaction that thereby suggests how, rather than investing aesthetic value in Shakespearean drama, we should see that drama as the origin of our valuation of the aesthetic. In Bourdieu's account, the invention of a pure aesthetic progressed at different rates, "according to the society and artistic field in question." In France, it was the absolute monarchy that ultimately prevented cultural producers from escaping the pole of power; but the abdication of Shakespeare's duke explains why, under pretext of protection by a nominal prince, his playhouse was able to anticipate "art for art's sake" by over two centuries (Bourdieu 1993: 113). For the mutual "indulgence" Prospero craves – "As you from crimes would pardoned be" (19) – is nothing less than that "pure gaze" of aesthetic appreciation which comes when art is at last emancipated from the imperatives of both patronage and profit.

"It shapes the fantasies by which it is shaped," declared a celebrated new-historicist chiasmus of Shakespearean drama, "begets that by which it is begotten" (Montrose 1992: 130); and Bourdieu's study of *The Rules of Art* suggests how this aphorism might allow literary criticism "to bypass the opposition between internal and external analysis" when articulated by his history of the literary field as "a world apart, subject to its own laws." New historicism has been much concerned to explore both the privileged poetics of Shakespeare's play-texts and the privileged conditions of his playgoers; but Bourdieu proposes that it is through his notion "of a homology between the space of works defined by their symbolic content and the space of their positions in the field of production," that this "opposition between structure and history will be overcome" (Bourdieu 1996: 205). After the new historicism, therefore, Bourdieu helps us to grasp how by dreaming of "cloud-capped towers" and "gorgeous palaces" (4. 1. 152) at Elsinore or Knowsley in playhouses on Bankside, Shakespeare's theatre was "stripped of mercantile traces," as Stephen Mullaney images "the place of the stage" in *Pericles*, "including its designation as a marketplace" (Mullaney 1988: 139). For the long road to artistic freedom that took the dramatist from Stratford to Southwark via the Earl of Derby's Lancashire household was replicated in each of his plays, by this account, in their negation of the pole of commerce by the pole of power. In this way they fulfilled their function as symbolic goods – in a market where Ann Jennalie Cook confirms that "quality of plays and players was equated with quality of audience" (Cook 1981: 266) – of demarcating the distinction between their "gentle hearers" and "they / That come to hear a merry bawdy play . . . with such a show / As fool and fight is" (*Henry VIII*, Prologue 13–19). Bourdieu would argue that it is by reason of his reflexivity about this exchange of economic for cultural capital that, like Flaubert, Shakespeare is the truest analyst of Shakespeare. For though they present themselves as art for art, by marrying patrician patron with paying public, his plays in fact remind us that "over that art" which they say "adds" to commerce, is an art that commerce makes:

This is an art
Which does mend nature – change it rather – but
The art itself is nature.

(*The Winter's Tale* 4. 4. 95–7)

Note

1 All references to Shakespeare are to the Arden editions of the plays.

9

Shakespeare's Globe?

CRYSTAL BARTOLOVICH

The recently opened "Shakespeare's Globe" on London's Bankside offers an especially compelling case study through which to consider the effects of "globalization" on "nation-state" and "culture" so highly contested in current debates both in and outside of Marxism.[1] Not only – as we shall see – has the building of the new Globe implicated it in quite complex "global" relations, but also the dissemination of "Shakespeare" all over the globe has made it increasingly difficult to locate "his" work nationally (as "Shakespeare's Globe" – in part, at least – purports to do). Such problems of location and possession seem to be multiplying geometrically under conditions of late capitalism as "globalization," on the one hand, works toward "the compression of the world into a single place" (Robertson 1992: 6), while "culture," on the other hand, remains bound up with particularization, serving (in Fredric Jameson's formulation) as "the vehicle through which the relationship between groups is transacted" (1993b: 34). Indeed, the 1970s, when the Globe Trust was formed and began to agitate for a "national" commitment to a reconstruction of "Shakespeare's" theater in Britain, are often seen as the years in which recognition of globalization became widespread as well, not least because of the various crises of "culture" which emerged as the New Social Movements, decolonization and diaspora changed the ways that groups sorted themselves and transacted their relations, locally and globally. One effect of these changes (in tandem with global economic restructuring) was a sense (contested, but widespread) that the nation-state was now under siege, and, hence, that the distinctiveness of "cultures" – presumed to be bound up with nation-states – too had been undermined. "Shakespeare's Globe" emerged in such a time of crisis, and cannot, I think, be properly understood aside from it.

The interrogative punctuation added to the proper name "Shakespeare's Globe?" in the title to my own essay signals that this quest for understanding will raise urgent questions about ownership – especially about what I will be calling here "possessive nationalism."[2] "Nation" and "possession" are conjured up by the Globe's promotional literature directly in its assertion that it is "*England's* most important theatrical heritage."[3] This particular claim about a site called "Shakespeare's Globe" cannot be extricated fully from colonial connotations ("internal" – in the privileging of "England" – as well as "external" given the force of the signifier "globe"), especially since "Shakespeare" has been called upon to play a role in "colonizing the minds" of subject peoples in the past.[4] However, how this "colonization" works under conditions of late capital, in which Britain is a relatively depleted global power, remains to be seen. In any case, the "return" of the "Globe" at this time invites interrogation as a symptom of globalization.

To this end, I will first consider the significance of the selection of *Henry V* – arguably the most overtly "nationalistic" and Anglophilic text in the Shakespearean canon – as the featured play of the Globe's opening season, examining in particular the view of the "English language" it attempts to promote. After indicating that the "English language" is a site of mixture and contestation – far more broadly than is usually noted in the criticism of that play – I explore the related conflicts which have been provoked by the building of the Globe itself, both "locally" (in the Globe Trust's disputes with Southwark Council), and "globally" (in its attempt to situate the theater locally, nationally and internationally all at once). These disputes reveal, I argue, how deeply both language and "culture" are (unhappily) implicated in an ideology of exclusive "possession" (as opposed to interconnection) in the contemporary world. Finally, I consider the implications of this possessiveness for "Shakespeare" as I examine the contestation within that powerful signifier and the work associated with that proper name, pushing the now highly influential studies on early modern "authorship" and material text in a *transnational* direction. Through this chain of examples of polyvocality and contestation, I make the case that, rather than speaking of "Shakespeare's Globe," we might more properly speak today of the globe's Shakespeare, a claim which entails a "socialized" perspective on culture.[5]

I. Henry's (French) kiss

In its opening season, Shakespeare's Globe seemed to take on (trans)-national issues directly through the decision to stage *Henry V.* Twentieth-century interpretations have long indicated the "nationalistic" overtones of this play, from E. M. W. Tillyard's (1944), Lily Campbell's (1947) and Laurence Olivier's (1944) earlier work, up through the most recent criticism, much of which has been concerned with the play's apparent attempt to mix together the "four nations" of Britain (England, Scotland, Wales and Ireland) into one.[6] David Baker, for example, argues that: "*Henry V* glorifies [Shakespeare's] own English nation, most especially in the person of Henry V. But in the other, equivocally English, displaced characters who share the stage with the king – especially MacMorris the Irishman and Fluellen the Welshman – Shakespeare implies the very discordances that this nation meant to eliminate" (1997: 24). As many critics have noted (whether they see them as ultimately smoothed over or silenced or not), the "discordances" to which Baker alludes here are marked linguistically in the play: although Henry's troops "handle an English cudgel" together, not all of them "speak English in the native garb" (Gurr [ed.] 1992: 5. 1. 75–7). The relationship between the English language and "cudgels," one might even say, is very much a matter with which the play concerns itself.

The playnotes for the Shakespeare's Globe performance of *Henry V* tell us, after all, that the play "celebrates the English language as a great *instrument* of inspiration and communication." But what sort of instrument – and whose? The playnotes don't tell us for sure, but imply that the "English language," like the Globe, is both a benign "instrument" and England's. However, with language and nation being bound up so often with each other in the modern problematic of "culture," it becomes imperative to examine what happens to "culture" when the "English language" has become so emphatically dispersed, in part through the cudgel of the British imperial project, and, later, through decolonization and "other" claims on "English" than Britain's – and other claims on Shakespeare as well. As one British cultural materialist has observed: "academic study of [Shakespeare's] work is dominated by U.S. scholars and critics" (Sinfield 1992: 7). These claims (and challenges) are not only "American," however, but range widely, from

N'gugi wa Thiong'o to Aimé Césaire, Michelle Cliff to Tayeb Salih, among many, many others. That English has been spread around the globe is indisputable; the significance of this dispersion for "culture" is less clear. I want to insist, however, that as long as "English" is not recognized as a broad site of struggle, but only as a metropolitan "possession" to which all other claims are secondary, the liberatory implications for "culture" of these diverse "global" claims will remain obscure.

That such claims on "English" are indeed made, is, of course, recognized, though often to fend them off. Writing one of his many mournful journalistic elegies to an England lost, the notorious Tory commentator Peregrine Worsthorne asserted in the *Daily Telegraph* that while the proud and confident English *nation-state* that he found celebrated in his boyhood (wartime) encounter with Shakespeare's *Henry V* is now dissipated by globalization, the *English language* he discovered in that play still carries the same power. Hence he reworks a favorite maxim culled from Cecil Rhodes for new times: "To be born speaking English, as only the English can, is to rewin the lottery of life" (Worsthorne 1998).[7] Faced with what he sees as a series of global "humiliations" for Britain abroad, as well as loss of respect for elites and, most gallingly, "history devalued so as to make it more acceptable to the sensibilities of multicultural society" at home, Worsthorne *advocates* the European Union (EU). He views joining the EU as preferable to life in a sovereign nation in which "superior people" are not appreciated and immigrants – such as Worsthorne's journalist colleague Darcus Howe, who was born in Trinidad – make shocking claims as, for example, that the "mix and meddle between master and slave . . . are as much your history as they are mine" (Howe and Worsthorne 1998).[8] Compared to the implications of *that* intermixture, Worsthorne finds the prospect of throwing in his lot with Europe an evident relief. In any case, he is solaced by his faith that the English still have "one possession that not even Brussels can interfere with or downgrade: the English language," which will continue to distinguish them and bring them honor (Worsthorne 1998). Raising the specter of intermixture, Worsthorne asserts the ability of the English language, as an English possession, to triumph over all threats to identity and coherence.

The view of *Henry V*, Shakespeare and the English language, promoted by the Globe playnotes, and evident in mainstream readings such as Worsthorne's, overlooks, however, how much "communication" – and indeed, the "English language" – is troubled in the play. As Andrew Gurr observes in the introduction to his edition:

From early in Act 3 the different dialects of the four captains and the

> scenes spoken in alien French offer an aural challenge to the claims for brotherhood. No play of Shakespeare's makes so much use of differences in language and has more language barriers. With one entire scene in French, another half in French, and the French nobles regularly starting their scenes by making use of French phrases, plus Llewellyn's, Macmorris's and Jamy's non-standard English, Pistol's theatrical and old-fashioned quasi-verse, together with Mrs. Quickly's malapropisms, the play puts up a considerable show of non-communication.
>
> (1992: 36)

Various characters "mistake each other" as they speak (3. 3. 134–5), or only "partly understand [each other's] meaning" (3. 6. 51). It is not surprising, then, that numerous critics, including Greenblatt (1985), Cairns and Richards (1988), Mullaney (1988), Newman (1991), Neill (1994), McEachern (1996) and Baker (1997), all emphasize language in their readings of the play. Its language, being neither transparent, unequivocal nor unifying, seems to require explaining.

Michael Neill has associated the extravagant display of languages in the play with its concern to use the stage to help forge just the sort of "national language" that Worsthorne seems to have in mind, a process Neill finds explicitly articulated in Thomas Heywood's *Apology for Actors* – though not in terms that Worsthorne would be likely to find particularly comforting. "Our English tongue," explains Heywood, "which hath been the most harsh, uneven, and broken language of the world, part Dutch, part Irish, Saxon, Scotch, Welsh, and indeed a gallimaufry of many, but perfect in none, is now by this secondary means of playing, continually refined . . . so that in process, from the most rude and unpolished tongue, it is grown to a most perfect and composed language, . . . [so] that many Nations grow enamored of our tongue (before despised)" (Neill 1994: 19). Rather than seeing "gallimaufry" as cause for celebration or a sign of the richness of human interchange, Heywood regards it with dismay, a condition to be overcome in the interests of a secure possession of "English" by the "English." Providing an imaginary solution to this perceived social crisis, *Henry V* displays emphatically this "gallimaufry of many" and, then, as Neill argues, "pass[es] off . . . in the guise of a national generosity that expands the idea of genus (or gens) . . . an act of aggressive assimilation that the subsequent course of Empire would make only too familiar" (1994: 20). To put this argument in the combined terms of the play and the Globe's playnotes, we might say that English acts as a "cudgel" in language's clothing, compelling the subordination of all other languages (and peoples) in its path.

But there remains a problem: where is this "English" to be located? No cudgel can entirely obliterate the dependence of "English" on "Dutch," "Irish," "Saxon," "Scotch," "Welsh" and all the un-named others which have contributed to it, pulling it in numerous directions, as Heywood so anxiously notes. "English" in Heywood's account is not an effect of the destruction of its multiple determinants (what would be left?), but of their *disavowal* in the interests of accomplishing a "composed" whole, that is to say, a language transformed into something distinct from its component parts, no longer owing anything to them, indeed now in a position to stand against them, and, apparently, assert superiority. As Heywood implies, and as *Henry V* illustrates, such singular, or exclusivist, possession of a multiply accented[9] cultural form can only be accomplished by the violence of boundary-setting and hierarchization, of denial and/or discounting of the multiple voices to which "English" remains (irreducibly) indebted.

To forge a language/nation/culture nexus is, then, it seems, not only to engage in the violent production of a disparaged "otherness," but to *forget* – and then maintain an ongoing "sanctioned ignorance" about – the alien(ated) elements and forces of ones "own" culture.[10] We must not allow ourselves to forget, however, that the intermixing is nonetheless ubiquitous, unavoidable and, indeed, desirable when not coerced:

> the history of all cultures is the history of cultural borrowings. Cultures are not impermeable; just as Western science borrowed from Arabs, they had borrowed from India and Greece. Culture is never just a matter of ownership, of borrowing and lending with absolute debtors and creditors, but rather of appropriations, common experiences, and interdependencies of all kinds among different cultures. This is the universal norm. Who has yet determined how much the domination of others contributed to the enormous wealth of the English and French states?
>
> (Said 1993: 217)

The cost of answering Said's question here, it seems to me, may well be the end of myths of "possessive nationalism" for *all* peoples. That is to say, even the subordinated "parts" must see the limits to their own "possession" of an intact and pure self. This is an important issue for it has bearings on strategy: should subordinated peoples primarily assert "distinct" cultures of their own against the aggressive assimilation of more powerful groups (as is often asserted in the recent criticism of

Henry V, which champions the right of the Irish, Scots and Welsh to their "own" cultures), or, alternatively, should the subaltern groups instead primarily work to show the dependence of all cultures on each other?

To begin to answer this question, I would like to return to *Henry V* to examine an aspect of its linguistic politics that has gone unnoted in the voluminous criticism: "French" disrupts "English" more forcefully in the play than is ordinarily admitted, especially by the play itself, and this has important implications for how we understand "culture." While the linguistic difference marked in the Welsh and Irish characters is presented as needing no translation, as already assimilated to "English" – though their accents, syntax and vocabulary mark their difference from the "standard" as well as their subordination to it – the play's treatment of French is quite different. The final scene (and the earlier "language lesson" scene), it is often remarked, move back and forth between "French" and "English," displaying to the audience that these languages are distinct and distancing – "alien" as Gurr puts it in the passage cited above. English, here, it is ordinarily assumed, unequivocally serves as a distinguishing possession and an instrument of power: English *over* French – as far more successfully over the Welsh, Irish, and Scottish languages. The French King speaks his lines in "English," apparently deferring to the English King, a gesture made all the more overt by his daughter's labored efforts at "English" later on, which Henry must bridge in his own attempts at "French." Because "French" retains its "own" vocabulary and structure, and is shown to give these up right on stage, England's military triumph can be displayed as a linguistic one as well.

Hence, in speaking to Katherine, whose hand he claims along with France, Henry banters with her in prose lines, slipping back and forth between two "tongues" with her as he maneuvers to secure "possession":

Katherine: Is it possible dat I sould love de ennemie of France?

King Henry: No it is not possible you should love the enemy of France, Kate; but in loving me, you should love the friend of France; for I love France so well that I will not part with a village of it; I will have it all mine. And, Kate, when France is mine and I am yours, then yours is France and you are mine.

Katherine: I cannot tell wat is dat.

King Henry: No, Kate? I will tell thee in French, which I am sure will hang upon my tongue like a new-married wife about her husband's neck, hardly to be shook off. Je quand sur le possession de France, et quand vous avez le possession de moi – let me see, what then? Saint Denis be my speed! – donc votre est France et vous êtes mienne. It is as easy for me, Kate, to conquer the kingdom as to speak so much more French. I shall never move thee in French, unless it be to laugh at me.

Katherine: Sauf votre honneur, le Francois que vous parlez, il est [meilleur] que l'Anglois lequel je parle.

King Henry: No, faith is't not, Kate; but thy speaking of my tongue, and I thine, most truly falsely, must needs be granted to be much at one.

(5. 2. 58–6)

Henry's protest in the final line betrays more than he is aware of, since, in a sense he clearly does not see, Katherine's observation (as well as his own) is quite insightful: their "speaking" *is* "much at one."

For is French as "alien" as the staging implies (and critics have insisted)? Demonstrably, French "hang[s] upon [Henry's] tongue" and can "hardly be shook off" even before he claims to have made any use of it: much of Henry's *English*, after all, *is* "French." To give just a short list from the above exchange: "possible," "enemy," "village," are all – as the metropolitan linguists like to call them – "loan words" from the French, as are, even more significantly, both "conquer" and "possession." How secure can the English "possession" of the "English" language be, if it is so evidently indebted? Scholars of the history of the "English" language emphasize that the influx of "French" after the Norman conquest was substantial; a consultation with any dictionary that provides etymological information will quickly attest to this – and, yet, apparently we learn such history only to immediately "forget" its significance, allowing the boundaries of nation-states to mystify it – at least in some cases. I point out this (usually unremarked) linguistic intermixing not in order to suggest that "French" and "English" are "the same" – obviously not the case – but rather as a reminder that all languages are, quite literally, "creole," if we understand by this term a linguistic site of cultural syncretism, though only some languages are *designated* creole, with all its baggage of implied secondariness, derivative-ness and impurity.

Whereas the stage "Irish" and "Welsh" in *Henry V* are displayed as mixtures, English *seems* to elude this fate by its position as the "standard" against which the "mixedness" of these "other" languages is judged. With an eye to undermining such a strategy, Ulf Hannerz has attempted to reinscribe the word "creole" for a "globalizing" world, and argues that "we are all being creolized" (1987: 557). Other cultural theorists, as Said above, emphasize – more appropriately to my mind – that we have all always been "creolized," though the form that this intermixing has taken – and its politics – change over time, sometimes radically. In other words, the "fact" of creolization is ubiquitous, but categorization as "creole" depends upon who is in a position to claim to be "standard," and thus is bound up with power. Because "mixture" has been associated with subordination and impurity in relation to "standard" languages, mixture becomes difficult to identify with and approve. The "standard" languages, too, however, are mixtures, though their speakers have historically had the power (military, economic, ideological) to represent that mixture as insignificant or invisible.

In recent postcolonial theory, exposing this syncretism has become a standard strategy to undermine the West's claim to be (and to have been) everything, leaving the non-West to occupy the position of the derivative, secondary and lacking. Wilson Harris, for example, insists on the importance of a "cross-cultural imagination" to combat the "monolithic character of conquistadorial legacies" (1983: xv), and such a sensibility finds its way into a huge segment of postcolonial writing, from the fiction of Salman Rushdie to the theoretical work of Arjun Appadurai, Paul Gilroy and Stuart Hall. While some Marxists (e.g. Brennan 1997, Ahmad 1992) have objected that possessive nationalism remains strategically necessary as a defensive gesture for the oppressed in an appallingly unequal world, the (poststructurally inflected) postcolonial theorists have emphasized that exploding all myths of self-identity and possession is necessary to undermine the ideological rationale for coercive assimilation (i.e. that the subaltern group lacks absolutely that which the conqueror provides – that "culture" only moves in one direction, osmotically, from a site of greater to one of lesser density). For Brennan, however, such claims, which often lead to formulations such as "we are all cosmopolitans" – or "creolized" as I put it earlier – are "complete as identity and incomplete as situation" (1997: 18); in other words, they are descriptively (perhaps even theoretically) accurate, but strategically dangerous, because they leave too much to the side the persistent problem of power, which mere discursive claims of heterogeneity alone are unlikely to unsettle. Instead, resistant alternatives to the self-proclaimed "standard" languages and cultures require the formation of (Fanon-ian) coherent and unified insurgent cultures, born of struggle (rather than merely dredged up out of the pool of archaic cultural forms).

As sophisticated as such a vision of resistance can be, many postcolonial theorists have rejected even this (strategic) "binarization" of the (neo)colonial relation, insisting on the formation of a mutual culture among ostensibly distinct groups, and worked to indicate the debts of dominant cultures to all that they would exclude in the act of defining themselves. This debate is of the greatest importance to any attempt to understand "Shakespeare," a site of intermixing, multiple claims and contestation that implicates far more peoples than those of the "four nations" of Britain in the (neo)colonial world. Henry's (and "Shakespeare's") triumphal speech cited above in the exchange with Katherine bears the trace of an earlier intermixing, unsettling any simple determination of "mine" and "thine" where the ostensibly "two tongues" of French and English are concerned. Before Henry ever kisses Katherine, her tongue has already been in his mouth, so to speak. To note this is by no means to discount the brutality of Henry's power play (or, for that matter, the earlier Norman one), but rather to unsettle the link between "culture" and "nation" which underwrites it. Such gestures may be *insufficient* as strategy, as Brennan asserts, but they are nonetheless crucial, I would argue, especially as "English" is not only multiply determined historically, but remains so today – even leaving aside its status as a global *lingua franca* – since it is spoken by and through divergent "cultures," among peoples living in Australia and Canada, the Caribbean, the United States, Africa and India, among others, severely troubling Raymond Williams's early claim that "the area of a culture . . . is usually proportionate to the area of a language rather than to the area of a class" – at least insofar as he took this to mean *a* culture of (the) English (1983: 320) – or even of the *British*. "English" is not an enclosure, or an object – certainly not "naturally" a possession – but is rather a process and site of continuous transformation and adaptation to new conditions – conditions which are never simply "local." England cannot contain it; and "Shakespeare's" plays, dependent as they are on a language that is dependent on so many others, cannot be localized absolutely in one place.

For what is the "area of a language"? How can we chart the contours of a process, or the extent of that which is not one? Nearly forty years before Heywood proposed that the "gallimaufry" of the English language was at last being regularized and distinguished by its usage on stage – its *performance* as English we might say – "E. K." (the putative "editor" of Spenser's *Shepherd's Calendar*) complained of exactly the opposite dynamic at work in poetry:

> our mother tongue, which truly of itself is both full enough for prose, and stately enough for verse, hath long time been counted most bare and barren of both. Which default whenas some endeavored to salve and recure, they patched up the holes with pieces and rags of other languages, borrowing here of the French, there of the Italian, everywhere of the Latin; not weighing how ill those tongues accord with themselves, but much worse with ours; so now they have made our English tongue a gallimaufry, or hodgepodge of all other speeches.
>
> (Spenser 1932: 5)

Rather than the myth of a chaos of "English" resolving itself into order at about 1612 when Heywood publishes his *Apology*, "E. K."'s origin myth, published in 1579, imagines an older vigorous and pristine English having fallen into disarray. What both writers share, however, is the conviction that the English actually in use between their moments of writing is not quite, well, *English*. "Gallimaufry" – itself a word "borrowed" from the French – becomes the sign of this displacement of English by its own users. All the plays attributed to Shakespeare – including, of course, *Henry V*, were composed and performed within this same period, when English was, apparently, believed to be not quite itself. A later myth would weave "Shakespeare" into this problem directly by declaring him to be the solution, claiming that "he" made the triumph of English over its gallimaufrosity possible, providing for the birth of the language and culture of "English" as such.[11] The interesting thing about this myth is that it recognizes the actual mixedness of English even as it attempts to abolish it.

Hence, the contestation has continued, albeit disavowed or discounted, such that in 1984 the Caribbean poet Kamau Brathwaite could observe of a different – but related – dilemma of intermixture, that the "English" language in which he wrote was not an "English" national possession: "English it may be in terms of some of its lexical features. But in its contours, its rhythm and timbre, its sound explosions, it is not English, even though the words, as you hear them, might be English to a greater or lesser degree" (1984: 13). Not only does Brathwaite refuse to have his mother tongue reduced to "dialect" or "creole" – a secondary, improper form of "English" – but he insists at the same time on the radical (in every sense) "difference" of what is often dismissed as a corrupted, or derivative, form of the same, and also claims that this "difference" has impacted on the metropolitan form of "English" which devalues his mother tongue: the "underground language [of slaves] was constantly transforming itself into new forms. It was moving from a purely African form to a form which was African but which was adapted to the new environment and adapted to the cultural imperative of the European languages. And it was influencing the way in which the English, French, Dutch, and Spaniards spoke their own languages" (1984: 7). Brathwaite refers here to a matter of "accent" in Voloshinov's sense of multiple uses and claims on the "same" language, which renders "English" (or any other language) incapable of reduction to a singular possession (1973: 23); thus we find ourselves returned to the assertion that so scandalized Peregrine Worsthorne: "the mix and meddle between master and slave . . . [is] as much your history as . . . mine" (Howe and Worsthorne 1998). At a moment when even the *Guardian* can pose as a serious question "What is a true Brit? Should Britishness be redefined to recognize black immigration?" (the title to the article in which the Howe/Peregrine exchange cited above unfolds), we need to attend carefully to these "nation"/"culture" debates.

As the example of the "French" words silently "performed" into "English" in the final scene of *Henry V* indicates, the "English" language(s) have been forged from intermixings which are often denied, disavowed or rendered invisible. A "celebration of the English language," then, as the Globe proposed to elicit in the performance of *Henry V*, would require the extension of invitations to many more peoples than "the English." Not only the "French," of course, but the "Dutch," the "Welsh" and various postcolonials, as well as all the other contributors and participants. But in the end even this gesture would be insufficient, assuming as it does that pre-existing cultures have "converged" into English, when the very possibility of any such coherence is in question. This observation does not mean that all celebrations are off; it simply means that what we need to celebrate changes: not the "English" possession of the "English language" as Peregrine Worsthorne and the Globe Trust propose, nor the division of English into component parts with each "separate" culture taking back "its own" (the "devolution" approach), but instead the remarkable human capacity for collective production as it manifests itself in English, though in a degraded form, marred as it has been by destructiveness and domination by elites. Under current conditions, such a celebration cannot occur without a struggle, first to make the liberatory collectivity visible out of the depths of forgetfulness and sanctioned ignorance, and, then, crucially, for that collectivity to wrest control of culture for itself.

II Buying into the Globe

The above reading of *Henry V*, with its emphasis on the mixture of which "English" is an effect, will provide a model for my investigation of the "ownership" of "Shakespeare's Globe," and the difficulty with determining it. The moment in which the Globe reconstruction got off the ground, so to speak – around 1970 – was, after all, a very troubled time for "Englishness." Decolonization was virtually complete, the postwar economic boom was a winding down, "American" popular culture had made (what was widely perceived to be) vast inroads on what was left of so-called "British" culture, and, most important, post-colonial diaspora had brought a continuous flow of immigrants with different languages, customs and appearance to mingle with a population that at least claimed to be homogenous.[12] In order to combat the ensuing identity crisis and rally voters under these conditions, British politics in the Tory years (Thatcher became Prime Minister in 1979) relied heavily on a certain celebration of "Englishness" and "tradition," which Patrick Wright (1985) has critiqued in his work on the "heritage industry." Given its self-representation as "England's most important theatrical heritage," at least, the simulated "Shakespeare's Globe" appears at first glance to be a made-to-order defense against the identity crisis which has troubled postwar Britain, offering its people a chance to discover, and, above all, *possess*, once again that ancient and settled national identity that the very name of "Shakespeare" is supposed to conjure up.

Indeed, since "Shakespeare" and the "Globe" are widely taken to be metonyms for "England" (and, by uneasy extension, "Britain"), the politics of the Globe can be seen to participate in a signification of England's place in the world. As Alan Sinfield (1992) has argued in his analysis of the use of an image of the Globe in a 1989 advertisement for the now privatized Royal Ordnance, so powerful is the Shakespeare myth that even a "British" munitions manufacturer has thought it fitting to deploy "the Globe" as a trope of its own "tradition" and "excellence." But there are signs even here that the narrative of national possession is troubled. The seemingly confident assertion on the part of Royal Ordnance that "after 400 years [it] still plays the globe, all of it," betrays a certain spatial ambiguity operating alongside nationalist pride (see Sinfield 1992: 2–3). Indeed, in the same Royal Ordnance advertisement which features the Globe so prominently as a metonym for "every theater of military operations," the ostensibly "British" aerospace company locates itself in Arlington Virginia, under a logo which depicts half a Union Jack (on the left) flying next to half of the Stars and Stripes (on the right). Reading from left to right, one might well wonder if that logo signals an equal partnership, or a displacement, especially in the context of Britain's postwar decline as the United States rose to superpower status, and the attendant shift of company headquarters for the formerly "national" enterprise.

A similar global politics has played itself out in the rebuilding of the Globe, which was instigated not by Thatcher, or popular agitation in Britain, or even local scholarly interest, as one might imagine, but rather by way of the efforts of an expatriate American actor, Sam Wanamaker, who had not just England, but the whole globe, in mind when he proposed a rebuilding of the Globe. As he explained in the course of a fascinating interview with Graham Holderness, he and the other Globe Trustees were on the one hand "looking North, across the river to the wider world beyond; [and on] the other facing south to the locality and to the people of Southwark . . . We never abandoned the belief that we were local, national and international in character" (Holderness 1988b: 18). The "national" reception of these efforts, as well as the "local" (in Southwark), however, ranged largely from indifference to resistance in Wanamaker's own account, an assessment confirmed by John Drakakis's (1988) blow-by-blow narrative of the Globe Trust's various dealings with the left-wing elements among Southwark residents and in the local Council, which at one point labeled the entire project "elitist, touristic and irrelevant to local needs" (Holderness 1988b: 16).[13] Not only were some Southwark residents apparently distrustful of the various business interests – many of which were not only not "local" but not even "British" – that Wanamaker had brought to the project in his endless quest for funds, but the Council claimed that it wanted to use the site on which the Globe reproduction now stands for public housing (Holderness 1988b: 17). Wanamaker found this plan preposterous: "to take the prime sites that have national and international significance and value – when housing could be built elsewhere – is the destruction of cultural and social values" (Holderness 1988b: 17). One is prompted to ask: whose cultural values?

Interestingly, in spite of the local dissent, Wanamaker attributes his position to *populist*, not elitist, views, and considered his own values to be those of "the people." Son of Jewish Ukrainian immigrants to New York, he described his motives in undertaking the Globe project to be entirely democratic, and saw the theater as potentially "a great force for social change" by disseminating the humanizing benefits of "common culture" to all "peoples of the world" (Holderness 1988b: 18). When his interviewer suggests gently that some people might see his view as "conservative," Wanamaker simply retorts: "Why should Shakespeare be available only to the educated?" as if there were no distinction between making "available" and thrusting (a certain version of) "Shakespeare" upon the world's peoples whether in Southwark or South Asia (Holderness 1988b: 20). Indeed, perhaps the most revealing aspect of the Globe project for the purposes of assessing the effects on "culture" of "globalization" is that in it supposedly "British" cultural symbols themselves become the agents of a perceived "cultural imperialism" *of Britain*, foregrounding how such signs remain active sites of struggle, and change their meaning under altered global conditions.[14] In any case, the poor fit between Wanamaker's sincere and well-intentioned humanist universalism (which assumes a "common culture") and the realities of contemporary geopolitics in an unequal world could hardly be more starkly illustrated than in his dispute over "value" with local residents in Southwark.[15]

Although the cultural politics elude him because he sees only one "universal" Shakespeare of inherent "common" value to "all peoples," even in the face of quite insistent charges that his own view was partial and interested, Wanamaker, nevertheless, displays considerable awareness of the impact of the geopolitical situation on culture when he explains why he had to resort to private funding to build his Globe:

> The economic crisis through which Britain has been passing since the war has been a crisis more severe than that experienced by other nations such as Germany and Japan, and has also been affected by the terrible transition from an imperialist power to a second or third-rate nation. These economic and political changes have far-reaching cultural consequences: among them a growing awareness that public funding for educational or artistic projects is likely to be increasingly restricted or denied.
>
> (Holderness 1988b: 19)

The "economic crisis" to which Wanamaker refers is an effect of the restructuring of the global economy in the postwar period, a process which is often (including in this essay) referred to as "globalization."[16] As Wanamaker himself notes, this process is not without its implications for "culture," though these implications are rather more complicated than the limits they impose on funding availability, as his analysis suggests.

What Wanamaker did not seem to see is that the conditions he describes not only make it difficult for "Britain" to finance the protection and propagation of its "own" culture, but, at the same time, make it more difficult for it to "possess" a culture at all, since these conditions give more weight in the global balance of power to the "international" bloc (specifically, the United States, Japan and the EU), represented by himself and the Trust's various transnational financial backers, than to "local," or "national" interests (unless congruent with the "international"). As a result, "Shakespeare" as deployed by the Globe Trust could be experienced as an imposition rather than an affirmation on Bankside. One particularly irate Southwark resident declares, for example: "if Shakespeare moves in 'ere, I'm moving out!" (cited in Drakakis 1988: 39). This outburst might, of course, be dismissed as (and may even *be*) anti-intellectualism, but I think such a charge is missing the point: if "locals" do not see "Shakespeare" *in the form offered* as representing them, in what sense can *this* Shakespeare serve as a "national" symbol, much less a "local" one? Above all, what we see in the Globe controversy is "Shakespeare" as a site of struggle over control of material and cultural space at a time when both have been brought into crisis by the ongoing "globalization" of capital. In the face of such a struggle, the point is not to return "Shakespeare" to his seemingly rightful place in Southwark, as Wanamaker undertook to do; there is no such place. To the contrary, we need to attend to such struggles and try to move toward a way of imaging "culture" beyond the national, without resorting to either a humanist (i.e. false) universal or a transnational corporate takeover.

I do not raise the specter of corporate takeover fancifully. Further complicating the "space" of the new Globe and London's "vital relation" to it claimed by the promotional literature, the opening season of plays was sponsored by the decidedly "global" corporations Unilever and Panasonic (Matsushita), whose transnational sphere of operations less invokes an old English imperial Paradise Lost than a New World Order in which Britain is decentered, even from financial support of what are (putatively) its "own" national symbols. Unilever was among the first modern multinationals, and later transnationals (on the *Fortune* Global 500 list, it now ranks 35). Although its remote origin was in shops and factories in late nineteenth-century Britain, Lever Brothers established production facilities and outlets for local consumption in a number of colonial countries at around the same time, most notably in

South Africa, where it maintains significant interests to this day, as it did throughout the colonial and apartheid periods. Furthermore, as early as 1929 Lever Brothers had merged with a Dutch margarine-production group to form Unilever, a new corporate entity, which a business historian has called a "bilingual international enterprise," among the very first of its kind (Fieldhouse 1978: 40). The "Englishness" of Lever brothers, already complicated by its dispersed and far-flung factories and markets, was decidedly decentered by this move, even though London became the headquarters of the merged companies, which were joined "without subordinating one to the other" (Fieldhouse 1978: 39). What the history of Lever Brothers manifests is the ways in which economic units of analysis don't always conform to national(ist) ones, indicating a need to carefully examine and analyze the relations among them. Unilever is, after all, in a global position now to help "colonize" Southwark as it once helped to colonize South Africa.

As for Panasonic (whose parent company, Matsushita, is number 23 on the *Fortune* Global 500 list), no lines, even tenuous, distantly historical ones, link it to any "British" corporations. Its investment in "Shakespeare's Globe" signals instead the increasingly explicit entangling of Asia with the cultures and economies of the "West." Indeed, on its web page Panasonic describes its sponsorship of *Henry V* as an anniversary present to itself after twenty-five years in Britain, and as a sister project to its earlier sponsorship of a reconstruction of the Globe in Tokyo, which was completed before its London counterpart.[17] I am not, of course, suggesting – economistically – that Unilever and Panasonic now "own" Shakespeare, but I am wondering what it means for how we understand "culture" when forces outside the nation "invest," in both senses, in its putative icons.

Analysis of such problems of "location" are crucial to any understanding of the current global situation, marked as it is with massive inequality. The 300 largest transnationals – Unilever and Panasonic among them – now control about one-quarter of the world's productive assets (Barnet and Cavanagh 1994: 15). Although they are headquartered in a handful of countries (the United States, Japan, Germany, France, Switzerland, Netherlands, the United Kingdom), their spheres of operation cross the boundaries of any given country; indeed, collectively, they have produced a network of economic activity on a scale "never before achieved by any world emperor or nation-state" (Barnet and Cavanagh 1994: 15). Because of the vast inequality characterizing the globe of global capital which enforces economic difference – both "in" and "among" states – "cultural difference" remains highly charged as well. On the one hand, it is used *by* capital: cultural difference offering opportunities for targetting consumers with specific "lifestyles," or commodified for sales to tourists and the sedentary adventurer alike ("ethnic" cuisines, The Body Shop, "world music" and so on), purveying the "exotic" without the bother and expense of jet travel and booking hotels.[18] On the other hand, cultural difference seems to provide a defense against an encroaching global sameness, which usually bears the name of "Americanization": McDonald's, blue jeans and Hollywood movies, as far as the eye can see. However, as Stuart Hall has argued, even "Americanization" can work "through" difference under conditions of late capital by "recogniz[ing] and absorbing . . . differences within the larger, overarching framework of what is essentially an American conception of the world . . . stage-manag[ing] independence within it" (1997: 228–9). "Difference" in itself, then, provides no necessary protection from "Americanization." In any case, the politics of "difference" is complex in a world dominated by a capitalism that is contradictory in its processes, and in which nation-states remain important for the negotiation of global power relations. What the Globe example makes evident, is that supposedly differentiating "national" symbols are being struggled over and re-coded at the "global" level – and not always in that "national" – much less the "local" – interest.

These struggles are, of course, not new, but they have been given a heightened urgency by the recent pace and strategies of globalization. Whereas in the earlier form of globalization over which Britain itself presided, "its" cultural forms were put to the use of securing the power of its elites, the new Globe adamantly signifies the loosening of that power. The complex politics of location indicated by this situation are foregrounded in Wanamaker's, perhaps unwitting, but certainly evocative, use of the language of "North" and "South" in his discussion (quoted above) on his view of spatial relations of the Globe (and globe). While Southwark is the "local" in Wanamaker's account, the "wider world" begins in "the North," right across the Thames in the City of London. London is, of course, what Saskia Sassen (1991) calls a "global city," which, through its international banking and insurance ties, is still indisputably powerful internationally even if Britain is only, by Wanamaker's assessment, a "second or third-rate nation," when compared to Japan, Germany or the United States. That Wanamaker invokes the North/South binary to describe the relation between Southwark and the City is especially apt, however, because it points out one of the paradoxes of capitalist modernity: that it is uneven both "locally" and globally.[19] The postwar economic crises in Britain have not affected all of its areas in the same way, leaving some, like Southwark, relatively underdeveloped, while the City, a few hundred yards away, thrives. And the City bears a similar relation to those places even further South – Africa, Latin America, the Caribbean – which remain so much poorer and less "developed" than the wealthiest Northern nations, where over 80 percent of the world's wealth flows and resides, to be distributed (unevenly, of course) among only 20 percent of the world's population.[20]

Understanding the spatial politics of conditions such as these, according to David Harvey (1995), requires a different optic than the usual (binaristic) appeals to center and periphery in Marxist critiques of imperialism. Specifically, how are we to make sense of globalization and culture in such a way that does not keep us locked in the enclosure of the nation-state, which has never been the only meaningful spatial unit of capitalism much less of "culture," and yet recognize that massive inequalities and power differentials (which do continue to break down along the North/South axis in many, if not all, respects) characterize the system? Another way to put this question, given my narrower focus here, is: can we imagine culture outside of "possessive nationalism" and still effectively contribute to a resistance to global power inequalities? Given this dual goal, perhaps the best way to come to terms with global culture is by analogy with labor and its "socialization," one of the concepts through which Marx theorized articulation-in-difference: the combination of many different labors into one. Where actual conditions of mixture and interdependence are mystified and diverted toward exclusive ownership under capitalism, socialization provides an alternative model for understanding human relations: cultural and social, as well as economic.

III The Globe's Shakespeare

I indicated in the last section that the Globe Trust's deployment of "Shakespeare" appears to have been the sign under which a certain "colonization" of Southwark has taken place, just as in an earlier moment, "Shakespeare" had been obliged to play a role in the British imperial project. However, whereas in the earlier case "Shakespeare" was confidently represented as a specifically "English" (or British) export, a cultural sign of "universal value" through which the "civilizing mission" of Britain was justified to other places, in the latter case, the justification of the "universal value" of "Shakespeare" seemingly comes *from* elsewhere *to* Britain: the United States and Japan, for example, as "outsiders" buy into the Globe. This state of affairs could be an occasion for outcry about "Britain's" loss of control over its "own" heritage. However, as John Drakakis (1988) rightly argues, this story in *both* its moments is largely the story of elites, of those who have deployed "Shakespeare" as a marker in a game of signifying "high" cultural value, largely to secure – consciously or not – their own interests. Sorrow for the "British" elites who have lost monopoly control of the Shakespeare industry is not really in order; as Raymond Williams observed of such dynamics of possession in another context: "it is a deep and persistent illusion to suppose that time confers on these familiar processes of acquisition an innocence which can be contrasted with the ruthlessness of subsequent stages of the same essential drives . . . If we have humanity to spare, it is better directed to the unregarded men who were making and working . . . in any event . . . under the old owners and the new" (1973: 50). To undermine this misplaced reverence for possession (and possessors), Judith Williamson has proposed a shift from an ideology of "belongings" to one of "belonging" – of recognized interdependence and conscious collective effort to a common good (1988: 205–7). However, even Williamson seems to imagine this "belonging" as predicated only on living in, working in and "loving" a particular place (her example is London) (1988: 206); I have been trying to indicate, alternatively, that interconnectedness is global, and has to be theorized as such. As Fredric Jameson has so evocatively observed, as capitalism develops, one of its effects is that "the truth of . . . experience no longer coincides with the place in which it takes place" (1988: 349). To get at this "truth" requires more than attention to *a* place, however loving.

Indeed, for people to free themselves from the tyranny of the commodity form, especially of labor as a commodity (as Williamson advocates) requires, according to Marx, a recognition of social interdependence which exceeds both the locality and the nation-state; he called this interconnection the "socialization of labor." Capital renders this "socialization" possible – but only in a degraded form, turned to the control and interests of private owners of capital rather than to everyone. As Ernest Mandel explains:

> [The] jobs [of workers in the capitalist mode of production] have become part of a co-operative totality which, potentially, once capitalism has been superseded by the reign of associated producers, will

> open up undreamt of possibilities for the development of individual talents and capacities too, precisely because this high level of objective cooperation of labor immensely widens the general scope of human endeavor and potential self-development . . . In this way too, capitalism prepares the ground for both the real unity of the human race and the real universality of the individual, made materially possible by this objective socialization of labor.
>
> (1990: 946)

On the one hand, then, in the capitalist privileging of "private property" the means of production are held exclusively by a minority who guide production in the interests of capital accumulation rather than social welfare. On the other hand, "socialization" moves toward the pooling of total social labor as a collective resource, potentially to the benefit of everyone. Hence, Mandel observes in the "objective socialization of labor" a "globalization" emerging that is not only the corporate "globalization from above" which fuels the dreams of contemporary capital, but is rather the prospect of a "globalization from below," a set of interconnections among peoples who take charge of themselves and their collective interests.[21] Such interests and dependencies are never merely a "local" matter: pollutants run down stream, raw materials are unevenly distributed, and production decisions made in one site affect the availability of jobs, resources and products in many others. "Socialization," then, is never limited to just one country. It is the general interdependence upon labors of peoples who might be very widely separated indeed. For this reason, it is difficult to imagine any "social" product to be entirely localizable – even "cultural" products.

To take a concrete "cultural" example: from this perspective, how might we imagine "Shakespeare" socially? One strand of Shakespeare criticism has especially suggestive implications for answering this question and rethinking "culture" in terms which destabilize it as an enclosure, an essence and, above all, a possession. Although the Globe Trust asserts confidently that the "Globe" belongs to "Shakespeare," some Shakespeare scholars have been rather less confident that a single-author model is applicable to the body of work that has been assigned that proper name. Many recent critics have indicated the construction of Shakespearean "authority" in modern editorial assumptions and procedures, a process – not incidentally – that is coincident with the construction of "national literatures" to underwrite the cultures of modern nation-states.[22] According to these critics, modern editorial practices tend to disavow the different conception of authorship as well as the plurality of practices and labors that characterized dramatic production on the early modern stage and in the printshop: compositors, prompters, censors, player improvisation and interpolation, and so on. Rather than viewing these agents as contaminating a previously pure Shakespearean script, these critics view the whole field of production as part of the texting in a time when possessive individualist authorship was only emergent. By putting the emphasis on the whole range of labors of which a text is an effect, rather than the individual genius of its nominal author, this criticism demystifies artistic production, and opens the possibility of understanding it as a social, rather than an individual, product. When examined in a global context, however, the implications of this criticism are more radical than even its proponents have suggested, since heretofore the play of signification and combination of labors appears magically to stop at the shoreline, crossing neither channel nor ocean. However, once "Shakespeare," or any other cultural nexus, is opened to the play of textuality, not even the formidable power of the state can stop it fully. Deconstructing "Shakepeare," given "his" force as a national icon, willy-nilly deconstructs the nation as well.

An influential strand of "postcolonial" theory has been arguing along these lines, suggesting that "global cities" such as London, too, are contestatory sites, as are the "nations" of which they are "part," and, thus that hybridity, syncretism and creolization are more characteristic of culture than purity and enclosure.[23] A focus on cultural intermixing and combined labor suggests a rather different understanding of what "Globe" might mean – as well as "Shakespeare" – from that which would emerge in a "heritage" celebration of "England" and "Englishness." I have drawn a parallel between the "decentering of the author" and the "decentering of the nation" to suggest that we might attach proper names to "nation-states" with the same falsely reifying effect that results from attaching them to "authors" and "works." Problematizing "authority" in early modern studies has been part of a project to historicize (and critique) "individualism" and "property" – concepts which have been of profound importance to the development of the modern nation-state, predicated as it is on the property of each "individual" in his own person and on the state protection of private property secured by those individuals.[24] It stands to reason, then, that the Shakespearean criticism which has focused on the "author" question, might have something to tell us about the "nation" as well. Just as the myth of authority serves certain interests, and reinforces (while mystifying) certain social relations, so, too, does the myth of the "nation." Specifically, just as the myth of authority requires a disavowal of the multiple labors involved in the production and circulation of texts, so, too, does the myth of nationhood require a disavowal of the multiple and (seemingly) "extraneous" labors and forces producing the nation, which purports to be an essence underwritten by a unique and independent "culture" (much as the sovereign subject purports to be an essence underwritten by a unique and independent "self").

As Paul Gilroy (1991, 1993) has complained, the problem with notions of purity and possession of culture and nation is not only that they require a misreading of historical production, given the massive interchanges and borrowings necessary to any cultural formation, but also that such mythical notions of purity are mobilized to racist and exclusionist ends. In resistance to such projects he has proposed not only new spaces of analysis, such as the Black Atlantic, but also, at the same time, deconstructed spaces such as the nation-state, long taken for granted as the containers of "authentic" cultures, with distinctive, self-generated "internal" development. For Gilroy and like-minded critics, homogeneity and autochthony are the products of a disavowal of the "movement and mediation" of which all cultures are effects (Gilroy 1993: 19). In the case of Shakespeare, old and new-historicist scholarship alike has already indicated that "Shakespeare's" plays were cobbled together from orts and fragments of other texts, many from places other than England – from continental and classical stories, the work of colleagues and other plays – and yet we describe the work to be "his" and – against all the evidence, like tea and sugar – to be somehow "English" through and through. As we have seen, however, even *Henry V*, an example of the ostensibly most "English" of the Shakespearean genres, the histories, speaks "French" more often than it is willing to admit – and it accumulates various other formal, linguistic and literary debts as well, not the least being the truly enormous number of labors required to free up labor for dramatic production in the first place. To these conditions at the remote origin, we must add as well the transformations in time and space of "Shakespeare" as "he" travels.[25] Given the extravagant syncretism of the cultural matrix we call "Shakespeare" – and the language in which "he" wrote – perhaps we might rethink not only the ascription of authorial possession but also the coherence of the nation it helps underwrite. In 1581, Elizabeth balanced the crown budget for the first time in her reign with pirated "Spanish" gold extracted by forced "Indian" labor from mines in the

Americas.[26] By these means, she stabilized the "English" economy, and made joint-stock investments with long-term consequences for "its" trade development. To leave the massive anonymous labors of those miners out of "English" history is to perpetuate the disavowal of interdependencies which underwrites "Englishness." To include them, however, explodes "Englishness" as it has been understood heretofore, even when it has been conceded to be a construct, since I am asserting that as a construct it is not – cannot be – merely "local."

I am suggesting something more here than the now commonplace (post)structuralist tenet that there can be no "self" without an "other," that we can only know the "English" by difference (that is, as not-French, not-American, not-Irish), and thus that the trace of the other is part of "Englishness," irreducibly necessary to its constitution. My point is, in addition, a rather old-fashioned materialist one: that there could have been no "Shakespeare" without a vast multiplicity of labors – including cultural and linguistic practices – not all of which are localizable in "England." In urging the broadest possible view of such interconnections, I am not suggesting that "difference" has no meaning – to the contrary, variations will be all the more evident when we understand them as an effect of geographically and historically specific combinations of globally shared elements and forces. Culture is not an enclosure, or a one-way street, but a network of mutual dependencies. It is never simply "local." Anthony Giddens uses the term "disembedding" to describe the " 'lifting out' of social relations from local contexts of interaction and their restructuring across indefinite spans of time–space" (1990: 21). It is linked in his understanding to "globalization," or "the intensification of worldwide social relations which link distant localities in such a way that local happenings are shaped by events occurring many miles away and vice versa" (1990: 64). In his model, there is never simply homogenization, because the nexus of cultural elements will be different in different locations, even if there are many shared elements in the entire cultural field. However, there is never simply a "local" culture either because pressures and intermixtures exerted from "elsewhere" always play roles in the "local" site – at least since the emergence of modernity. Whether we are talking about "Shakespeare's Globe," or *Henry V*, or "English," the effects of those "disembedded" forces can be traced. Hence, it is imperative, I am suggesting, that we learn to think other spaces besides the nation-state.

It is imperative to do so because the "possessive individualisms" of nation-states with armies (and other cudgels, ideological and economic) to support them make it possible for them to claim creolized cultures as "their" own while relegating others to the status of borrowers or derivatives, excluded or marginalized. How best to resist this theft-and-imposition dynamic remains an open question. My task in this essay has been simply to indicate that exclusion and oppression have been the culprits in this dynamic, not mixture and interconnection, though the latter are often demonized, not only on the Right, but also on the Left as critics attempt to "reclaim" distinct cultures of/for the oppressed. The "socialization" of culture, I have argued, suggests a different approach.

Against a possessivist and exclusivist view of language, culture and nation, C. L. R. James, devoted as he was to a Marxist internationalism, once observed: "No account of Western civilisation could leave out the names of Toussaint L'Ouverture, Alexander Hamilton, Alexander Dumas (the father), Leconte Delisle, José Maria de Heredia, Marcus Garvey, René Maran, Saint-John Perse, Aimé Césaire, George Padmore, Frantz Fanon . . . and Alejo Carpentier" (1980: 190). By inserting "others" into "its" cultural heritage James effectively deconstructs "Western" presumption. Hurling together cultural and revolutionary heroes of the Americas, Europe and Africa, he reminds us that so-called "Western history" and "culture" were built by countless peoples who are excluded from them, and calls into question the very concept of "the West" as ordinarily conceived. Rethinking cultural signs and the uses to which they are put is part of this process, rendering "Shakespeare's Globe" a matter of global consequence.

What will happen now in a world in which Shakespeare's work is circulated to, and appropriated by, nations and institutions with more (as well as less) global clout than Britain? One possibility is a turn to "heritage" (Worsthorne) and/or humanist universalism (Wanamaker) to defend Britain's claim to "its" national poet on the grounds of the value he has for human kind as a whole; another will be the displacement of the nation in favor of a corporate transnationalism which draws on the best of each to ornament global capital's elites; another option, however, would be not to "humanize" or "corporatize" Shakespeare, but rather to *socialize* him, that is, to make him the globe's as James might do: by recognizing not only the numerous hands and labors that participated in the production of the plays that bear his name, but also the numerous ostensibly "alien" hands, voices and labors which helped produce the language and nation-state which Shakespeare's name has been called upon so often to underwrite. At such a time, everyone might be seen to have a "legitimate" claim to share in the fruits of that labor, not just the few. Then, and only then, will we have not merely "Shakespeare's Globe," but, truly, the globe's Shakespeare.

Notes

I would like to thank the various colleagues who have helped shape this essay (though, of course, not always just as they might have liked): Dympna Callaghan, Eric Cheyfitz, Margreta de Grazia, John Elliot, Jean Howard, Peter Hulme, Rosemary Kegl, Brian McCord, Bill Sherman and Scott Shershow.

1 In so-called "strong globalization" (Lazarus 1999) theses, in (and outside of) Marxism, the nation-state is viewed as depleted or imperiled (e.g. Dirlik 1994 , Jameson 1991, Miyoshi 1993), while other theorizations, especially among Marxists (e.g. Ahmad 1992, Brennan 1997, Smith 1997), are more skeptical about the progress – and deleterious impact on the (metropolitan) nation-states – of "globalization," arguing that the states of the North still maintain a neo-imperial stronghold on the states of the South (with destructive implications for "cultures" of the latter as well as the global economy).
2 I deploy the phrase "possessive nationalism" in analogy with "possessive individualism" as theorized by C. B. Macpherson (1964).
3 All citations attributed to the promotional literature are culled from brochures published for the 1997 season: "Opening Season" and "Shakespeare's Globe Exhibition."
4 John Gillies (1994) has discussed the "globe"/"world" link, as well as the connection between theater and cosmography in *Shakespeare and the Geography of Difference*. In addition, an interesting collection of recent essays takes up the relationship of Shakespeare to (trans)national culture; see John Joughin (ed.), *Shakespeare and National Culture* (1997). The phrase "colonizing the mind" derives from N'gugi wa Thiong'o, who has argued that "the domination of a people's language by the languages of the colonizing nations was crucial to the domination of the mental universe of the colonized" (1994: 442). For a discussion of the role of "Shakespeare" and other literary texts in such colonization, see Viswanathan (1989). Also see the essays collected in Loomba and Orkin (eds) (1998) for ensuing "appropriations" and counter-claims.
5 By the "globe's Shakespeare" I mean to suggest something more than that numerous Shakespeares have been fashioned in different places around the globe, as has been tracked, for example, in books and articles by Orkin (1987), Bristol (1990), Kennedy (ed.) (1993), Hattaway et al. (eds) (1994), Zhang (1996), Trivedi (1996) and Loomba (1997). I am interested as well in "Shakespeare" as always already "global" – an effect of conditions of possibility and forces that are not localizable within the borders of "England."

6 See, for example, Sinfield (1992), chap. 6. These "nationalistic" claims have co-existed with observations about the "ambivalence" of the play toward Henry as a character, warfare as a means of achieving nationalist ends, or even about "power" itself. See McEachern (1996), chap. 3.
7 The Rhodes version (as reported by Worsthorne) is: "to be born English is to win the lottery of life."
8 This sentence is culled from the pages of an epistolary debate between Worsthorne and Howe, written while the pair were making a Channel 4 documentary "England, my England," a "programme about Britishness" according to the *Guardian*, which ran the feature, co-authored by Worsthorne and Howe, under the title "What is a true Brit? Should Britishness be redefined to recognize black immigration?"
9 Voloshinov (1973) reads "accent" (in a broad sense of multiple uses of the "same" language) as marking the "struggle in language" and its irreducible polyvocality (see pp. 17–24). I take this struggle to include more (e.g. gender, race, in particular, though not exhaustively) than the "class" accent on which Voloshinov focuses.
10 Benedict Anderson emphasizes this in *Imagined Communities*, citing Ernest Renan: "Or l'essence d'une nation est que tous les individus aient beaucoup de choses en commun, et aussi que tous aient oublie bien des choses" (1991: 6). "Sanctioned ignorance" is the phrase Gayatri Chakravorty Spivak uses to describe this forgetfulness (and ongoing failure to see) in a specifically (neo)imperial context (1988: 291).
11 For a discussion of the myth of Shakespeare as the origin of "proper" English, see Holderness and Murphy (1997).
12 The postwar scene in Britain has been described in a number of books, of which I will name here a few that focus in particular on cultural matters: Chun (1993), Dworkin (1997), Hall (1988), Sinfield (1989).
13 The *New York Times* described the British government's response to Wanamaker's plans as "apathy" (Obituary, 1993); the *Los Angeles Times* reported that he had to overcome "bureaucratic obstacles and occasional hostility," and quoted Wanamaker as attributing these problems to his ethnicity: "because I am an American, they assumed I was going to create a Disneyland or that I was interested in property development and personal profit" (Folkart 1993).
14 Drakakis observes this "colonial" theme in the Globe project, and situates it not only in the "cultural imperialism" of investors such as Leona and Harry Helmsley (US real-estate magnates), but also in British elites, custodians of "high culture," who eventually threw in their lot with the Globe Trust (1988: 32).
15 A Marxist critique of Wanamaker is, of course, complicated by his own evident leftward leanings, which led to his black-listing in the United States in the 1950s, and migration to Britain for stage work, which put him into contact with the network which would later facilitate his attempt to get the Globe project off the ground.

16 David Harvey (1995) provides a good basic description of the commonly cited forces of "globalization" (or, as he prefers, "uneven spatio-temporal development") in "Globalization in Question."
17 The *Daily Telegraph* even reported that the construction of the Globe in London was slowed because the builders of the Tokyo "Elizabethan village" purchased so much "English Oak" that "supplies . . . dried up" and were unavailable for Shakespeare's Globe (Obituary, 1993).
18 Judith Williamson (1986) has discussed the ideological implications of the "exotic" as a Western consumer category in "Woman is an Island."
19 On the complexity of contemporary "uneven-ness" of capital, see McIntyre (1992).
20 These figures are derived from the UN *Human Development Report 1994*. For a discussion of globalization with particular emphasis on world-scale inequality as described by this report, see Robinson (1996).
21 On "globalization from below," see Brecher and Costello (1994).
22 See, for example, Masten (1997), Stallybrass and de Grazia (1993), de Grazia (1991), Orgel (1988).
23 See, for example, King (1990).
24 See note 1 above.
25 For a discussion of this "travel" in the case of a theoretical text, see "Traveling Theory" in Said (1983).
26 On Elizabeth's judicious use of plunder, see Scott (1968), chap. IV.

10

The Shakespeare film and the Americanization of culture

DENISE ALBANESE

I

With its pre-millennial award for Best Picture to John Madden's *Shakespeare in Love*, the Motion Picture Academy of America seems to have made it official: Shakespeare and film have finally reached a rapprochement. Indeed, scarcely a month passes without a new Shakespeare-oriented project's being scheduled or publicized. Kenneth Branagh, already responsible for three films, has made a deal with Intermedia Films to produce several plays for cinematic distribution, with each production not to exceed an hour and a half in running time; a version of *The Taming of the Shrew*, *Ten Things I Hate About You*, was released in the spring of 1999; and Julie Taymor, director of *The Lion King* on Broadway, has filmed a *Titus Andronicus* that is, according to the April 1999 issue of *Vanity Fair*, "a triumph of avant-garde gore." Although as recently as 1984 Richard Burton stated that Shakespeare films were "box office poison," on this evidence, at least, it appears they have turned into something more widely and commercially palatable (quoted in Levine 1988: 53).

But before joining in the general wonderment at this cinematic wealth, we would do well to ask the nature of the phenomenon we're considering. Does the undeniable increase in the number of films indicate a burgeoning public gusto for Shakespeare, as my speculation about commercial viability seems to suggest? Or does the fact of these films demand juxtaposing box-office appeal with the economic and ideological conditions that might bring together Shakespeare on the one hand, and the film industry – particularly the US film industry – on the other? After all, the production agendas of the cinema can scarcely be modeled by the simple law of supply and demand, even given Hollywood's dubious penchant for turning yesterday's success into today's formula, and the handy fact that Shakespeare's scripts are essentially in the public domain (and so comparatively quick and cheap to develop). Given Burton's remark, it is an irony that Shakespeare has a legible place in the tense priorities of commodity culture, where his name stands as a free-floating signifier for quality – consider Terence Hawkes's (1992) resonant "meaning by Shakespeare."[1] (As I write, I have before me a shopping bag from Trader Joe's, a chain of food stores, which features Shakespeare's visage – eyes blocked out, the better to pretend to disguise him – and the legend "A famous name we cannot reveal" over a narrative about its high-quality private-label goods.) Even if a given Shakespeare film is not a box-office success, then, the prestige of involvement might compensate filmmakers and subsidizing producers for any unsatisfactory profit margins.

To talk of immaterial compensation, however, is necessarily to engage with cinema's particular flexibility as a site of ideological production, for which, albeit in a more limited register, Hollywood has been demonized by social critics who deem mass representations the agents of moral collapse. Such critics have also been notable among those bemoaning the apparent eclipse of Shakespeare by mass culture in the Academy: witness the media furor that occurred when Georgetown University ceased requiring English majors to take a course in Shakespeare. The many excoriations of what was, after all, only a local curricular decision, one already quietly adopted by many colleges, indicates that in public discourse Shakespeare represents stable literary (and, by extension, ideological) values currently under siege because of academic practice, which mirrors the country's irresponsible fascination with Hollywood, among other forbidden objects (Innerst 1997).[2] Given the general esteem in which *Shakespeare in Love* has been held, it is thus nicely ironic that a series of intensely familiar propositions about Shakespeare-as-author is being purveyed by a medium – film – presumed antithetical to the very values Shakespeare has been held to embody.

This conjuncture of events suggests that the Shakespeare film explosion of the 1990s is uniquely well positioned to take the heat off the culture industry for its putative excesses, and incidentally to repair the defects of the fall – by which I mean not only recent acts of apostasy in the Academy, but potentially also the lack of enthusiasm towards Shakespeare felt by much of the US population. By this token, the Shakespeare film operates as a sugar-coated pill for the masses, as well as a loss-leader for the accountants. While such considerations probably are pertinent to the bardolatrous cinematic glut, I'd like to get at the issue another way: by examining the category "Shakespeare film" itself. Behind its connotative front it has worked as a highly interested counter in recent discussions of the films, demanding nothing so much as acquiescence with the happy fact of proliferation. But should the adaptation of *Shrew*, for instance, which like *Clueless*'s version of *Emma* is translated to the demotic of a modern US high school, be considered categorically indistinguishable from Taymor's production, featuring the much lauded and classically trained Anthony Hopkins as Titus, and located in a postmodern Roman *mise en scène* that suggests Jarman's *Edward II* in its temporal indiscriminacy? Is it enough that mall movie and art cinema have the apparition of Shakespeare in common for us to forget all the differences in direction, style, language, and cast – not to mention budget, production, and distribution – that would mark them as importantly distinct? Indeed, as I have argued, the contrary. Just as reading Kurosawa's *Throne of Blood* and *Ran* as evidence of Shakespeare's infinite translatability elides what is *not* Shakespearean in Kurosawa's Japanese films, so the false genre called "the Shakespeare film" seems to insist on the stability of Shakespeare as a sign, and on the transparency of the film industry as a screen upon which Shakespeare is projected. In the process, what is occluded is the fact that the films, precisely *as* films, constitute a referendum on Shakespeare's value at the end of the twentieth century.

Lawrence Levine has suggested that Shakespeare was the object of one such referendum at the beginning of this century, when the formation of discourses of the "highbrow" and the "lowbrow," the elite and the mass-cultural form, first came into play (Levine 1988). Given the pervasiveness of mass culture, that by now reflexive division of the cultural field is all but exhausted as an analytic, even as the economic relations that brought the division its material potency continue to mutate. Although most US subjects experience a mixture of resistance toward and intimidation by Shakespeare, the alienated reading and writing practices by which they come to his texts are less indicative of the inhibiting force of the elite as a category than an indictment of educational fantasies about accessibility, high literacy, and upward mobility. At any rate, the social transformations typical of industrialized modernity have rendered Shakespeare a "tutelary deity" (Bristol 1990: 19) in the US classroom (particularly at the secondary level) and so in the US imaginary, within a more general and idealist dispensation that deems the study of literature an enabling form of distinction. The recent cinematic phenomenon with which I'm concerned, however, represents a struggle over Shakespeare's place in US culture that is occurring most importantly outside academic circles. While there has been much crucial work scrutinizing the role Shakespeare is asked to play in hegemonic formations, its direct effect on public discourse in the United States is at best hard to assess: academics surely do not commission, fund, or motivate Shakespeare films, and far too often they do not even conceptualize such films as economic, as opposed to ideological, agents (e.g. Boose and Burt [eds] 1997).

What is not hard to assess, however, is the increasing dominance of the market in arbitrating questions of value capitalism was once content not to control directly. In such a regime, it may not be sufficient to have Shakespeare serve as a loss leader. Witness the film industry's targeting the education system, a market thus far dominated by the extremely expensive BBC/Time-Life video releases of the 1970s and 1980s. Publicity materials for Al Pacino's *Looking for Richard* – a film whose box-office revenues were not particularly impressive – evince Hollywood's efforts to expand its audience (and in some sense to supplement, even supplant trained educators) by offering to provide exercises to be used in class along with a video of the film. That Hollywood has begun its march on such heretofore neglected arenas suggests the way to characterize the referendum for which the films constitute effective evidence: as a contest between increasingly triumphal market forces on the one hand, and literature as a regressive formation exempt from direct market instrumentality on the other. While such regressive formations around the esthetic tend to dominate in the US imaginary – witness the Georgetown controversy – that such a struggle is being staged in the cinematic forum changes the questions, and makes the commodity status of filmed Shakespeare itself both a register of the debate and a marker of the terms of success, especially given the increasingly global cinematic market that extends from the United States outwards.

Hence my interest in two 1996 productions: Kenneth Branagh's *Hamlet* and Baz Luhrmann's *William Shakespeare's Romeo and Juliet*, in distribution, in the United States and elsewhere, at approximately the same time. Their simultaneity on the one hand, and their marked differences as filmed commodities on the other, make it possible to consider them as embodiments of the struggle over Shakespeare I've described. On the one hand, Kenneth Branagh's lavish and prestigious film embodies an increasingly regressive notion of cultural capital that is, in the United States and rather like Branagh himself, associated with the literary legacy of Great Britain. In this regressive dispensation, the obvious value of *Hamlet* demands that it be filmed with reverence, and that purely economic considerations take a back seat to creating a cinematic canon. On the other, Baz Luhrmann's film (like *Shakespeare in Love*) gives Americans a Shakespeare without tears – a Shakespeare, that is, devoid of the conventional trappings of "quality cinema" and an elite theatrical tradition. The text's domestication to the esthetics of US-derived mass media signals the consonance between Shakespeare and the economic agendas of cinematic commodity culture. In each case, a proposal about Shakespeare, either as burnished (and imported) cultural good, or else as locus of excitement and irony already naturalized to the United States, informs and is subtended by the test of the market. As I have suggested, what is at stake is a new national articulation around Shakespeare.

The comparative analysis that follows represents only a gesture at the specific financial underpinnings of the two films. A more comprehensive study of the Shakespeare film in United States, and ultimately in global commodity culture, would take seriously the fiscal maneuvers necessary to bring any Shakespearean text to the screen: it would remember how both the market for Shakespeare films, and all questions of funding, are changing historical phenomena, and recognize the increasing importance of the United States for all cinematic productions; it would factor in the role of transnational production coalitions in attempts to make niche-marketed cinema viable; it would learn more about how budgets are secured in relation to casting decisions; it would study how distribution deals are crafted in relation to larger studios, with the increasingly global market for cinema in mind; it would investigate whether and how video revenues are projected and factored in, in advance of production; finally, it would read all local phenomena in the light of changing global trade policies (e.g. GATT) concerning film as a cultural product.

Of course, the fiscal practices of the film industry offer but a start at understanding the larger business of Shakespeare – the financial resources that go into reproducing, publishing, disseminating, and professing the poems and plays, dispersed over a variety of practices and institutions – that make it possible for us to continue to debate his significance. Studying these quite literally material aspects of the

Shakespeare industry would reveal at least as much about his shifting place in the United States in these peri-millennial years as any curriculum controversy. And, if one takes Terence Hawkes's hint that "Bardbiz [is] merely the continuation of American foreign policy by other means" (1992: 153), such revelations might, like Hollywood itself, have more than local, and more than ideological, influence.

II

My point of departure concerning recent film versions of the plays is the naturalistic narrative lines along which they have mostly been constructed. As James L. Loehlin has usefully indicated, "[t]he realist Shakespeare film is characterized by the sort of mid-range naturalistic acting, cinematography and editing that is used in most Hollywood films. The characters are presented as "real people," in plausible make-up and costumes, and the film relates the narrative straightforwardly, without calling attention to the medium" (Loehlin 1997: 67). While earlier films, such as Olivier's *Henry V* and *Hamlet*, invoke the conventions of the stage for the sound set (or else those of art film as art, via highly self-conscious camera work), many Shakespeare-inflected films since then seem to have accepted that film is a "natural" medium for presenting the plays, debates about adaptations notwithstanding (e.g. Bulman and Coursen [eds] 1988; Davies and Wells [eds] 1994). Shakespeare films may not be able to count on the ordinariness of television, the sense, according to Graham Holderness, of a medium completely interpenetrated with everyday life, present almost by default (Holderness 1988a: 174–9). Nevertheless, like most films in distribution, such Shakespearean productions put a semblance of the ordinary on offer – even if a subset of the audience demands that those watching a Shakespeare movie follow the protocols of theater, rather than movie-going. Indeed, that some spectators approached Branagh's *Hamlet* with the same reverence they would bestow on a live performance indicates the connection to be found between cinematic realism and correspondingly "ordinary" (which is to say conventional), even retrograde, propositions about the intrinsic value of the Shakespearean scripts on which these realist Shakespeares are based. In this sense, the disposition toward Shakespeare undergirding the category of "Shakespeare film" which I want to call into question seems most in operation when the audience conventions that hold true for film in general are *not* – when, that is, audiences expect Shakespeare films to be special cases of the cinema.

Kenneth Branagh's *Hamlet*, which follows on his film debut as *Henry V* (1989) and his subsequent production of *Much Ado About Nothing* (1993), will be my primary evidence for this case. The two earlier films have clearly established Branagh as the cinematic successor to Laurence Olivier – which is to say as the crossover actor, the classically trained British star who when he moves from stage to sound set carries along with him the prestige both of originary country and elite genre, and who in a US context therefore operates as a guarantor of quality cinema. But however much the first films marked Branagh as a precocious and prematurely autobiographical phenomenon in the United States, neither *Henry* nor *Much Ado* signifies sufficiently as a canonical masterpiece. Not so with *Hamlet*, the consecrated vehicle for the reproduction of an influential model of male subjectivity, and the presumable center of the Shakespearean canon in the public imaginary, both here and abroad.

Not surprisingly, the cultural importance generally ascribed to this text, which is sustained by cinematic as well as theatrical and critical history, has left ample trace on Branagh's film. His *Hamlet* is innovative in detail; nevertheless, it reveals Branagh's fidelity to modes of representation that are both reactionary in ideological terms and a contradiction in terms of the market for Hollywood-inflected realist cinema, to which it owes its primary esthetic allegiance. Clearly, Branagh's at times gratuitous casting reveals his investment in the nexus of value that is the Hollywood star system: witness the number of big-name American actors in minor parts, who are as likely there to secure funding as to represent the universality of the Shakespearean dispensation. Moreover, Branagh's directing serves to focus audience attention on his own performance, a performance that offers many instances of what Theodor Adorno has called regressive fetishization – moments, that is, whose only cogency comes from their nature as set pieces designed to generate a momentary affective response, rather than from their integral relation to a sustained narrative, experience, or interpretation of the play (Adorno 1978).

Perhaps the most egregious instance of such a set piece occurs as Hamlet looks at Fortinbras's troops arrayed against the Polacks. When the movie was on theatrical release, it was the last scene before a much anticipated intermission. With its swelling music, slowly craned camera rising up and up and framing Hamlet against a sea of men (a perhaps deliberate echo of the rousing patriotism of the Crispin's day speech in Branagh's more cogent film), the speech might manage to extort sentiment even from a spectator interested in reading the ambiguity of

Hamlet's ever-diminishing form against the triumphalism of the music. The crescendo that accompanies "My thoughts be bloody or be nothing worth!" propelled viewers into the light of the auditorium, having halted the action by implying that Hamlet's meandering quest for revenge has finally crystalized into resolve. When the lights were low again, however, that impetus was revealed (as the fidelity to script must inevitably reveal it) as purely sensational, beholden (like the chandelier-swinging, or the visually impressive yet illogically simultaneous eruption of Fortinbras's soldiers from behind the mirrored doors whose chambers don't communicate with one another) to a momentary cinematic effect that is for Adorno the sign of Hollywood's power to imprint the commodity esthetics of mass culture on all comers, especially reproductions of the classics.

Yet however much his direction reflects the values of mainstream Hollywood cinema, Branagh's much remarked upon insistence that his *Hamlet* be filmed from an uncut script militates against the logic of the film market, which increasingly demands action-packed, and hence export-friendly, products rather than magniloquent four-hour epics. On the evidence of Branagh's practice, Shakespeare's *Hamlet* is a sign of exceeding preciousness: hence the play around the monumental inscription of the dead king's name, especially at the end of the movie. Despite the strong weight of performance practice throughout history, for Branagh not one word of the play can be lost without peril. Nor, apparently, can inference or recitation pass without being inserted into the cinematic plenum, without, that is, being illustrated: thus the movie provides scenes from the fall of Troy, the panic of Hecuba, the private recollections of Ophelia. That at times the film seems to illustrate *Hamlet*'s narrative moments emphasizes its author's position as a *literary* icon, rather than, say, purely as a dramatist.

Thus Branagh's apparently perverse – and apparently counter-productive – notion of copiousness is not so innocent of market logic after all, if by that phrase one signifies an appeal to the niche occupied by fairly literate fans of cinematic adaptations of nineteenth-century novels, the presumable addressees for the "Shakespeare film" in all its unreconstructed glory. The conservative amplitude of the script, for instance, is well served by the seeming anachronism of its setting in nineteenth-century Europe, with Blenheim Palace made to stand in for Elsinore. In this regard, Branagh's *Hamlet* approximates the period and style of Masterpiece Theater and Merchant–Ivory productions, aligns itself with them in interpellating a US audience interested in, and comfortable with, British-inflected representations of texts from the distant – but not too distant – past. Given the attention to luxurious settings and interiors that characterizes these films, this time before might be called the upholstered past, made for ease and relaxation, a past that is domesticated, effortlessly knowable. In Branagh's view of *Hamlet*, the nineteenth-century setting enables the audience to recognize a cultural fantasy of history and Shakespeare both as all-inclusive: via the liberal and anachronistic palliative of color-blind casting, Branagh neutralizes the historical imbrication of the nineteenth-century nation-state in imperialist formations, and turns the court of Elsinore into a fiction of millennial diversity.[3] (That actors of color are given comparatively few speaking parts reveals the impoverishment of this dispensation.)

Like the productions of the BBC and Merchant–Ivory I've mentioned, indeed, like *Shakespeare in Love*, Branagh's *Hamlet* therefore participates in a belated discourse of bourgeois prestige, where movie attendance demands, at the very least, a nodding acquaintance with a prior tradition of high (verbal) literacy, a competence entirely befitting the conservatism of Branagh's interpretation itself, despite his articulated desire to render Shakespeare accessible to all. If dominant cultural formations around the pre-eminence of the esthetic artifact work to maintain their hold through reproduction, then this *Hamlet*, like some of the other films to have appeared recently, serves to sustain elitism in the apparently paradoxical form of a mass cultural artifact. The splendors of the *mise en scène* Branagh has deployed provide a precise counterpart for the film's status as a visual rendition of traditional literary capital, and thus, it seems, an effective reassurance to recent polemicists that Shakespeare is still a locus of familiar value.

And yet this traditional capital is a form of wealth not highly valued by the largest segments of the current market, among them the youth market, at whom several of the forthcoming Shakespeare films are aimed. Branagh's difficulty in getting the film funded – and the promise, recorded in his introduction to the filming diary for *Hamlet*, to cut it drastically for video distribution – betray a recurrence of the sentiment with which I began: Shakespeare and the movies don't mix (Branagh 1996a: xiv). Given his film's grosses in cinematic release, it seems that Branagh's attempt to revivify the discourse of humanistic cultural capital is one his distributor, Castle Rock Entertainment, might well have found less than economically compelling.[4] The discourse that ratifies *Hamlet* is too attentive to an audience doomed to recede as the exchange value of a specific model of high literacy recedes to succeed in any but the niche market I have described. Branagh's *Hamlet* might via its own auteur's efforts propose a Shakespeare recognizable, even appealing, to those who opposed Georgetown's decision to cease requiring a course devoted to the author. Indeed, it might even be considered as an interesting supplement by the film industry to the perceived deficiencies of higher education – be read, that is, as evidence that the market has become interested in re-securing cultural dominants perceived to be under siege, as I indicated in connection with *Looking for Richard* earlier in this chapter. But in itself the film can only account for the value of a cultural good to those who, in one form or another, are already disposed to ascribe value to that good. Branagh's deal with Intermedia Films means that he will surely continue to make "Shakespeare films": indeed, it is unlikely so prominent and useful a cultural entrepreneur could disappear from the scene, especially given the comparative profitability of both *Henry V* and *Much Ado About Nothing*. But restricting his future releases to ninety minutes or less indicates the relative failure of his grandiose and marmoreal comprehensiveness, and of the insolvency of bourgeois Shakespeare at the end of the twentieth century.

III

Branagh's bourgeois Shakespeare is, at base, recognizable as the Shakespeare of residual Anglophilia. When he claims that "the man [Shakespeare] is for everyone" – and then undergirds that claim by prominently featuring US comedians like Billy Crystal and Robin Williams – his directorial broad-mindedness turns the film itself into a spectacle of postimperial British largesse eager to extend itself ever further into the US imaginary.[5] But is Shakespeare still Britain's to control, especially as a cinematic commodity? Consider in response Baz Luhrmann's brilliantly polished, exciting, and troubling *William Shakespeare's Romeo and Juliet*, whose Hollywood energy cannot but stand in stark contrast to Branagh's more stately, more stereotypically British, film. Set in a fictive and rundown Verona Beach but filmed comparatively cheaply in an economically depressed Mexico City (and jointly produced by companies in Australia and Canada as well as the United States), *Romeo and Juliet* offers a siting of Shakespeare more appropriate for, and symptomatic of, the neocolonialism of the global youth market that emanates from the United States outwards. As most readers might suspect, Luhrmann's film has proven far more profitable than Branagh's: approximately two-thirds of its budget of $14.5 million was recouped in its opening weekend in the United States. Indeed, that the

Internet Movie Data Base provides some indication of European grosses, and documents rental revenues in excess of $22 million, attests to the fact that Luhrmann's movie has been positioned as something of a phenomenon.

Some of the reasons for its comparative success are not far to seek. Luhrmann's direction clearly locates *Romeo and Juliet* in cinematic, rather than literary, history (it alludes to Hollywood westerns in the brawls between Montague and Capulet, for example) in more structurally and thematically relevant ways than does Branagh's film. And the MTV-esque aspects of the editing, the soundtracks, and the movie's fashionable costuming are obvious components of its success, insofar as they already indicate the movie's exuberant capitalization on the prevalent mass esthetics of that global youth market.

Much more could be said about how the film reworks as well as exploits the codes of mass cinema; but this kind of attention obscures how the film functions as a commodity, how it stokes mainstream desires while apparently wearing its "Shakespeare" with a radical difference. Particularly striking is the way the film glamorizes its essentially conservative invocation of racial, ethnic, and gender diversity. Unlike *Hamlet*, *Romeo and Juliet* has major parts played by actors whose non-whiteness is significantly foregrounded; however, the way in which they are exoticized resonates better with US policy retrenchments around affirmative action and minority rights in the post-Reagan years than with any genuinely progressive casting agenda. Despite the possibility that Leonardo DiCaprio functions as an object of attraction across genders, it is Mercutio – played by Harold Perrineau, an African-American actor – who is assigned sole responsibility for any homoerotic subtext in his relationship to Romeo.[6] This is shown most spectacularly in his drag performativity, but also revealed by his terminal encounter with Tybalt, whose taunting and enraging query about "consorting" with Romeo is staged so as to become the verbal equivalent of gaybaiting. It is also troubling that a character played by a black actor is additionally responsible for illustrating the downside of pharmaceutical stimulation, as his "Queen Mab" speech repositions a potentially inspired poetic fantasy as hallucinatory and incoherent raving. (In contrast, Romeo's poeticizing is shown to be controlled and self-conscious, inscribed in a notebook and then validated as poetic by the uncomprehending plainspokenness of Dash Mihok's Benvolio.)

Even if the obvious collision of raced body and illicit activity is read as a durable figment of the white imaginary, as edited and scored (the music signals "trouble") the scene does not invite a reassessment of its hoary staging of the black junkie so much as pile one form of othering, of outlawry, onto another. Harold Perrineau is an arresting, talented actor; however, like Des'ree, performing at the Capulet ball, or Quindon Tarver, the young choir boy who sings "When Doves Cry," he isn't allowed to steal the film so much as give it piquancy, entertainment value, "color." Similar arguments could also be made concerning John Leguizamo's Tybalt, whose Latin menace, conjoined with his implicit homophobia, are played off against the comparatively decent, tremulous, and Anglo-Saxon-seeming Benvolio; or Paul Sorvino's operatic wife-beating grandee Capulet.[7] In contrast to many of their friends and relatives, the matching complexions of DiCaprio's Romeo and Claire Danes's Juliet suggests young love as a kind of haven for the epidermal elite of North America, caught in a phantasmatic hothouse of untrammeled and exotic passions.

Yet in presenting the ruling houses of Montague and Capulet as competing corporate entities in iconic skyline shots, Luhrmann images that phantasmatically ripe and overdone violence as somehow related to capitalism rather than to blood and family, as in the original, or to race, as its spectacular casting suggests. It is clear enough that capitalism may provide a ready equivalent for the mixture of power, rivalry, and privilege that subtend the original enmity between Montague and Capulet – and, further, that racism and capitalist violence might be fruitfully conjoined. Still, that the competing families are also corporate entities is not, at first glance, of much consequence for the diegesis: obviously, for all of Shakespeare's vaunted ability to offer up structures of feeling for emergent capitalism, he cannot have predicted the particular form of its violence. But if for Luhrmann capitalism seems significant only insofar as it adds to his image repertory, the production of his film cannot escape being embedded in its logic. The looming corporate presences on the skyline of Verona Beach – are they brand names? or, like "Trump," simply twin signs of well-funded egotism? – therefore become my way into an analysis of how the commodity status of this particular Shakespeare film, and a good measure of its appeal, are secured by exploiting the benefits of location. After all, part of the reason Luhrmann chose Mexico City for the setting of this film is that, given the country's recent economic crises, "Everything was for sale" there, as at least one magazine story had it.

Or on sale: the Hollywoodized film industry, like many other Northern enterprises, confronts the comparatively high labor costs of US centers by working in locations where such costs can be kept down. While Toronto is a preferred venue for many film and television ventures that seek a generic metropolis as backdrop, the producers of *William Shakespeare's Romeo and Juliet*, it seems, have followed the lead of other types of industries in looking to the South to minimize production costs and maximize profit, to a place where, by Hollywood standards, everything is for, or on, sale. Michael Denning has remarked in passing that Mexico has long stood as "Hollywood's other"; the Mexico that enables *Romeo and Juliet* to be produced affordably, however, and that the film in turn puts on display, is less purely and mythically primitive, more the secondary and disadvantaged partner in the North American economic relations structured by the shibboleth of the free market and dominated by US-based formations like NAFTA (Denning 1997: 401). Evidence that Mexico is being positioned to function as the neocolonial outpost of its more highly capitalized neighbor to the north may be read in the insistence among reviewers and publicists that the movie's fictional venue be likened to Venice Beach or to Miami – to some place, that is, within the United States. Of course, that the characters speak English might be one argument for the phantasmatic translation; but insofar as having Italians speak English didn't bother Shakespeare, it seems less than convincing here as a reason. Rather, the displacement insists on the ineluctable centrality of the United States as a site for economic and cultural production, with consequences for the movie's positioning of Shakespeare.

The surplus value for *Romeo and Juliet* – its comparative success as a film commodity – that Mexico City makes possible is extracted from the exoticized bodies of performers to whom I've already alluded: Leguizamo's Tybalt and Perrineau's Mercutio, in particular, endow the movie with the stylistic effects of its aspirations to the global postmodern. While this argument cannot engage meaningfully with the actual working conditions under which the movie was made – exactly how, for instance, shooting in Mexico kept costs down – it can at least consider the diegesis as a symbolic guide. In bringing the narrative together with film's status as commodity I want to draw on Marx's theory of surplus value to uncongeal how signification is secured in the manufacture of a cultural good that, like *Romeo and Juliet*, capitalizes on the benefits of an increasingly world-wide production system. It is the "exoticism" of Mexico City itself – the atmospherics provided by its hallucinoid pollution, its monumental statues, totems of Catholic devotion that loom at least as large as the family signs – that makes possible a productive accretion of value around *this* version of Shakespeare. This local color revalorizes *Romeo and Juliet* as a product designated for knowing, and Northern, consumers of postmodern kitsch, ironists toward a system of belief that, exteriorized, acquires status as a marker of style.

Thus the cinematic *mise en scène* reveals a canny sense of how to adapt multiculturalism for stylistic purposes that require no concession to understanding the complexity of racial or ethnic formations, a tendency already borne out by the casting. Consider the movie's proliferation of religious iconography, which constitutes perhaps the most striking element of its visual style, and which is the scenic counterpart of its significantly raced bodies. I have already mentioned the thrilling faux-totalitarianism of the immense religious statues around which action seems to pivot. But the indigenous Catholicism of Mexico has been mined for greater contributions to the look of the movie. The Madonnas, angels, candles, and florid bleeding hearts emblazoned on shirt and chest all serve to index the "passion" to be found in the script, and thus to supplement its suspiciously pallid and Anglicized "star-crossed lovers," whose underplayed performances were widely praised for a realness constituted precisely in relation to the excess (I use the term advisedly) that characterizes the rest of the movie. These iconic elements in their original siting are strongly associated with Latin American devotional practices to be found, presumably, in the very Mexico City where filming took place. In the film, however, they have been deracinated from context and character investment and set loose to signify the mainstreaming of a certain mode of cynical, ironic consumption of global difference.

In a discussion of the way Latin American iconographic material has become transmogrified into trendy knick-knacks, Celeste Olalquiaga notes that such iconography is originally meant to materialize an impalpable, and, indeed, ineffable spiritual experience, whose very "tackiness" becomes an inverted measure of the sublime it records (Olalquiaga 1992: 41–2). Yet even the perspective that passes judgement on artifacts in terms of the decorum of elite art (even when that art is devotional), already presupposes a distancing between assessor and object, a failure to share the framework of devotion and a consequent substitution of a slumming esthetics removed from the emotive intensities of religious practice. As Olalquiaga notes, "Ethnicity and cultural difference have exchanged their intrinsic values for the more extrinsic ones of market interchangeability" (1992: 39). To put it more precisely, in the regime of kitsch, objects associated with specifically non-market rituals of exchange have come to supply cheap commodities, by means of which an ironic sensibility can be secured. In *Romeo and Juliet*, Latin American Catholic paraphernalia constitute an extra-diegetic compliment to this ironized spectator, offering, instead of the bourgeois esthetics of Branagh's *Hamlet*, the sophisticated bricolage of the multicultural market, on offer to the young consumers toward which the movie and its tie-in products seem principally to have been addressed.

The distance between such objects and those in their ambit that is the precondition of kitsch is modeled throughout the diegesis. When the very Anglo-seeming Juliet kneels to pray amid a wealth of angels, for instance, or when neon crosses proliferate in her tomb, the tableaus are visually arresting, but they are not to be read as meaningful articulations of faith or character; they cannot be used to consolidate a "reading" of a Juliet steeped in Latinity, or to provide verisimilar evidence of Verona Beach's generally fervent Catholicism. These possibilities map out a paradox. On the one hand they depend on more orthodox understanding of the ends, both esthetic and interpretive, which Shakespearean instantiations ought to serve, by asking for a focus on character. On the other, to the extent that they thoroughly Latinized *Romeo and Juliet*, they would demand a dislocation of such traditional sensibilities, and a movement toward the radically different Shakespeare that the film apparently puts on offer. Rather than engage with either possibility, however, Luhrmann's direction, unlike Branagh's, never presents Shakespeare as a focus of reverence; nor does it propose the text as a site for a genuinely critical engagement. Rather, what the film's icono-fetishism reflects is the extent to which the vicarious experience proffered by kitsch can be extended even in the direction of (cinematic) Shakespeare. Taken to its logical conclusion, this would be to read the Shakespearean itself in *Romeo and Juliet* as something alien to the principal subjects addressed by the film, an object given value through the process of market exchange. In a word, Shakespeare would be little distinguishable from kitsch.

IV

Should Baz Luhrmann's *William Shakespeare's Romeo and Juliet* be read primarily as a Shakespeare film? Even given the preceding analysis, this appears a perverse question, given the title's trumpeting of authorship: unlike Branagh's *Henry V*, where Shakespeare's name was suppressed from all advertisements, Luhrmann's film clearly revels in the connection (for Branagh, see Hedrick 1997: 57). That Shakespeare's name was not perceived to be a further selling point for a film directed by and starring a British actor then little known to a wider public may explain

Henry V's laconic title; after all, so soon after Burton's remark that Shakespeare is poison at the box office, why should Branagh have made the risk to commercial success greater than it already was? By this logic, then, it would follow that *William Shakespeare's Romeo and Juliet* was already so assured of a market that it could risk affiliation with what Branagh's initial film feared to look upon.

Given that Baz Luhrmann, whose only previous US release was the critically acclaimed but hardly blockbuster *Strictly Ballroom*, is far from a household name, and given, too, the smart idiosyncracies of this particular film, its distributors could hardly have been so assured, despite whatever audience guarantees DiCaprio and Danes might have seemed to provide. If the title *William Shakespeare's Romeo and Juliet* is indeed a marketing strategy, it represents a far more sophisticated sense of audience, and consequently of the film's position in the market, than in the prior case. Here, the relation between film and title, and hence between script and author, is one of both affiliation and disavowal: while nowhere is the connection to Shakespeare hidden – indeed, the script is faithful to Shakespeare's original – the very style of the film seems to deny relation. Deny it, that is, if one's sense of what a Shakespeare film ought to be like is extrapolated from *William Shakespeare's Romeo and Juliet*'s cinematic antecedents, from a reserve of ideological propositions about literacy, mass popularization, and the work the Bard must be seen to do, the difference he must be asked to mark from consumer culture.

What I am *not* saying, I hope, is that Luhrmann's film gives us a Shakespeare for the 1990s: my suspicion is that his success will not be duplicated by other youth-oriented Shakespeare productions, which ought to put paid to continuing arguments about making the dramatist "relevant." Besides, if anecdote can be a nonce substitute for ethnography, Luhrmann's conception generated some resistance among the usual audiences for Shakespeare films: several colleagues can echo my experience in being asked by generally well-educated (and generally, although not exclusively, middle-aged) people whether we found the film offensive, which I take to be at least partly that audience's projection onto the Academy of a fixed and bourgeois esthetics naturalized to the Bard. But what gives this particular film its provocative hold on other types of spectators can be read in the editing – not simply because of the pace it establishes, but because of the repeated collisions it stages between text and referent, which in this analysis might stand in for the collision between "Shakespearean" esthetics and those of cinematic commodity culture, fabled (and pilloried) for its glamorization of violence. Take, for instance, the textual "swords" that are insistently represented by guns: the bracing anachronism is reinforced by tightly focused shots on those menacing, gleaming weapons, totemic icons of American movies. The camerawork at these early moments, which by metonymic focus establishes the world of the diegesis, cannot but force the issue of incongruity between what is said and what is seen, between what literary tradition demands as visual cue and what film, as a medium, proffers in (self-conscious?) response.

In the broadest possible sense, *William Shakespeare's Romeo and Juliet* works at such an incongruity. Throughout, what is said is certainly Shakespeare's language (although not conventionally recognizable as such), but what the film puts on offer is anything but "Shakespearean," in the same conventional sense that Branagh's *Hamlet* is pre-eminently Shakespearean. Indeed, even the spoken is suspect, insofar as the prosaic articulations of the cast were sometimes read by film critics as robbing the play of its poetry, as though the paradoxical effect of Luhrmann's own species of textual fidelity were to consolidate by negation the essentialist quality of Shakespearean language. This reaction occurred despite the fact, as I have already argued, that the film gives us to understand when a speech is "properly" poetical and when it is to be understood otherwise. In establishing its own conventions about Shakespearean language, *Romeo and Juliet* puts aside the magniloquent tradition of classical acting styles characteristic of Shakespeare films like Branagh's and those of his predecessors, in favor of representing such language as, in the main, everyday speech, akin to the speech of advertising or of banal emotions. Such non-declamatory vocalizing actually manifests the subsumption of a recognizably Shakespearean "voice" under the regime of the cinematic: what is seen – the gun, the bleeding heart, the star – cannot but be more important than what is said (if not sung) or by whom the script was produced.[8] The priority of the visual over the linguistic insists on a new American identity for Shakespeare.

Rather than claim that *William Shakespeare's Romeo and Juliet* is a Shakespeare for now based on any simple-minded sense of its "relevance," then, I propose instead that the film gives us a masterful accommodation of Shakespeare to the US horizon, that it marks perhaps the first time that the dominant esthetics of Hollywood are fully set loose to do their work on a text and author which, though naturalized already to the US framework by educational and research institutions, tend to be reproduced as other, and as anterior to those institutions.[9] What, indeed, does it mean to claim that Shakespeare is "at home" in the United States? Certainly it does not mean, as Al Pacino seems to have believed in making *Looking for Richard*, ignoring the ideological apparatuses that have already made Shakespeare pervasive here (the scholars and actors from whom he mostly seeks advice are British): in fantasizing that US audiences only need to see Hollywood stars genuflect before a British deity to be brought to worshipful attention, Pacino errs as readily as Branagh. Rather, given the millennial dream that we have witnessed the end of history with the demise of the Cold War, and the persistent fantasy that the predicted global triumph of the free market may precisely be read as the success of the American economic plan, to make Shakespeare at home in the United States is to render him, too, a direct apparatus of the market.

In his exceptionally useful account of Shakespeare's institutionalization in the United States, Michael Bristol has argued that the Americanization of Shakespeare that began with John Adams in the late eighteenth century represents "a massive transfer of authority and cultural capital [from Britain] to American society" (Bristol 1990: 10). This transfer of assets has gone along with a sustaining connection (both ideological and material) with British national traditions; but it has also been accompanied by an increasingly flexible recasting of those traditions – among them, the relationship between financial capital and the cultural capital to which Bristol alludes, which is to say between a "vulgar" but undeniable marker of class, and its shadowy, if metonymic, counterpart. Under current US economic conditions, when part-time jobs in the humanities indicate that even academia has reconfigured labor for the age of flexible accumulation, possessing a wealth of literary knowledge seems more a guarantor of downward mobility than a muted and enabling echo of the prestige of money and birth. Luhrmann's *Romeo and Juliet* repositions Shakespeare for the realities of this millennial market, where, as I have argued concerning its religious iconography, surplus value is secured via what seems a familiar US gambit: neocolonial outsourcing.

V

William Shakespeare's Romeo and Juliet is undeniably a smart and seductive text, even for a reader who insists that it not be interpreted as a found object. Consider only how the fleeting glimpses of advertisements in Shakespearean language seem already to adumbrate the preceding analysis. They tantalize as parodies of contemporary advertising's opportunistic appropriations of the Bard as a sign of excellence –

remember that Trader Joe's shopping bag. At the same time, those very advertisements take seriously the films's necessary proposition that Shakespeare scripts the discourse of the diegetic everyday, which is to say of its own fictional representation of public culture. To acknowledge these and other such complexities, to note the film's capacities to generate sophisticated readings, is to heed the way it interpellates a number of ideal readers: *William Shakespeare's Romeo and Juliet* has something for the semiotically inclined college professors who love mass culture, as well as for the DiCaprio fans who saw the movie five or six times, which is to say for those who foreground the Shakespearean connection and those who, potentially, might disavow it, even see it as kitschy. But to say as much is also to acknowledge that *Romeo and Juliet* fulfills the role of the film commodity with particular expertness – at least, for one with a script by Shakespeare produced at the end of the century.

For these purposes, it simply does not matter that the film has the capacity to ironize the very formations around millennial Shakespeare that it supersedes. There was a time when, it seems, irony was considered to be the basis of an oppositional political practice, when, as Roland Barthes expresses it in *Mythologies*, "sarcasm [was] the condition of truth" (Barthes 1972: 12). I wonder whether such a modeling of distance ever did have the effectivity he claimed for it: Barthes himself scripted a sad fate for the leftist mythographer, cut off, alienated, from the center of culture, and from those whose consciousness s/he would attempt to re-form. Nevertheless, it needs no ghost to tell us that cynical distance has gone mainstream. Like the English majors many of us have trained as resistant, canny spectators, debunkers of cultural myths who are now working in the advertising industry, irony has become a part of the sales repertory of capitalism. If I can be forgiven a thumping, unsubtle conclusion: When the global force of free market policy has set itself the task of vanquishing alternative cultural logics, it can even sell Shakespeare – if not "Shakespeare films."

Notes

I wish to thank Crystal Bartolovich and the Group for Early Modern Cultural Studies for the opportunity to first try out this argument. It has subsequently benefitted from readings by, and conversations with, Jean Howard, David Levy, Scott Shershow, and Paul Smith.

1 It should be noted that Hawkes's account does not quite make the point for

which I use his title. Rather, he argues against textual essentialism (with meaning as the "product" sold by its supreme author) in favor of understanding specific instantiations dialectically.

2 Innerst is reporting on a survey of "70 leading colleges and universities" conducted by the National Alumni Forum in light of the Georgetown controversy. For information about and documentation of events at Georgetown, I am grateful to Kim Hall and Henry Schwartz.

3 Consider Branagh's remarks concerning his casting choices for *Hamlet* during a public discussion at the Smithsonian Institution in Washington, DC in December, 1996:

> In the end . . . I don't think you can second guess the audience or think that somehow to provide those people in those parts is to guarantee you a certain kind of audience, because I've been aware over the years, in fact for a lot of people, the knee-jerk reaction is lack of acceptance and a suspicion. And in fact I think it can do you more harm than good . . . There would be a price to pay for some people. I'm sure it won't work for everyone, but for me it was a great treat to see all those different approaches come together. I believe the man belongs to everyone, you know, across the world, and across cultures, across sexes, and so implicitly I wanted to suggest that with the accent-blind, nationality-blind, color-blind casting.
>
> (Transcription made by Diane Williams)

For a more substantial analysis of race-blind casting in *Hamlet* and *Much Ado About Nothing*, see Denise Albanese, "Black and White, and Dread All Over: The 'Photonegative' *Othello* and the Body of Desdemona," in Callaghan (ed.) 2000: 226–77.

4 The most recent data from the Internet Movie Data Base indicate that *Hamlet* has yet to recoup its production costs: budgeted at $18 million, the movie's total US gross was given as $4.4 million. The Internet Movie Data Base (www.indb.com), the source for my figures, must be used with caution, for there is reason to suspect its accuracy. In consulting Shakespeare movies listed on the site over a period of several months, I found the data were infrequently updated and unevenly collected: the international data are comprehensive in some cases, scattered in others, and non-existent in still others. Nevertheless, indb.com is roughly useful, if only as a preliminary basis for an argument about profitability.

5 The quotation comes from the transcription cited in note 3.

6 The claim is Richard Burt's (1997: 244). His words on the movie demand quoting in full: "*Romeo and Juliet* portrayed Mercutio as a bi-sexual, gun-toting cross-dresser who 'consorts' with Romeo. (It is worth noting that Leonardo DiCaprio, who played Romeo, is a gay icon and that the actor who played Tybalt, John Luguizamo [sic], had appeared the year before as a character in drag." It may be true that DiCaprio has wide erotic appeal

(and not just to men), and that Leguizamo's other cinematic roles might leave a regendering trace across his performance as the parodically macho Tybalt (who is shown as the favorite of Juliet's mother). Nevertheless Burt's troubling indiscriminacy effaces the extent to which the script demands that only Mercutio of the three be read as sexually ambiguous. The distinction is important to maintain, given the film's insistent conjoining of race and other forms of exoticism.

7 I have hazarded the approximate "Anglo-Saxon" as a description of Benvolio because of Dash Mihok's red hair and fair skin – as well as the costume he wears to the Capulet ball, an odd combination of Viking helmet and Scottish kilt (all the costumes are resonant of mythic characterizations; thus Dave Paris's astronaut garb, Romeo's knight in shining armor, and Juliet's angel).

8 The commercially successful soundtrack also functions to de-emphasize the importance of the script.

9 This piece was formulated in large part in response to Michael Bristol's *Shakespeare's America, America's Shakespeare* (1990) and to subsequent conversations with him.

11
Measure for Measure: Marxism before Marx

KIERNAN RYAN

I The lost horizon

Most recent criticism of Shakespeare shaped by Marxist assumptions and modes of analysis has laboured under the double burden of its retrospective gaze and its diagnostic attitude to the plays. The recurrent aim is to return the text in question to the matrix from which it emerged in order to explain it and expose it to the critique of hindsight. The price of such radical historicist critiques has too often been a blindness not only to the plays' capacity for resistance and dissent, but also to what remains incalculable in them because it belongs to the future, not the past, because it points beyond the horizon of their own time rather than back to an intractably anterior world. In "The Soul of Man under Socialism," Oscar Wilde declared that "A map of the world that does not include Utopia is not worth even glancing at" (Wilde 1994: 1184). And if Wilde were still around to remark on the state of the world of literary studies, he might well be moved to add that criticism which forgets the future is unlikely to have much of a future itself. For the approaches to literature that now prevail, in their keenness to collapse texts into their original contexts, have indeed neglected the dimension of futurity, and nowhere is the cost of that neglect more evident than in what now passes for progressive Shakespeare criticism.

In this essay I want to argue the case for mining a different vein in the modern Marxist tradition in order to do justice to the complexity and prefigurative power of Shakespeare's plays. In the work of Walter Benjamin, Herbert Marcuse and above all Ernst Bloch, a rich theoretical legacy still lies waiting to be claimed by radical critics in the English-speaking world. The value of that legacy was made clear thirty years ago in Fredric Jameson's trailblazing study *Marxism and Form* (1971), whose failure to have the widespread impact that it deserved to have on both sides of the Atlantic remains one of the tragedies of recent critical history. For what Jameson brought within reach through his accounts of these giants of modern German Marxism was a conception of literature and art diametrically opposed to that which informs most radical criticism at the present time. Despite the striking differences of mind and method they display, Benjamin, Marcuse and Bloch are united by their commitment to redeeming the repressed utopian spirit of Marxist philosophy and activating the dormant utopian powers of literature and art to speed the transfiguration of late capitalist society. Their adoption of a historical perspective and their vigilant pursuit of the hermeneutics of suspicion do not preclude their allegiance to the proleptic logic that Marx himself perceived at the core of revolutionary struggle:

> So our campaign slogan must be: reform of consciousness, not through dogma, but through the analysis of that mystical consciousness which has not yet become clear to itself. It will then turn out that the world has long dreamt of that of which it had only to have a clear idea to possess it really. It will turn out that it is not a question of any conceptual rupture between past and future, but rather of the completion of the thoughts of the past.
>
> (letter to A. Ruge, 1843, quoted in Jameson 1971: 116)

As a consequence, none of them had any difficulty discerning in the great art of the past vivid premonitions of a dispensation whose advent we still await.

For Benjamin, to immure any literary text in its moment of genesis is a deeply reactionary ruse, whatever the political credentials of the critic, and however conscious the critic may be of the fact that every historicist reading is warped by its own modernity. Benjamin "leaves it to others to be drained by the whore called 'Once upon a time' in historicism's bordello," as he so delicately puts it in his "Theses on the Philosophy of History" (1970: 264). He advocates instead an approach propelled by the understanding that "As flowers turn toward the sun, by dint of a secret heliotropism the past strives to turn toward that sun which is rising in the sky of history" (1970: 257). And there is no better place to catch that "secret heliotropism" in action than the realm of art, because "One of the foremost tasks of art has always been the creation of a demand which could be fully satisfied only later" (1970: 239).

For Bloch, too, "historicism involves the sterile incarceration of history," as a result of which "the dead dog of yesterday can run around in the park and romp just as merrily as the dangerous lion of today or tomorrow" (1988: 43–4, 47). What makes great art so invaluable, in Bloch's view, is its knack for giving "the dead dog of yesterday" the slip by disclosing within the consciousness of the past a *future unconscious*, which lies below the horizon ahead of us. This "unconscious of what is yet to come," as Jameson calls it (1971: 129) is what Bloch terms the *Novum*. By this he means an intuition of the eventual in the previous or the present so startling and strange that it can be communicated only in the cryptic codes devised by the individual artistic genius, or by the collective ingenuity of the people at work in fairy tale and fable. The key task of the radical critic is thus to reclaim "the future in the past that is significant to the degree that the genuine agent (*Täter*) of cultural heritage reaches into the past, and in this very same act the past itself anticipates him, involves him and needs him" (Bloch 1988: 46–7).

For a shrewd guide to where the signs of a work's commerce with futurity are most likely to be found, the critic need look no further than Marcuse, whose last major work, *The Aesthetic Dimension*, concludes that "The critical function of art, its contribution to the struggle for liberation, resides in the aesthetic form . . . The encounter with the truth of art happens in the estranging language and images which make perceptible, visible and audible that which is no longer, or not yet, perceived, said and heard in everyday life" (1979: 8, 72). Those for whom Marcuse is no longer modish enough to merit quotation will be relieved to find this conclusion succinctly endorsed by Bakhtin: "Form serves as a necessary bridge to new, still unknown content" (1986: 165).

My reason for invoking the utopian esthetics of Benjamin, Bloch and Marcuse is not to advocate the mechanical application of their interpretive methods to Shakespeare, but merely to buttress my plea for radical critics to bring a wider range of expectations to bear on Shakespeare's plays. That Shakespeare's drama is steeped in the oppressive ideas and attitudes of his day – that it could not help but be as much "a document of barbarism" as a "document of civilization," as Benjamin would put it (1970: 258) – may be readily conceded, and the importance of explaining the nature and degree of its embroilment in the barbarism of its time can scarcely be underestimated. But, by the same token, the contribution of his drama to the civilizing process should not be discounted either, and, unless the utopian initiative in Marxist criticism is to be dismissed as entirely misconceived, there is a fair chance that there is more to Shakespeare's scripts than collusion with the monarchy and market capitalism. If we are prepared to grant the possibility that Shakespeare's early modern imagination was able to anticipate the shapes that late modern reality would take, and perhaps foreshadow "the forms of things unknown"[1] beyond our horizon too, then we might just find stored in the language and structure of his plays a vision of his world that would transform Shakespeare's political significance.

What we might find, to put the point provocatively, is that Shakespeare was a Marxist long before Marx. Marx's passionate, life-long love of Shakespeare is well known, and the pervasive debt of his political and economic writings to the creator of *Hamlet* has been documented in S. S. Prawer's monumental study, *Karl Marx and World Literature* (1976). Marx knew that Shakespeare had plenty to teach him, as his enlistment of Timon's speech on gold to make a vital point in *Capital* makes clear (Prawer 1976: 78–80). My own hunch is that Marx learned much of his Marxism at the knee of his mighty precursor – as well as from other titans of world literature – and that Marxism has more to learn from Shakespeare today than ever before. Shakespeare, needless to say, did not write critiques of political economy or revolutionary manifestos. But he did write plays that were driven by a commitment to the same fundamental principles and values that motivated Marx. Shakespeare's plays always knew what Marx came to know over two centuries later, *but they knew it in a different form.* They knew it in the concrete, theatrical form of dramatized predicaments and situated speech rather than through abstract, discursive analysis and argument; which is why they also know more than Marxism alone, however supple and adaptable it may become, can ever hope to discover.

II The theatre of complicity

On the face of it, however, it must be confessed, to claim that Shakespeare's radical utopian vision is embodied in *Measure for Measure*, that twisted, queasy comedy in which, as Hazlitt noted, "our sympathies are repulsed and defeated in all directions" (1930: 346), would appear to be the rankest folly – "utopian" indeed, in the usual, contemptuous sense of futile and self-deluding. But there are at least three good reasons for testing the viability of the approach advocated in the first part of this essay against this particular play. The first reason, of course, is because it seems so certain to prove a hostile witness, which makes whatever corroboration it can provide more valuable than the testimony of a more convivial comedy, such as *As You Like It* or *Much Ado*. The second is because, as the title of the play proclaims, it is expressly concerned with the question of justice, the quest for which was a consuming obsession of both Marx and Shakespeare, as Derrida has recently reminded us in *Specters of Marx* (1994). And the third is because *Measure for Measure* has come to be regarded as the play that demonstrates, more clearly than almost any other in Shakespeare's canon, "the effectiveness and complexity of the ideological process of containment" (Dollimore 1994a: 15) which his drama supposedly served, and which it is the role of the progressive critic to unmask and disarm. Thus Jonathan Dollimore's seminal account of *Measure for Measure* in *Political Shakespeare* concludes that the play is "a reactionary fantasy, neither radical nor liberating . . . the very disclosure of social realities which make progress seem imperative is recuperated in comedic closure, a redemptive wish-fulfilment of the status quo" (Dollimore 1994b: 84); while Kathleen McLuskie's equally influential essay in the same volume finds ample warrant in the same play to condemn its author as "the patriarchal Bard" (McLuskie 1994).

The most cogent critiques of the play to date contend, indeed, that *Measure for Measure* is a perfect dramatization of the grim tale told by Foucault's *Discipline and Punish* (1979). Nor is it hard to see why: *Measure for Measure* might have been written in order to vindicate Foucault's analysis of the origins of the carceral society. The play provides a textbook instance of the transition from a culture in which power asserts itself through spectacular, public displays of punitive violence, to one which secures subjection by subtler strategies of surveillance, concession and repressive tolerance. As a result, the play seems to finger itself as a pawn of power and its author as the secret agent of authority – as one of the "King's Men" indeed, in the more sinister sense that lurks within that designation.

"In Shakespeare's drama," according to Leonard Tennenhouse, "stagecraft collaborates with statecraft in producing spectacles of power. The strategies of theater resembled those of the scaffold, as well as court performance . . . in observing a common logic of figuration that both sustained and testified to the monarch's power" (1986: 15). Thus in *Measure for Measure*, Tennenhouse maintains, the Duke's "powers of disguise, of substitution, of staging scenes which transfer authority or reveal a crime, characterize the Jacobean theater as surely as they do the monarch's statecraft" (1986: 157). As a figure of the dramatist himself, Duke Vincentio epitomizes the complicity of theatre and throne in deepening the mystique of the monarchy and sealing its supremacy against dissent. The play's plot contrives a situation of corruption, confusion and crisis, which can only be resolved by the omniscient intervention of the patriarchal principle incarnate, who reclaims mastery over the instruments of state by regulating the sexual behaviour of his subjects through marriage. The Duke contrives for his surrogate Angelo a trap which catches him in a treacherous act of lechery, and entangles the principal characters in a deadly web of culpability, from which the Duke's omnipotence alone can free them in a publicly staged spectacle of exposure and remission.

"My business in this state / Made me a looker-on here in Vienna" (5. 1. 312–13), explains the man Lucio dubs "the old fantastical Duke of dark corners" (4. 3. 147–8). The Duke vanishes, only to return in a form which allows him to police those dark corners of his realm unimpeded, and penetrate the hidden reaches of its citizens' hearts and minds. In the person of this invisible voyeur it is difficult not to see a prevision of the modern society in which power imposes itself not through force, but through the tyranny of transparency, by exposing everyone to the impersonal ubiquity of its remorseless gaze:

> *Angelo*: Oh, my dread lord,
> I should be guiltier than my guiltiness
> To think I can be undiscernible
> When I perceive your grace, like power divine,
> Hath looked upon my passes.
>
> (5. 1. 359–63)

In *Discipline and Punish*, Foucault finds the architectural epitome of this regime in Bentham's *Panopticon*, whose principal objective is "to induce in the inmate a state of conscious and permanent visibility that assures the automatic functioning of power" (1979: 201). It would plainly be inaccurate to describe the Duke's Vienna as a fully fledged panopticon *avant la lettre*, but it seems not unreasonable to suggest that it affords us a remarkable image of the culture of incarceration in embryo, as it evolves within a more primitive, but still potent, society of the spectacle. The Vienna of *Measure for Measure* revolves, after all, around the prison, to which most of the *dramatis personae* gravitate, blurring the normally blatant boundary between the world within and the world beyond its walls.

Consider also Angelo's eagerness to forfeit his life in retribution for his crime, once he apprehends the Duke's omniscience: "I crave death more willingly than mercy. / 'Tis my deserving, and I do entreat it" (5. 1. 469–70). If that is put together with the Duke's deliberate creation of anxiety in Isabella by withholding his knowledge of her brother's safety, consigning her to prison and putting her through the pantomime of begging for her would-be rapist's life, it is impossible to deny that *Measure for Measure* has more than a glancing insight into the psychological manipulation that attends the culture of surveillance, turning subjects into willing agents of their own subjection. The problem is that the critics who espouse this angle on the play want to go much further: they want to insist on the culpable collusion of Shakespeare's play in this oppressive process of conditioning. Foucault remarks of the cells of the panopticon that "They are like so many cages, so many small theatres, in which each actor is alone, perfectly individualized and constantly visible" (1979: 200). Critics have not been slow to take such hints as their cue to arraign the theatre of the Bard, and *Measure for Measure* in particular, as powerful implements for expanding the visibility of contemporary conduct. By making every private nook and cranny of experience conspicuous, so the argument runs, Shakespeare's theatre actively adapts the spectating citizen to the nascent imperative of internalized surveillance. "These are the measures of *Measure for Measure*," concludes Jonathan Goldberg, "the principle of representation that prescribes a single law for the state and the theater" (1983: 239).

In *Will Power*, Richard Wilson sums up the charges levelled against the play by radical historicist criticism. *Measure for Measure* provides, in Wilson's view, "a conspectus of the Damoclean methods of the disciplinary state" (1993: 126) – "Damoclean" because they work by breeding a constant state of trepidation from the prospect of punishment, from the suspension of penalties that may be exacted at any moment by an obscure authority. Nor is the activation of this state of mind confined to the characters. The sustained tension of the plot is generated for the audience by the impending doom of Claudio and our anxiety that his death be averted. Once it has been averted, the Duke concocts a fresh batch of ad-libbed anxieties (the prospect of Isabella's imprisonment, the death sentences on Angelo and Lucio) to keep us attentive by keeping us apprehensive. "From the outset," argues Wilson, "this play presents a power that has learned the lesson of modernity, that subjection is obtained not by oppression, but by self-repression. The state over which Vincentio presides has long ago begun the experiment of abandoning its public violence in return for private discipline of its citizens, and it knows its legitimacy depends upon its incitement of transgression" (1993: 126). Shakespeare is implicitly indicted for rationalizing the new disciplinary regime, for creating a play whose cultural function is to serve as midwife to a far more insidious form of oppression by making it plausible and admirable:

> *Measure for Measure* is a mirror for magistrates, then, in which Angelo, who begins his rule "Hoping [to] find good cause to whip them all" (II.i.136), discovers that the quality of mercy is such as to subjugate more completely than the axe or lash; that, in the words of the commonplace, "the more power he hath to hurt, the more admirable is his praise, that he will not hurt" (Sidney, *The Countess of Pembroke's Arcadia*, II, 15). So, what the play dramatises is the wisdom of the cryptic *Sonnet 94*, that "They that have power to hurt and will do none", are those installed in regality: "They rightly do inherit heaven's graces." "Mercy", Isabella assures the judge, "will breathe within your lips, / Like man new made" (II.ii.78–9); but the "new man" so made is "the demi-god, Authority" (I.ii.112), as omnipotent as "Merciful Heaven" (115). Thus we glimpse in the text a strategy of power that will "make mercy . . . play the tyrant" (III.ii.188) more effectively than any "pelting petty officer" (II.ii.113).
>
> (Wilson 1993: 127–8)

The Duke's resort to mercy is exposed, on closer inspection, as not the exemplary virtue of a wise, benevolent ruler, but yet another ruse of tyranny at its most devious. By placing his formidable dramatic skill and rhetorical ingenuity at the service of the Duke's charade of "apt remission" (5. 1. 491), Shakespeare duplicates in the theatre, it is alleged, the Duke's duping of his subjects. The Bard blinds his audience to the face of domination behind the mask of mercy by contriving their relieved applause for the Duke's last-minute reprieves. If there is indeed "A single law for the state and the theater," as Goldberg believes, when it comes right down to it, there is no telling the Duke from the dramatist.

III 'Poetical justice"

That, at least, is what the new-historicist and cultural-materialist consensus on *Measure for Measure* would have us believe, and up to a point this account of the play is convincing and illuminating. *Measure for Measure* does portray with extraordinary prescience the emergence of an unprecedented mode of hegemony, which is all the more effective for being obscure and diffuse, and whose latest manifestation in postindustrial Western cultures is arguably so successful as to have become truly impalpable. But to maintain that Shakespeare is the willing or unwitting prop of dominion's dark designs on his audience is to part company with credibility, for such a proposition can be sustained only by screening out the devices Shakespeare employs to demystify the ploys of power and subject them to a lethal critique.

That critique is sharpened by the fact that *Measure for Measure* comes clean about its implication in the structures of subjection it depicts, inciting us to be wary of art's incriminating compact with power, the devil's deals which even the most unbiddable authors must strike with authority. Shakespeare did not need Benjamin to advise him that every document of civilization is also fated to be a document of barbarism, which leaves its imprint on art whether art likes it or not. In *The Tempest*, that recognition is encapsulated in the casting of Prospero as Duke and dramatist, as a character who is both the benevolent agent of comedic resolution and the embodiment of the repressive regime that he transmutes. And the same recognition is built into Duke Vincentio's doubling as dramatist in *Measure for Measure*. Even Shakespeare's breeziest, upbeat comedies are also comedies of coercion, which bend the intractable, tragic stuff of history to their festive will. In the figure of the manipulative Duke of Vienna, who inflicts comedic closure on a play which is, as Swinburne protested, "in its very inmost essence a tragedy" (Swinburne 1880: 203), Shakespeare blows the gaff on the violence involved in representation, on the cost of capitulating to convention in both art and life. *Measure for Measure* has the nerve to put itself and its author in the dock alongside the cast. It *displays* the liability incurred by the act of dramatic duplication, by this theatrical doubling of the real, even as it undoes the authority of what counts as reality in its time.

A less myopic view of *Measure for Measure* than that of the politically correct critics I have been quoting is supplied by Walter Pater's inspired essay on the play in *Appreciations* (1889). Pater applauds the play hissed by Coleridge as "a hateful work, although Shakspearian throughout" (Coleridge 1990: 62):

> Out of these insignificant sources Shakespeare's play rises, full of solemn expression, and with a profoundly designed beauty, the new

> body of a higher, though sometimes remote and difficult poetry, escaping from the imperfect relics of the old story, yet not wholly transformed, and even as it stands but the preparation only, we might think, of a still more imposing design. For once we have in it a real example of that sort of writing which is sometimes described as *suggestive*, and which by the help of certain subtly calculated hints only, brings into distinct shape the reader's own half-developed imaginings. Often the quality is attributed to writing merely vague and unrealised, but in *Measure for Measure*, quite certainly, Shakespeare has directed the attention of sympathetic readers along certain channels of meditation beyond the immediate scope of his work.
>
> (Pater 1889: 179)

What our attention is being directed towards is an intimation of what Pater terms "poetical justice" :

> The action of the play, like the action of life itself for the keener observer, develops in us the conception of this poetical justice, and the yearning to realise it, the justice of which Angelo knows nothing, because it lies for the most part beyond the limits of any acknowledged law . . . It is for this finer justice, a justice based on a more delicate appreciation of the true conditions of men and things, a true respect of persons in our estimate of actions, that the people in *Measure for Measure* cry out as they pass before us; and as the poetry of this play is full of the peculiarities of Shakespeare's poetry, so in its ethics it is an epitome of Shakespeare's moral judgments.
>
> (Pater 1889: 190)

Pater never brings to satisfactory definition what he means by this ulterior "poetical justice", allowing his intuition to evaporate into evocative rhetoric. But he seizes upon something absolutely central to *Measure for Measure* with his idea that the play points towards a moral perspective which cannot be encompassed or enacted, because it lies beyond the purview of the characters, because it is a perspective which only the sympathetic reader or spectator is placed to discern and develop. It is vital, however, that this prospective morality is distinguished from the established morality that it subverts. In this regard, Pater's view of the Bard chimes perfectly with that of Hazlitt, whose reflections on *Measure for Measure* in his *Characters of Shakespear's Plays* lead him to conclude that "In one sense Shakespear was no moralist at all: in another, he was the greatest of all moralists" (1930: 347). Hazlitt rightly suspects, moreover, although he does not elaborate the point, that *Measure for Measure*'s assault on the moral dispensation of the day is spearheaded by Barnardine, whom he hails as "a fine antithesis to the morality and the hypocrisy of the other characters of the play" (1930: 346).

IV The quality of mercy

Barnardine is indeed the key to *Measure for Measure*, because he marks the boundary of the moral universe by which the denizens of Vienna are circumscribed. By his defiant insistence on dwelling beyond that boundary, he allows us to identify the dilemmas of Vienna as the consequences of its constitution, and, at the same time, he affords us a position uncontaminated by the codes that constrain the rest of the cast. In Barnardine we behold the embodiment of the point to which the play as a whole strives to transport us. For one brief, uncanny moment, a stance that resists absorption into the assumptions upon which the Duke's plan depends becomes incarnate in the shambling guise of Barnardine, who refuses point blank to comply with Vincentio's version of the comedy. "A man that apprehends death no more dreadfully but as a drunken sleep: careless, reckless, and fearless of what's past, present, or to come" (4. 2. 125–7), a man who would not bother to escape even if he were invited to, Barnardine proves immune to punishment and pardon alike, confounding the Duke's devices by his sublime indifference to his fate. In fact, Barnardine's impassivity lends him a strange, mesmeric power over his executioners, who are compelled to dance attendance on his disposition: "I will not consent to die this day, that's certain . . . I swear I will not die today for any man's persuasion" (4. 3. 47–8, 51).

Barnardine is the outward sign of the play's inward drive to clear a space within which a superior conception of justice can secretly flourish. I say "secretly," because the play's visionary displacement of the Viennese regime is mainly achieved by subliminal means, by the structural manipulation of perspective and supposition rather than by overt assertion. This is not to deny that overt assertion plays a crucial role in complicating our assumptions and uncoupling us from the imperative of subjection. The first arresting instance occurs when Escalus seeks clemency for Claudio from Angelo by asking him to search his own conscience:

> Had time cohered with place, or place with wishing,
> Or that the resolute acting of your blood
> Could have attained th' effect of your own purpose,
> Whether you had not sometime in your life
> Erred in this point which now you censure him,
> And pulled the law upon you.
>
> (2. 1. 11–16)

Angelo is ready for that and meets it with icy objectivity: " 'Tis one thing to be tempted, Escalus, / Another thing to fall" (2. 1. 17–18). But, like the aspersions that Lucio casts on the Duke's moral character, the argument Escalus initiates will not go away: it sticks like a burr.

Angelo has a much tougher time resisting it when it crops up again one scene later in the mouth of Isabella, who puts the case far more forcibly than Escalus:

> *Isabella*: If he had been as you, and you as he,
> You would have slipped like him, but he like you
> Would not have been so stern.
> *Angelo*: Pray you be gone.
> *Isabella*: I would to heaven I had your potency,
> And you were Isabel: should it then be thus?
> No. I would tell what 'twere to be a judge,
> And what a prisoner.
>
> (2. 2. 65–71)

The thrust of Isabella's speech is that Angelo should imagine himself in Claudio's place and be merciful, on the grounds that there but for the grace of God goes he. But the terms in which she puts the point, and especially her astute reversal of roles and confusion of identities, make it cut deeper than a mere summons to compassion. Within a hundred lines, it becomes clear just how deep:

> Go to your bosom,
> Knock there, and ask your heart what it doth know
> That's like my brother's fault. If it confess
> A natural guiltiness, such as his,
> Let it not sound a thought upon your tongue
> Against my brother's life.
>
> (2. 2. 140–5)

In case we still cannot see where this is heading, Angelo delivers the irrefutable conclusion that spells it out for us:

Oh, let her brother live:
Thieves for their robbery have authority
When judges steal themselves.

(2. 2. 179–81)

This catapults us to the core of the matter. As characters locked inside their predicament, Isabella's conscious concern is to secure her brother's reprieve by begging for mercy, while Angelo is intent on agonizing over his right to judge Claudio for succumbing to the appetites to which Angelo himself is about to capitulate. But the arguments of both characters unleash a logic which ends up undermining the validity of the plot and the rationale of mercy itself. The same lethal logic can be observed at work in two stunning speeches from two other plays, in which Shakespeare turns an equally ruthless gaze on the legitimacy of the law and what masquerades as justice.

The first occurs in the trial scene of *The Merchant of Venice*. Castigated by the Christians for his merciless bloodlust, Shylock reminds them that in the eyes of their own law – as they themselves concede – he is "doing no wrong." On the contrary, as Shylock proceeds to point out:

You have among you many a purchased slave,
Which, like your asses and your dogs and mules,
You use in abject and in slavish parts
Because you bought them. Shall I say to you,
"Let them be free! Marry them to your heirs!
Why sweat they under burdens? . . . "
. . . You will answer,
"The slaves are ours." So do I answer you.
The pound of flesh which I demand of him
Is dearly bought; 'tis mine, and I will have it.
If you deny me, fie upon your law:

(4. 1. 90–101)

Here Shylock makes nonsense of the Christians' appeal for clemency by demonstrating that his "wolvish, bloody, starved, and ravenous" desires (4. 1. 138) are the very foundation and institutionalized norm of Venice, whose inhumanity is ratified as "justice" by its laws.

Even more penetrating are the deranged King Lear's lines to Gloucester, lines which Edgar's subsequent aside prompts us to hear as "matter and impertinency mixed, / Reason in madness" (4. 5. 166–7):

Lear: . . . A man may see how this world goes with no eyes; look with thine ears. See how yon justice rails upon yon simple thief. Hark in thine ear: change places, and handy-dandy, which is the justice, which is the thief? Thou hast seen a farmer's dog bark at a beggar?

Gloucester: Ay, Sir.

Lear: And the creature run from the cur? There thou mightst behold the great image of authority. A dog's obeyed in office.
Thou rascal beadle, hold thy bloody hand.
Why dost thou lash that whore? Strip thy own back.
Thou hotly lusts to use her in that kind
For which thou whip'st her. The usurer hangs the cozener.
Through tattered clothes great vices do appear:
Robes and furred gowns hide all. Plate sin with gold,
And the strong lance of justice hurtless breaks;
Arm it in rags, a pigmy's straw does pierce it.
None does offend, none, I say none. I'll able 'em.
(4. 5. 144–60)

This speech, which was probably written within a year or so of *Measure for Measure*, hammers home the point of that last quotation from Angelo, and throws more light on *Measure for Measure* than most modern critics of the play combined. Like Shylock's speech, it demands the understanding that there can be no justice in a constitutionally unjust society, which is programmed to preserve its unequal distribution of status, wealth and power. How can a structurally immoral social order indict anyone for transgressions of which it is the precondition, for the immorality which it does not merely foster but *requires* in order to ratify its authority, to sanction its sway? To Lucio's question, "Whence comes this restraint?" Claudio replies, "From too much liberty, my Lucio, liberty" (1. 2. 106–7). The exchange neatly captures the reciprocity of licence and legality, virtue and depravity, the spurious moral poles between which the populace of Vienna are doomed to shuttle.

What counts as licit and illicit, however, as Pompey knows full well, is actually the arbitrary construction of a given culture at a given time. It is what those who rule decide to define and enforce until it becomes expedient to change it. "Is it a lawful trade?" asks Escalus reproachfully of Madam Mitigation's right-hand man. "If the law would allow it, sir," retorts Pompey, deftly whipping the magistrate's assumptions from under his feet. The law and its administration in a divided world are not the source of the solution but part of the problem, and the same goes for mercy. In *The Merchant of Venice*, Portia's celebrated eulogy of mercy is revealed as the contemptible hypocrisy of those who can afford the luxury of that virtue, because they have the power to bestow it. In *Measure for Measure* likewise, the mercy that Isabella begs Angelo to show Claudio, and the Duke's climactic display of mercy to all those whom he has placed at his mercy, are revealed as the symptoms of the disease for which they are touted as the cure. To put it another way, the author of *Measure for Measure* would have found the opening stanza of Blake's poem "The Human Abstract" instantly intelligible:

> Pity would be no more
> If we did not make somebody Poor;
> And Mercy no more could be
> If all were as happy as we.
>
> (Blake 1972: 217)

Measure for Measure demystifies mercy, which feeds off the oppressive hierarchy it secretly consolidates – the power structure that produces the need for mercy in the first place. As a consequence, the critical view of the play as endorsing the Duke by staging his compassionate finale collapses. But it collapses not only because of the visible pressure exerted upon it by the speeches I have quoted, but also because its foundations are eroded by the implicit perspective that governs the play. The unjust justice and the immoral morality of Vienna depend for their authority and efficacy on hierarchy, on the stratified system of social differences to which they are keyed and which they serve to sustain. But *Measure for Measure* dramatizes the lives of individuals trapped within that system from a viewpoint that unhinges hierarchy, even as it records the crippling consequences of its dominion.

V Double trouble

How the play does that is best explained by explaining its obsession with doubles and doubling, its compulsive multiplication of alter egos and substitutes. The Duke appoints Angelo his deputy, addressing him in the opening scene as "one that can my part in him advertise" and commanding him "In our remove be thou at full ourself" (1. 1. 41, 43). We are invited to read Angelo's subsequent career not only as a wilful departure from the Duke's design, but also as a manifestation of the Duke himself, a pursuit by his double of the course Vincentio might have taken, had he not had this stand-in to hand. The Duke is certainly happy to step into Angelo's shoes at the end, to hijack as his bride the woman whom Angelo has plagued in his name and placed within his power. The difference that divides the Duke from Angelo, and both of them from their supposed inferiors, those whom they have the power to consign to the dungeon or the gallows, is also blurred by the parallels between the couples Angelo and Mariana, Claudio and Juliet, Lucio and Kate Keepdown, and even poor Elbow and his wife, who (like her counterparts in this licentious list) "was respected with him before he married with her" (2. 1. 167), if Pompey at least is to be believed. The chain of substitution and analogy binds everyone in the play to each other, playing havoc with official social and moral distinctions. Escalus stands in for Angelo in the cod trial of Pompey and deputizes for the Duke at the denouement. Mariana takes the place of Isabella in the infamous bed-trick, of which the Duke observes: "the doubleness of the benefit defends the deceit from reproof" (3. 1. 240–1). Mariana's maidenhead is exchanged for the unmuffled head of Claudio, which has itself been replaced by the head of Ragozine, which in turn had been swapped for the stubborn bonce of Barnardine. And Pompey Bum swaps his life as a pimp for the hangman's hood without batting an eyelid: all his former clients are now banged up in the slammer after all, making the difference between knocking-shop and nick purely academic.

Duplication and exchange swarm through the body politic of Vienna like a contagious disease, infecting high and low, the virtuous and the vicious alike, and thereby erasing the divisions upon which such discriminations rest. The phrasing of the script gets in on the act, too, tuning us to the play's seditious frequency at every turn. From its self-mirroring title down to its final lines, *Measure for Measure* is riddled with locutions framed to convey symmetry, equivalence, inversion or repetition. The Duke closes the play with a perfect instance of chiasmus, when he promises the astounded Isabella: "What's mine is yours, and what is yours is mine" (5. 1. 529). It is a trick of speech that he shares, not surprisingly, with his surrogate: "When I would pray and think, I think and pray," says Angelo at 2. 4. 1. *Geminatio* ("twinning") is translated by Thomas Wilson in *The Arte of Rhetorique* as a "doublet," which occurs, he explains, "when we rehearse one and the same word twice together" (Wilson 1909: 200). This tic of repetition is equally at home on the tongue of Elbow: "Thou art to continue, now, thou varlet, thou art to continue" (2. 1. 162–3); Angelo: "What's this? What's this?" (2. 2. 167); Isabella: "Seeming, seeming" (2. 4. 151); the Duke: "Go mend, go mend" (3. 2. 24); and the anonymous boy who serenades the melancholy Mariana with his echoing refrain: "bring again, bring again . . . sealed in vain, sealed in vain" (4. 1. 5–6).

The play's constant resort to cloning and transposition is equally apparent in the organization of its scenes. The structural principle of switching between the rulers and the ruled, between the upholders and the violators of the law, from the corridors of power to the jail and the bordello and back again, begins by reinforcing points of contrast and discrimination. But the cumulative impact of this oscillation transforms an initial acceptance of disparity into the realization of resemblance, as the grounds of incongruity dissolve. Which indeed is the wiser (to echo Escalus), Justice or Iniquity? By commuting between different classes and their distinct moral codes, *Measure for Measure* transfigures the fact of degree and discord into the potential for union and consensus.

"Though you change your place," Pompey assures Mistress Overdone, "you need not change your trade" (1. 2. 90). Or as the hangman Abhorson prefers to put it: "Every true man's apparel fits your thief" (4. 2. 34). Detail and structure conspire in *Measure for Measure* to dismantle the scaffolding of hierarchy and expose the fragility of the class distinctions and moral oppositions on which the action is built. By revealing the tide of consanguinity that flows beneath the threshold of social difference, by disclosing the repressed identity that mocks impositions of disparity, *Measure for Measure* unravels the divisive dispensation that the Duke's plot defends and that radical critics have accused it of endorsing. The persons of the play, the citizens of Vienna, are fated to remain bound by the terms and limits of the fictional universe they inhabit. But *our* understanding of *Measure for Measure* is released from that bondage by our vantage point as audience or readers, whose vision of that universe is dramatically different from theirs. Shakespeare does indeed direct our sympathies, as Pater surmised, "along certain channels of meditation beyond the immediate scope of his work," "beyond the limits of any acknowledged law," in quest of the "still more imposing design" of a "finer justice," the as yet purely "poetical," as yet merely imaginary, justice for which "the people in *Measure for Measure* cry out as they pass before us." Even as it completes its ostensible contract with the ideology of subjection, and frankly admits its complicity in the comedy of coercion, *Measure for Measure* forges for us, from this bleak narrative of constraint, the prospect of an egalitarian community, on whose basis alone the true justice for which our own world still hungers might one day prove attainable.

Note

1 *A Midsummer Night's Dream*, 5. 1. 15. All textual references are to the New Cambridge Shakespeare editions listed in the Bibliography.

12
Shakespeare beyond Shakespeare

SCOTT CUTLER SHERSHOW

> The first literary result of the foundation of our industrial system upon the profits of piracy and slave trading was Shakespeare. It is our misfortune that the sordid misery and hopeless horror of his view of man's destiny is still so appropriate . . . that we even to-day regard him as not for an age, but for all time. But the poetry of despair will not outlive despair itself.
>
> (Bernard Shaw, *An Unsocial Socialist*)

I

The power of esthetic universality as an idea lies in its professed ability to circumscribe and circumvent its own critique. In early modern studies, for example, the idea of a universal Shakespeare survives despite all the many recent efforts to place him within his own period and document the historical construction of his cultural status. Such projects, under the aspect of universality, can always be viewed as merely "a testimony to Shakespeare's intrinsic strength" (Kirsch 1990: 221). Correspondingly, any *particular* theoretical approach to Shakespeare (such as Marxism, feminism, and the like) may be seen as merely striving "to appropriate Shakespeare for its own ideology" and thus subordinating him "to the imperialism and self-advancement of the particular group" (Vickers 1993: x–xii). Even as scholars increasingly agree that "Shakespeare" finally exists only as a process of shared and shifting interpretation, they still manage to conclude that the "brisk circulation" of his texts in theory and popular culture suggests "a more durable basis for the value and authority of these artifacts" (Bristol 1996: xii). Shakespeare is thus reaffirmed as an immanent, durable, self-renewing center of value and authority, at once thoroughly susceptible to appropriation and yet, precisely as such, finally invulnerable to all "extrinsic" claims.

To be sure, critics of both left and right commonly concede that a variety of "economic" issues (in publishing, the theater, the university, and so forth) condition the historical existence of "Shakespeare" as cultural text. But the rhetoric I have cited indicates that, beyond all such considerations, a certain symbolic economy underlies this defense of Shakespeare's universal value. I will argue here that these formulations evoke the central terms of a theoretical conversation that begins with Marcel Mauss's *The Gift* (1990), and continues in the work of Georges Bataille and in readings of the latter by Jacques Derrida, Jean-Luc Nancy, and others. At the heart of this continuing debate is Mauss's claim that archaic human societies around the world were not organized around the production and conservation of scarce resources (like capitalist societies) but, instead, around mutual gift-giving and ritualistic expenditure, such as the famous "potlatch" (see Mauss 1990). Bataille elaborates and eventually transforms Mauss's anthropological observations into a theoretical opposition between what he calls "restricted" and "general" economies. In brief, a "restricted" economy assumes that the central economic issue is *scarcity*, and thus emphasizes production, accumulation, and the profit or "return" that may be expected from all economic practices. A "general" economy, by contrast, assumes that the central economic issue is *surplus*; and therefore emphasizes gifts, sacrifices, and reckless expenditures, with the prospect of loss without return or reserve.

With these terms in mind, it becomes clear that the rhetoric of Shakespearean universality associates an approach such as Marxism with the "restricted" economy: that is, with the self-interest and calculation, the *economism*, that Max Weber famously identified as the organizing "spirit" of capitalism itself. The universalizers suggest that the Marxist critic strives to make Shakespeare her own property, and exploits Shakespeare in the expectation of "self-advancement." Correspondingly, Shakespeare himself becomes the site of a kind of "general" economy of abundance, "infinite variety," and a surplus of value that overflows any attempt to harness or contain it. Harold Bloom, for example, exemplifies precisely this strategy in his lengthy paean to a universal Shakespeare. Bloom argues, on the one hand, that after every specific interpretation of Shakespeare, "there is always a residuum, an excess that is left over," and, on the other hand, that what he calls the "ideologues" of the contemporary Academy "themselves are caricatures of Shakespearean energies" (Bloom 1998: 718, 12). Thus, in a rhetorically effective but quite illogical inversion, the universalizers insist, in effect, that the singular author is "broad" but the whole field of theory is "narrow."[1]

Various other scholars specifically invoke Mauss in defense of some version of this humanist estheticism.[2] Perhaps the best-known example is Lewis Hyde's *The Gift*, which argues that all "creative life" takes place within a "gift economy." Hyde concedes that works of art often become literal commodities, and discusses at length the tension between such commercialization and art's alleged generosity, but he also insists that "where there is no gift there is no art" (Hyde 1983: xiii). Bataille's own text sometimes seems to license this kind of argument by similarly discovering, within the esthetic, a certain resistance to the utilitarian calculus of classical economic theory. In the end, however, "general economics," as elaborated across the full range of Bataille's vast and sometimes fragmentary corpus, finally leads in quite a different direction. Indeed, Bataille's work announces a profoundly radical critique of traditional Western standards of representation and knowledge, a critique which might be said to begin with a quintessentially Marxist vision of the unity of material and symbolic production. He suggests that the central problem of all material existence is how to expend the surplus energy that flows unceasingly to the Earth from a Sun that "gives without ever receiving" (Bataille 1991: vol. 1, 28). This literal surplus of energy in the terrestrial biosphere cannot, in principle, be fully expended, and so "can only be lost without the slightest aim, consequently without any *meaning*" (cited in Derrida 1978: 270). Therefore, epistemology must come to terms with the terminal absence of meaning beyond all "aim," all traditional operations of knowledge, and thus, too, beyond the aiming or knowing Subject. Classical philosophic systems are therefore restricted *theoretical* economies that construe the world as limited or "restricted" enough to be graspable by thought, and assume that intellectual work will be rewarded with the wages of knowledge. Such systems thus might be understood as forms of epistemological capitalism, in which knowledge, like any other resource, is produced, expanded, accumulated, and conserved.

By contrast, using an ingenious French pun that opposes "thought" (*pense*) to "expenditure" (*depense*), Bataille calls prophetically for a "general" theoretical economy that has subsequently emerged in post-structuralist philosophy: systems in which there is always a *surplus* of signification, and in which meaning is therefore open, infinitely disseminated, and forever uncontainable. Such a project, Bataille also argues, remains faithful to a radically materialist Marx whom he envisions in one early essay as the Shakespearean "old mole" burrowing beneath all theoretical idealisms, whose revolution "hollows out chambers in a decomposed soil repugnant to the delicate nose of the utopians" (Bataille 1985: 34–5).[3] At the farthest horizons of his thought, correspondingly, Bataille projects what Jean-Luc Nancy calls a "literary communism," a community manifest in a writing or a voice that indeed must "be *offered*, that is to say, presented, proposed, and abandoned on the common limit where singular beings share one another" – but that, conversely, "has nothing to do with the myth of communion through literature" (Nancy 1991: 64, 73). If there are moments in Bataille's texts which may be thought to license a certain arcadian nostalgia or humanist estheticism, they are but the traces of Bataille's own struggle to think the unthinkable and hold fast to a value construed as negative rather than positive, destructive rather than creative, reckless and wasteful rather than prudent and thrifty.

In the rest of this essay, I will sketch the early modern roots of the familiar theoretical strategy which envisions Shakespeare (or his text) as the source of a radically non-economistic generosity and abundance. Pierre Bourdieu has, of course, described at length the historical construction of a universal esthetic in Kantian philosophy and elsewhere (see Bourdieu 1984, 1993); and many other scholars have documented how, in early modern Europe, a range of material practices were gradually reinterpreted as constituting literary "authorship." Here, I will approach similar conclusions from a different direction, using Bataille's terms to illuminate how, in early modern discourse, conventional ideas about authorship, representation, and subjectivity itself seem to be rooted in the period's "economic" ideas. From a Marxist point of view it would be, of course, no surprise that "economic" and "literary" discourses should be genetically and conceptually linked. But these particular homologies reveal the traces of that broad historical process by which the esthetic, construed as a kind of "gift" – a value absolutely distinguished from mere economic value – would as such become a crucial underpinning of a system otherwise insisting on the "restricted" economic values of thrift, calculation, and self-interest. In other words, the idea of a universal esthetic seals itself off from "economic" considerations, but only so as to allow the latter free reign everywhere else. As Bourdieu has memorably expressed it, "art for art's sake" is just another way of saying "business is business."

II

Bataille sometimes follows Mauss in projecting a "basic movement in history" (Bataille 1991: vol. 1, 38) in which a new general economy, a reborn ethic of generosity, was inexorably approaching. Derrida, even as he gestures toward this utopian reading in the title of his seminal reading of Bataille, "From Restricted to General Economy," later stipulates that the relation between the two economies is "neither of identity nor of contradiction," and that they therefore do not exist as autonomous historical modes which might be chosen or rejected once and for all (Derrida 1981: 4). I will use the terms here to refer to two poles of thought that co-exist in a wide variety of discourses from the early modern to the postmodern.

Both economies were certainly available, as figures of longing or moral aspiration, in the Bible itself and in the loose network of ideas and tropes that constititute what I will call the "moral economy" of early modern England. On the one hand, early modern preachers and pamphleteers rarely tire of affirming that as you sow so shall you reap; but on the other hand, also enjoin their readers (as Jesus did his disciples) to "freely give," and to "lay not up for yourselves treasures upon earth" (*Matt* 10: 8; 6: 19). Similarly, early modern homiletic discourse conventionally portrays the divine as an inexhaustible plenitude, and social life as a condition of absolute mutual indebtedness. As Bishop Edwin Sandys summarizes:

> Every man is to his neighbor a debtor, not only of that which himself borroweth, but of whatsoever his neighbor needeth; a debtor not only to pay that he oweth, but also to lend that he hath and may conveniently spare; to lend, I say, according to the rule of Christ, "Lend, looking for nothing thereby."
>
> (Sandys 1841: 202–4)

Sandys' concluding injunction, always a central formula in the profusion of anti-usury texts published in the sixteenth and early seventeenth centuries, also affirms a kind of general economy in which human life is envisioned as a condition of perpetual and mutual giving with no thought of return. To some extent, the opposition of restricted and general economies seems to correlate with the theological opposition of salvation by works or by grace; and Luther, as is well known, understood himself to be rejecting the spiritual economism of the Roman church's chantry chapels, indulgences, and the like. Nevertheless, it would be an oversimplification to identify the two economies as simply Catholic or Protestant. In a celebrated paradox, Protestantism in early modern England would embrace at once a theological idea of salvation by God's "free gift" of grace (a kind of general economy), and a moral doctrine of "justification by success" that epitomizes a restricted economy (investment and return) and, as Weber and later scholars have argued, entwines or co-operates with the ideologies of capitalism itself.

It is only in retrospect, however, that capitalism appears as Weber's Ben Franklinesque "spirit" of frugality and thrift, the very paradigm of a restricted economy. Bataille himself undoubtedly envisioned capitalism in these terms, and positioned the idea of general economics in opposition to the values of a bourgeois class who (he claims) gave the very word "economic" its "vulgar sense" (Bataille 1985: 124). The bourgeoisie consumes the surplus of material production while remaining otherwise devoted to economic restriction both in the material sense (the reinvestment and reproduction of accumulated value) and in the theoretical sense (an Enlightenment empiricism that sees the knowing subject as capable of grasping the world).

Writers of the early modern period did not, however, see things quite this way. To be sure, one conventional discourse laments the decline of rural hospitality and denounces an alleged new "covetousness" in social life. Just as frequently, however, the discourse seems to envision nascent capitalism as a fearful general economy of loss, in which a newly energized commercial marketplace was draining away the nation's lifeblood. From the fifteenth to the seventeenth centuries, for example, writers repeat a particular denunciation of international trade – in which, it is claimed, England was exporting staple commodities (such as tin, wool, or even grain) in return for "superfluous" luxuries. The anonymous author of the *Libelle of Englyshe Polycye* (1436) complains that for "Apes and japes and marmusettes taylede, / Nifles, trifles, that litell have availed," merchant ships "bere hens oure beste chaffare" [i.e. merchandise]; and

> bere the golde oute of thy londe
> And souke the thrifte awey oute of oure honde;
> As the waffore [i.e. wasp, drone] soukethe honye fro the bee,

So mynúceth oure commoditie.

(Warner [ed.] 1926: ll. 249–50, 375, 396–9)

Various statutes prohibiting the import of luxury goods were passed over the course of the sixteenth century. In 1559, for example, Parliament was debating, in virtually the same terms as the late medieval satirist, whether it should order "that no merchant . . . bring into the realm caps, pins, points, dice, gilt stirrups, etc . . . for they are not only false and deceitful wares, rather serving for the gaze than any good use, but for such trifles they filch from us the chief and substantial staple wares of the realm" (Tawney and Power [eds] 1924: vol. 1, 327).

The economic doctrine today known as mercantilism that develops in the writings of Thomas Mun and several others in the early decades of the seventeenth century represents, at least in part, a systematic theoretical answer to this conventional denunciation of international commerce. Mun's *Discourse of Trade from England unto the East-Indies* (1621) contains his first statement of the so-called "balance of trade," the idea he would later develop fully in the famous *England's Treasure by Foreign Trade* (c. 1623, published 1664). Mun asserts as a basic principle that "in those Kingdomes, which with great care and warinesse doe ever vent out more of their home commodities, than they import and use of forren wares; . . . the remainder must returne to them in treasure" (Mun 1621: 1). The usefulness of this concept lies in the way it ingeniously restores a restricted economy (economic "return" and "reserve") to the traditional image of a pernicious economy of loss. In Mun's schema, the abundant "venting out" of goods returns as "treasure." Nevertheless, Mun still feels himself immediately forced to concede that if the English themselves, "through wantonesse and riot . . . overwaste both forren and domestike wares; there must the money of neccessitie be exported, as the meanes to helpe furnish such excesse." It is in this way, Mun concludes, that "manie rich countries are made exceeding poore" (Mun 1621: 1–2).

Histories of economic theory commonly describe the mercantilists as the beginning of a tradition of "political" economy that continues, in England, through Adam Smith, David Ricardo, and their successors. This political economy, it is claimed, superseded the pre-existing body of ideas and texts that would only retrospectively (and in an oppositional spirit) be named the "moral economy."[4] Yet mercantilism, as Mun's lines above suggest, was every bit as "moral" in its intentions and formulations, and even shares a common structure of thought with the sermonists and biblical commentators of the period. For both, a model of restricted economy (you must sow that you may reap) is the standard by which any practice is to be judged. The venting of national products returns as treasure, the endeavors of all men in their "callings" return in the form of what sermonist William Perkins calls an "abundance" which "it is the pleasure of God to bestow . . . upon them" (Perkins 1612: 770). But this model is flanked, so to speak, on the one side by a pernicious general economy of consumer desire and commercial greed and, on the other side, by an idealized general economy manifest either in divine plenitude or human generosity.

III

The tension between restricted and general economic visions can also be followed in a conventional debate about the so-called "parable of the talents" from the Gospel of St. Matthew, which also appears in slightly different form in the Gospel of St. Luke. This became a particularly contested passage within the larger debate about usury that intensifies around the turn of the seventeenth century. In the parable, Jesus compares the kingdom of heaven to a master who travels to a far country, leaving with each of his three servants five, two, and one "talents" respectively, and then demands an accounting on his return. The first and second servants double their talents by "trading" with them, but the third hides his talent so as, he later claims, to be able to return it safely. To this third servant, the master replies (citing the Geneva Bible of 1560): "Thou evil servant, & slothful . . . Thou oughtest therefore to have put my money to the exchangers, and then at my coming should I have received mine own with vantage" (*Matt.* 25: 26–7). This parable presents a confusing mixture of the two economies. On the one hand, the master commands, in what has recently been called the most "frightening" line in the whole Bible (Gomes 1996: 293), that "unto every one that hath shall be given, and he shall have abundance: but from him that hath not shall be taken away even that which he hath." On the other hand, the master seems, at least on the literal level of the parable's narrative, to enjoin not only the general idea of commercial profit but even usury itself. Two different anti-usury texts from 1604 cite an anonymous defense of usury then apparently circulating in manuscript that claims that, in the parable of the talents, "our Savior speaketh of usury as of a lawful gain: and withal signifieth, that it is better for a man . . . to put forth his money to usury, than to have it idle by him."[5] The standard way to refute this literal interpretation of the passage was to insist on a strictly figural interpretation. As far back as the Church fathers, the parable was understood to be referring, not to money, but to what are commonly called "spiritual gifts and graces"; and the parable thus enjoins, not financial usury, but the profitable employment of one's skills and abilities. Indeed, the personal sense of the word "talent" that now prevails in English derives from the conventional figural interpretation of this parable.

But this division between literal and figural readings seems, in the various articulations of this conventional argument, to have a further discursive effect. Here, for further example, is how sermonist Henry Smith phrases his version of this point:

> He which used his Talent, doubled it; and he which hid his Talent, lost it: even so to every man God hath given some gift, of judgment, of tongues, of interpretation, or counsel, to employ and do good; and he which useth that gift which God hath given him, to the profit of others, and Gods glory, shall receive more gifts of God, as the servant which used two Talents, received two more: but he which useth it not, but abuseth it, as many doe, that gift which he hath, shall be taken from him, as the odd Talent was from the servant which had but one: showing, that one gift is too much for the wicked, and therefore it shall not stay with him. One would think it should be said, Whosoever hath not, to him shall bee given: and whosoever hath, from him shall bee taken: for God bideth us give to them which want. But this is contrary: for he taketh from them which want, and giveth to them which have. It is said, that our thoughts are not like Gods thoughts: and so our gifts are not like Gods gifts: for he giveth spiritual things, and we give temporal things. Temporal things are to be given to them which have not, but spiritual things to them which have.
>
> (Smith 1622: 321–2)

The opposition between the literal and the figural, seen as essential to the proper interpretation of the parable, seems to carry this writer by its own rhetorical momentum toward an analogous opposition between the temporal and the spiritual. This shift, however, slightly alters the logical terms of the argument. With the original opposition, the literal reading (God permits or even enjoins the putting out of money for "vantage") must be *rejected* in favor of the proper figural reading (God requires the profitable employment of personal "gifts" and "graces"). With the new opposition, conversely, the temporal simply *accompanies* the spiritual, as a distinct mode of practice. This new experiential division is necessary to explain the apparent injustice of the parable's conclusion, which then really refers to how personal gifts should be used to produce spiritual profit; and also to eliminate any possible interpretation that might question the idea of *charity*: the giving of "temporal things . . . to them which have not."

What happens in this discourse, then, is a kind of splitting, an assumption of two distinct modes of social practice: one subjective, concerned with personal "talents" and "graces"; the other objective, concerned with quantitative "increase" and financial profit. In other words, the discourse has constructed a sphere of interiority, the site of what is often called "spiritual usury," even as it also assumes an absolute division between it and a "temporal" sphere in which, "for the generation of this world," business is business. Either of these spheres is entirely individual in emphasis, and such individuality remains in constant tension with the discourse's simultaneous affirmation of community, its frequent assertions that each individual must use his personal gifts for "his neighbors profit" and "for the common good" (Geneva Bible, marginal annotation on *Matt.* 25: 27; Downame 1604: 287). This injunction also applies to the temporal practices of borrowing and lending, in which one must "Lend to . . . poor neighbors in time of their great need," looking neither for "vantage" nor even "so much as for the principal again" (Wilson, n.d. [1572]: 189). Both this charitable lending (or giving) and the corresponding injunction to make profitable use of one's personal talents are metaphorically linked as practices which produce a "multiplication of the gifts and graces of god" (Wilson, n.d. [1572]: 190). The discourse mandates that your lands, your money, your "stock," and your personal "talents" must be developed and employed; indeed, human beings are *permitted* gain in the temporal sphere, but *compelled* to enlarge themselves spiritually.

Moreover, since the patristic period it had been conventional to understand the work of the preachers and moralists in producing the moral economy as itself the paradigm of this profitable employment of spiritual gifts, which Smith envisions above as "of judgment, of tongues, of interpretation, or counsel." In the fourth century, for example, Saint John Chrysostom understands the parable to be enjoining that "He that hath a gift of word and teaching to profit thereby, and useth it not, will lose the gift also; but he that giveth diligence, will gain to himself the gift in more abundance" (Chrysostom 1851: 472). One of the emblems in Geffrey Whitney's well-known compilation from the sixteenth century, similarly, depicts two scholars reading, with the motto:

> We may not haste, our talent to bestow,
> Nor hide it up, whereby no good shall grow.
>
> (Whitney 1586: 177)[6]

In producing the moral economy, then, these writers were practicing what they preached; and the act of reading this discourse, correspondingly, manifests the spiritual "profit" which justifies its production. "I doubt not," declares Samuel Hieron in *Truths Purchase: or A Commodity which no man may either neglect to buie, or dare to sell*, "but as a man having publicly bought a commodity, may privately husband it, to his own best behoof, so that which is delivered openly may, (nay ought) by private reading, prayer, meditation, and conference, be increased" (Hieron 1606: sig. D2r). Here, the process of figural analogy, as usual, evokes the secondary opposition of temporal and spiritual practices, but then links the assumed moral propriety of personal economic gain with a realm of private spiritual experience. Similarly, Alexander Niccholes, in his *Discourse of Marriage and Wiving* (1615), urges young men not to postpone marriage (in terms reminiscent of Shakespeare's sonnets) by "hiding in the earth their talents from use, which might have been otherwise multiplied, by a lawful usury, to a happy increase" (Oldys [ed.] 1809: 163). The rhetoric of these injunctions suggests clearly how such texts, as it were, produce subjects by enjoining them to reproduce themselves, by an operation of (spiritual and physical) capital in which personal "graces" and "talents" contribute, not to the common good, but to a wholly individual process of happiness and self-fulfillment.

In this, the moral economy reaches an impasse. It demands of each individual subject a willingness to give and "look for nothing thereby"; and conceives the spiritual sphere from which the subject emerges as the very site where humanity echoes and confirms the divine plenitude with its own generosity. But the same formulations envision the subject as *produced by* a restricted economy, a process of spiritual self-development in which writers and readers alike employ their stock of talents in the expectation of "return." Thus, in this discourse, the general economy is doubly marginalized even as it is profusely affirmed. On the one hand, it is largely split off from the practical behavior expected of "the generation of this world"; on the other hand, it is entrusted to a subject who has been constituted by (and is condemned to labor within) a restricted economy of accumulation and conservation.

IV

Just as the paradigm of spiritual usury was the literal production, the reading and writing, of the moral economy itself, so the mercantilists commonly imagine trade in terms which relate it to a prevailing quasi-Platonic model of language and representation. In text after text, commerce is described as a process involving the "venting" or, to use another common word, "uttering" of English commodities (e.g. Wheeler 1601: 8; Mun 1621: 50; Roberts 1641: 60). That *to utter* means both *to speak* and *to sell* indicates how both speaking and selling are envisioned in what Derrida has called "logocentric" terms. In both cases, that is, value descends from heaven or ascends from the earth, and is then transported or transmitted from the inside to the outside, from self (England) to other (the world marketplace).

The word *utter*, however, commonly meant not simply "to sell" but, more precisely, to engage in a practice such as "regrating" or "forestalling" the market – that is, buying cheap to sell dear, profiting from discrepancies of price between different markets. In the moral economy, the distribution of staple products is always enjoined to be "so far as possible, *direct*, from the farmer to the consumer" (Thompson 1993: 193). Therefore the discourse always condemns a man who buys something "in order that he may gain by selling it again unchanged and as he bought it" (Gratian, *Decretum*, cited in Tawney 1936: 34–5). The verb *utter* commonly refers to the practices of these despised "middle men," who seem to conjure up profit in excess of the intrinsic value (the "just price") of the product. For example, Thomas Kyd in his *Householders Philosophie* (1588) denounces as "most injust" the merchant who "having bargained for the commodities of a Countrey, retaileth them or selleth them againe in the same place, watching the opportunitie and time when they may *utter* them unto theyre most advantage" (Kyd 1801: 276; my emphasis). Early modern discourse also related such practices to what Aristotle calls "chrematistics" or "money-making," a mode of economic behavior opposed to true "economy" or "household management." In an early modern annotation of the *Politics*, chrematistics is defined as "the artificiall and crafty meanes of getting of money by engrossing up of commodities, and *uttering* them againe for gaine" (Aristotle 1598: 51; my emphasis).

The two meanings of *utter* converge precisely in the equally conventional image of the huckstering merchant, the very emblem of a restricted economism. Thus the playwright Robert Wilson denounces merchants who "with lying, flattering and glosing . . . must *utter* your ware" (Wilson 1988: 11); and Henry Crosse writes of "shop-keepers" who "keep small conscience in *uttering* their ware, their shops, shops of deceit, for now almost all men crye out, that there is nothing but cosonage in buying and selling" (Crosse 1603: sig. H4r). These writers suggest, in other words, that merchants utter (dishonestly) so as to utter (dishonestly), a circularity which indicates a pitfall in this conventional line of thought. The logocentric model in which (as Ben Jonson puts its) "likeness is always on this side truth" (Jonson 1925–63: vol. 8, 590), involves an economy of loss, an inevitable dilution of "truth" that takes place within all representation. Therefore, this model of linguistic utterance, precisely *in* its figural analogy to material commerce, seems to confirm the conventional anxiety about the latter as a draining away of the national substance.

As though in response, and as we have already in part seen, early modern discourse strives to reinscribe the practices of speaking, writing, and selling within a restricted economy in which one ex-pounds or ex-ports in the expectation of (spiritual or material) profit. Mercantilism reimagines commerce as a profitable "balance" or circulation of trade; while the discourse of moral economy constructs a human subject who constantly seeks to *grasp* the world, and who "never gives anything without calculating, consciously or unconsciously, its reappropriation, its exchange, or its circular return" (Derrida 1992: 101). Accordingly, the moral economy would always cherish, as a central trope, the Gospel image of preaching as a spiritual "ploughing," a symbolic and subjective husbandry in which, as George Gifford puts it, "The seede is the word of God," "the sower of it is the Preacher," and the mind and heart are "the ground . . . unto which it falleth" (Gifford 1582; cf. Latimer, "Sermon of the Plough," in Chandos 1971). Still, if commerce is somehow like language (and vice versa), then both are what Derrida has called "guilty," for the economism imposed on either process never extinguishes a nostalgic yearning for the lost and absent center of value that sets in motion the circulation of linguistic signs or staple goods. This is the very place of the famous "anxiety" of early modern England, which a whole range of scholarly work locates in some ambiguous conjunction of literary representation (especially in the theater) and a new and larger presence of "the market" in social life – an anxiety, as I have argued elsewhere, of subjects who come into being already lost to some mysterious expropriating power at once linguistic and commercial (Shershow 1995).

In other words, early modern discourse longs for, and in so doing constructs, an imagined center of plenitude and presence, a fantasy of a value which need never be submitted to utterance or exchange. Michael Drayton, in a flattering poem to King James on behalf of the goldsmiths of London, first repeats the conventional accusation that merchants merely bring to England

> sleight gauds and womanish devices,
> Of little use and of excessive prices.
> Good home-made things with trifles to suppresse,
> To feede luxurious riot, and excesse.

– and then claims, by contrast, that among James's other subjects,

> harts are heap'd with those innumberd hoords,
> That tongues by uttrance cannot vent in words.
> (Drayton 1604: sig. B1v–r)

In such lines, the conventional anxiety about trade is displaced by a vision of the generous subject, of the subject *as* generosity: the heart "heap'd" with the love that cannot be spoken and that yet, of course, *is* being spoken, written, uttered. In the terms of this conventional structure of thought, it is then only logical to celebrate the literary Author – the one who speaks and gives and gives through speaking – as the very site and conduit of this transcendental plenitude. In Heming and Condell's famous epistles to the first folio edition of Shakespeare's works, they insist that they publish these plays "without ambition . . . of self-profit" even as they urge potential readers to "buy" and "reade" the book. Correspondingly, it is their highest praise of Shakespeare that "what he thought, he uttered" (Shakespeare 1974: 62–3).

V

At one level of interpretation, Shakespeare's own representation of these economic issues remains wholly within the basic symbolic economy, and even the specific network of conventional ideas and tropes I have been considering here. In *The Merchant of Venice,* for example, Shakespeare obviously seems to oppose a benevolent and extravagant generosity to mere selfish, money-grubbing economism. I scarcely need to cite the familiar lines which make clear how all the good characters of this play are givers and spenders. Antonio pledges his "extremest means" (1. 1. 138) to Bassanio, who himself wins Portia by his willingness to "give and hazard all he hath" (2. 7. 9). Portia offers to resolve Antonio's debt of three thousand ducats by offering to pay "six thousand," and then to "Double six thousand, and then treble that" (3. 2.

299–300). Jessica spends "fourscore ducats" at a single dinner and a significant portion of her patrimony on a honeymoon spree. These characters will eventually unite in opposition to Shylock, whose greatest joys are his "bargains" and his "well-won-thrift" (1. 3. 50). This thematic structure has licensed the interpretations of generations of students and critics in which the play is seen as suggesting that "economic" values (contracts, investments, usury) must be properly subordinated to "human" values (love, friendship, community). Frank Kermode argues, for example, that *Merchant* "begins with usury and corrupt love" and "ends with harmony and perfect love" (Kermode 1961: 224).

By contrast, Marxist critics such as Walter Cohen and Michael Ferber, with their careful elucidations of the play's historical context, have pierced the veil of this thematic allegory to reveal how Shakespeare at most attacks a kind of precapitalist hoarding – so that, in the end, the play "is quite obviously procapitalist" (Cohen 1982: 768). Indeed, I would suggest that, as far as he could understand "capitalism" at all, Shakespeare envisions it here in what Marx argues is its progressive aspect: how it opens doors, breaks up the medieval hoards, puts money in circulation, and fosters that very "universality" in whose name Shakespeare himself would one day be celebrated.[7] In the wake of such insights, perhaps the one thing that remains to be stated a little more strongly is the sheer speciousness of a play which indulges us with what Bataille might have called loss *with* return: the double luxury of generosity and abundance. The play's alleged "harmony," as Lawrence Danson puts it, "is *earned* by Shakespeare for his characters and the audience" (Danson 1978: 11; my emphasis). The peculiarly appropriate verb I have emphasized indicates clearly, even if unintentionally, how the play presents us with a seductive fantasy of the general economy (infinite risk, infinite generosity) which remains wholly in service of a (literal and figural) economism. To put it simply, in this play Antonio gives and invests and risks – and profits; and Bassanio "gives and hazards all he hath," and in the end "hath" Portia and love and money and all. Such a strategy at one level merely replicates the specious providentiality of the early modern moral economy itself, a discourse which also commonly promises to reward its readers if they will give without *expectation* of reward. For example, the marginal annotations of the Geneva Bible to Luke 6: 35 ("lend, looking for nothing againe") clarifies that one should lend "Not onely not hoping for profite, but to lose the stocke and principall, for as much as Christ bindeth himselfe to repay the whole with a most liberall interest." William Perkins argues, similarly, that "to seeke for abundance is not lawful";

but that "If God give abundance when we neither desire it nor seeke it, we may take it, hold and use it" (Perkins 1612: 126).

Even more broadly, however, the play also contributes to the profound ruse with which capitalism, both then and now, grounds itself in economic restriction (investment with "return") and at the same time cloaks itself with an ethic of generosity and the gift. As Michael Ferber has shrewdly argued, in *Merchant*, "Shakespeare invented an imaginary alternative to the Weber Thesis" and "tied capitalism to a sort of anti-Calvinist Christianity that encouraged uncalculating acts of sacrifice and risk" (Ferber 1990: 447–8). In this, Shakespeare even seems to anticipate contemporary capitalist apologists such as George Gilder, who celebrates what he calls the "essential generosity" of capitalism and even claims that "giving is [its] vital impulse and moral center" (Gilder 1981: 30). If one wishes, one may give Shakespeare credit for the imaginative prescience with which his play anticipates the ideological strategies of contemporary capitalism. But let us also acknowledge that, in this, he does little more than contribute to the mystifications which continue to bedevil our practice and our thought.

Later in his career, Shakespeare would, of course, devote an entire play to an explicit consideration of the general or "gift" economy. But *Timon of Athens* remains a nearly unperformable curiosity precisely because it can approve neither Timon's extravagant imprudence nor the dog-eat-dog world of untrammeled self-interest that brings him down. Shakespeare simply cannot imagine any realistic social model beyond these two alternatives, and since the play deplores both it has absolutely nowhere to go. Shakespeare had, however, already performed a slightly more complex staging of this economic opposition in two celebrated scenes of *King Lear*. In the first, Lear pauses before leaving the storm, in order, he claims, to "pray." But he addresses his prayer, not to the gods, but rather to the

> Poor naked wretches, wheresoe'er you are,
> That bide the pelting of this pitiless storm.

And Lear's prayer ends, of course, with the injunction to

> Take physic, pomp,
> Expose thyself to feel what wretches feel
> That thou mayst shake the superflux to them.
>
> (3. 4. 27–36)

Slightly later, the blind Gloucester gives his purse to someone he believes to be a beggar, and instructs the "heavens" to "deal so still":

So distribution should undo excess
And each man have enough.

(4. 1. 66–71)

These obviously parallel scenes, as the work of various commentators join to suggest, are susceptible to two opposite interpretations. Is Shakespeare transmitting what Annabel Patterson calls a "popular voice" of early modern England, a grassroots tradition of primitive communism (Patterson 1989)? – and is he even, as some might argue, literally anticipating Marx by imagining a truly collective economy? Or is Shakespeare simply affirming *charity*: that is, the paternalistic responsibility, in a world of scarce resources, to give generously "to them which have not"?[8]

Even if one concedes this interpretive crux to be insoluble, however, it leads to a still larger question. In Bataille's terms, are we to understand that charity, generous giving, is (as it sounds) a veritable general economy? To do so is to remain within the ideological confines of the early modern moral economy itself, which always assumes (in the words of Henry Bullinger) that God "granteth to his disciples a propriety and possession of peculiar goods, wherewith they may frankly do good unto other . . . For if all things be common, then doest thou give nothing of that which is thine, but all that thou spendest is of the common riches" (Bullinger 1577: 260).[9] So shines a good deed in a naughty world! As Bullinger's formula makes all too clear, charity and generosity are about transferring value from haves to have-nots; and they thus require a world of properties and subjects, a world in which the poor you have always with you. To ignore this insight and identify mere charity, mere gift-giving, with the general economy is also, presumably, to relegate the other alternative – Marxism, communism, collectivity – to the restricted economy. This, we may recall, is precisely what the formulations I critiqued at the beginning of this essay are doing.

But there is another way to understand the clash of ideologies and economies in Shakespeare's famous lines. This time, we would recognize that charity and generosity themselves remain under the horizon of the restricted economy, for they merely involve loss *with* return: giving in the expectation that God, or someone else, or one's own generous heart, will repay the gift with interest. Marxism would then be located, correspondingly, under the horizon of the general economy, precisely as it seeks to think a community in which there could no longer be charity, or even justice, or even virtue; where there would be no giving because there would be no subjects to give or properties to receive. And whereas the first formulation, as we have seen, inevitably leads back to an esthetic universality, this formulation permits and requires us to give up the spurious abundance of authorship and art, "to strip away and discard the enchanted impression of aesthetic autonomy" (Greenblatt 1988: 5).[10]

In seeing this, however, one must always grasp that the commodity and the gift, the restricted and general economies, exist only *in relation*, and therefore, merely to oppose one to the other is to see the opposition as itself an essentially (and merely) *moral* one – and so, finally, to replicate the theoretical errors I have tried to describe here. I am calling, in other words, for a theoretical movement of double inversion that does not merely reinstate the original opposition. Whereas esthetic critics view Shakespeare as a general economy and Marxism as a restricted economy, I insist first on an inversion that recognizes "Shakespeare" as "restricted" in two senses. On the one hand, he is wholly bound within the horizons of early modern thought; on the other hand, he remains himself a product of economistic "return," a continuing instance of what Bourdieu calls "cultural" capital. But this moment of recognition returns us at the same time to a "Shakespeare" who, as even the universalizers are constrained to agree, exists only in a (general) economy of "endless interpretation" (Bloom 1998: 728).[11] In such an economy, each individual reading or performance, as an instance of value, is always "restricted" or contingent; and yet, by the same token, always exposed, given, offered to be shared. True enough, the discourse of esthetic universality takes Shakespeare as *given* and hence as *a gift*; but always reveals at the same time that such a gift (like the divine "talents," like a rich man's proffer of charity) comes *with obligation*. How else could the universalizing critics (retreating from their spurious general economy back to a "restricted" empiricism) attack the Marxist critic in the name of some allegedly "truer" interpretation? By contrast, I argue that Shakespeare, like any other writer, like any other writing or reading or effort of thought, like language itself, can finally be nothing more nor less than what Marx calls the "product" and the "presence" of the community, "a presence which goes without saying" (Marx 1973: 490). But of Shakespeare himself, this means, as Nancy stipulates, that

> he is not the author, nor is he the hero, and perhaps he is no longer what has been called the poet or what has been called the thinker; rather, he is . . . this singular voice, this resolutely and irreducibly

singular (mortal) voice, *in common*: just as one can never be "a voice" ("a writing") but *in common*.

(Nancy 1991: 70)

What else have we ever been hearing in the intoxicating sonorities of his pentameter, in the fierce interrogatories ("who's there?") and disconcerting iterations ("to be or not to be") of his theater and his book, but the call of the community that is "*to come*," that "is always *coming*, endlessly, at the heart of every collectivity" (Nancy 1991: 71)? The fact remains, however, that the Bard himself "could see nothing in the world but personal aims" (Shaw 1963: vol. 3, 510). To read Shakespeare, to perform Shakespeare, to profess Shakespeare, is therefore to embark on a path that can only lead beyond Shakespeare. In his end is our beginning.

Notes

1 The recently founded Association of Literary Scholars and Critics, in a promotional letter dated April 24, 1998, claims to "uphold *broad* conceptions of literature, rather than the *narrow*, highly politicized ones too often encountered today" (my emphases).

2 The pitfalls of the idea of a "gift" economy are clearly represented by Fumerton 1991, which relies heavily on Mauss and more recent anthropologists such as Marshall Sahlins and Chris Gregory in discussing aristocratic gift-giving in the English Renaissance. This line of thought leads Fumerton to claim, for example, that the art-collecting of King Charles I "was born of the same energies" (24) as the revolution which toppled his regime!

3 See Peter Stallybrass's essay in this volume (chapter 2) for more on how Marx himself construed the Shakespearean "mole" as a symbol of proletarian revolution.

4 Thompson 1993 suggests that the term "moral economy" was coined in the late eighteenth century to oppose the "political economy" of Adam Smith and his successors.

5 Downame 1604: 284. Virtually this same passage appears in Pie (1604). On how anti-usury texts from the early seventeenth century preserve an otherwise lost manuscript defense of usury, see Jones 1989: 153.

6 Milton would later, of course, employ a similar pun in the famous sonnet on his blindness, relating his own poetic aspirations to profit from the "talent which is death to hide."

7 The image of Jessica, bearing "ducats" and climbing from Shylock's windows into streets filled with carnival, despite his orders to "lock up my doors" and "stop my house's ears" (2. 5. 29–34), is perhaps the play's most

vivid libidinal image of how a new economy would bring freedom, mobility, and pleasure.

8 See Kronenfeld 1992 for a detailed historical elucidation of the ambiguity in these two passages.

9 Bullinger's collected sermons became required reading for English clergymen in the late sixteenth century. See Tawney 1936 (181).

10 I here cite but contradict Greenblatt's point.

11 In making this point, however, they always evade the essential further conclusion to which it inexorably leads: that, as Terence Hawkes (1992) argues, "We have no access to any 'essential' meaning nestling within Shakespeare's texts and awaiting our discovery," but instead, "*use* them to generate meaning" (3).

Bibliography

Adorno, T. (1978) "On the Fetish Character in Music and the Regression of Listening," in A. Arato and E. Gebhart (eds) *The Essential Frankfurt School Reader*, New York: Urizen.

Agnew, J. (1993) "Coming up for Air: Consumer Culture in Historical Perspective," in J. Brewer and R. Porter (eds) (1993).

Agrippa, C. (1509 [1542]) *A Treatise of the Nobilitie and Excellencye of Woman Kynde*, trans. D. Clapham, London.

Agrippa von Nettesheim, H. C. (1509) *Declamatio de nobilitate et praecellentia foeminei sexus*.

Ahmad, A. (1992) *In Theory*, London and New York: Verso.

—— (1994) "Reconciling Derrida: 'Spectres of Marx' and Deconstructive Politics," *New Left Review* 208: 88–106.

Alpers, S. (1988) *Rembrandt's Enterprise: The Studio and the Market*, Chicago: University of Chicago Press.

Anderson, B. (1991) *Imagined Communities: Reflections on the Origin and Spread of Nationalism*, London and New York: Verso.

Andrews, K. R. (1984) *Trade, Plunder and Settlement: Maritime Enterprise and the Genesis of the British Empire, 1480–1630*, Cambridge: Cambridge University Press.

Anon. (1678) *A Warning for Bad Wives: or, the Manner of the Burning of Sarah Elston*, London.

—— (1700) *Baron and Feme. A Treatise of the Common Laww Concerning Husbands and Wives*, London: John Walthoe.

—— (1732) *A Treatise of Feme Coverts: Or, the Lady's Law*, London: Bernard Lintot.

—— (1973) *The True Chronicle History of King Leir and his Three Daughters*, in G. Bullough (ed.) (1957–75) Vol. 7.

Anthony, K. (1945) *The Lambs: A Story of Pre-Victorian England*, New York: Knopf.

Appleby, J. (1993) "Consumption in Early Modern Social Thought," in Brewer and Porter (eds) (1993), 162–73.

Archer, J. M. (1994) "Antiquity and Degeneration: The Representation of Egypt and Shakespeare's *Antony and Cleopatra*," *Genre* 27: 1–27.

Aristotle (1598) *Aristotles Politiques*, trans. Loys le Roy, called Regius, London.

Aughterson, K. (1995) *Renaissance Woman: A Sourcebook, Constructions of Femininity in England*, New York: Routledge.

Bailey, F. A. (1951) "The Elizabethan Playhouse at Prescot, Lancashire," *Transactions of the Historical Society of Lancashire and Cheshire* 103: 69–81.

Baker, D. J. (1997) *Between Nations: Shakespeare, Spenser, Marvell, and the Question of Britain*, Stanford: Stanford University Press.

Bakhtin, M. (1986) *Speech Genres and Other Late Essays*, ed. C. Emerson and M. Holquist, trans. V. W. McGee, Minneapolis: University of Minnesota Press.

Bal, M. (1994) "Scared to Death," in M. Bal and I. E. Boer (eds) *The Point of Theory: Practices of Cultural Analysis*, New York: Continuum.

Barker, F. (1984) *The Tremulous Private Body: Essays on Subjection*, London: Methuen.

Barnet, R. and Cavanagh, J. (1994) *Global Dreams: Imperial Corporations and the New World Order*, New York: Simon and Schuster.

Bartels, E. C. (1997) "*Othello* and Africa: Postcolonialism Reconsidered," *William and Mary Quarterly*, 3rd series, 54: 45–64.

Barthes, R. (1972) *Mythologies*, trans. A. Lavers, New York: Hill and Wang.

Bashar, N. (1983) "Rape in England between 1550 and 1700," in London Feminist History Group (ed.) *The Sexual Dynamics of History*, London: Pluto Press.

Bataille, G. (1985) *Visions of Excess: Selected Writings, 1927–1939*, ed. A. Stoekl, trans. A. Stoekl et al., Minneapolis: University of Minnesota Press.

—— (1991) *The Accursed Share: An Essay on General Economy*, 3 vols., trans. R. Hurley, New York: Zone Books.

Baudrillard, J. (1981) *For a Critique of the Political Economy of the Sign*, trans. C. Levin, St. Louis: Telos Press.

Baxandall, L. and Morawski, S. (eds) (1973) *Marx and Engels on Literature and Art*, New York: International General.

Beardsworth, R. (1996) *Derrida and the Political*, New York: Routledge.

Benjamin, W. (1970) *Illuminations*, ed. H. Arendt, trans. H. Zohn, London: Jonathan Cape.

Berry, L. E. (1969) "Introduction," in *The Geneva Bible: A Facsimile of the 1560 Edition*, Madison: University of Wisconsin Press.

Beuttner, B. (1996) *Boccaccio's Des cleres et nobles femmes: Symptoms of Signification in an Illuminated Manuscript*, Seattle: College Art Association.

Bevington, D. (1998) "A. L. Rowse's Dark Lady," in M. Grossman (ed.) (1998).
Billingsley, M. (1618) *The Peis Excellence*, London.
Blackburn, R. (1997) *The Making of New World Slavery: From the Baroque to the Modern, 1492–1800*, London: Verso.
Blackstone, W. (1979) *Commentaries on the Laws of England: A Facsimile of the First Edition*, vol. 1, Chicago and London: University of Chicago Press.
Blake, W. (1972) *Complete Writings*, ed. G. Keynes, Oxford: Oxford University Press.
Blanchot, M. (1986) "Marx's Three Voices," trans. Thomas Keenan, *New Political Science* 15: 17–20.
Bloch, E. (1988) *The Utopian Function of Art and Literature: Selected Essays*, trans. J. Zipes and F. Mecklenburg, Cambridge, Mass., and London: MIT Press.
Bloom, H. (1973) *The Anxiety of Influence: A Theory of Poetry*, New York: Oxford University Press.
—— (1998) *Shakespeare: The Invention of the Human*, New York: Riverhead Books.
Bonfield, L. (1983) *Marriage Settlements, 1601–1740*, New York and Cambridge: Cambridge University Press.
Boose, L. E. (1975) "Othello's Handkerchief: The Recognizance and Pledge of Love," *English Literary Renaissance* 5: 360–74.
Boose, L. and Burt, R. (eds) (1997) *Shakespeare the Movie: Popularizing the Plays on Film, TV, and Video*, London and New York: Routledge.
Bourdieu, P. (1971) "Intellectual Field and Creative Project," trans. S. France, in M. Young (ed.) *Knowledge and Control: New Directions for the Sociology of Education*, London: Collier-Macmillan.
—— (1984) *Distinction: A Social Critique of the Judgement of Taste*, trans. R. Nice, London: Routledge; Cambridge, Mass.: Harvard University Press.
—— (1993) *The Field of Cultural Production*, trans. R. Johnson, Cambridge: Polity Press; New York: Columbia University Press.
—— (1996) *The Rules of Art: Genesis and Structure in the Literary Field*, trans. S. Emmanuel, Cambridge: Polity Press.
Bowen, B. E. (1999) "Aemilia Lanyer and the Invention of White Womanhood," in S. Frye and K. Robertson (eds) (1999).
Bradford, E. (1956) *The Elizabethan Woman*, London.
Branagh, K. (dir.) (1989) *Henry V* videocassette, CBS/Fox.
—— (dir.) (1993) *Much Ado About Nothing*, videocassette, Tristar.
—— (1996a) *Hamlet by William Shakespeare: Screenplay, Introduction, and Film Diary*, New York: Norton.
—— (1996b) *Hamlet*, videocassette, Columbia Tri-Star.
Brathwaite, E. K. (1984) *History of the Voice*, London: New Beacon Books.
Brecher, J. and Costello, T. (1994) *Global Village or Global Pillage: Economic Restructuring from the Bottom Up*, Boston: South End Press.
Brennan, T. (1997) *At Home in the World: Cosmopolitanism Now*, Cambridge, Mass.: Harvard University Press.

Brenner, R. (1993) *Merchants and Revolution: Commercial Change, Political Conflict, and London's Overseas Traders, 1550–1653*, Princeton: Princeton University Press.

Breton, N. ([1600] 1875–9) *The Works . . . of Nicholas Breton*, vol. 2, ed. A. B. Gosart, Edinburgh.

Brewer, J. and Porter, R. (eds) (1993) *Consumption and the World of Goods*, New York: Routledge.

Brewer, J. and Staves, S. (1996) *Early Modern Conceptions of Property*, New York and London: Routledge.

Bristol, M. (1990) *Shakespeare's America, America's Shakespeare*, London and New York: Routledge.

—— (1996) *Big Time Shakespeare*, London and New York: Routledge.

Brotton, J. (1998) *Trading Territories: Mapping the Early Modern World*, Ithaca, N.Y.: Cornell University Press.

Brubaker, R. (1993) "Social Theory as Habitus," in C. Calhoun, E. LiPuma, and M. Postone (eds) (1993).

Bullinger, H. (1577) *Fiftie Godlie and Learned Sermons, Divided into Five Decades*, London.

Bullough, G. (1957–75) *Narrative and Dramatic Sources of Shakespeare*, 8 vols., London: Routledge and Kegan Paul.

Bulman, J. C., and Coursen, H. R. (eds) (1988) *Shakespeare on Television: An Anthology of Essays and Reviews*, Hanover, N.H.: University Press of New England.

Burke, P. (1978) *Popular Culture in Early Modern Europe*, London: Temple Smith.

—— (1992) *The Fabrication of Louis XIV*, New Haven, Conn.: Yale University Press.

Burt, R. (1997) "The Love That Dare Not Speak Shakespeare's Name: New Shakesqueer Cinema," in L. Boose and R. Burt (eds) (1997).

Burton, R. (1982) *The Anatomy of Melancholy*, ed. Thomas C. Faulkner et al., Oxford: Clarendon Press.

Bynum, C. W. (1982) *Jesus as Mother: Studies in the Spirituality of the High Middle Ages*, Berkeley: University of California Press.

Cain, M. and Hunt, A. (1979) *Marx and Engels on Law*, London, New York, and San Francisco: Academic Press.

Cairns, D. and Richards, S. (1988) *Writing Ireland: Colonialism, Nationalism and Culture*, Manchester: Manchester University Press.

Calhoun, C. (1993) "Habitus, Field and Capital: The Question of Historical Specificity," in C. Calhoun, E. LiPuma, and M. Postone (eds) (1993).

Calhoun, C., LiPuma, E. and Postone, M. (eds) (1993) *Bourdieu: Critical Perspectives*, Cambridge: Polity Press.

Callaghan, D. (1989) *Woman and Gender in Renaissance Tragedy*, Atlantic Highlands, N.J.: Humanities.

—— (1999) *Shakespeare without Women*, New York: Routledge.

—— (ed.) (2000) *The Feminist Companion to Shakespeare*, Oxford: Blackwell.

Camden, C. (1972) *The Elizabethan Woman*, Houston: The Elsevier Press.

Campbell, L. (1947) *Shakespeare's "Histories": Mirrors of Elizabethan Policy*, San Marino: Huntington Library.

Chambers, E. K. (1923) *The Elizabethan Stage*, vol. 4, Oxford: Oxford University Press.

Chandos, J. (ed.) (1971) *In God's Name: Examples of Preaching in England from the Act of Supremacy to the Act of Uniformity, 1534–1662*, London: Hutchinson.

Charles, L. and Duffin, L. (eds) (1985) *Women and Work in Pre-Industrial England*, London: Croom Helm.

Chaytor, M. (1995) "Husband(ry): Narratives of Rape in the Seventeenth Century," *Gender & History* 7, 1: 378–407.

Chaytor, M. and Lewis, J. (1982) "Introduction," in A. Clark, *Working Life of Women in the Seventeenth Century*, London: Routledge.

Cholakian, P. F. (1991) *Rape and Writing in the Heptaméron of Marguerite de Navarre*, Carbondale: University of Southern Illinois Press.

Chrysostom, St. J. (1851, rpt. 1956) *The Homilies of St. John Chrysostom on the Gospel of St. Matthew*, vol. 10 of *A Select Library of the Nicene and Post-Nicene Fathers*, ed. P. Schaff, trans. G. Prevost, Grand Rapids, Mich.: Wm. B. Eerdmans.

Chun, L. (1993) *The British New Left*, Edinburgh: Edinburgh University Press.

Cixous, H. (1986) "Sorties," in H. Cixous and C. Clément, *The Newly Born Woman*, trans. B. Wing, Minneapolis: University of Minnesota Press.

Clark, A. ([1919] 1982) *Working Life of Women in the Seventeenth Century*, ed. M. Chaytor and J. Lewis, London: Routledge.

Clarkson, L. A. (1971) *The Pre-Industrial Economy in England 1500–1750*, London: B. T. Batsford.

Cohen, W. (1982) "*The Merchant of Venice* and the Possibilities of Historical Criticism," *English Literary History* 49, 4: 765–89.

—— (1985) *Drama of a Nation: Public Theater in Renaissance England and Spain*, Ithaca, N.Y.: Cornell University Press.

Coleridge, S. T. (1990) *The Collected Works of Samuel Taylor Coleridge*, vol. 14: II, *Table Talk II*, ed. C. Woodring, London: Routledge; Princeton, N.J.: Princeton University Press.

Collins, H. (1982) *Marxism and Law*, Oxford: Clarendon Press.

Cook, A. J. (1981) *The Privileged Playgoers of Shakespeare's London, 1576–1642*, Princeton, N.J.: Princeton University Press.

Coote, E. (1614) *The English Schoole-Master*, London.

Cornell, D. (1995) *The Imaginary Domain: Abortion, Pornography and Sexual Harassment*, New York: Routledge, 1995.

Crashaw, R. (1972) *The Complete Poetry of Richard Crashaw*, ed. G. Walton Williams, New York: New York University Press.

Crosse, H. (1603) *Vertues Common-wealth, or the Highway to Honour*, London.

Dalton, C. (1995) "Where We Stand: Observations on the Situation of Feminist Legal Thought," in F. E. Olson (ed.) *Feminist Legal Theory*, vol. 1, New York: New York University Press.

Dalton, M. (1635) *The Countrey Justice*, London.

Danson, L. (1978) *The Harmonies of The Merchant of Venice*, New Haven, Conn.: Yale University Press.
Davies, A. and Wells, S. (eds) (1994) *Shakespeare and the Moving Image: The Plays on Film and Television*, Cambridge: Cambridge University Press.
de Grazia, M. (1991) *Shakespeare Verbatim: The Reproduction of Authenticity and the 1790 Apparatus*, Oxford: Oxford University Press.
—— (1996) "Imprints: Shakespeare, Gutenberg, Descartes," in T. Hawkes (ed.) *Alternative Shakespeare 2*, New York: Routledge.
de Grazia, M. et al. (eds) (1996) *Subject and Object in Renaissance Culture*, Cambridge: Cambridge University Press.
Dekker, T. (1967), *The Gull's Hornbook*, ed. E. D. Pendry, London: Edward Arnold.
Denning, M. (1997) *The Cultural Front*, London: Verso.
Derrida, J. (1978) "From Restricted to General Economy: A Hegelianism without Reserve," in his *Writing and Difference*, trans. Allan Bass, Chicago: University of Chicago Press.
—— (1981) "Economimesis," *diacritics* 1, 1: 2–25.
—— (1989) *Of Spirit: Heidegger and the Question*, trans. G. Bennington and R. Bowlby, Chicago: University of Chicago Press.
—— (1992) *Given Time: I Counterfeit Money*, trans. P. Kamuf, Chicago: University of Chicago Press.
—— (1993) *Spectres de Marx: l'état de la dette, le travail du deuil et la nouvelle Internationale*, Paris: Galilée.
—— (1994) *Specters of Marx: The State of the Debt, the Work of Mourning and the New International*, trans. P. Kamuf, London and New York: Routledge.
—— (1998) *Resistances of Psychoanalysis*, trans. P. Kamuf, P. Brault, and M. Naas, Stanford: Stanford University Press.
Dickenson, D. (1997) *Property, Women and Politics: Subjects or Objects?*, New Brunswick, N.J.: Rutgers University Press.
Dirlik, A. (1994) *After the Revolution: Waking to Global Capitalism*, Hanover, N.H., and London: Wesleyan University Press.
Dodd, J. and Cleaver, R. (1598) *A Godlie Forme of Householde Government*, London.
Dolan, F. E. (1999) "Household Chastisements: Gender, Authority, and 'Domestic Violence,'" in P. Fumerton and S. Hunt (eds) (1999).
—— (ed.) (1996) *The Taming of the Shrew: Texts and Contexts*, Boston and New York: Bedford Books of St. Martin's Press.
Dollimore, J. (1994a) "Introduction: Shakespeare, Cultural Materialism and the New Historicism," in J. Dollimore and A. Sinfield (eds) (1994).
—— (1994b) "Transgression and Surveillance in *Measure for Measure*," in J. Dollimore and A. Sinfield (eds) (1994).
Dollimore, J. and Sinfield, A. (eds) (1994) *Political Shakespeare: Essays in Cultural Materialism*, 2nd edn, Manchester: Manchester University Press.
Donaldson, Ian. (1982) *The Rapes of Lucretia: A Myth and Its Transformations*, Oxford: Clarendon Press.
Downame, G. (1604) *Lectures on the XV Psalme*, London.

Drakakis, J. (1988) "Theatre, Ideology, and Institution: Shakespeare and the Roadsweepers," in G. Holderness (ed.) (1988).

Drayton, M. (1604) *A PæanTriumphall. Composed for the Societie of the Goldsmiths of London: congratulating his Highnes magnificient entring the Citie*, London.

Duplessis, R. S. (1997) *Transitions to Capitalism in Early Modern Europe*, Cambridge: Cambridge University Press.

Dutton, R. (1991) *Mastering the Revels: The Regulation and Censorship of English Renaissance Drama*, London: Macmillan.

Dworkin, D. (1997) *Cultural Marxism in Postwar Britain*, Durham, N.C., and London: Duke University Press.

E., T. [Thomas Edgar?] (1632) *The Lawes Resolutions of Womens Rights: Or, The Lawes Provision for Woemen*, London.

Edwards, P. (1968) *Shakespeare and the Confines of Art*, London: Methuen.

Elias, N. (1978) *The History of Manners*, trans. E. Jephcott, New York: Pantheon Books.

Elyot, T. (1540) *Defense of Good Women*, London.

Erickson, A. L. (1993) *Women and Property in Early Modern England*, London and New York: Routledge.

Essex ROD/B3/3/208, no. 14.

Fedoseyev, P. N. (1973) *Karl Marx: A Biography*, trans. Y. Sdobnikov, Moscow: Progress Publishers.

Ferber, M. (1990) "The Ideology of *The Merchant of Venice*," *English Literary Renaissance* 20, 3: 431–64.

Ferguson, M. W. (1994) "Moderation and its Discontents: Recent Work on Renaissance Women," *Feminist Studies* 20, 2: 349–66.

Fiedler, L. A. (1972) *The Stranger in Shakespeare*, New York: Stein and Day.

Fieldhouse, D. K. (1978) *Unilever Overseas*, London: Croom Helm.

Fleming, J. (1994) Review of *Writing Women in Jacobean England* by B. K. Lewalski, *Huntington Library Quarterly* 57, 2: 199–204.

Folkart, B. A. (1993) "Sam Wanamaker: Actor Led Globe Theater Effort," *Los Angeles Times*, December 19: A46.

Foucault, M. (1979) *Discipline and Punish: The Birth of the Prison*, trans. A. Sheridan, New York: Vintage Books.

Fox-Genovese, E. and Genovese, E. D. (1983) *Fruits of Merchant Capital: Slavery and Bourgeois Property in the Rise and Expansion of Capitalism*, Oxford: Oxford University Press.

Fraser, N. and Nicholson, L. (1988) "Social Criticism without Philosophy: An Encounter between Feminism and Postmodernism," in A. Ross (ed.) *Universal Abandon? The Politics of Postmodernism*, Minnesota: University of Minnesota Press.

Freccero, C. (1991) "Rape's Disfiguring Figures: Marguerite de Navarre's *Heptaméron*, Day 1: 10," in L. A. Higgins and B. R. Silver (eds) (1991).

Frye, S. (1999) "Sewing Connections: Elizabeth Tudor, Mary Stuart, Elizabeth Talbot, and Seventeenth-Century Anonymous Needleworkers," in S. Frye and K. Robertson (eds.) *Maids and Mistresses, Cousins and*

Queens: Women's Alliances in Early Modern England, Oxford: Oxford University Press.

Fumerton, P. (1991) *Cultural Aesthetics: Renaissance Literature and the Practice of Social Ornament*, Chicago: University of Chicago Press.

Fumerton, P. and Hunt, S. (eds) (1999) *Renaissance Culture and Everyday Life*, Philadelphia: University of Pennsylvania Press.

Geneva Bible, The, (1560) *The Bible and Holy Scriptures conteyned in the Olde and Newer Testament*, Geneva.

Giddens, A. (1990) *The Consequences of Modernity*, Stanford: Stanford University Press.

Gifford, G. (1582) *A Sermon on the Parable of the Sower*, London.

Gilder, G. (1981) *Wealth and Poverty*, New York: Bantam.

Gillies, J. (1994) *Shakespeare and the Geography of Difference*, New York: Cambridge University Press.

Gilroy, P. (1991) "*There ain't No Black in the Union Jack*," Chicago: University of Chicago Press.

—— (1993) *The Black Atlantic: Modernity and Double Consciousness*, Cambridge, Mass.: Harvard University Press.

Goldberg, J. (1983) *James I and the Politics of Literature: Jonson, Shakespeare, Donne, and their Contemporaries*, Baltimore and London: Johns Hopkins University Press.

Gomes, P. J. (1996) *The Good Book: Reading the Bible with Mind and Heart*, New York: William Morrow.

Gowing, L. (1994) "Language, Power, and the Law: Women's Slander Litigation in Early Modern London," in G. Walker and J. Kermode (eds) (1984).

Gravdal, K. (1991) *Ravishing Maidens: Writing Rape in Medieval French Literature*, Philadelphia: University of Pennsylvania Press.

Greenblatt, S. (1980) *Renaissance Self-Fashioning: From More to Shakespeare*, Chicago: University of Chicago Press.

—— (1985) "Invisible Bullets: Renaissance Authority and its Subversion, *Henry IV* and *Henry V*," in J. Dollimore and A. Sinfield (eds) *Political Shakespeare: New Essays in Cultural Materialism*, Ithaca, N.Y., and London: Cornell University Press.

—— (1988) *Shakespearean Negotiations: The Circulation of Social Energy in Renaissance England*, Berkeley and London: University of California Press.

—— (1989) "Towards a Poetics of Culture," in A. Veeser (ed.) *The New Historicism*, London: Routledge.

—— (1990a) *Learning to Curse: Essays in Early Modern Culture*, London: Routledge.

—— (1990b) *Shakespearean Negotiations: The Circulation of Social Energy in Renaissance England*, Oxford: Oxford University Press.

—— (1997) "The Mousetrap: In Memory of Louis Marin," *Shakespeare Studies* (Japan) 35: 1–32.

—— (ed.) (1993) *New World Encounters*, Berkeley: University of California Press.

—— et al. (1997) (eds) *The Norton Shakespeare Based on the Oxford Edition*, New York: Norton.

Grossman, M. (ed.) (1998) *Aemilia Lanyer: Gender, Genre, and the Canon*, Lexington: University of Kentucky Press.

Guibbory, A. (1998) "The Gospel According to Aemilia: Women and the Sacred," in M. Grossman (ed.) (1998).

Gurr, A. (1980) *The Shakespearean Stage: 1574–1642*, Cambridge: Cambridge University Press.

—— (ed.) (1992) *King Henry V*, Cambridge: Cambridge University Press.

H., N. (1694) *The Ladies Dictionary; Being a General Entertainment for the Fair Sex: A Work Never attempted before in English*, London.

Hakluyt, R. (ed.) (1927) *Principal Navigations, Voyages, Traffiques and Discoveries of the English Nation*, London: J. M. Dent.

Hall, K. F. (1995) *Things of Darkness: Economies of Race and Gender in Early Modern England*, Ithaca, N.Y.: Cornell University Press, 1995.

Hall, S. (1988) *The Hard Road to Renewal*, London and New York: Verso.

—— (1992) "Cultural Studies and its Theoretical Legacies," in L. Grossberg et al. (eds) *Cultural Studies*, New York: Routledge.

—— (1997) "The Local and the Global," in A. King (ed.) *Culture, Globalization and the World System*, Minneapolis: University of Minnesota Press.

Halpern, R. (1991) *The Poetics of Primitive Accumulation*, Ithaca, N.Y.: Cornell University Press.

—— (1997) *Shakespeare among the Moderns*, Ithaca, N.Y.: Cornell University Press.

Hanawalt, B. A. (ed.) (1986) *Women and Work in Preindustrial Europe*, Bloomington: Indiana University Press.

Hannerz, U. (1987) "The World in Creolization," *Africa* 57, 4: 546–59.

Harris, J. G. (1994) " 'Narcissus in thy face': Roman Desire and the Difference It Fakes in *Antony and Cleopatra*," *Shakespeare Quarterly* 45: 408–25.

Harris, W. (1983) *The Womb of Space: The Cross-Cultural Imagination*, Westport, Conn.: Greenwood Press.

Hartman, S. V. (1997) *Scenes of Subjection: Terror, Slavery, and Self-Making in Nineteenth-Century America*, Oxford and New York: Oxford University Press.

Hartmann, H. (1981) "The Unhappy Marriage of Marxism and Feminism: Towards a More Progressive Union," in L. Sargent (ed.) *Women and Revolution: A Discussion of the Unhappy Marriage of Marxism and Feminism*, Boston: South End Press.

Harvey, D. (1995) "Globalization in Question," *Rethinking Marxism* 8, 4: 1–17.

Hattaway, M., Sokolova, B. and Roper, D. (eds) (1994) *Shakespeare in the New Europe*, Sheffield: Sheffield Academic Press.

Hawkes, T. (1992) *Meaning by Shakespeare*, London and New York: Routledge.

—— (ed.) (1996) *Alternative Shakespeares 2*, New York: Routledge.

Hazlitt, W. (1930) *The Complete Works of William Hazlitt*, vol. 4, ed. P. P. Howe, London and Toronto: Dent.

Hedrick, D. (1997) "War is Mud: Branagh's Dirty Harry V and the Types of Political Ambiguity," in L. Boose and R. Burt (eds) (1997).

Hegel, G. W. F. (1928) *Sämtliche Werke*, vol. 19, Stuttgart: Fr. Frommans Verlag.

—— (1955) *Lectures on the Philosophy of History*, trans. E. S. Haldane and F. H. Simson, vol. 3, London: Routledge and Kegan Paul.
—— (1977) *Phenomenology of Spirit*, trans. A. V. Miller, New York: Oxford University Press.
Helgerson, R. (1992) *Forms of Nationhood: The Elizabethan Writing of England*, Chicago: University of Chicago Press, 151–91.
—— (1999) "The Women's World of Shakespeare's Windsor," in P. Fumerton and S. Hunt (eds) (1999).
Hendricks, M. (1998) "'Tis not the fashion to confess': Shakespeare–Postcoloniality–Johannesburg, 1996," in A. Loomba and M. Orkin (eds) (1998).
Heywood J. (1607) *The Fair Maid of the Exchange*, London.
Hieron, S. (1606) *Truths Purchase: or A Commodity which no man may either neglect to buie, or dare to sell*, London.
Higgins, L. A. and Silver, B. P. (eds) (1991) *Rape and Representation*, New York: Columbia University Press.
Higgins, L. A. and Silver, B. R. (1991) "Introduction," in Higgins and Silver (eds) (1991).
Hinds, H. (1996) *God's Englishwomen: Seventeenth-Century Radical Sectarian Writing and Feminist Criticism*, Manchester: Manchester University Press.
Hobby, E. (1988) *Virtue of Necessity: English Women's Writing 1646–1688*, London: Virago.
Holderness, G. (1988) *The Shakespeare Myth*, Manchester: Manchester University Press.
—— (1988a) "Boxing the Bard: Shakespeare and Television," in G. Holderness (ed.) (1988).
—— (1988b) "Sam Wanamaker" (interview), in G. Holderness (ed.) (1988).
Holderness, G. and Murphy, A. (1997) "Shakespeare's England: Britain's Shakespeare," in J. Joughin (ed.) *Shakespeare and National Culture*, Manchester and New York: Manchester University Press.
Hollier, D. (ed.) (1988) *The College of Sociology (1937–39)*. Minneapolis: University of Minnesota Press.
Honan, P. (1998) *Shakespeare: A Life*, Oxford: Oxford University Press.
Honoré, A. M. (1961) "Ownership," in A. G. Guest (ed.) *Oxford Essays in Jurisprudence*, Oxford: Oxford University Press.
Howard, J. E. (1999) "Producing New Knowledge," in S. Frye and K. Robertson (eds) (1999).
Howe, D. and Worsthorne, P. (1998) "What is a True Brit?" *Guardian*, April 25: Features, 2.
Howell, M. C. (1986) *Women, Production and Patriarchy in Late Medieval Cities*, Chicago: University of Chicago Press.
—— (1996) "Fixing Movables: Gifts By Testament in Late Medieval Douai," *Past and Present* 150: 3–45.
Hufton, O. (1998) *The Prospect before Her: A History of Women in Western Europe 1500–1800*, New York: Vintage.

Hull, S. (1982) *Chaste, Silent, and Obedient: English Books for Women 1475–1640*, San Marino: Huntington Library.
Hults, L. (1991) "Dürer's Lucretia: Speaking the Silence of Women," *Signs* 16, 2: 205–37.
Hunter, G. K. (1967) "Othello and Colour Prejudice," *Proceedings of the British Academy* 53: 139–63.
Hutson, L. (1992) "Why the Lady's Eyes Are Nothing Like the Sun," in I. Armstrong (ed.) *New Feminist Discourses: Critical Essays on Theories and Texts*, London: Routledge, 155–75.
Hyde, L. (1983) *The Gift: Imagination and the Erotic Life of Property*, New York: Random House.
Hyppolite, J. (1974) *Genesis and Structure of Hegel's Phenomenology of Spirit*, trans. S. Cherniak and J. Heckman, Evanston: Northwestern University Press.
Ingram, M. (1984) "Ridings, Rough Music and the Reform of Popular Culture," *Past and Present* 105.
Innerst, C. (1997) "The Bard Draws a Pass to Pop Culture on Campus: Many Colleges Skipping Shakespeare," *Washington Times*, December 17, 1997: A1 and A20.
International Movie Data Base (www.imdb.com).
James, C. L. R. (1980) *Spheres of Existence: Selected Writings*, Westport, Conn.: Lawrence Hill.
Jameson, F. (1971) *Marxism and Form: Twentieth-Century Dialectical Theories of Literature*, Princeton, N.J.: Princeton University Press.
—— (1981) *The Political Unconscious: Narrative as a Socially Symbolic Act*, Ithaca, N.Y.: Cornell University Press.
—— (1988) "Cognitive Mapping," in C. Nelson and L. Grossberg (eds) *Marxism and the Interpretation of Culture*, Urbana and Chicago: University of Illinois Press.
—— (1991) *Postmodernism, Or the Cultural Logic of Late Capitalism*, Durham, N.C.: Duke University Press; London: Verso.
—— (1993a) "Actually Existing Marxism," *Polygraph* 6, 7: 170–95.
—— (1993b) "On 'Cultural Studies,'" *Social Text* 34: 17–52.
—— (1995) "Marx's Purloined Letter," *New Left Review* 209: 75–109.
Jankowski, T. (2000) ". . . in the Lesbian Void: Woman–Woman Eroticism in Shakespeare," in D. Callaghan (ed.) (2000).
Jed, S. H. (1989) *Chaste Thinking: The Rape of Lucretia and the Birth of Humanism*, Bloomington: University of Indiana Press.
Johnson, N. P. (1997) "Canonicity and Identity: Mythologies of English Renaissance Writing," unpublished Ph.D. thesis, Cornell University.
Jones, A. R. (1991) "New Songs for the Swallow: Ovid's Philomela in Tullia d'Aragone and Gaspara Stampa," in M. Migiel and J. Schiesari (eds) *Refiguring Woman: Perspectives on Gender in the Italian Renaissance*, Ithaca, N.Y.: Cornell University Press.
—— (1996) "Dematerializations: Textile and Textual Properties in Ovid, Sandys, and Spenser," in M. de Grazia et al. (eds) (1996).

Jones, N. (1989) *God and the Moneylenders: Usury and Law in Early Modern England*, Oxford: Basil Blackwell.

Jonson, B. (1925–63) *Ben Jonson*, 11 vols., Oxford: Clarendon Press.

—— (1966), *Sejanus his Fall*, ed. W. F. Bolton, London, Ernest Benn.

Jordan, C. (1990) *Renaissance Feminism: Literary Texts and Political Models*, Ithaca, N.Y.: Cornell University Press.

Joughin, J. (ed.) (1997) *Shakespeare and National Culture*, Manchester and New York: Manchester University Press.

Jouhard, C. (1994) "Power and Literature: The Terms of the Exchange, 1624–42," in R. Burt (ed.) *The Administration of Aesthetics: Censorship, Political Criticism, and the Public Sphere*, Minneapolis: University of Minnesota Press.

Julius, P. (1892) "Diary of the Journey of the Most Illustrious Philip Julius, Duke of Stettin-Pomerania . . . through . . . England, . . . 1602," in. G. von Bulow (ed.) *Transactions of the Royal Historical Society*, n. s. [2nd series], 6.

—— (1976) "The Rape in Shakespeare's *Lucrece*," *Shakespeare Studies* 9: 45–72.

Kahn, C. (1991) "*Lucrece*: The Sexual Politics of Subjectivity," in London Feminist History Group (ed.) *Rape and Representation*, New York: Columbia University Press.

Kapp, Y. (1972) *Eleanor Marx*, vol. 1, New York: Pantheon Books.

Kegl, R. (1994a) "'The Adoption of Abominable Terms': The Insults that Shape Windsor's Middle Class," *English Literary History* 61: 2.

—— (1994b) *The Rhetoric of Concealment: Figuring Gender and Class in Renaissance Literature*, Ithaca, N.Y.: Cornell University Press.

Kennedy, D. (ed.) (1993) *Foreign Shakespeare: Contemporary Performance*, Cambridge: Cambridge University Press.

Kenny, C. S. (1879) *The History of the Law of England as to the Effects of Marriage on Property and on the Wife's Legal Capacity*, London: Reeves and Turner.

Kermode, F. (1961) "The Mature Comedies," in his *Early Shakespeare*, Stratford-on-Avon Studies 3. London.

Kernan, A. (1995) *Shakespeare, the King's Playwright: Theater in the Stuart Court, 1603–1613*, New Haven, Conn.: Yale University Press.

King, A. (1990) *Urbanism, Colonialism, and the World-Economy*, London and New York: Routledge.

King, M. L. (1999) "Women's Voices, the Early Modern, and the Civilization of the West," *Shakespeare Studies* 25: 21–31.

Kirsch, A. (1990) "Between Bardolatry and Bardicide," *Times Literary Supplement*, April 20–6: 421–2.

Korda, N. (1996) "Household Kates: Domesticating Commodities in *The Taming of the Shrew*," *Shakespeare Quarterly* 47: 109–31.

Kronenfeld, J. (1992) "'So Distribution Should Undo Excess, and Each man Have Enough': Shakespeare's *King Lear*—Anabaptist Egalitarianism, Anglican Charity, Both, Neither?" *English Literary History* (59): 755–84.

Krontiris, T. (1992) *Oppositional Voices: Women as Writers and Translators of Literature in the English Renaissance*, London: Routledge.

Kuryluk, E. (1991) *Veronica and Her Cloth: History, Symbolism and Structure of a Love Image*, Cambridge, Mass.: Blackwell.

Kyd, T. (1801) *The Works of Thomas Kyd*, Oxford: Clarendon Press.

Laclau, E. (1995) "The Time is out of Joint," *diacritics* 25, 2: 86–96.

Lamb, M. E. (1990) *Gender and Authorship in the Sidney Circle*, Madison: University of Wisconsin Press.

—— (forthcoming) "Margaret Roper, the Humanist Political Project, and the Problem of Agency," in P. Herman (ed.) *Opening the Borders*, Wilmington: University of Delaware Press.

—— (forthcoming) "Patronage and Class in Aemilia Lanyer's *Salve Deus Rex Judaeorum*," in J. Donawerth (ed.) *Women, Writing, and the Reproduction of Culture in Tudor and Stuart Britain*, New York: Syracuse University Press.

Lanyer, A. (1993) *The Poems of Aemilia Lanyer: Salve Deus Rex Judaeorum*, ed. Susanne Woods, New York: Oxford University Press.

Lash, S. (1993) "Pierre Bourdieu: Cultural Economy and Social Change," in C. Calhoun, E. LiPuma, and M. Postone (eds) (1993).

Lawrence, B. E. (1884) *The History of the Laws Affecting the Property of Married Women in England*, London: Reeves and Turner.

Lazarus, N. (1999) *Nationalism and Cultural Practice in the Postcolonial World*. Cambridge: Cambridge University Press.

Le Hardy, W. (1935) *Calendar to the Sessions Records*, new series, vol. 1: 1612–14, London.

Le Moyne, P. (1647) *La Gallerie des Femmes Fortes*, Paris.

Levine, L. W. (1988) *Highbrow Lowbrow: The Emergence of Cultural Hierarchy in America*, Cambridge, Mass.: Harvard University Press.

Lewalski, B. K. (1993) *Writing Women in Jacobean England*, Cambridge, Mass.: Harvard University Press.

Limon, J. (1985) *Gentlemen of a Company: English Players in Central and Eastern Europe, 1590–1660*, Cambridge: Cambridge University Press.

Loehlin, J. L. (1997) "'Top of the World, Ma': *Richard III* and Cinematic Convention," in L. Boose and R. Burt (eds) (1997).

Loomba, A. (1996) "Shakespeare and Cultural Difference," in T. Hawkes (ed.) (1996).

—— (1997) "Shakespearian Transformations," in J. Joughin (ed.) *Shakespeare and National Culture*, Manchester and New York: Manchester University Press.

Loomba, A. and Orkin, M. (eds) (1998) *Post-Colonial Shakespeares*, London: Routledge.

Luhrmann, B. (dir.) (1996) *William Shakespeare's Romeo and Juliet*. Videocassette, Twentieth-Century Fox Video.

Lupton, J. and Reinhard, K. (1993) *After Oedipus: Shakespeare in Psychoanalysis*, Ithaca, N.Y.: Cornell University Press.

McDonald, R. (1996) *The Bedford Companion to Shakespeare: An Introduction with Documents*, Boston: Bedford Books.

McEachern, C. (1996) *The Poetics of English Nationhood, 1590–1612*, Cambridge: Cambridge University Press.

McGee, A. (1987) *The Elizabethan Hamlet*, New Haven: Yale University Press.
McGrath, L. (1991) "Metaphoric Subversions: Feasts and Mirrors in Aemilia Lanyer's *Salve Deus Rex Judaeorum*," *LIT: Literature, Interpretation, Theory* 3: 101–13.
Macherey, P. (1995) "Remarx: Derrida's Marx," trans. T. Stolze, *Rethinking Marxism* 8, 4: 18–25.
McIntyre, R. (1992) "Theories of Uneven Development and Social Change," *Rethinking Marxism* 5, 3: 75–105.
McLellan, D. (1973) *Karl Marx: His Life and Thought*, New York: Harper and Row.
—— (ed.) (1981) *Karl Marx: Interviews and Recollections*, London: Macmillan.
McLuskie, K. (1991) "The Poets' Royal Exchange: Patronage and Commerce in Early Modern Drama," in C. Brown (ed.) *Patronage, Politics and Literary Traditions in England, 1558–1658*, Detroit: Wayne State University Press.
—— (1994) "The Patriarchal Bard: Feminist Criticism and Shakespeare: *King Lear* and *Measure for Measure*," in J. Dollimore and A. Sinfield (eds) (1994).
McMillan, S. (1987) *The Elizabethan Theatre and The Book of Sir Thomas More*, Ithaca, N.Y.: Cornell University Press.
McNeill, F. (1999) "Gynocentric London Spaces: (Re)Locating Masterless Women in Early Stuart Drama," *Renaissance Drama* 28: 195–244.
Macpherson, C. B. (1964) *The Political Theory of Possessive Individualism*, Oxford and New York: Oxford University Press.
Macray, W.D. (ed.) (1886) *The Pilgrimage to Parnassus*, Oxford: Clarendon Press.
Mandel, E. (1990) "Introduction [to Appendix]," in K. Marx, *Capital*, vol. 1, trans. B. Fowkes, London: Penguin Books.
Mann, D. (1991) *The Elizabethan Player: Contemporary Stage Representation*, London: Routledge.
Marcuse, H. (1979) *The Aesthetic Dimension*, London: Macmillan.
Marston, J. (1965) *The First Part of Antonio and Mellida*, ed. G. K. Hunter, London: Edward Arnold.
Marx, E. (1895) "Recollections of Mohr," in S. K. Padover, *Karl Marx: An Intimate Biography*, New York: McGraw-Hill.
Marx, K. (1852a [1963]) *The Eighteenth Brumaire of Louis Bonaparte*, New York: International Publishers.
—— (1852b [1985]) *Der 18. Brumaire des Louis Bonaparte*, in *Werke*, vol. 11, Berlin: Dietz Verlag.
—— (1856 [1980]) "Speech at the Anniversary of *The People's Paper*," in K. Marx and F. Engels, *Collected Works*, vol. 14, New York: International Publishers.
—— (1970) *A Contribution to the Critique of Political Economy*, New York: International Publishers.
—— (1973) *Grundrisse*, trans. Martin Nicolaus, London: Penguin.
—— (1976) *Capital*, vol. 1, trans. Ben Fowkes, New York: Penguin.
—— (1978) "Theses on Feuerbach," in R. C. Tucker (ed.) *The Marx–Engels Reader*, 2nd edn, New York: Norton.

Marx, K. and Engels, F. (1958) *Werke*, Band 3, Berlin: Dietz Verlag.
—— (1976), *Collected Works*, vol. 5, New York: International Publishers.
—— (1982) *Collected Works*, vol. 38, New York: International Publishers.
Masten, J. (1997) *Textual Intercourse: Collaboration, Authorship and Sexuality in Renaissance Drama*, New York: Cambridge University Press.
Mauss, M. ([1924] 1990) *The Gift: The Form and Reason of Exchange in Archaic Societies*, trans. W. D. Halls, New York: Norton.
Mehlman, J. (1977) *Revolution and Repetition: Marx/Hugo/Balzac*, Berkeley: University of California Press.
Mehring, F. (1962) *Karl Marx*, trans. E. Fitzgerald, Ann Arbor: University of Michigan Press.
Mendelson, S. and Crawford, P. (1998) *Women in Early Modern England 1550–1720*, Oxford: Clarendon Press.
Middleton, C. (1985) "Women's Labour and the Transition to Pre-industrial Capitalism," in L. Charles and L. Duffin (eds) (1985).
Mignolo, W. (1995) *The Darker Side of the Renaissance: Literacy, Territoriality, and Colonization*, Ann Arbor: University of Michigan Press.
Miyoshi, M. (1993) "A Borderless World?" *Critical Inquiry* 19, 4: 726–51.
Montrose, L. (1992) "*A Midsummer Night's Dream* and the Shaping Fantasies of Elizabethan Culture," in R. Dutton and R. Wilson (eds) *New Historicism and Renaissance Drama*, London: Longman.
—— (1996) *The Purpose of Playing: Shakespeare and the Politics of the Elizabethan Theatre*, Chicago: Chicago University Press.
Mukerji, C. (1983) *From Graven Images: Patterns of Modern Materialism*, New York: Columbia University Press.
Mullaney, S. (1988) *The Place of the Stage: License, Play and Power in Renaissance England*, Chicago and London: University of Chicago Press.
Mun, T. (1621) *A Discourse of Trade from England unto the East-Indies*, London.
Munro, J. (1909) *The Shakespeare Allusion Book*, London: Chatto and Windus.
Nancy, J. (1991) *The Inoperative Community*, trans. P. Connor et al. Minneapolis: University of Minnesota Press.
Neill, M. (1994) "Broken English and Broken Irish: Nation, Language and the Optic of Power in Shakepeare's Histories," *Shakespeare Quarterly* 45: 18–22.
—— (1997) *Issues of Death: Mortality and Identity in English Renaissance Tragedy*, Oxford: Clarendon Press.
Nelson, K. (1998) "Annotated Bibliography: Texts and Criticism of Aemilia Bassano Lanyer," in M. Grossman (ed.) (1998).
New Caucus, The (1999) *The New Caucus Response to the Schmidt Report*, <http:\\www.newcaucus.org>.
Newman, K. (1991) *Fashioning Femininity and English Renaissance Drama*, Chicago: University of Chicago Press.
Obituary: "Sam Wanamaker." (1993) *Daily Telegraph*, December 20: 21.
Obituary: "Sam Wanamaker." (1993) *New York Times*, December 19: sec. 1, 62.
Olalquiaga, C. (1992) "Holy Kitschen," in *Megalopolis: Contemporary Cultural Sensibilities*, Minneapolis: University of Minnesota Press.

Oldys, W. (ed.) (1809) *The Harlein Miscellany*. London.
Olivier, L. (dir.) (1944) *Henry V*, film.
Orgel, S. (1975) *The Illusion of Power: Political Theater in the English Renaissance*, Berkeley: University of California Press.
—— (1988) "The Authentic Shakespeare," *Representations* 21: 1–25.
—— (1996) *Impersonations: The Performance of Gender in Shakespeare's England*, Cambridge: Cambridge University Press.
Orkin, M. (1987) *Shakespeare against Apartheid*, Johannesburg: Ad. Donker.
Orlin, L. C. (1994) *Private Matters and Public Culture in Post-Reformation England*, Ithaca, N.Y.: Cornell University Press.
—— (1999) "Three Ways to be Invisible in the Renaissance: Sex, Reputation, and Stitchery," in P. Fumerton, and S. Hunt (eds) (1999).
Pacino, A. (dir.) (1996) *Looking for Richard*, videocassette, Twentieth Century Fox.
Padover, S. K. (1978) *Karl Marx: An Intimate Biography*, New York: McGraw-Hill.
Parker, P. (1994) "Fantasies of 'Race' and 'Gender': Africa, *Othello*, and Bringing to Light," M. Hendricks and P. Parker (eds) *Women "Race," and Writing in the Early Modern Period*, London: Routledge.
Pater, W. (1889) *Appreciations*, London: Macmillan.
Patterson, A. (1989) *Shakespeare and the Popular Voice*, Cambridge, Mass.: Blackwell.
Perkins, W. (1612) *The Workes of that Famous and Worthy Minister of Christ . . . Mr. William Perkins*, vol. 1, London.
Pie, T. (1604) *Usuries Spright Conjured, or a Scholastiall Determination of Usury . . . with his Answere to a Treatise, written in defence of Usurie*, London.
Post, J. B. (1978) "Ravishment of Women," in J. H. Barker (ed.) *Legal Records and the Historian*, Cambridge: Cambridge University Press.
Prawer, S. S. (1976) *Karl Marx and World Literature*, Oxford: Oxford University Press.
Prest, W. R. (1991) "Law and Women's Rights in Early Modern England," *The Seventeenth Century* 6, 2: 169–87.
Rambuss, R. (1998) *Closet Devotions*, Durham, N.C.: Duke University Press.
Richey, E. (1998) " 'To Undoe the Booke': Cornelius Agrippa, Aemilia Lanyer and the Subversion of Pauline Authority," *English Literary Renaissance* 27, 1: 106–28.
Rivers, G. (1639) *The Heroinae: or, The Lives of Arria, Pauline, Lucrecia, Dido, Theutulla, Cypriana, Aretaphila*, London.
Roberts, L. (1641) *The Treasure of Traffike. Or A Discourse of Forraigne Trade*, London.
Roberts, M. (1985) " 'Words they are Women, and Deeds they are men': Images of Work and Gender in Early Modern England," in L. Charles and L. Duffin (eds) (1985).
Robertson, R. (1992) *Globalization*, London: Sage.
Robinson, W. (1996) "Globalisation: Nine Theses on Our Epoch," *Race and Class* 38, 2: 13–31.

Rollins H. E. (1922) *A Pepysian Garland: Black-Letter Broadside Ballads of the Years 1595–1639*, Cambridge: Cambridge University Press.
Ross, L. J. (1960) "The Meaning of Strawberries in Shakespeare," *Studies in the Renaissance* 7: 225–40.
Rymer, T. (1693) *A Short View of Tragedy*, London.
Said, E. (1983) *The World, the Text and the Critic*, Cambridge, Mass.: Harvard University Press.
—— (1993) *Culture and Imperialism*, New York: Knopf.
Salmon, M. (1986) *Women and the Law of Property in Early America*, Chapel Hill and London: University of North Carolina Press.
Sanders, E. R. (1998) *Gender and Literacy on Stage in Early Modern England*, Cambridge: Cambridge University Press.
Sandys, E. (1841) *The Sermons of Edwin Sandys*, vol. 41, Parker Society, Cambridge: Cambridge University Press.
Sassen, S. (1991) *The Global City*, Princeton, N.J.: Princeton University Press.
Scarry, E. (1987) *The Body in Pain: The Making and Unmaking of the World*, New York: Oxford University Press.
Schlegel, A. W. von and Tieck, L. (trans.) (1841) *Hamlet, Prinz von Dänemark*, in *Shakspeare: Dramatische Werke*, vol. 6, Berlin: Reimer.
Schmidgall, G. (1981) *Shakespeare and the Courtly Aesthetic*, Berkeley: University of California Press.
Schoenbaum, S. (1975) *William Shakespeare: A Documentary Life*, Oxford: Oxford University Press.
—— (1977) *William Shakespeare: A Compact Documentary Life*, New York: Oxford University Press.
Scott, W. R. (1968) *The Constitution and Finance of English, Scottish and Irish Joint-Stock Companies to 1720*, vol. 1, Gloucester, Mass.: Peter Smith.
Shakespeare, W. (1604) *The Tragicall Historie of Hamlet, Prince of Denmarke* (Q2), in P. Bertram and B. W. Kliman (eds) *The Three-Text Hamlet*, New York: AMS Press, 1991.
—— (1971) *The Merry Wives of Windsor*, ed. H. J. Oliver, The Arden Shakespeare, London: Methuen.
—— (1974) *The Riverside Shakespeare*, ed. G. B. Evans, Boston: Houghton Mifflin.
—— (1976) *The Poems*, ed. F. T. Prince, The Arden Shakespeare, London: Methuen.
—— (1981) *The Taming of the Shrew*, ed. B. Morris, The Arden Shakespeare, London: Methuen.
—— (1984) *A Midsummer Night's Dream*, ed. R. A. Foakes, New Cambridge Shakespeare, Cambridge: Cambridge University Press.
—— (1985) *Hamlet, Prince of Denmark*, ed. P. Edwards, New Cambridge Shakespeare, Cambridge: Cambridge University Press.
—— (1987) *The Merchant of Venice*, ed. M. M. Mahood, New Cambridge Shakespeare, Cambridge: Cambridge University Press.

—— (1991) *Measure for Measure*, ed. B. Gibbons, New Cambridge Shakespeare, Cambridge: Cambridge University Press.
—— (1992) *The Tragedy of King Lear*, ed. J. L. Halio, New Cambridge Shakespeare, Cambridge: Cambridge University Press.
—— (1995) *Titus Andronicus*, ed. J. Bate, The Arden Shakespeare, New York: Routledge.
—— (1997a) *Othello*, ed. E. A. J. Honigmann, The Arden Shakespeare, London: Thomas Nelson.
—— (1997b) *The Norton Shakespeare*, ed. S. Greenblatt et al., New York: W. W. Norton.
—— (1997c) *The Riverside Shakespeare*, 2nd edn., Boston: Houghton Mifflin, 1997.
Shammas, C. (1993) "Changes in English and Anglo-American Consumption From 1550–1800," in J. Brewer and R. Porter (eds) (1993).
Shaw, B. (1963) *Complete Plays with Prefaces*, 6 vols., New York: Dodd, Mead.
Shepherd, S. (1992) "What's So Funny about Ladies' Tailors? A Survey of Some Male (Homo)sexual Types in the Renaissance," *Textual Practice* 6, 1: 17–30.
Shershow, S. C. (1995) "Idols of the Marketplace: Rethinking the Economic Determination of Renaissance Drama," *Renaissance Drama*, n. s. 26: 1–27.
Shoemaker, I. H. and Brown, E. (1981) *The Engravings of Marcantonio Raimondi*, Lawrence, Kans.: Spencer Museum of Art.
Shuger, D. K. (1994) *The Renaissance Bible*, Berkeley: University of California Press.
Sim, A. (1996) *The Tudor Housewif*, London: Sutton.
Sinfield, A. (1989) *Literature, Culture and Politics in Postwar Britain*, Berkeley: University of California Press.
—— (1992) *Faultlines: Cultural Materialism and the Politics of Dissident Reading*, Berkeley: University of California Press.
Skura, M. A. (1993) *Shakespeare the Actor and the Purposes of Playing*, Chicago: Chicago University Press.
Smith, H. (1622) *The Sermons of Master Henry Smith*, London.
Smith, P. (1997) *Millenial Dreams*, London and New York: Verso.
Somerset, A. (1994) "How Chances it They Travel: Provincial Touring, Playing Places, and the King's Men," *Shakespeare Survey* 47, Cambridge: Cambridge University Press.
Spenser, E. (1932) *The Shepherd's Calendar*, New York: Dutton.
—— (1988) "Can the Subaltern Speak?" in C. Nelson and L. Grossberg (eds) *Marxism and the Interpretation of Culture*, Urbana and Chicago: University of Illinois Press.
Spivak, G. (1995) "Ghostwriting," *diacritics* 25, 2: 65–84.
Sprinker, Michael (ed.) (1999) *Ghostly Demarcations: A Symposium on Jacques Derrida's 'Spectres of Marx'*, London and New York: Verso.
Stallybrass, P. (1992) "The Body Beneath," in S. Zimmerman (ed.) (1992).

—— (1996) "Worn Worlds: Clothes and Identity on the Renaissance Stage," in M. de Grazia et al. (eds) (1996).
Stallybrass, P. and de Grazia, M. (1993) "The Materiality of the Shakespearian Text," *Shakespeare Quarterly* 44, 3: 255–83.
Staves, S. (1990) *Married Women's Separate Property in England, 1660–1833*, Cambridge, Mass., and London: Harvard University Press.
Stimpson, C. (1986) "Preface," in M. C. Howell (1986).
Strier, R. (1995) *Resistant Structures: Particularity, Radicalism, and Renaissance Texts*, Berkeley: University of California Press.
Stubbes, P. ([1597] 1877–9) *The Anatomy of Abuses*, ed. F. J. Furnivall, London.
Swinburne, A. C. (1880) *A Study of Shakespeare*, London: Chatto and Windus.
Tasso, T. (1588) *The Householders Philosophy*, trans. T. K., London.
Tawney, R. H. (1936) *Religion and the Rise of Capitalism*, London: John Murray.
Tawney, R. H. and Power, E. (eds) (1924) *Tudor Economic Documents*, 3 vols, London: Longmans.
Taylor, J. (1624) *The Praise of Cleane Linnen*, London.
—— (1634) *The Needles Excellency*, London.
Tennenhouse, L. (1986) *Power on Display: The Politics of Shakespeare's Genres*, New York and London: Methuen.
Thiong'o, N. wa (1994) "The Language of African Literature," in P. Williams and L. Chrisman (eds) *Colonial Discourse and Postcolonial Theory*, New York: Columbia University Press.
Thompson, E. P. (1993) "The Moral Economy of the Crowd in the Eighteenth Century," in his *Customs in Common*, New York: New Press.
Tillyard, E. M. W. (1944) *Shakespeare's History Plays*, London: Chatto.
Todorov, T. (1987) *The Conquest of America: The Question of the Other*, trans. R. Howard, New York: Harper Torchbooks.
Trill, S. et al. (eds) (1997) *Lay By Your Needles Ladies, Take the Pen: Writing Women in England, 1500–1700*, London: Arnold.
Trivedi, H. (1996) *Colonial Transactions: English Literature and India*, Manchester: Manchester University Press.
Underdown, D. E. (1985) "The Taming of the Scold: The Enforcement of Patriarchal Authority in Early Modern England," in A. Fletcher and J. Stevenson (eds) *Order and Disorder in Early Modern England*, Cambridge: Cambridge University Press.
Vaughan, R. (1542) *A Dyalogue Defensyve for Women, Against Malycyous Detractours*, London.
Viala, A. (1985) *Naissance de l'écrivain: sociologie de la litterature a l'age classique*, Paris: Minuit.
Vickers, B. (1993) *Appropriating Shakespeare: Contemporary Critical Quarrels*, New Haven, Conn.: Yale University Press.
Vickers, N. (1985) "The Blazon of Sweet Beauty's Best: Shakespeare's *Lucrece*," in P. Parker and G. Hartman (eds) *Shakespeare and the Question of Theory*, New York: Methuen.

Vickery, A (1993) "Women and the World of Goods: A Lancashire Consumer and Her Possessions, 1751–81," in J. Brewer and R. Porter (eds) (1993).
Viswanathan, G. (1989) *Masks of Conquest: Literary Study and British Rule in India*, New York: Columbia University Press.
Vives, J. L. (c. 1553) *The Office and Duetie of an Husband*, trans. T. Paynell, London.
Voloshinov, V. N. (1973) *Marxism and the Philosophy of Language*, trans. L. Matejka and I. R. Titunik, New York and London: Seminar Press.
Wacquant, L. J. D. (1993) "Bourdieu in America: Notes on the Transatlantic Importation of Social Theory," in C. Calhoun, E. Lipuma, and M. Postone (eds) (1993).
Walker, G. (1994) "Women, Theft and the World of Stolen Goods," in G. Walker and J. Kermode (eds) (1994).
—— (1998) "Rereading Rape and Sexual Violence in Early Modern England," *Gender & History* 10, 1: 1–23.
Walker, G. and Kermode, J. (eds) (1994) *Women, Crime and the Law Courts in Early Modern England*, Chapel Hill: University of North Carolina Press.
Wall, W. (1993) *The Imprint of Gender: Authorship and Publication in the English Renaissance*, Ithaca, N.Y.: Cornell University Press.
Walter, J. (1980) "Grain Riots and Popular Attitudes to the Law: Maldon and the Crisis of 1629," in J. Brewer and J. Styles (eds) *A Governable People: The English and their Law in the Seventeenth and Eighteenth Centuries*, London: Hutchinson.
Warner, G. (ed.) (1926) *The Libelle of Englyshe Polycye: A Poem on the Use of Sea Power, 1436*, Oxford: Clarendon Press.
Warnicke, R. (1993) "Private and Public: The Boundaries of Women's Lives in Early Stuart England," in J. R. Brink (ed.) *Privileging Gender in Early Modern England*, Kirksville, Mo.: Sixteenth Century Journal Publishers.
Wayne, V. (1999) "The Sexual Politics of Textual Transmission," in T. Berger and L. Maguire (eds) *Textual Formations and Reformations*, Wilmington: University of Delaware Press.
Weber, M. (1930) *The Protestant Ethic and the Spirit of Capitalism*, trans. T. Parsons, London: George Allen and Unwin.
Wentersdorf, K. P. (1980) "The Queen's Company in Scotland in 1589," *Theatre Research International*, 6: 33–6.
Wheeler, J. (1601) *A Treatise of Commerce*, Middelburgh.
Whitney, G. (1586) *A Choice of Emblemes, and other devises*, Leyden.
Wilde, O. (1994) *Complete Works of Oscar Wilde*, Glasgow: HarperCollins.
Wiles, D. (1998) "The Carnivalesque in 'A Midsummer Night's Dream,'" in C. Brown and R. Knowles (eds) *After Bakhtin: Shakespeare and the Politics of Carnival*, London: Macmillan.
Williams, G. (1994) *A Dictionary of Sexual Language and Imagery in Shakespearean and Stuart Literature*, Atlantic Heights, N.J.: Athlone Press.
Williams, R. (1973) *The Country and the City*, New York: Oxford University Press.
—— (1983) *Culture and Society*, New York: Columbia University Press.

Williamson, G. C. (1922) *Lady Anne Clifford, Countess of Dorset, Pembroke, and Montgomery, 1590–1676: Her Life, Letters and Work*, Kendal: Wilson.

Williamson, J. (1986) "Woman is an Island," in T. Modleski (ed.) *Studies in Entertainment*, Bloomington: Indiana University Press.

—— (1988) *Consuming Passions*, London and New York: Marion Boyars.

Wilson, Robert (1988) *Three Ladies of London and Three Lords and Three Ladies of London*, The Renaissance Imagination 36, ed. H.S.D. Mithael, New York: Garland.

—— (1993) *Will Power: Essays on Shakespearean Authority*, Hemel Hempstead: Harvester Wheatsheaf.

Wilson, T. ([1560] 1909) *Wilson's Arte of Rhetorique 1560*, ed. G. H. Mair, Tudor and Stuart Library, Oxford: Clarendon Press.

—— (n.d. [1572]) *A Discourse Upon Usury*, ed. R. H. Tawney, New York: Harcourt Brace.

Wolfson, A. J. (1990) "Explaining to her Sisters: Mary Lamb's Tales from Shakespear," in M. Novy (ed.) *Women's Re-Visions of Shakespeare: On the Responses of Dickinson, Woolf, Rich, H. D., George Eliot, and Others*, Urbana and Chicago: University of Illinois Press.

Wolfthal, D. (1999) *Images of Rape: The "Heroic" Tradition and its Alternatives*, Cambridge: Cambridge University Press.

Woodbridge, L. (1984) *Women and the English Renaissance: Literature and the Nature of Womankind, 1540–1620*, Urbana: University of Illinois Press.

Worsthorne, P. (1998) "Farewell to England's Nation-State Independence," *Daily Telegraph*, June 29: 14.

Wright, P. (1985) *On Living in an Old Country*, London: Verso.

Xenophon (1532) *Treatise of Householde*, trans. G. Hervet, London: Thomas Berthelet.

Zhang, X. Y. (1996) *Shakespeare in China*, Newark: University of Delaware Press.

Zimmerman, S. (1992) *Erotic Politics: Desire on the Renaissance Stage*, London: Routledge.

Žižek, S. (1989) *The Sublime Object of Ideology*, New York: Verso.

Index

Printed in Great Britain
by Amazon.co.uk, Ltd.,
Marston Gate.